Creating the Couple

Creating the Couple

Love, Marriage, and Hollywood Performance

Virginia Wright Wexman

PRINCETON UNIVERSITY PRESS
PRINCETON, NEW JERSEY

Published by Princeton University Press, 41 William Street,
Princeton, New Jersey 08540
In the United Kingdom: Princeton University Press,
Chichester, West Sussex

Library of Congress Cataloging-in-Publication Data

Wexman, Virginia Wright.
Creating the couple : love, marriage, and
Hollywood performance / Virginia Wright Wexman.
p. cm.
Includes bibliographical references and index.
ISBN 0-691-06969-7 (cl) ISBN 0-691-01535-x (pb)
1. Motion pictures—Social aspects—United States.
2. Motion picture acting. 3. Love in motion pictures.
4. Marriage in motion pictures.
I. Title.
PN1993.5.U6W45 1993
302.23′43′0973—dc20 92-36398 CIP

This book has been composed in Adobe Goudy

Princeton University Press books are printed on
acid-free paper and meet the guidelines for permanence
and durability of the Committee on Production Guidelines
for Book Longevity of the Council
on Library Resources

Printed in the United States of America

1 3 5 7 9 10 8 6 4 2

1 3 5 7 9 10 8 6 4 2
(pbk.)

Portions in Chapter 2 have previously appeared in
Virginia Wright Wexman, "Suffering and Suffrage: Birth, the Female Body,
and Women's Choices in D. W. Griffith's *Way Down East*"
from *The Velvet Light Trap*, No. 29, Spring 1992;
reprinted by permission of the University of Texas Press.

FOR JOHN, KIM, TODD, AND SARA

CONTENTS

PREFACE

HOLLYWOOD has created a cinema of actors. Stars sell Hollywood movies and are themselves sold in fan magazines and other media discourses. As a popular art form, Hollywood film has sought to capitalize on the willingness of audiences to empathize with the visible human presences that movies set before them. The relationship between Hollywood stars and their audience involves the stars' ability to model cultural norms and practices for a society that is largely bereft of more traditional modes of transmitting values.

Building on Edgar Morin's seminal study, this book argues from the assumption that movie stars function primarily as romantic ideals. The films in which they appear can be understood as part of Hollywood's project of defining the myriad of possible relationships encompassed in the category that cinema scholars have labeled "the couple." As a form of modern popular ritual, movies define and demonstrate socially sanctioned ways of falling in love. For a culture that organizes itself in large part around the social rituals embodied in the modern mass media, stars enact acceptable romantic fantasies. In what follows I analyze how Hollywood conventions of acting relate to changing styles of courtship and marriage, focusing on the implications of the appearance and behavior of these well-known figures as they manifest themselves within specific cinematic texts. My method is inspired by what Mikhail Bakhtin has called "sociological poetics," which emphasizes the interrelationships between textual reading and social history.

Unlike some other writers on film performance such as Charles Affron, Richard Dyer, and James Naremore, I have not attempted to define general principles that can be applied to all acting in the cinema. The work of these scholars has provided vocabularies and concepts upon which I have freely drawn. My own project, however, is more narrowly defined. Just as Charles Maland has traced the interaction between the evolving image of Charlie Chaplin and the culture's responses to it, I am concerned with the relationship between specific

Hollywood performers and developments in American society; but rather than focusing on the shifting political ideologies that Maland treats, I deal with changing norms of romantic love and marriage. I have viewed Hollywood actors as part of a cultural mechanism that models social behavior; but instead of examining the formation of the star system itself as Richard de Cordova does, I examine the ways in which this modeling function expresses itself in the films Hollywood has produced.

To understand the meanings of star performer/characters in cinematic texts, one must approach these figures in terms of the narrative contexts that define them. Thus, though actors and their bodies are the ultimate objects of my analyses, my discussions of individual films refer to matters of plotting and cinematic technique as well. Nor have I limited my discussion to actors' creations of characters in individual films; instead, I have freely drawn on the intertextual and extratexual material with which the Hollywood star system has surrounded each role a major actor undertakes; for movie stars are not just "actors"—in some sense they always play "themselves." My approach features intensive analyses of a few well-known Hollywood films in which acting is foregrounded either because performances featured in them have been recognized as preeminent, exemplary, or influential, or because they are films that thematize or problematize performance.

The book is organized around major trends in performance styles. Following an introductory section that defines and illustrates the basic terms and assumptions of the study as a whole, the book is composed of three parts, each of which takes up the interaction between various styles of film performance and shifting social norms concerning marriage and romantic love. Part 2, entitled "Patriarchal Marriage and Traditional Gender Identities," focuses on the way in which traditional marriage norms relate to issues of authorship and genre respectively: chapter 2 treats the Griffith-Gish collaboration in the context of a struggle over the terms of patriarchal marriage that took place during the early part of the century as feminists fought for suffrage, whereas chapter 3 explores John Wayne's relationship to the Western genre as a function of a property-centered conception of traditional marriage which I call "dynastic marriage." The next section, entitled "Companionate Marriage and Changing Constructions of Gender and Sexuality," explores evolving ideas about male and female stardom in terms of the culture's move toward a model of courtship and marriage in which companionship was valued: chapter 4 takes up the issues of the love goddess, and chapter 5 examines the impact of method acting on Hollywood's ideals of maleness. The book's final section, "Beyond the Couple," considers the recent breakdown in the ideal of monogamous marriage as the sole acceptable life-style for adults as it has interacted with Hollywood's experimentation with self-reflexive acting styles, using *Nashville*, *House of Games*, and *Do the Right Thing* as its major examples.

In charting trends in film performance I have focused on the discourse that acting constructs about the human body. Some theorists, working from a psychoanalytic model, have tended to assume that the body is defined solely by its capacity for sexual desire. However, as Elaine Scarry has remarked, "Though desire is an important fact about the body, it is only one of many" ("Work and the Body" 117). My own consideration of the relationship between romantic love and marriage and Hollywood acting styles is obviously concerned in large part with issues of sexuality, but I have not posited sexual desire as a simple Freudian drive. Rather I have approached sexuality as a cultural construct which is intimately related to changing social conditions, or what Jürgen Habermas has termed "the grammar of everyday life." I share the presuppositions of social scientists like Sherry Ortner and Harriet Whitehead, who have written, "What gender is, what men and women are, what sorts of relations do or should obtain between them—all of these do not simply reflect upon biological givens, but are largely a product of cultural processes" (1).

Because my argument is based on the notion of romantic love and marriage as social ideologies, I have attempted to historicize terms like *patriarchy*, *sexuality*, and indeed *the couple* itself, which have sometimes been used in film theory as though they represented phenomena that are monolithic and unproblematic. My exploration of the relationship between performance styles and discourses surrounding the body emphasizes the significance of specific historical moments and considers the shifting and overlapping nature of discourses that necessarily characterize any such moment. At the same time I have not attempted to write a history in the sense of providing a survey of significant actors, performance modes, or marriage conventions. Instead, I have isolated a few exemplary issues and filmic texts that open up a variety of perspectives on the ways in which Hollywood creates the couple. The purpose of my study is to suggest a new strategy for the textual analysis of Hollywood cinema rather than to stand as a history. The films that I subject to intensive scrutiny reflect the differing concerns and arguments of each chapter. My aim is similar to Terry Eagleton's attempt in *The Ideology of the Aesthetic* "to reunite the idea of the body with more traditional political topics of the state, class conflict, and modes of production through the mediatory category of the aesthetic."[1]

In relating various historical issues to the reading of cinematic texts, I have learned from the example of the literary new historicists. Unlike some members of this group, however, I do not regard all historical information as discourse that must be given equal weight; my approach comprehends concepts such as "the historical real" and "facts." As David Simpson has stated: "Only a method based in materialist beginnings can provide any base for the reconstruction of a *possible* whole; only a materialist procedure can produce evidence that must, for any serious scholarly purpose, be unignorable" (746). For example, Rock Hudson's death from AIDS is accepted by most people as being of a different order of verisimilitude than is his status as a doctor, although he played such a role in *Magnificent Obsession*. Although Hollywood has notoriously manipulated the former kind of "factual" information about the stars' offscreen activities in order to foster the credibility of the latter "fictions" concerning the characters that they create onscreen, this distinction should not be lost sight of—even by those who remain committed to the proposition that the historical real is ultimately unknowable.

I have attempted to balance my emphasis on historical data with an equal emphasis on the power of discourse to shape and order these facts in complex and circuitous ways. To account for this complexity I have made use of Raymond Williams's concept of culture as a dynamic process created through the interplay of dominant, residual, and emergent discourses. This approach argues that cultural hegemony is continually being renegotiated; in Williams's words, "What the cultural sociologist or the cultural historian studies are the social practices and social relations which produce not only 'a culture' or 'an ideology' but, more significantly, those dynamic actual states and works within which there are not only continuities and persistent determinations but also tensions, conflicts, resolutions and irresolutions, innovations and actual changes" (*The Sociology of Culture* 29). Adapting Williams's emphasis on the interplay between residual, dominant, and emergent discourses has led me to pose textual readings in which the gaps and contradictions that are sometimes taken as signs of a subversive "progressivity" are understood somewhat differently. My discussion of such provocative textual moments may see them as revealing an emergent discourse, but it may also read them as vestiges of one which is residual.

Throughout the book I draw heavily on the insights of anthropology as a way of understanding the interaction between art and culture, and between sexuality and social organization. The comparativist perspective of anthropology, however, raises the difficult question of the privileged position claimed by interpreters of social processes. From what position of authority can I claim to speak if all interpretations are themselves placed within culture and history? I have responded to this dilemma by appealing to a notion of progress: one can thus distinguish between an all-encompassing relativism and a polysemy that would allow for varied responses to and uses of cultural products but that understands these variations as part of a larger social process in which progress is an operative principle.

Such a principle of progress, founded on Enlightenment values, would propose that scholarship has often been able to profit from its past accomplishments, at least in the sense of gaining a firmer grasp of the complexity of the phenomena with which it must come to grips and perhaps even in the sense of learning how to approach more productively the relationship between these phenomena and their cultural context. The modest proposition that the true is the useful has recently been updated by scholars like Richard Rorty and Nancy Fraser, whose work offers an escape from tendencies inherent in much recent poststructuralist theory toward the dissociation between intellectual endeavor and social responsibility.[2] Scholarship that derives its agenda from pragmatically conceived provisional "truths" has the hope of advancing our knowledge rather than simply revising it. This study is an attempt to contribute to that project.

I owe whatever strengths my argument may have largely to the generous intellectual contributions of colleagues, students relatives, and friends. In particular, I have greatly profited from discussions with, among others, Susan Tax Freeman, Christopher Hine, Chris Messenger, Chon Noriega, David Spurr, and Sylvia Vatuk, many of whom also offered valuable bibliographic leads. Parts of the manuscript were read and commented on by Alan Friedman and Linda Williams, and Judy Belfield patiently proofread the finished version. A quarter-long sabbatical leave and a year-long fellowship at the University of Illinois at Chicago Institute for the Humanities allowed me uninterrupted periods of time for research and writing; I greatly appreciate the support that the university provided for these leaves. Lachlan Murray was very helpful in locating important printed materials, and Joyce Drzal greatly facilitated my access to relevant films and videos. The frame enlargements that appear throughout the text were assembled with the help of Albert Richardson at the *Chicago Reader* and Cary Carr, Eugene Clardy, and Chuck Edelman at Helix Camera. Charles Silver at the Museum of Modern Art arranged for me to view the restored version of *Way Down East* along with a number of other Griffith films. Paolo Cherchi Usai at George Eastman House generously supplied me with the 35-mm frame enlargements from *Way Down East* and *Orphans of the Storm* (courtesy of the International Museum of Photography at George Eastman House), and Kristin Thompson provided general advice on related matters. Costs were covered by a grant from the UIC Research Board. The book's cover illustration was created by my daughter-in-law, Sara Swan. Joanna Hitchcock, Mary Murrell, and Colin Barr at Princeton University Press were unfailingly patient and helpful, and Barbara Grenquist was a meticulous and sensitive copy editor. All have my warmest appreciation. As always, my husband, John Huntington, has given me the benefit of his invaluable judgment and suggestions from the beginning; because of his unstinting contributions, this study represents, more than most, a collaborative enterprise.

Introduction: The Movies as Social Ritual

ROMANTIC LOVE, CHANGING MARRIAGE NORMS, AND STARS AS BEHAVIORAL MODELS

Undirected by culture patterns—organized systems of significant symbols—man's behavior would be virtually ungovernable, a mere chaos of pointless acts and exploding emotions, his experience virtually shapeless.

—CLIFFORD GEERTZ, The Interpretation of Culture

The deployment of sexuality has its reasons for being, not in reproducing itself, but in proliferating, innovating, annexing, creating, and penetrating bodies in an increasingly detailed way and in controlling population in an increasingly comprehensive way.

—MICHEL FOUCAULT, The History of Sexuality

Are not two loves essentially individual, hence incommensurable, and thus don't they condemn the partners to meet only at a point infinitely remote? Unless they commune through a third party: ideal, god, hallowed group . . .

—JULIA KRISTEVA, "In Praise of Love"

IN THEIR MONUMENTAL STUDY *The Classical Hollywood Cinema*, David Bordwell, Janet Staiger, and Kristin Thompson have calculated that 85 percent of all Hollywood films made before 1960 have romance as their main plot, and 95 percent have romance as either the main plot or a secondary plot. This empirical data corroborates a commonly held perception: in most Hollywood films, romantic love is a major concern. As in contemporary American culture generally, romantic love in Hollywood has traditionally been seen as properly culminating in marriage; thus, these movies are overwhelmingly preoccupied with what received Hollywood wisdom knows as its most reliable formula: boy meets girl, boy loses girl, boy gets girl. Raymond Bellour has called this convention "the creation of the couple" and has identified it as a pattern that "organizes, indeed constitutes, the classical American cinema as a whole" ("Alternation" 88).

Hollywood's emphasis on courtship and romantic love is a function of the movies' place within American—and indeed world—culture as a commercial enterprise based on the concept of mass entertainment. With its orientation toward box-office receipts and elaborate promotional strategies, Hollywood has positioned itself as a social institution. In the past, scholars have sometimes defended film as an art by celebrating the survival of the director's personal vision in the face of these commercial demands. Creatively ambitious filmmakers have often fostered this view by arguing that the "love interest" in their films is the result of the influence of crassly commerical producers and studio executives, who have thereby compromised the development of more "significant" themes.[1] However, such an opposition between "art" and "commerce" need not form the basis of critical interest in popular cinema, for it can also be claimed that Hollywood film is important because it constitutes a significant cultural practice, the conventions of which are related to the way we live. A close reading of filmic texts can be carried out against the background of American social history.

Raymond Williams has distinguished this approach to art as a practice from the more traditional view of it as a set of cultural objects. "The relationship between the making of a work of art and its reception is always active, and subject to conventions which in themselves are forms of (changing) social organization and relationship," Williams writes, "and this is radically different from the production and consumption of an object" (389). Terry Eagleton expands on this description of art as cultural practice when he defines it as "forms of *activity* inseparable from the wider social relations between writers and reader, orators and audience, [filmmakers and spectators,] inseparable from the wider social purposes and conditions in which they [are] embedded" (*Literary Theory* 206). Such an approach understands Hollywood filmmaking as an activity that occupies a position in contemporary culture analogous to the place that ritual occupies in more primitve societies. Anthropologist Victor Turner has characterized such ritualistic functions as follows: "When we act in everyday life we do not merely re-act to indicative stimuli, we act in frames we have wrested from the genres of cultural performance" (*From Ritual to Theatre* 122).

In a society in which the choice of marriage partners is, in theory at least, completely free, marriage patterns will be influenced by cultural institutions. As Pierre Bourdieu has argued: "The constraints surrounding every matrimonial choice are so tremendous and appear in such complex combinations that the individuals involved cannot possibly deal with them consciously, even if they have mastered them on a different level." Bourdieu's term for this largely unconscious level of social patterning is *habitus*. "[Marriage] strategies are the product of *habitus*," he writes, "meaning the practical mastery of a small number of implicit principles that have spawned their own pattern, although they are not based on obedience to any formal rules" ("Marriage Strategies" 141). Hollywood film, which has traditionally been addressed primarily to young people, can be seen as an institution that aids in the formation of such a *habitus* by modeling appropriate courtship behavior.[2]

Theories of Marriage and Romantic Love

To point to Hollywood's obsession with stories of romantic love tells us little if we are unable to specify a more precise meaning for the concept of love itself. Romantic love has, in fact, been the subject of widely diverse discussions conducted by philosophers, psychologists, sociologists, and anthropologists, among others. I will not attempt to digest the vast outpouring of material on this topic that has been produced by scholars in all these fields—not to mention the thousands of popular books on the subject. Instead, in what follows I will confine myself to considering a representative selection of diverse arguments about love so as to define my own approach in relation to some of the major traditions that now prevail.

Though philosophers from Plato onward have been fascinated by the subject of love, their concerns are typically both too abstract and too judgmental to be of much use for the kind of sociologically oriented investigation that I have engaged to undertake here. To cite a recent example, in *The Modern Age*, the last book of his trilogy *The Nature of Love*, Irving Singer distinguishes between a number of philosophical definitions of this phenomenon. He concludes that romantic love can be compatible with marriage in the modern world if it comprehends "falling in love," "being in love" and "staying in love," assuming that "human beings who develop properly . . . will be able to achieve a satisfying and desirable completion to love" (372). Whatever the merits of such discriminations, a normative procedure like this one, which is typical of the approach followed in most philosophical considerations of love, is of little use when dealing with a social formation that involves great numbers of people, both "proper" and "improper." A view of the subject of romantic love that accommodates itself more readily to actual social practices must be sought.[3]

Probably the most widely accepted theory of romantic love today is that of Freud, who focused his attention on the process by which children learn to direct their ability to love through their early experiences within the nuclear family. Freud distinguished between two kinds of object choices: the anaclitic type that results when children successfully resolve the Oedipus complex and learn to look outside of their immediate families in search of long-term sexual relationships with partners of the opposite gender, ordinarily in marriage arrangements; and the narcissistic type that results when children's libidos become fixated at an early stage in their sexual development and they fail to achieve this ideal of long-term heterosexual coupling.[4]

Freud's theory has been a particularly fruitful one for film analysis. However, its ahistorical model of social development within the nuclear family, its exclusive focus on sexuality conceived as a drive, and its idealization of love in relation to monogamous marriage make it an inadequate explanation of the role played by romantic love in organizing a variety of social arrangements in different times and places—arrangements that do not always emphasize connections among love, sexuality, and marriage. As Lawrence Stone has observed, "romantic love—this unusually brief but very intensely felt and all-consuming attraction towards another person—is culturally conditioned, and therefore common only in certain societies at certain times, or even in certain social groups within those societies—usually the elite with the leisure to cultivate feelings" ("Passionate Attachments" 16).[5]

Anthropological accounts of love and marriage in other cultures emphasize its role in organizing social and economic arrangements rather than its capacity for providing the kind of emotional fulfillment specified by the Freudian model. Sherry Ortner and Harriett Whitehead, for example, have stated: "The erotic dissolves in the face of the economic, questions of passion evaporate into questions of rank, and images of male and female bodies, sexual substance, and reproductive acts are peeled back to reveal an abiding concern for military honors, the pig herd, and the estate" (24). Explanations of romantic love that rely solely on Freudian psychology have no way of accounting for the kind of social and economic factors implied in descriptions such as these.

A more culturally relativistic account of romantic love is offered in Michel Foucault's *History of Sexuality*, which conceptualizes erotic desire as a modern ideology whereby social control is exercised by organizing the ways in which the body experiences pleasure. Foucault's emphasis on the changing meanings of the body and his understanding of the idealizing tendency of romantic love as a mask for strategies of power relations is a valuable concept. However, as Jürgen Habermas points out in *The Philosophical Discourse of Modernity*, Foucault's approach lacks a Utopian dimension. Though Foucault advocates the study of the socially marginal as a way of overcoming power differences, the concept of social equality is inimicable to his theory because he comprehends social organization solely in terms of shifting power relationships. Where there is only power, there can be no justice. An approach to romantic love that seeks to encompass the notion of social progress must therefore expand its theoretical horizen beyond Foucault.

Habermas himself has put forward a concept of communicative action as a way around the nihilism he finds in Foucault and other modern theorists who have denied the possibility of subject-centered reason. Habermas writes, "If we assume that the human species maintains itself through the socially co-ordinated activities of its members and that this co-ordination is established through communication—and in certain spheres of life, through communications aimed at reaching agreement—then the reproduction of the species *also* requires satisfying the conditions of a rationality inherent in communicative action" (397). Though there is cause to doubt that the notion of communicative action finally does away entirely with hidden agendas of power that thinkers since Nietzsche have attributed to subject-centered reason, by focusing on the potential for reciprocity in human relationships Habermas's approach does provide for the possibility of social systems that can be held up as superior to others because they are more egalitarian. I will briefly explore the implication of the utopian dimension of Habermas's formulation and its relationship to romantic love in the epilogue of this study; for the moment, however, it is important to note that his concept opens up the possibility of cohesive human interaction that is not determined solely by motives of power and narrow self-interest.[6]

In order to define an avenue of approach to the ways in which romantic love has been used as a social ideology in a variety of cultures, a theoretically oriented history of the subject is helpful. One such history has been put foward by the German sociologist Niklas Luhmann in his book *Love as Passion*. Using imaginative literature as his main evidence, Luhmann conceptualizes the history of romantic love in the West as a series of discursive formations, noting the different role such formations have played within different national traditions. He argues, "We assume that the thematic choices and guiding principles informing literary, idealizing, and mythicizing portrayals of love are not arbitrary, but rather represent reactions to the respective society and the trends for change within it" (20). These systems rely heavily on a network of established symbolic discourses through which they can be organized and regulated. Luhmann writes, "Taking a chance on love and the correspondingly complicated, demanding reorientation of everyday life is only possible if one has cultural traditions, literary texts, convincingly evocative linguistic patterns and situational images—in short, if one can fall back on a timeworn structure of semantics" (39). In the modern world Hollywood cinema may be construed as constituting such a semantic structure.[7]

Luhmann analyzes shifts that occurred from one system of romantic love to another as a function of shifting class and gender relations, focusing especially on the contradiction between the concept of romantic love as an intense, all-consuming passion that is by its nature short-lived and its status in the modern world as the cornerstone of lifelong monogamous marriage. Hollywood film has elided this contradiction through the convention of representing weddings (or the promise of weddings) as the culmination of its romantic-love fantasies; thus, romantic love after marriage need not be portrayed.

Luhmann sees contemporary culture as having fostered an ideology of romantic love centered on the ideal of sexual fulfillment and characterized primarily by notions of freedom and individuality. Here his insights need to be qualified, however, for our society is not as free as he implies. Anthropologists Ellen Ross and Rayna Rapp have pointed out that "[a]lthough the movement toward self-conscious sexuality has been hailed by modernists as liberatory, it is important to remember that sexuality in contemporary times is not simply released or free-flowing. It continues to be socially structured" (68).

The models of courtship and marriage put forward in Hollywood cinema make a significant contribution to the process of structuring the modern social *habitus* regarding romantic love. Sex researcher John Money has referred to the development of such a *habitus* on the individual level as the creation of a "love blot." When falling in love, he claims, "the person projects onto the partner an idealized and highly ideosyncratic image that diverges from the image of the partner as perceived by other people" (65). This image is tied to the proceptive phase of sexual arousal in which "imagery . . . is not only perceptual but also fictive" (76). Hollywood has traditionally supplied a steady stream of such fictions.

To account for the changes that the concept of romantic love has been subject to over the years it is necessary to consider the changing role of marriage and the family. Two influential accounts of the social origins of the family are associated with the names of Claude Levi-Strauss and Friedrich Engels. In *The Elementary Structures of Kinship* Levi-Strauss argues that the original mode of social organization centered on the use of women as objects of exchange. Like the exchange of gifts, the exchange of women between families ensured a social network of rights and obligations. According to Levi-Strauss, the need to exchange women among different families in order to create a social network accounts for the ubiquity of the incest taboo. He writes, "The prohibition of incest is less a rule prohibiting marriage with the mother, sister, or daughter than a rule obliging the mother, sister, or daughter to be given to others. It is the supreme rule of the gift" (481). Although Levi-Strauss concerns himself only with primitive cultures, his theory can be extrapolated to apply to more complex societies in which the concept of exchange can be used to promote a social network in groups with similar interests within the larger society. As Gayle Rubin states the matter: "The incest taboo imposes the social aim of exonomy and alliance upon the biological events of sex and procreation. . . . Specifically, by forbidding unions within a group it enjoins marital exchange among groups" (113).

The nature of such group interests and their role in promoting an ethic of endogamy as well as one of exogamy has been explored by Engels in his book *The Origin of the Family, Private Property and the State*. Engels argues that female subjugation within the family unit originated as a function of the ownership of private property.[8] He claims that the concept of private property induced men to enforce a division of labor in which they would be owners while women labored under their domination. By thus controlling women, men could devote their attention to acquiring more property and, by means of social strategies such as the institution of monogamous marriage, they could also ensure that their property would remain with their heirs. He writes, "Monogamy arose from the concentration of considerable wealth in the hands of a single individual—a man—and from the need to bequeath this wealth to the children of that man and of no other. . . . The man took control of the home . . . ; the woman was degraded and reduced to servitude; she became the slave of his lust and a mere instrument for the production of children" (138, 121). As one anthropologist recently stated the implications of Engels's theory: "Husbands are important mainly as fathers; that is to say, as men who give their name, and the right to inherit their property, to the children of the women with whom they have made a particular contract" (Mair 17). This argument stresses the use of marriage as a means of shepherding resources in the name of patriarchal interests. In complex societies such interests can be seen as including one's class and ethnic group as well as one's family. Thus marriages within class and ethnic boundaries would come to be seen as more desirable than more extreme forms of exogamic practices.[9]

Engels's theory complements that of Levi-Strauss; together they create a picture of social organization in which patterms of endogamy and exogamy in complex cultures are governed by class and ethnic interests. Marriages between various families of the same class and ethnic group will be fostered so as to promote group solidarity, but marriages across group lines however they are designated will be discouraged so as to ensure that social rewards will remain group specific. As anthropologists Sherry Ortner and Harriet Whitehead have noted, marriage in complex societies serves the function of "preserving or enhancing the purity or pedigree of the group" (22). Jack Goody has described the situation as follows: "Intermarriage would make it impossible to maintain extensive differences in behavior between individuals and groups, since it would lead to a merging of the subcultures that distinguish them" (*Production* 102). Thus, as Kingsley Davis has observed, "A cardinal principle of every stratified social order is that the majority of those marrying should marry equals" (quoted in Goody, *Production* 102).

As I have suggested, such a model of social organization, centered on the patriarchal family, can be understood as operating in modern cultures that profess to value individual freedom as well as in more traditional ones. In such societies an ideology of romantic love guides marriage choices at an unconscious level, thereby promoting the ideal of freedom of choice while at the same time discouraging sexual alliances both within individual families and between ethnically and class-segregated groups by engendering and supporting patterns of *habitus*. As Bourdieu argues: "a happy love, that is, a socially approved and success-bound love, [is] the same thing as that *amor fati*, love of one's own social destiny, which brings together socially compatible partners by way of a free choice that is unpredictable and arbitrary in appearance only" ("Marriage Strategies" 140).

In such a cultural configuration, extreme forms of endogamy (incest) and exogamy (miscegenation) will be seen as taboo because such practices run counter to the cementing of intragroup bonds and the conservation of resources around which the social fabric is constructed. Homosexual alliances and alliances between older women and younger men may also be disparaged, not because they may result in the wrong kind of family but because they imply no family structure at all—they neither produce heirs nor involve a woman who can be "given away" by her father upon marrying. In contrast to romantic love within the family or across class and racial lines, homosexual and older women–younger men alliances can be seen as excessive rather than as actively counterproductive. In a social economy that strives to channel people's emotional energies into creating familial bonds, however, these kinds of romantic ties will also be discouraged.[10]

Though an important strand of film theory has analyzed the way in which cinematic texts operate to constitute the couple, the concept of the couple is sometimes referred to as if it were a single monolithic entity. But *the couple* is a term with many meanings. As histories of sexuality and romantic love show, the function of romantic love can vary from culture to culture and over time.[11] Jeffrey Weeks, for example, states: "'Sexuality' is not an unproblematic natural given, which the 'social' works upon to control, but is, on the contrary, an *historical* unity which has been shaped and determined by a multiplicity of forces, and which has undergone complex historical transformations" (*Sex, Politics, and Society* xi). Joan Kelly's feminist study of the Renaissance makes a similar point in relation to a particularly historical case. She writes: "One index of a heightened patriarchal outlook among the Renaissance nobility is that love in the usual emotional and sexual sense must lead to marriage and be confined to it—for women, that is" (39). However, despite such historical shifts and constraints, romantic love has continued to thrive under a variety of cultural conditions.

In American society ethnic divisions have historically played a more prominent role in marriage patterns than have more strictly class-oriented considerations. However, as Werner Sollars's study *Beyond Ethnicity: Consent and Descent in American Culture* shows, Americans have a history of having balanced their commitment to preserving ethnic ties against an equally strong commitment to the concept of romantic love and free choice. "Romantic love became identified with America," Sollars states. "American allegiance, the very concept of citizenship developed in the revolutionary period was—like love—based on consent, not on descent, which further blended the rhetoric of America with the language of love and the concept of romantic love with American identity. . . . Since the eighteenth century American culture has in an exceptionally intense way emphasized this naturalized construct of romantic love as the basis for marriage" (112, 166–67).

Cultural historians generally agree that the emphasis on romantic love and its association with marriage and personal fulfillment first took hold in the nineteenth century as part of the romantic cult of individualism. As Ellen Rothman has stated, "In the middle decades of the nineteenth century, romance was fast losing its negative connotations and emerging as the only acceptable basis for intimacy between women and men. Romance was redefined as the key to domestic harmony rather than a threat to it. As Romantic love became something to celebrate rather than mistrust, 'falling in love' would become an increasingly normative part of middle-class courtship" (102).

By the early twentieth century the emergence of a public sphere fostered the development of a youth culture centered on courtship rituals largely cut off from supervision by the older generation. Social historians attribute this change to a variety of factors, including mobility, the weakening of family ties, increasing age segregation, a growing climate of material abundance, and newly available forms of commercial amusement. John Modell describes "a new system of social relations governed informally but firmly by young people themselves. . . . a date was away from home, unchaperoned, and not subject to parental veto" (92, 93). Modell suggests that it was "not the occurrence of emotional or physical intimacy but the question of whose advice guided young people in developing heterosexual ties that was the critical difference between dating and 'keeping company,' which it supplanted. . . . [The date] was a step in an ongoing negotiation with rules defined and deviation punished by age peers" (93, 94). Beth Bailey describes the evolution of this process in terms of the discovery of the movies: "couples courted on the streets, sometimes in cheap dance halls," she writes, "or eventually at the movies" (18). John D'Emilio and Estelle Freedman concur, stating that "in the early twentieth century, movies became meeting places for romantic trysts" (197). As a favored activity among members of the new youth culture and especially among courting couples, the movies were ideally positioned to instruct audiences about the changing mores governing romantic love.

The meanings of the romantic couple underwent further shifts during the early part of the century when traditional patriarchal forms of marriage began to give way to a newer idea of companionate marriage. Although romantic love was thought to be a necessary prelude to both, patriarchal marriage was based on the concept of separate spheres for husbands and wives—women as mothers and domestic managers and men as rule makers and breadwinners—while the companionate ideal stressed partnership and communication in the domestic sphere. At the same time sexual fulfillment came to be regarded as a significant by-product of romantic attachment and happy marriages. It perhaps goes without saying that the companionate model was less problematic in theory, where it could be posed in terms of an ideal of equal partnership, than in practice, where it was customarily interpreted as a wife who offered enlightened support to her husband's activities and values; nonetheless, the companionate ideal radically altered the ways in which most people thought about coupledom. In more recent years "the couple" has developed still other meanings that imply neither marriage nor heterosexuality. Further, sexual pleasure is today increasingly viewed as a means of self-expression and a mainstay of identity rather than as simply a means of forging stable heterosexual bonds using romantic love as glue. Each of these large categories contained an infinite number of variations. As historian Lawrence Stone has cautioned, "Chronological and class discrepancies will always thwart attempts to chart a neat pattern of development." Stone further states that the modern period has seen "a growing diversity of family types, a widening pool of cultural alternatives (*Marriage* 658).[12]

Traditional mainstream filmmaking practice has heavily promoted the ideal of monogamous marriage to a "suitable" partner. Besides following the general social taboo against incest, Hollywood, until very recently, included a clause in its production code prohibiting the portrayal of miscegenation as well. More subtle restrictions on accepted exogamic and endogamic practices decisively shaped the ways in which Hollywood moviemakers conceived of plots and characterizations. Over the years the movies' depictions of heterosexual romance moved from an acceptance of the Victorian notion of separate spheres to the companionate ideal to the validation of romance as a key to individual identity. Such shifts, and the modes by which they are defined against competing discourses, have had a profound and subtle effect on Hollywood filmmaking practice.

To illustrate the way in which a more sociologically and historically oriented approach to the issue of the couple would affect the reading of Hollywood storytelling practices, let us consider Hitchcock's 1954 *Rear Window*, a much-written-about film that has often been seen as one preoccupied with perverse sexuality, in particular voyeurism and castration. Such analyses rarely note, however, that the central problem faced by the film's main characters, L. B. Jeffries and Lisa Fremont (James Stewart and Grace Kelly), does not involve sex at all—in fact, the film goes to some length to emphasize the powerful and mutually satisfying sexual attraction that binds them together and motivates them to attempt to resolve the differences in their life-styles. These differences prevent them from creating a relationship that involves companionship as well as sex. Lisa's life revolves around women's fashion, whereas Jeff is committed to a career of adventure-oriented photojournalism. It is this level of incompatibility rather than sexual disfunctionality that disturbs Jeff and that lies at the center of the film's narrative complications.

The struggle between Jeff and Lisa can thus be understood as a struggle for power in a romantic relationship based on a principle of companionship. The failure of Jeff's nurse, Stella (Thelma Ritter), to calm his doubts about Lisa's suitability as a partner for him is due to the fact that her arguments reflect the views of an older generation for whom the notion of separate spheres makes the concern with companionship less central. Lisa herself presents yet another problem, for her superior economic resources and the elevated class status implied by her life-style and manner initially cause her to assume that she can adopt a leadership role in her marriage; she thus threatens Jeff's image of himself as a marital companion who at the same time occupies a superior position as a provider and as the partner who defines the couple's values and life-style. This power struggle must be resolved before "the couple" can be harmoniously constituted.

Lisa first attempts to define the companionate model in her own terms by trying to tempt Jeff with gourmet restaurant cuisine and visions of his future as the proprieter of a photography studio specializing in the feminized areas of fashion shoots and portraiture. When these ploys fail, she attempts to win him by helping him to capture a criminal, thereby entering into his life of adventure. The narrative implies that it is Lisa's enthusiasm for this enterprise that finally convinces Jeff that she can make a suitable mate for him and adapt to his world.

The final shot of Lisa in blue jeans putting down a book of travel adventure and picking up a fashion magazine while Jeff dozes off attests to the contradiction inherent in her position as the female partner in a companionate relationship in which she is expected to be both a sidekick and an object of erotic desire. (An earlier shot of Lisa posing for Jeff in her chic negligee suggests that her ability to enhance her aura of sexual desirability through the commodities proffered by the fashion industry is not an insignificant aspect of her attraction for him.) Though Lisa may acknowledge the work associated with the former role, she must mystify the work associated with the latter.

When considered from this perspective, the activities of the couples across the courtyard from Jeff's apartment acquire connotations quite different from those that have sometimes been attributed to them. For example, the newlywedded husband who loses his job because his sexually voracious wife has exhausted him suggests that marriages should involve satisfactions beyond the erotic ones. The attraction between Miss Lonelyhearts and her composer-neighbor suggests the importance of similar interests as well as sexual rapport in romantic attachments, and the reunion between Miss Torso and her sailor-husband suggests that marital fulfillment need not necessarily be founded on an attraction to a mate whose appearance conforms to culturally constructed criteria for erotic desirability. The older couple who sleep on the fire escape are posed as people who have reached a stage of marital relations at which sexuality has ceased to be a significant issue; instead, the complementary and mutually supportive roles they enact in relation to their little dog hint at the shared parental responsibilities that are conceived as part of the companionate model. Finally, Thorwald, the murderer, may be understood in terms of the desperate lengths to which a husband may be driven if he forms a marriage alliance with a wife who is not companionable.

Hitchcock has embedded this story of the struggle over the definition of acceptable parameters governing the companionate couple within a visual milieu that abounds with Freudian allusions to sexual anxiety and perversion; and he has further constituted the film's visual strategies so that the audience feels implicated by these allusions because of the voyeuristic activity that we indulge ourselves in by the very act of watching what the director puts in front of us. However, none of the many readings that explore this dimension of the film attempt to account for the discrepancy that exists between the movie's sexually charged visual subtext and its story; that is, these readings fail to establish that the narrative complications that problematize the creation of the couple are sexual rather than economic in nature. In the absence of such a connection Hitchcock's teasing allusions to sexual trauma must be regarded as at best playful titillations and at worst as an attempt to mystify the cultural issues at stake by distracting the audience with provocative hints about sexual complications which sophisticated modern filmgoers will be only too eager to seize upon. Like the police detective Tom Doyle (Wendell Corey), the audiences—and scholars—of Hollywood cinema may be readily distracted from problematic social issues by suggestions that may be taken as connoting the presence of material of a daring sexual nature. Just as Jeff twice cautions Tom to "be careful" about becoming sidetracked in this way, so may Hitchcock be warning his audience to ignore his sexual "Maguffins." In *The History of Sexuality* Michel Foucault similarly warns his readers about the distracting proliferation of discourses on sexuality in modern culture. By ignoring such warnings and placing an essentialized conception of sexual normality at the center of every Hollywood film, critics risk obscuring the historical and cultural factors involved in the creation of the couple.

Romantic Love and the Conventions of Star Performance

Besides serving as a guide to the creation of its staple boy meets girl–boy loses girl–boy gets girl–scenarios, Hollywood's romantic ideology of the idealized heterosexual couple has governed its creation of actors as symbols of romantic desirability. In so doing it has built on a long tradition of performance strategies. As Joseph Roach has observed, "The techniques whereby the body is prepared for performance, the particular bodily expressions whereby the public accepts the truth of performance, and the imagery whereby the body is eroticised in performance, illuminate at any given cultural moment the relationships between sexuality and power" (101).

As has frequently been pointed out, in the medium of cinema, the erotic potential of performance is particularly pronounced. In his seminal study *The Stars* Edgar Morin has argued that Hollywood film promotes its mythology of romantic love by presenting its stars as romantic ideals, thereby exploiting the spectator's dreamlike engagement with the cinematic experience. "The great lovers rule the screen, focusing love's magic upon themselves, investing their interpreters with divinizing virtues," Morin writes. "[T]hey are created to love and be loved, to fasten upon themselves that immense affective surge which constitutes the participation of the spectator. The star is above all an actress or an actor who becomes the subject of the myth of love, to the point of instigating a venerable cult" (40). As John Ellis was later to state, the star phenomenon "produces a relationship of desire between spectator and star performer that is intensified by the photo-effect of cinema itself" (108). The stars thus intensify the sexual charge inherent in the act of watching films, promoting a cult of romantic attraction that connects the rituals of love with an ideal of physical beauty.

Like romantic love itself, this ideal of physical beauty is culturally conditioned. To comprehend the extent of such conditioning one has only to compare art historian Kenneth Clark's book *Feminine Beauty* with anthropologist Robert Brain's book *The Decorated Body*. Clark's book poses a "timeless ideal" of physical beauty as represented in the work of great artists of the Western tradition; Brain's book, by contrast, documents the widely diverse standards of beauty held by different cultures as represented in photographs of people from around the world who have carefully cultivated features that appear grotesque to modern Americans: elongated necks and skulls, shrunken feet, and scarred and tattood torsos. Contemporary Western culture associates beauty especially with the bodies of women. In chapter 4 I explore the ways in which our culture and its movies mask the economic aspects of this operation by reifying female beauty, conceiving of it as a gift of nature, the product of luck and lineage rather than an investment of money and labor.

Although appearance is central to almost all performance, it is typically far more crucial in screen acting than it is in acting for the stage. Yet the significance of appearance as a dimension of film performance is rarely acknowledged. Instead, discussions of this topic commonly rely on criteria derived from the theater. The one distinction between the two kinds of performance commonly acknowledged in theory although rarely in practical criticism is the reduced distance between actors and spectators made possible by close-up photography. Although critics commonly recognize the more subtly nuanced gestural repertoire in screen performance that results from this distinction, the differences in the means by which actors control their appearance in each medium is largely ignored. On stage actors are prone to use wigs, makeup, and costume to project a variety of images. On screen they are more likely to employ less-obvious strategies such as hair coloring, plastic surgery, and weight control to project a single image that operates intertextually.[13]

If close-up photography has influenced the subtlety with which emotions and information are signaled through performance, it has also privileged a particular element associated with romantic attraction: the kiss. Lena Tabori's recent picture book of Hollywood kisses attests to the photogenic power of this representational strategy. The movie kiss represents a privileged moment of romantic bonding, the prelude to which is designed to foreground the emotional expressivity of the actor's face. Customarily this moment is designed to highlight the expression of romantic fulfillment on the face of the woman, who is foregrounded by a key light while her male partner remains in the shadows. Contemporary responses to the movies' early preoccupation with the kiss bear out its claim to significance: at the beginning of the century a New York newspaper proclamed, "For the first time in the history of the world, it is possible to see what a kiss looks like" (quoted in Freedman and D'Emilio 197); in 1909 a sixteen-year-old boy wrote to Florence Lawrence, "Your acting is realistic in many way[s], mostly the way you make love" (quoted in Gunning, *D. W. Griffith* 231).

A number of femininst film theorists have pointed to cinema's obsession with making female sexuality visible; conventional Hollywood representations of the romantic kiss exemplify this preoccupation. Hollywood's traditional stories of courtship and marriage have typically focused on the woman's resistance to romantic attachments; therefore, the kiss often represents a significant moment of change for her and documents her surrender to the erotic will of the man. Hollywood's highlighted close-ups of the actress's face at such moments emphasize her pleasure and even relief in this abandonment of separation and independence. Not coincidently, it is at this moment when she is at her most beautiful: expertly made up, exquisitely coiffed, and elegantly costumed. Herman Buchtman's book on screen makeup reveals that the practices of Hollywood cosmeticians are designed to enhance this effect of the woman spotlighted during romantic close-ups. He writes, "A practical rule requires the male performer's skin tones to be two or three shades darker than those of the female performer" (28).

Traditional Hollywood films often made use of kisses as a means of effecting narrative closure: the final fade-out followed the long-awaited clinch. David Bordwell provides empirical evidence of this practice in his *Narration in the Fiction Film* when he reports that of over one hundred randomly sampled Hollywood films from the studio era, over sixty ended with a display of the united romantic couple (159). Presumably a good proportion of these displays occurred as kisses. As John Belton has pointed out, even as early as *True Heart Susie* (1918) D.W. Griffith employed the device of the frustrated kiss to structure his story and win sympathy for his heroine, whose poignant looks of expectation followed by disappointment could be captured in lingering close-ups (166). The 1937 version of *Stella Dallas* also makes use of the kiss as a structuring element, this time in a somewhat self-reflexive manner. Early in the story, Stella is enchanted by the vision of actors kissing in a movie; at the end she watches her daughter engaging in a similar kiss through a window whose dimensions echo those of the movie screen that initially established her vision of human fulfillment as a kiss. Significantly, it is Stella's expression of rapture as she observes this privileged moment that is focused on, for the story has positioned the kiss in terms of the vicarious pleasure of those who, like moviegoers, witness this activity rather than the romantic couples who participate in it.

In recent years the increasing reliance on sexual explicitness in the depiction of romantic coupling has made it difficult to design love stories that could privilege the actor's faces as revealed in climactic close-ups. One reason for the success of the 1990 hit *Pretty Woman* is that it managed to revive the structuring power of the kiss as an erotic crescendo by positioning it as a signal of a love that transcends sex. The prostitute-heroine (Julia Roberts) confides early on that she never kisses clients; the audience then waits for the moment when she will break this rule with the film's hero (Richard Gere), thereby attesting that their sexual relationship has gone beyond the level of a casual business transaction.

Realism, Formalism, and the Hollywood Star System

Actors' portrayals of romantic passion as well as their depictions of other characterological features may be judged using a variety of standards.[14] As I discuss in chapter 5 V. I. Pudovkin's conception of character types in film defines screen acting in terms of casting skills rather than performance skills, thus crediting the director as the sole creator of screen characters. "In order to create a required appearance, the stage actor tries to find and create the necessary make-up, altering his face," Pudovkin has written. "For this reason one cannot build up a required type artificially for the screen; one must discover him" (*Film Technique* 134–35). Subsequently, European directors such as Robert Bresson, Werner Herzog, and the Italian neorealists have followed a similar aesthetic of character "typage" in their films by casting non-actors whose appearance corresponded to the type of a given character. Bresson has defended his practice of using models by commenting, "An actor, even (and above all) a talented actor, gives us too simple an image of a human being, and therefore a false image" (Schrader 65). Such an approach has never been plausible in Hollywood films, which rely heavily on the promotion of star personalities as a marketing strategy. But even in European films, the theory of typage, although it emphasizes the importance of appearance, denies the role that actors play in shaping their appearance.

In an essay entitled "On Acting and Non-Acting" drama scholar Michael Kirby has schematized commonly held realist views of acting by representing them on a continuum from what he calls nonmatrixed performance to what he calls complex acting. Although Kirby denies that value judgments enter into his scheme, the term *complex acting* in itself suggests that he regards such acting in a different light from non-matrixed performance, which he also calls "non acting." Merely wearing a costume or makeup on stage is not, for Kirby, acting, which only occurs when "emotions are 'pushed' for the spectator" (103). The problem inherent in such a formulation appears when one begins to question how "pushed" emotions are to be discerned by an observer-critic, for Kirby claims that "the motionless performer may convey certain attitudes and emotions that are acting even though no physical actions are involved" (104).

Kirby's view of performance recapitulates the emphasis on the interior life of the actors espoused by theories of Method acting and, more generally, by traditional realistic theories of acting that look for a "true-to-life" quality. Such theories are of little use as critical tools, for they disallow consideration of specific acting techniques in favor of a rhetoric that valorizes the actor's inner feelings and their putative authenticity. By concerning themselves solely with the emotional content of performance seen from the actor's point of view, such theories hold up standards for performance that are beyond the power of the critic to analyze. How are commentators to distinguish between an actor's portrayal of emotion and the emotion of a person who is actually experiencing a given state? Although actors may express pain in performance, their emotion has a different status from the feelings of a person who is genuinely in pain. The concept of "pushed" emotions makes a great deal of this distinction but offers no way of analyzing it.

An alternative approach to acting, historically associated with Diderot's essay on the subject, stresses technique over feeling. Diderot's approach avoids the problem of trying to determine when actors are being authentic and when they are faking. More recently, Erving Goffman has suggested that all behavior can be seen as a kind of performance and that "acting" can be identified simply as performance within a theatrical "frame." Such a approach to acting allows the critic to bypass Kirby's troublesome distinctions between emotions that are genuine, "pushed," or merely false and concentrate instead on constructing technical descriptions of all the dimensions of performance.[15]

However, this approach, too, presents problems. First, the extensive studies of social-science researchers like Ray Birdwhistle, Edward Hall, and Erving Goffmann notwithstanding, it remains doubtful that any scientific principles of kinesic activity could prove fruitful for film analysis, in part because, as Roberta Pearson has pointed out, the sheer complexity and indeterminacy of the kinesic information which would necessarily be involved in any such analysis mitigates against these kinds of applications. Further, as Richard Schechner and Cynthia Mintz have observed, performance is continuous (or, to cite their term, *anologic*) while its analysis must approach this phenomenon in terms of discrete (or *digital*) units. Thus, though kinesic data may serve as evidence for critical argumentation about performance techniques, it must be combined with and weighed against other kinds of evidence and methodological strategies in order to produce persuasive and consequential conclusions.

A second problem inherent in a strictly formalistic analysis of Hollywood performance concerns its emphasis on textuality to the exclusion of what may be termed "the historical real." Social scientists working in this tradition see all behavior as performance—as text—thus they, like Kirby, have no way of distinguishing between performance and nonperformance. Yet the Hollywood star system was developed in part to bridge a perceived gap between these two modes. While Hollywood film has fostered performances that read as seamless wholes, exhibiting what James Naremore has called "expressive coherence," the Hollywood star system has built on the realistic identification between performer and role by positioning stars as people who are simply "being themselves" on screen. Stanley Cavell states the case aphoristically when he writes, "For the stage, an actor works himself into a role; for the screen, a performer takes the role onto himself" (*The World Viewed* 27). The success of stars as performers is often explained by referring to the "magic" of their personalities rather than to their skills as actors. As Manohla Dargis comments, "The predominant style in mainstream American films today is a carefully modulated 'realism,' one that attempts to erase its own footprints as the movie unfolds" (32).

Film historians' understanding of the origins of the star system as an extratextual popular discourse has undergone considerable revision in recent years. In her essay "Seeing Stars" Janet Staiger has argued that Carl Laemmle's promotion of Florence Lawrence in 1910, which had formerly been taken as the beginning of the popular discourse on stars, was not an isolated event but rather the culmination of a number of previous moves in that direction. Further, Richard de Cordova points out in his book *Picture Personalities* that for a time following the promotion of Lawrence and other early motion-picture players actors were identified only with their on-screen roles; their personal lives remained private. De Cordova distinguishes between full-fledged stars and early picture personalities like Lawrence whose offscreen activities were not publicized. Only after the star system was fully developed did the relationship between a star's offscreen persona and an individual performance become a topic of popular discourse.

Once in place, this discourse quickly became complex and indeterminate. In his seminal study *Stars*, Richard Dyer employs the term *structured polysemy* to reflect "the finite multiplicity of meanings and effects they embody and the attempts so to structure them that some meanings and aspects are foregrounded as others are masked or displaced" (51). Dyer distinguishes between four different levels of discourse surrounding star images: promotion (controlled by the star or studio), publicity (out of the control of the star or studio), films, and criticism and commentary. These discourses are commonly perceived as having varying relationships to the historical real.[16]

One can explore the implications of these variations while avoiding some of the epistemological difficulties with which poststructuralist theory has surrounded the concept of the historical real by invoking the less troublesome notion of regimes of verisimilitude. To draw on the terms employed by Tvsetan Todorov in *The Poetics of Prose*, stars can be understood as representing a means by which Hollywood could invest the *generic verisimilitude* of its stories with the *cultural verisimilitude* of the major players who took part in these stories.[17] Through practices like typecasting and personal publicity, Hollywood used the star system to give its productions a greater—and qualitatively different—aura of realism. One need not adopt a posture of naive credulity regarding all the "facts" that Hollywood purveys about its stars in order to argue that the film audience has traditionally percieved this information as being endowed with a kind of authenticity that it does not grant to the fictional forms of the films themselves. The disbelief that people suspend when they go to the movies becomes a less-significant factor when they read the fan magazines.[18] When they read reports in the "legitimate" press, such disbelief is rarely brought into play at all. Despite Hollywood's notorious history of creating backgrounds for its players that conform to their on-screen images, such information retains a special status in relation to the stars' fictional roles, investing these roles with a degree of verisimilitude that allows not only the actors themselves to be positioned as social models but also the characters they play. As Barry King puts it in his essay "Articulating Stardom," star performers are commonly understood as *personators* rather than *impersonators*.

At times the cultural verisimilitude associated with an actor's off-screen persona is introduced into the cinematic text itself to further enhance the impression that the stars are merely playing themselves, as when Spencer Tracy silences Katharine Hepburn in *Adam's Rib* (1949) by commenting, "Now don't give me that Bryn Mawr stuff again." A more sustained strategy of this type can be observed in Marlon Brando's rambling speech in *Last Tango in Paris* (1972) delivered beside the body of the character's dead wife and widely read as autobiographical. Similarly Dexter Gordon in *'Round Midnight* (1988), ostensibly portraying fellow jazz musician Bud Powell, expresses seemingly genuine and unrehearsed feelings about his sense of professional calling when he is interviewed by a hospital social worker. Both of these speeches are read by many members of the audience as confessions of highly personal experiences in the lives of the actor-speakers.

Hollywood is also adept at exploiting sensational events in the lives of the stars to promote films that play upon the audience's knowledge of these events in the manner of *films à clef*. Thus Cheryl Crane's putative attachment to the boyfriend of her mother, Lana Turner, the subject of a widely publicized murder trial, was played upon in Douglas Sirk's 1959 *Imitation of Life*; and Rob Lowe's amorous activities with two young women and a video recorder became the focus for the marketing strategy of his 1988 vehicle *Bad Influence*.

In a more general sense, the customary Hollywood practice of tailoring dialogue to the speech patterns of particular actors and the inclination of many stars to rewrite or improvise dialogue to suit their taste heighten the audience's sense of actors who are merely being themselves on-screen. Writer-comedians like Mae West and W. C. Fields are perhaps most conspicuously identified with this practice, but it has always been widespread in the Hollywood film industry. Perhaps the Hollywood actor most successful at merging persona and role in all these areas was John Wayne, whose achievement in investing the Western genre with an aura of realism will be explored in chapter 3.

The status of the stars as historical personages is significant not only in relation to the added dimension of verisimilitude which is thereby invested in their performances but in its own right as well. As social historican Elaine Tyler May states, "Perhaps even more than media images, the widely publicized 'private lives' of motion picture celebrities had a profound impact across the nation" (75). To an extraordinary degree, these media stories of the stars' lives are framed as scenarios of romantic attraction. Richard de Cordova has observed that "the star system, and arguably twentieth century culture in general, depends on an interpretive schema that equates identity with the private and furthermore accords the sexual the status of the most private, and thus the most truthful, locus of identity" (*Picture Personalities* 140). As is now well known, in the heyday of the studio system dates were routinely arranged between contract players. Expectations that the stars would always be romantically involved led many to engage in a series of publicized relationships. The contradiction that then emerged between such a pattern of behavior and the ideal of long-term monogamy was customarily resolved by structuring the narratives of their lives so that these tales climaxed with the revelation of a single "great" love that was tragically destroyed as a result of death, "career pressures," or some other impediment (for example, Clark Gable and Carole Lombard, Humphrey Bogart and Lauren Bacall, Frank Sinatra and Ava Gardner, Elizabeth Taylor and Richard Burton).[19] The stars thus represent a particular form of pleasure related not simply to a regime of hedonistic sexual activity but also to the formation of the romantic couple. Further, the discourse of sexual fulfillment in which this ideal is embodied is perceived as ahistorical and ineffable; in actuality, however, it represents specific political and economic concerns.

Courtship Conventions and Performance Styles: Humphrey Bogart in The Maltese Falcon *and* The Big Sleep

To exemplify the way in which the three variables that I have adduced—evolving ideologies concerning romantic coupling, narrative patterns, and acting technique—interact in Hollywood filmmaking practice, it is useful to compare two films starring Humphrey Bogart: *The Maltese Falcon* (1941) and *The Big Sleep* (1946). In both films Bogart plays a hard-boiled detective, a character type closely identified with his star persona and thus widely perceived as a "natural" expression of his "true" character. At the same time, Bogart's highly mannered style invites an analysis in which issues of performance technique as well as strategies of cultural verisimilitude can come into play.[20]

Both *The Maltese Falcon* and *The Big Sleep* were produced during a period of cultural upheaval when heterosexual relations were strongly marked by volatility and flux. One can read *The Maltese Falcon* as a cynical prognosis about future prospects for the traditional style of patriarchal marriage; its story is built around a struggle for male dominance in which the strength and independence of the woman ultimately disallows the possibility of a stable portrait of traditional romantic coupling. *The Big Sleep*, on the other hand, presents a similarly independent woman, but the Bogart hero regards her more as a potential partner than a potential threat. The film's depiction of their romance understands their relationship as a model for the newer companionate ideal rather than as an opportunity to indict the older practice of patriarchal marriage. Both narratives also articulate discourses on class and ethnicity which play a significant role in determining the operative definition of romance. The films' figuration of the body and Bogart's performance style reveal significant differences that relate to these differing views of courtship and marriage.[21]

In order to understand the way in which Bogart's depiction of the romantic hero operates in each of these films, we must first trace the route by which the hard-boiled detective figure became part of his star persona. *The Maltese Falcon* and *The Big Sleep* were important in establishing the actor's matinee-idol status during the forties and later; but prior to that time he had developed a screen image grounded in class rather than sexual issues. The strong class associations that surrounded the Bogart persona by 1940 play a major role in defining his tough-guy detective in *The Maltese Falcon* and *The Big Sleep* as a romantic hero who could articulate in a compelling way the relationship between class issues and the formation of the heterosexual couple.

Bogart was an ideal choice for the proletarian figure of the hard-boiled detective not because such roles reflected his actual background. In fact, Bogart the man was quite different from Bogart the star image. Born to an affluent social-register family in New York City, he grew up attending private schools. His first roles on stage and in films were consistent with his upbringing: he became typed as the kind of characrter who enters a scene asking, "Tennis anyone?" Although these parts were similar to his previous life experience, he did not have great success playing them. Instead, his breakthrough as an actor came in a role completely alien to him, that of a lower-class gangster. The vehicle was Robert Sherwood's *The Petrified Forest*, which Bogart starred in first on Broadway and then on the screen in 1936. The role of underworld thug Duke Mantee was well adapted to the image that Bogart projected. Though the actor was, in reality, a blue-blooded WASP society boy, his swarthy complexion and heavy features gave him the look of a southern European immigrant; and the dissipation in his face suggested a man who had known life in some of its unsavory aspects. His voice fit the image, too; it had a harsh, nasal edge that took readily to the tough-guy diction of Duke Mantee.

As effective as Bogart was in the role of Duke Mantee, however, his performance in the film version of *The Petrified Forest* is marred by broad, overdrawn effects that he had carried over from the stage, and it took several more years in Hollywood before he was able to develop a more subtle technique suitable for films. As Duke Mantee, he walks awkwardly, hunched over with his arms dangling loosely in front of him to give the impression of an apelike man with limited intellectual resources (fig. 1.1). His street-wise accent is virtually a caricature, typified by phrases like "Nevah hoid of it," and "Wadda you tink?" Most significantly, he never puts his hands to his face—a habit he was to cultivate with a myriad of elegant variations later in his career. In *The Petrified Forest* Bogart found a tough-guy image that he could develop, but he had yet to learn about acting in close-up.

By the time he starred in John Huston's *The Maltese Falcon* in 1941, however, Bogart's cinematic technique had matured. Even more importantly, the role was ideally suited to his type. The hard-boiled detective hero shared the lower-class origins and experience-hardened demeanor of the gangster heavies the actor often played during the late 1930s. But the detective was a more admirable figure; although he was threatened by the brutality of the urban milieu that surrounded him, he had the toughness and wit to triumph over it. Moroever, unlike Bogart's earlier screen incarnations, this figure was seen as one who was attractive to women.

Bogart was an appropriate choice for the hard-boiled detective role in part because of his height. He was not as tall as Western heroes like John Wayne and Gary Cooper, who, as I will argue in chapter 3, convey a certain moral superiority on-screen merely by virtue of their towering stature. But neither was Bogart as short as such archetypal film gangsters as James Cagney and Edward G. Robinson, who appear visually at a disadvantage with others and whose contentious temperaments invariably set them at odds with the world around them in encounters that foreground the negotiation of power relations. Bogart was of average height: short enough to share some of the gangster's pugnaciousness, but tall enough to partake in some of the Western hero's dignity. In addition, his wiry build gave him the fast-moving agility commonly associated with urban film heroes, and his rapid-fire delivery of dialogue suggested a quick-witted man who could cope with the complex milieu of the big city.

The tough-guy heroes that Bogart created in *The Maltese Falcon* and in Howard Hawks's *The Big Sleep* in 1946 were both of this type; yet they were by no means the same character. The distinction between them is a function of their contrasting attitudes toward romantic love. The scenarios of the two films gave their protagonists appreciably different roles in relation to women: the former is a misanthropic bachelor, whereas the latter initiates a romance plot which increasingly dominates the action. Bogart's perfomance style helped in distinguishing these figures by drawing on the wide range of expressions, gestures, and movements that he had developed during his prolific moviemaking activities in the late thirties. The contrasting visual strategies for representing the human body employed by Huston and Hawks support this differentiation in the characterization of the romantic hero.

In *The Maltese Falcon* the role of Dashiell Hammett's detective hero Sam Spade is that of a cynically defensive loner who is suspicious of all relationships, romantic and otherwise. This hostility has its source in his unesay relationship to a class identity. The worldly adventurers whom he confronts, including the connoisseur Kasper Gutman (Sydney Greenstreet) and his two associates Joel Cairo (Peter Lorre) and Wilmer (Elisha Cook, Jr.), are in quest of a fabulous art object (the eponymous falcon). The film's climax centers on the discovery that this object is a forgery, a revelation designed to emphasize the perverse monomania of the upper-class art collector. ("For seventeen years I have wanted that little item," Guttman asserts when he learns that the bird is a fake. "If I must spend another year on the quest—well, sir . . .") The woman in the case, Brigid O'Shaughnessy (Mary Astor), may be either Spade's adversary or his ally, but she is clearly more at home in the film's sophisticated world of international intrigue than he is.

Spade's distrust of this world leads him to assume that others are not to be trusted: "Everybody has something to conceal," he remarks at one point. Spade himself hides behind a variety of masks: the soothing father figure ("Suppose you tell me about it from the very beginning."), the volatile negotiator ("Keep that gunsel out of my way while you're making up your mind. I'll kill him if you don't. I'll kill him."), the irrespressible jokester ("Well, boys and girls, we put it over nicely!"), or the declamatory orator ("You getting this all right, son, or am I going too fast for you?"). In each case we understand that Spade is shamming. Such poses cloak his real interests and motives, "making it easier to deal with the enemy." And in *The Maltese Falcon* everyone is potentially Spade's enemy. The menacing, unpredictable character of his environment repeatedly asserts itself through the prevailing low-angle shots and odd, jarring compositions; the intensity of the threat is expressed in the high percentage of close-ups.

In such a setting height is all-important because it confers dominance and authority. Accordingly, Spade is taller than Wilmer, Cairo, and Guttman, whom he is destined to outsmart (although Guttman gains a certain aura of stature during the film's middle sections by virtue of Huston's strategy of shooting him from a low angle [fig. 1.2]). The police, on the other hand, represent the more solid power of social justice that must, in the end, be accommodated; hence they are taller than the hero (fig. 1.3). Most problematic are the women, including Brigid, his secretary, Effie (Lee Patrick), and his dead partner's wife, Ida Archer (Gladys George), each of whom brings an unpredictable element of sexual allure to the struggle for power. They are all nearly as tall as Spade: he is able to control them, but only with the greatest difficulty, as is made clear in his final confrontation with Brigid (fig. 1.4).

In *The Maltese Falcon* one way of wielding power is through displays of status and wealth. Spade must play this game with the others, but his appearance suggests that he is ill equipped for it. The dandified formality of his double-breasted suits and his slicked-back hair are belied by Bogart's clipped, nasal enunciation as well as by his heavy-featured ethnicity and by the scar that is clearly visible on his upper lip in the movie's many close-ups (fig. 1.5). The status trappings thus emerge as only another of Spade's masks, adopted so that he can deal on an equal footing with the continental Joel Cairo and the urbane Guttman, who speaks with a slight British accent and occupies a luxurious flower-filled hotel room. The equally cosmopolitan Brigid O'Shaughnessy, who buys her clothes in Hong Kong, constitutes, as we shall see, the most problematic challenge to Spade's shaky claim to social status.

Spade's sleek, carefully groomed exterior functions as a smooth armature holding in the tension that continually seethes inside him, a tension emanating from a fear that his masks will be swept aside and the vulnerability within exposed. Despite his brave front, Spade is not a secure man, as Bogart's watery eyes and moist lower lip communicate only too clearly (fig. 1.6).[22] And the actor's neurotically defensive gestures bear out the impression that his appearance projects. He smokes constantly. At moments of stress he pulls his upper lip back over his teeth or puts his hand to his face, stroking his jaw, rubbing his nose, or pulling at his lower lip (figs. 1.7, 1.8, 1.9, and 1.10). At times, the tension in these movements is underlined by a trembling muscle in Bogart's right cheek.

The meaning of these mannerisms is made more explicit by Bogart's actions in relation to the people around him, when the compulsion to dominate others overwhelms the desire for closeness. As Sam Spade, Bogart often stands with his hands challengingly on his hips or jabs his finger at those who question his authority (figs. 1.11 and 1.12). After vanquishing an adversary, he claps his hands and grins in triumph or blows smoke in the face of his foe (figs. 1.13 and 1.14). When he touches others, he clutches them, leading his secretary (Lee Patrick) to protest at one point that he is hurting her arm (fig. 1.15). When he takes Wilmer's guns away or tries to hit Lieutenent Dundy (Barton MacLane), his aggressive reflexes operate with the speed of an instinctive response.

These obsessive gestures, protective of the self, hostile toward others, determine Spade's demeanor in relation to his erotic life as well. William Luhr has argued that the love story "has very little to do with the story of *The Maltese Falcon*," which centers on "deviant sexuality, . . . Gutman's fetishistic obsession and his possible homosexual acolytes" (10). But this film suggests that all expressions of sexuality are involved with displays of power and status. Peter Lorre's effeminate Joel Cairo represents the least-palatable sexual threat to the machismo-obsessed proletarian hero. As Cairo enters the detective's office, Spade is seen in close-up licking his cigarette paper (fig. 1.16). Cairo, as he talks, fondles the handle of his umbrella; and later Spade, a cigarette dangling out of the side of his mouth, grins sadistically as he delivers a gratuitous blow to his effete visitor, as though taking pleasure in punishing Cairo for responding to his initial teasing come-on (figs. 1.17 and 1.18). The strong homoerotic overtones of the scene pointed to by critics like Vito Russo and Richard Dyer ("Homosexuality in Film Noir") are played up by Bogart's performance, which emphasizes the character's triumphantly homophobic reaction to a sexual invitation that constitutes a disturbing challenge to his sense of masculine superiority—a challenge complicated by the Europeanized upper-class image here associated with homosexuality. The gleeful relish with which Spade treats Guttman's sexually ambiguous "gunsel" Wilmer constitutes a further instance of the character's homophobia.[23]

All these motifs come together in the film's love plot, where Spade's obsession with power and status overcomes his sexual attraction to a formidable woman. When he first kisses Brigid, Spade holds her roughly by the throat, thereby brutally shielding himself from the threat of intimacy by asserting his ability to control her physically (fig. 1.19). The film's climactic confrontation between the two similarly stresses dominance over bonding (figs. 1.4 and 1.6), and the final image of Brigid descending in an elevator flanked by two policemen graphically depicts her downfall in terms of diminished status.

The Maltese Falcon thus features a hero who is unable to achieve romantic satisfaction because he is caught between two ideologies of coupledom. On the one hand, his affair with his partner's wife reveals him as a character who craves excitement and challenge in his romantic attachments and who rejects traditional sexual proprieties. For this reason, a traditionally submissive woman like his secretary bores him. Nonetheless, because of his insecure sense of class affiliation, the more provocative prospect of a relationship with a sophisticated, self-reliant woman posed by the newer companionate ideal and represented in the film by the charcter of Brigid threatens his sense of masculine superiority. The character's ambivalent emotions of attraction and repulsion are played out in a romantic scenario with strong sadomasoschistic overtones and ultimately lead to a romantic standoff.

If the need to dominate others—especially in the sexual realm—overwhelms the desire to be close to them in Bogart's interpretation of Sam Spade, the opposite holds true of his portrayal of Raymond Chandler's Philip Marlowe in *The Big Sleep*. Here the script is designed to capitalize on the romantic pairing of Bogart and Lauren Bacall, who had just created a popular sensation in Hawks's 1945 *To Have and Have Not*. And the director's predilection for witty repartee and high-spirited adventure furthers this romantic emphasis. Bogart's Marlowe begins by forming a strong bond with the wealthy General Sternwood (Charles Waldron), Marlowe's client and the father of Bacall's character Vivian Rutledge. In the course of his quest to find Sternwood's former employee Shawn Regan, the detective also relieves Vivian of the burden of protecting her emotionally unstable sister Carmen (Martha Vickers) from the blackmailer Eddie Mars. Vivian is thereby freed to pursue a romance with Marlowe, the man who has rescued her.

Though *The Big Sleep* boasts eight murders and a gloomy *film noir* ambience, the prevailing tone is lighter than that of *The Maltese Falcon*. Hawks likes to focus on the bonds between people as represented in tightly knit social groups; for this reason, the tension between the hero and the police, which is so conspicuous in *The Maltese Falcon*, is absent from *The Big Sleep*. And the director's lavish use of eye-level medium shots of several characters within a single frame means that the mood is less intense and more convivial than in Huston's film. Hawks's version of the hard-boiled–detective formula is about cooperation rather than competition, about getting together rather than getting ahead. In *The Big Sleep* a residual discourse of male dominance which is understood as having reached an impasse in *The Maltese Falcon* gives way to an increasingly hegemonic discourse on romance as companionship and an expression of sexual equality.[24]

This emphasis on the companionate couple, which overlies the tough-guy formula that was by then part of the Bogart persona, resulted in some strains during the film's production. To play up the romance elements in the film, Hawks shot additional footage of Bogart and Bacall together subsequent to the primary shooting schedule. Moreover, the logic of the mystery plot, in particular the question of who killed the Sternwoods' former chauffeur, Owen Taylor, was the subject of considerable debate both during the development of the script and after the film was released. (For histories and analyses of this controversy, see Shatzkin; Bordwell, *Narration* 345–46; and Mast, *Howard Hawks* 277.) In interviews Hawks dismissed these shifts and lapses in narrative consistency as unimportant, arguing that the crucial consideration was to "make good scenes" (McBride 104). However, the finished film, especially considered in relation to the well-publicized Bogart-Bacall romance, follows a clear narrative logic which positions the mystery plot as a device that initially serves to provide a plausible underpinning for Bogart's character and later functions as a means of bringing the two stars together as a romantic couple. Once this latter purpose is achieved, the mystery loses narrative interest; thus, despite its narrative gaps and confusions, *The Big Sleep* achieves, for most audiences, a satisfying sense of closure.

Approaching *The Big Sleep* as a study in the creation of a companionate couple allows for an understanding of the film that avoids the generality of Raymond Bellour's reading in his essay "The Obvious and the Code," which sees it as yet another Hollywood rendering of an undifferentiated notion of heterosexual bonding. Critics such as Annette Kuhn, Christopher Orr, and Judith Mayne have argued for a more discriminating understanding of the film's discourse on sexuality, pointing to traces of male homoeroticism and female bonding. However, in addition to these sexually "scandalous" features, the film's depiction of the heterosexual couple itself can be differentiated from that portrayed in other mainstream productions, even a film as similar as *The Maltese Falcon*. These differences are in turn related to the films' differing representations of class and ethnicity.

The marks of Hollywood's evolving conception of romantic love affect Bogart's portrayal of the hard-boiled–detective figure at many levels. In the later film the issue of height is defused. Almost all the characters in Hawks's film are relatively equal in stature, and there are few if any of the low-angle shots that invest tall people with such menace in *The Maltese Falcon*. Instead, the superior-inferior relationship established among characters of varying heights is replaced by a motif of circling, which signifies both the desire to size others up from all sides before committing one's trust to them or, on a more intimate level, the protectiveness of physical enclosure. To express this idea, Bogart's movements are orchestrated to complement those of the film's other characters. Marlowe participates in a series of dancelike sequences in which he is alternately a passive or active agent in the process of circling. When he meets Carmen, she walks around him appraisingly, just as Mars's two "boys" do in a more aggressive manner when they confront him (figs. 1.20 and 1.21). Marlowe himself uses this device as a means of getting to know others when he circles Joe Brody (Louis Jean Heydt) as he questions him about the murdered pornographer Arthur Gwynne Geiger and, in a more benign mood, when he moves around General Sternwood as he is listening to the old man's problem (figs. 1.22 and 1.23).

Of course, it is in the love affair between Marlowe and Vivian that the greatest degree of trust is developed, and the progress of their romance is subtly measured by the shifting pattern of Bogart and Bacall's movements in relation to each other. The first encounter between the two lovers is marked by Vivian restlessly pacing around the detective as Marlowe remains relatively stationary; she, suspicious and nervous, appears to be stalking him, while he, relaxed and uninvolved, coolly appraises her (fig. 1.24). Later, however, as he kisses her in his car following the attempted robbery at Mars's casino, he encloses her with his body, visually echoing the protective role that he has assumed in her life (fig. 1.25). Once he has solved her problem, he turns her gently toward him in what is the film's final gesture, a concluding use of the circling motif that resonates with the accumulated meaning of all that has preceded (figs. 1.26 and 1.27).

The tentative process by which the lovers establish rapport is documented by the alternating inflections of their bodies toward or away from each other as the action progresses. As she talks about Carmen's photograph in Marlowe's office, Vivian sits on the edge of his desk leaning anxiously forward, needing the detective's help but afraid to ask for it. He sits back comfortably in his chair, still uncommitted (fig. 1.28). In the subsequent restaurant scene, both lean foward during their conversation until Marlowe reasserts his mistrust by lounging back in his seat as he challenges Vivian's sincerity ("Why did you try [sugar] on me then?") (fig. 1.29). But his cool indifference is negated just before the scene ends when a careless passerby pushes him against the woman with whom he is falling in love in spite of himself. With Vivian in his car later, Marlowe leans forward as Vivian reclines back, a sign that he has assumed the burden that caused her inital tension (fig. 1.30). During the final scene at Geiger's house, Vivian sits quietly in a chair as Marlowe nervously perches on the arm of it considering how best to cope with the dangerous sitation that he has involved himself in for her sake (fig. 1.31). Here again the cumulative effect is like that of a dance—in this case, a dance of courtship.

Marlowe's role as Vivian's lover seems a natural one not only because of the graceful patterning of their movements in relation to each other during their scenes together but also because of the ease with which he fits into her upper-class world. Unlike *The Maltese Falcon* where Spade's lower-class image puts him at a disadvantage in his romance with the international adventuress Brigid O'Shaughnessey, in *The Big Sleep* Marlowe appears to occupy a social station if not equal to then at least not significantly distant from that of Vivian Sternwood. In this film Hawks includes few close-ups, thereby deemphasizing Bogart's ethnic features and coloring. At the same time, it is clear that the actor is older in *The Big Sleep* than he had been when he played Sam Spade in *The Maltese Falcon*. His more mature appearance gives him the air of a man who has already settled the question of his position in life. This sense of class security is reinforced by Bogart's more dignified, relaxed delivery. The lower-class pronounciation which at times crept into his diction as Sam Spade is now gone, and the virtual absence of long set speeches allows him to deliver his lines in the later film without the histrionic flourishes that supplied the necessary feeling of factitiousness to his earlier performance. To fit his character into Sternwood's milieu, Bogart used not only his voice but also his face and body. In the film's first scene Marlowe walks into the Sternwood mansion comfortably swinging his hat in his hand and openly curious as he looks at the objects in the entry hall (fig. 1.32). His expression of concern for the general confirms the notion that this is an environment in which he could feel at home. Even before he meets Vivian, this interview establishes him as a man her father approves of. All these indications operate to make Marlowe's working-class surroundings seem more a matter of whim than of necessity. Unlike Sam Spade, who could don a mask of upper-class sophistication only with difficulty, Bogart's Philip Marlowe appears to be a man who feels comfortable at any level of society. As a result, the aristocratic Vivian appears an appropriate romantic partner for him.

To create a character who is open to the possibility of romantic partnership rather than one who is obsessed with the necessity of control, Bogart radically altered his manner of expressing the quality of his internal life for his role in *The Big Sleep*. The defensive gestures that marked his portrayal of Sam Spade are toned down or eliminated; in their place are indications of relaxation and thoughtfulness. Marlowe dresses casually, his open jackets allowing him to put his hands in his pockets or to hook his thumbs in his belt, which he often does (figs.

1.33 and 1.34). If he grins, it is more likely to be at himself than at those around him, as shown by his self-depreciating chuckle just before he enters Geiger's bookstore in the guise of a prim scholar (fig. 1.35).[25] He smokes to be with others, not to divert his attention from them as Sam Spade often seemed to do—a quality announced in the film's opening credits, which show two cigarettes in a single ashtray (fig. 1.36), and later reasserted by General Sternwood's comment "I enjoyed your cigarette as much as you did." Marlowe's most characteristic gesture is pulling on his ear, which he does whenever he is thinking: as he listens to the general's recital of Carmen's indiscretions, for instance, or considers Eddie Mars's explanations of his noninvolvement in the case (figs. 1.37 and 1.38). Although Bogart had developed these mannerisms during the later 1930s, he eschews them in his portrayal of Sam Spade, for their connotations of comfortable openness would have been out of place in Huston's film.

Whereas Spade's explosive nature means that he injects an element of violence even into sexual encounters, Marlowe's easygoing affability gives him an air of detachment when he participates in violent acts. Although Marlowe is skilled in the use of violence, he does not relish it, as Spade sometimes seems to. Before he punches the thug Eddie Mars has sent to rob Vivian, the detective rubs his fist against his lapel, thereby indicting that the action is a rationally considered one rather than one that erupts out of an instinctively sadistic impulse (fig. 1.39). He pauses in a similar way before shooting Canino (Bob Steele). Even when he kicks Geiger's houseboy and companion, Carol Lundgren (Tom Rafferty), he does so without the obvious glee that Spade displays when he attacks Joe Cairo. Such demonstrations of restraint suggest that, although Marlowe can accommodate his actions to a world in which viciousness and brutality are rampant, he is not part of that world in the way that Sam Spade is. It further intimates an absence of the kind of psychic investment in homophobic sadism that characterizes the Huston character. Spade uses violence to build up his self-image at the expense of others; Marlowe uses it in a sportsmanlike way to advance the goals of his team and to cement a romantic parntership.

Through alterations like these, Bogart modifies his portrayal of the hard-boiled detective to express, first, the concern with class insecurity and male supremacy in a changing world that characterizes Huston's vision of the tough-guy hero, and, in the later film, the Hawksian theme of male camaraderie adapted to emphasize the creation of the modern companionate couple. In each case the films' visual and narrative design interacts with the star's performance mannerisms and with the class and ethnic connotations carried by his appearance and persona to construct heroes whose attitudes toward romance—as well as their chances of success in this realm—are demonstrably dissimilar. This kind of interaction between star persona, performance, and cinematic narratives is central to Hollywood's construction of a realistic discourse involving romance and marriage.

Patriarchal Marriage and Traditional Gender Identities

STAR AND AUTEUR: THE GRIFFITH-GISH COLLABORATION AND THE STRUGGLE OVER PATRIARCHAL MARRIAGE

One can make a persuasive case for Griffith's having a major, and perhaps the major influence upon the course which film acting would take in the American cinema.

—Henry Walthall

Lillian Gish is one of the few American stars who has enjoyed the reputation of being both a great beauty and a great performer. In both of these areas, her reputation has been largely shaped by D. W. Griffith, her first director and, for many years, her mentor. Gish was an ideal Griffith type, and the director fashioned stories and techniques to bring out some of her best qualities. Gish starred in more Griffith features than any other actor, and she is prominent in all the Griffith films that are today remembered as his best: *Birth of a Nation* (1915), *Intolerance* (1916), *Broken Blossoms* (1919), and *Way Down East* (1920). The period from 1914 to 1921, during which these works were produced, has been called Griffith's "Gish period," a designation that indicates that Gish was as significant in the evolution of Griffith's art as Griffith was in the evolution of hers.

The preoccupation of male directors with their female stars has recently been the object of intensive analysis. Of particular interest are Gaylyn Studlar's study of Von Sternberg and Dietrich and Donald Spoto's description of the relationship between Hitchcock and Tippi Hedren in his biography *The Dark Side of Genius: The Life of Alfred Hitchcock*. The Griffith-Gish collaboration holds special interest, however, because it coincided both with the early development of the star system itself and with the emergence of institutionalized Hollywood practices related to the creation of the couple. Because of Griffith's place as one of the primary architects of the classical Hollywood style, Gish's influence on him indirectly influenced the shape taken by some of the major conventions of this style and the vision that informed it. During their collaboration, Griffith elaborated a series of cinematic fantasies centered on the theme of romantic love in which Gish's fair-haired frailty represented an idealized image of woman's place within patriarchal marriage. In order fully to appreciate what was at stake for Griffith in such representations, it is necessary to approach them in the context of emergent discourses on film authorship and women's roles.

The Emergence of a Discourse on Film Authorship

In the early years of cinema, the issue of authorship was moot. Audiences paid to see "actualities" and "trickfilms," which foregrounded either documentary content or the novel technology of the camera itself. However, the growing demand for films led producers to turn increasingly to fictional formats, which featured actors rather than trains arriving at stations or spaceships landing on the moon (de Cordova, *Picture Personalities*). During this period the film companies retained control of their product by marketing movies in terms of their identification with studios rather than stars (thereby following what Eileen Bowser has called a "brand name" concept [*The Transformation of Cinema*]). Only after audiences demanded to know the names of such figures as "the Biograph Girl" and "the Vitagraph Girl" did film companies respond by turning actors into celebrities. By so doing, they positioned actors in the eyes of the public as the "authors" of their films insofar as the intertextual and extratextual discourses that developed around these cultural icons were exploited to create expectations and govern reading strategies in relation to the films in which stars appeared. Subsequent developments such as fan magazines, promotional tours, and the Academy Awards ceremony all reinforced the public's perception that stars and not directors stood at the center of the creative endeavor or Hollywood filmmaking. If as M. H. Abrams has claimed, modern ideas of authorship center on the fantasy that by experiencing an artwork each member of the audience can "come to know an author more intimately than his own friends and family" (21), then Hollywood stars can be said to represent perhaps the most highly elaborated instance of this phenomenon.

One can only speculate about what Griffith's feelings might have been as he watched this process unfold. He had played a pivotal and contradictory role in the development of the star system. On the one hand, his lavish use of close-ups and his leadership in Hollywood's move to full-length features were major factors in making movie actors into recognizable and seductive public figures. Moreover, a number of the earliest stars began their careers under Griffith's tutelage, including Florence Lawrence, Blanche Sweet, and Mary Pickford. However, as both Eileen Bowser (*The Transformation of Cinema*) and Tom Gunning (*D. W. Griffith*) have noted, Griffith's own company, Biograph, had enjoyed an undisputed preeminence under the earlier "brand name" system due to the high-quality productions crafted by its accomplished director. When actors' names began to be publicized, Biograph was the last company to use this marketing device; not until 1913, more than three years after the other film companies had adopted this policy, did Biograph follow suit.

The role that Griffith personally played in this strategy of resistance is unknown. It is clear, nonetheless, that there was good reason during these early years of filmmaking to imagine that producer-directors rather than actors would be the people who would be widely recognized as the authors of Hollywood movies. Griffith himself took a number of steps to ensure that his own name would remain a factor in the public's reception of his films. Most obviously, he credited himself above the titles and inscribed his initials on the intertitles. He also relied on a stock company of performers and, in the early years especially, habitually shifted actors between major and minor roles. When actors like Mary Pickford and Blanche Sweet became famous enough to demand high salaries, Griffith's customary practice was to release them from their contracts with him so that they could seek higher wages elsewhere. Even the shape of some of Griffith's most highly regarded films suggests a resistance to the star mystique: the epic sweep of *Birth of a Nation* and the quartet of story lines in *Intolerance* prevented any single actor from dominating either of these films; they were thus read by the public as D. W. Griffith productions rather than as showcases for their favorite stars. After the relative failure of *Intolerance*, Griffith settled into what were by then more conventionally organized narrative patterns centering on a single star protagonist.

In the sentimental melodramas that Griffith favored these protagonists were usually women, just as women were, in many cases, the stars whom Griffith created. If these newly powerful women altered Griffith's own vision of patriarchal privilege, it was not apparent in the organization of his production facilities. In the working environment that he set up for himself, the male director was the only star. His favorite female actors were women in their teens or early twenties, who were often chaperoned by widowed mothers or grandmothers. "I am inclined to favor beginners," he said in an interview in 1923. "They come untrammeled by so-called techniques, by theories, by preconceived ideas. I prefer the young woman who has to support herself and possibly her mother" (Walker 60–61).

In contrast to most of his other actors, Gish worked under Griffith for far longer than purely financial considerations would have justified. As she grew older and more celebrated in her own right, however, Griffith himself turned away from the relationship. His personal involvement with Gish gave way to an infatuation with the younger and less well known Carol Dempster, and in 1920 he instructed his business-manager brother to advise Gish to accept one of the many lucrative offers that she had been receiving to work elsewhere.

The threat of masculine disempowerment represented by the rise of female stars like Gish was closely tied to larger social issues associated with the contemporary women's movement. As Michael Rogin and Miriam Hansen ("The Hieroglyph and the Whore") have pointed out, themes identified with this movement found their way into Griffith's films.[1] Griffith's Gish period coincided with the final push for women's suffrage, which passed into law in 1920. The wide-ranging significance of this emergent discourse on suffrage in the beginning of the century—what Ellen Carol Dubois has heralded as "the first independent movement of women for their own liberation (iv)"—is evident from the number of related issues that developed around it, especially the right to birth control, the right to education, the right to work outside the home, and the right to sexual freedom. These issues, which derived additional impetus from the disruption in gender roles occasioned by the First World War, were tied together by the philosophic implications that contemporary feminists perceived in the cause of suffrage itself. Mary Fainsod Katzenstein has observed, "Above all [suffrage] was about the right of women to be recognized as public persons. It was about the right of women to address matters that extended outside of the purview of the household, to join together with other women to protest, to lobby, thereby to occupy a place in the public domain. Suffrage was in one single measure the symbol of women's right to become citizens of the *republic*" (11).

While this widespread movement for women's rights was at its height, Griffith was creating films largely animated by a residual discourse that celebrated the patriarchal family and women's place within it. His attitude toward woman's suffrage was perhaps expressed most explicitly in the opening title to his 1919 film *True Heart Susie*, which states, "Woman is supposed to be allowed her choice, yet not one in ten ever have a chance to marry any but one man."[2] Marriage and the family are here judged as being far more significant choices for women than the choices that were then opening up to them to participate in larger political processes by helping to choose public officials. Lillian Gish's special qualities as a performer as well as her growing stature as a star can be viewed in relation to such sentiments. In what follows, I will examine the stylistic tropes that distinguish their collaborative productions in terms of the way in which they function as responses to the social and institutional pressures I have described.

Griffith, Gish, Romantic Love, and Patriarchal Marriage

In Griffith's films, contemporary debates about women's freedom were recast as threats against the patriarchal family. The director represented these threats as emanating not from women themselves but from external forces, usually in the form of nefarious males. To portray women as the villains that menaced traditional family life would be to see them as possessing a power that Griffith was loathe to grant them. Whatever he may have feared about the potential of women's free choice to undermine the patriarchal family, he depicted women who were helpless victims passively enduring threats to the family mounted by others. Griffith's emphasis on female suffering in such portrayals implicitly expressed the rage that he harbored against the women whom he explicitly idealized. As Kenneth Lynn has observed, "The fear that women might victimize him was . . . kept secret in the movies he made; instead he portrayed the victimization of women by men" (261). The extent of Griffith's rage against women and the suspect nature of his idealization of patriarchal marriage are suggested by the fact that he himself assiduously avoided the domesticity that he so enthusiastically championed in his films, preferring the life-style offered by hotel rooms and a series of romances with his leading ladies. Because he remained married to, although separated from, his first wife, Linda Arvidson, for many years, these romances could never lead to marriage.

Griffith's idealization of the patriarchal family was founded on an ideology of romantic love that culminated in marriages between "suitable" partners—deemed "suitable" largely by virtue of culturally sanctioned standards of physical beauty. The coming together of these suitable romantic partners was intimately connected with the stylistic innovations traditionally associated with Griffith's name, in particular, two narrative devices that were to become staples of the classical Hollywood style: parallel editing and close-up photography.[3]

Griffith's use of parallel editing is described by Tom Gunning as follows: "The first two shots frequently introduce two characters (or two groups of characters) before they have actually met. The characters' stories will be intercut in the opening sections of the film until a scene where they are finally narratively linked. Such interweavings seem to be Griffith's basic narrative schema" ("Weaving" 19). In his classic essay on Griffith, Sergei Eisenstein argued that these two groups of characters reflected a world of haves and have nots (234). But Griffith's parallel montages most typically involve a relationship not between rich characters and poor ones but between men and women. By portraying the romantic adventures of the hero and heroine in the form of a parallel montage, Griffith depicts them as two halves of a single whole that come together in the final frames. This strategy recapitulates a conception of romantic love as a man and a woman who are incomplete by themselves but form a satisfying whole when they merge. For Griffith, parallel montage is a way of constituting the couple.

Griffith's parallel editing is most dramatically used in his climactic rescue sequences, where suspense is built up by intercutting shots of victims and rescuers. Although Griffith did not originate this strategy, he did a great deal to develop and popularize it as a standard trope of the classical hollywood style.[4] The other conventional Hollywood use of parallel editing is the chase, still a standard technique for structuring comedies. Both of these editing strategies exploit the suspense created by dynamic movement within and between frames to build stirring climaxes. Chases, however, usually involve only two types of characters—protagonists and antagonists—whereas rescues typically involve three—antagonists, rescuers, and victims. Thus rescues can culminate in the kind of emotion-laden scenes of reunion that suited the melodramatic love stories that Griffith favored.

In his Biograph shorts, Griffith's rescue montages often featured victimized children, who were prominent figures in seminal early films such as *Rescued by Rover* (1905) and *Rescued from an Eagle's Nest* (1908), the first movie in which Griffith himself appeared as an actor in a featured role. As Griffith's directorial career moved him toward longer narratives centered on love stories, however, he developed a predilection for depicting women as victims and their future husbands as rescuers. In *The Unseen Enemy* (1912), the first Griffith film in which the Gish sisters appeared, their ambiguous status as both children and women is conspicuous, for the young girls/women are rescued by two men: one is their older brother and the other a suitor.

As David Bordwell has observed, parallel editing is a device whereby the spectators are told more than the central character (Bordwell et al. 48). In rescues the technique dramatizes the limited knowledge of victims who might not be aware of their danger or of the imminence of their deliverance from it. When Griffith portrays a man's rescue of a woman, his montage suggests that the woman needs a male even if she herself believes otherwise or does not recognize her peril or helplessness. Nick Browne has argued that "if there is a fantasy animating Griffith's narrative project, which cross-cutting and the threat of rape come to symbolize, it has to do . . . with the seduction and at the same time the defense of the woman by his symbolic possession of her through his art" (79). This impulse to possess women typically occurs in Griffith's films not only on a symbolic level but also on a narrative one, for his chivalrous heroes usually rescue the heroines in order to earn the right to marry them. The rescue scenario typically implies that the male hero's superior physical strength and familiarity with weapons will enable him to succeed where the woman alone has failed. In short, parallel editing enabled Griffith to undercut the woman's perception of danger and persuade the audience that she needed a male to protect her.

The sources of such a stylistic predilection are complex. Russell Merritt has argued that Griffith's years in the theater had exposed him to many sexually assertive and promiscuous women, a circumstance that he responded to with terror and revulsion. He expressed these feelings in theatrical scenarios that featured masochistic and humiliated heroes. When he moved from theater to film, however, the self-abasing men that stood at the center of his many unproduced theatrical melodramas gave way to victimized women and triumphant rescue scenes. Merritt argues that Griffith's scenarios changed because he wanted to conform to the conventions of movie plots, which were "rooted in the liberating aspects of direct action" (17). But Griffith's development of the rescue montage undoubtedly arose from other causes as well. As a film director, he was a success rather than the failure he had been in the theater, and he could exercise much more control over his working environment. On the other hand, his status with the public as the sole author of his films was being threatened by the growing power and fame of his female stars. This threat to the director's newly established position of privilege was echoed in the society at large by the intensifying debate surrounding women's independence. These conditions formed the background for the changing preoccupations evident in Griffith's films: the hostility that he had directed inward onto the masochistic heroes of his plays now found more complicated expression in his emphasis on the heroine in distress who is unable to function without a man.[5]

Griffith's use of parallel editing to represent the rescue of women constitutes a form of violence against the female victim not only because of the exploitation of her suffering and terror that is occasioned by the narrative situation, but also because of the violation of realistic conventions of temporality that are encouraged by the technique itself. Intercutting can draw out the spectacle of women's suffering by slowing down the time frame.[6] When directors slow the temporal progression without slowing the action (as happens in slow motion), they create a nightmarish sense of static frenzy, an atmosphere of traumatized hysteria in which frantic action makes little headway. By thus overstating the situation Griffith's technique participates in the formal excess typical of melodrama in general, in which issues that cannot be acknowledged in the narrative often find an outlet in an overwrought style. As Geoffrey Nowell-Smith has stated, "In the melodrama, where there is always material which cannot be expressed in discourse or in the actions of the characters furthering the designs of the plot, a conversion can take place into the body of the text" ("Minnelli and Melodrama" 73–74).

Griffith's parallel montage typically works with his use of close-ups by alternating medium and long shots of an active male rescuer with close-ups of the tortured face of an entrapped woman. Thus the director can be said to have been the one to have consolidated the Hollywood convention that positions men as actors and women as spectacle, a convention that Laura Mulvey has pointed to in her influential discussion of classical Hollywood practice. That Griffith himself understood his technique in these terms is clear from a statement he made in 1915. "Man is a moving animal," he claimed. "It isn't so with woman. Their natures are different" (Geduld 28–29).

Close-ups allowed Griffith to place more emphasis on character, a shift that has been seen as a decisive factor in the move to longer narratives (Gunning, "Weaving"; Bordwell et al.) This move, in turn, was related to the development of a new "realistic" acting style that focused more on the emotions communicated by facial expression than on the broad bodily pantomime that was favored in the earliest films and that survived throughout the silent era in slapstick comedies (Bordwell et al.; Pearson; Staiger, "The Eyes"). In 1914 Griffith himself connected the close-up and the new acting norms.

> It is this learning step by step that brought about the "close-up." We were striving for real acting. When you saw only the small, full-length figures, it was necessary to have exaggerated acting, what might be called "physical acting," the waving of the hands and so on. The close-up enabled us to reach real acting, restraint, acting that is a duplicate of real life (quoted in Bordwell et al. 190–91).

With close-ups Griffith could focus his images of the victimized woman on her emotional state of suffering and need.

The persona that Gish created was ideally suited for this purpose. Although Pudovkin argued in *Film Acting* that in Griffith's films "various women express the same emotional states by the same external means" (139), Gish stood apart from all the other Griffith performers. She was the most adept of any of them at inventing means of expressing anxiety. As one contemporary critic commented, "She achieves greatness of effect through a single plane of emotion—namely hysteria" (Walker 77). In *The Mothering Heart* (1913) she throws her head back and lets her mouth gape in a silent scream. In *Broken Blossoms* she twirls frantically around in a tiny closet. In *True Heart Susie* she giggles to avoid crying. And in *Hearts of the World* (1918) she reacts to the death of her mother by lapsing into a catatonic stupor. Gish could develop these reactions by means of carefully modulated expressive changes; thus, these climactic moments of suffering could be depicted in close-up shots that could be held on her face for extended lengths of time without appearing static. Audiences were deeply moved by such expressions of suffering not only because they could observe Gish's facial expressions closely but also because she invested these moments with a strong aura of realism. One critic has reported that Gish's mother was shocked to discover whip marks on her daughter's back during the filming of *Broken Blossoms*, and Gish herself states in her autobiography that it was her idea to trail her hand in icy water for the climactic sequence of *Way Down East* and that she has experienced pain in this hand during spells of cold weather ever since (233).[7]

Griffith's close-ups of Gish emphasized her role as a victim by highlighting not only her suffering but also her aura of vulnerability. As Charles Affron has observed, "Her vulnerability to menace was sublimely appropriate to the complex of reverence and sadism that qualified women in his imagination" (38). This aura was conveyed by the childlike quality of her beauty. She possessed a slender, undeveloped body, long, wispy hair, a round face, large eyes, and a small nose. Her lips were made up in a rosebud style to make them appear less mature, and to maintain the impression that her mouth was childishly small she rarely smiled on-screen. Her seriousness set her apart from Mae Marsh, her nearest rival, whose capacity to project pathos was compromised by her quality of playfulness.

That Gish's on-screen appearance was, at least in part, her own creation was attested to by Griffith's first wife, Linda Arvidson, who recalled in her memoirs that Gish customarily arrived at the studio an hour or so early so that she could have cameraman Billy Bitzer make tests of her with different kinds of makeup (230). Bitzer himself corroborated the notion that Gish was preoccupied with her appearance in his autobiography, where he wrote that she "only wanted to be beautiful" (quoted in Schickel, *D. W. Griffith*, 176). As she grew into her twenties, an age that, as Griffith's biographer Richard Schickel has observed, was "old for a Griffith heroine," she persuaded her mentor to hire photographer Hendrik Sartov, whose soft-focus images could disguise her years and enhance her aura of childlike vulnerability (*D. W. Griffith* 385).[8]

The quality of Gish's beauty also readily lent itself to Griffith's racial themes, for her fair skin and hair set against the images of black or Asian men who threatened her virtue made her appear not only as a helpless child but also as a symbol of the purity of Northern European womanhood.[9] Her major role in *Birth of a Nation* came about one day when she substituted for Blanche Sweet in a rehearsal of the scene in which Elsie Stoneman is accosted by a mulatto. "During the hysterical chase around the room, the hairpins flew out of my hair, which tumbled below my waist as Lynch held my fainting body in his arms," Gish has recalled. "I was very blonde and fragile-looking. The contrast with the dark man evidently pleased Mr. Griffith, for he said in front of everyone, 'Maybe she would be more effective than the more mature figure I had in mind'" (133).

For such reasons as these, Griffith's close-ups of Gish created a memorable focus of victimized femininity around which to construct his rescue montages. Gish's status as the paradigmatic symbol of a woman in need of rescue was well known at the time. One contemporary observer, for example, suggested that there should be "a society for the preservation of Lillian Gish," and another defined an optimist as "a person who will go to the theater expecting to see a D. W. Griffith production in which Lillian Gish is not attacked by the villain in the fifth reel" (quoted in Slide 95).

Griffith tied Gish's aura of feminine helplessness to women's role in the family by portraying her as a mother in a number of films, including *The Mothering Heart* (1913), *Pathways of Life* (1913), *The Battle of Elderbush Gulch* (1913), *Judith of Bethulia* (1913), *Intolerance*, and *Way Down East*. Even in films where she is not explicitly depicted as a mother, she is often portrayed in a mothering relation to other characters, as in *House of Darkness* (1913), *True Heart Susie*, *Hearts of the World* and *Orphans of the Storm* (1921). And in *Broken Blossoms* she mothers a doll. As E. Ann Kaplan observed in her essay "Mothering, Feminism, and Representation" in Griffith's films "the good woman is always a mother" (125), and this characterization is especially applicable to Gish. If she herself typically appears as a victim, her babies are portrayed even more dramatically so, for in *The Mothering Heart* and *Way Down East* the babies die, and in *The Battle of Elderbush Gulch* the baby is placed in mortal danger. Gish recalls that for her first mother role in *The Mothering Heart* she augmented her bosom to make her figure appear more matronly, but thereafter she used her immature body to create an image of mothers who are themselves children.

Way Down East: *Marriage Choices*

As the family-identified heroine in all Griffith's major scenarios of romantic love, Gish's dilemma invariably concerns the question of whom she is to marry. Griffith's most memorable vehicles for Gish between 1915 and 1920, *Birth of a Nation*, *Broken Blossoms*, and *Way Down East*, can be seen as repeated attempts to define a suitable partner for the Gish heroine by charting a middle course for her between endogamy and exogamy, a choice represented in its most extreme form as one between incest and miscegenation. The motif of incest has often been recognized in these films (for example, by Browne, Hansen ["The Hieroglyph and the Whore"], Lesage, and Rogin ["The Sword Became a Flashing Vision"]). However, the representation of miscegenation as a taboo that is portrayed as complementary to incest has not been explored as it applies to cultural mores.[10]

In *Birth of a Nation*, Griffith's first full-length feature, Gish's romantic relationship with Henry Walthall is represented as a microcosmic resolution to the problems faced by America as a whole. Gish's Elsie Stoneman, a northerner, is rescued at the end of the film by Walthall's Ben Cameron, the southern leader of the Ku Klux Klan and Elsie's suitor. This romantic union between North and South is pointedly contrasted to the sexual threat posed to Elsie's honor by the mulatto Silas Lynch (George Siegmann), who has acquired his miscegenistic ambitions as a result of the position of power that he has been placed in by Elsie's father, a powerful politician who has himself entered into a miscegenistic alliance with his housekeeper. At the same time, Elsie's own relationship with her father is surrounded by an aura of sensuous intimacy. Thus, Ben rescues her from the threats of both miscegenation and incest.

Broken Blossoms, which followed *Birth of a Nation*, features no mediator such as Ben, and the alternatives for Gish are polarized as a choice between incest or miscegenation. She plays the daughter of a brutal boxer (Donald Crisp), who murders her after finding her consorting with a "yellow man" (Richard Barthelmess). Though the young girl is presented as virginal, the element of illicit sexuality represented by both of the male figures is suggested by the fact that her father beats and murders her on a bed, and she appears ensconced on another bed while with the "yellow man." The morally depraved quality that Griffith associates with miscegenation is emphasized during some of the film's early scenes, which portray decadent interracial couples consorting in an opium den. Later, an openly lecherous Asian man called "Evil Eye" makes unwelcome advances to the innocent girl played by Gish. In contrast, Barthelmess's heroic Asian explicitly renounces his carnal desires in order to worship the girl as an ideal. Given the impossible situation that Griffith sets up here, it is not surprising that the yellow man's attempted rescue of Gish at the film's conclusion fails.

The unreconcilable opposition of marriage choices depicted in *Broken Blossoms* resolved itself in *Way Down East*, the last film that Griffith made with Gish while she was still working exclusively under him. The film was based on a popular stage melodrama which was itself derived from a number of well-known melodramatic tales of the time, including Thomas Hardy's *Tess of the D'Urbervilles* and Harriet Beecher Stowe's *Uncle Tom's Cabin.*[11] Although Gish had strong reservations about Griffith's choice of such old-fashioned material, Griffith seized this opportunity to exploit Victorian conventions to their fullest. Released in 1920, the year that women's suffrage became law, *Way Down East* is Griffith's strongest defense of the patriarchal family. In this film he created a frame for Gish's acting talents that has caused her performance to be called the finest produced in the silent era (Gunning, "Rebirth"; Stanley Kauffmann). Gish's acting tour de force in *Way Down East* was made possible by the film's unprecedented exploration of the relationship between romantic love and the patriarchal family in terms of issues related to the female body.

The film's opening title states that "Today woman brought up from childhood to expect ONE CONSTANT MATE possibly suffers more than at any moment in the history of mankind, because not yet has the man-animal reached this high standard, except perhaps in theory." Thus, the film begins by suggesting that women were suffering at that historical moment not because they were moving toward a position in which they would be dividing their energies between public life and the family but because men were becoming more unfaithful. In a climactic confrontation scene, Gish delivers a spirited denunciation of the sexual double standard, thereby attesting to the film's moral fervor about the necessity for full male participation in the institution of monogamy. Men's sexual loyalty is presented as the key that would allow women to remain happy within a traditional family structure.[12] Through such appeals Griffith's film displays its sensitivity to the issue of women's rights by focusing on the rights that were due women within the family. In fact, however, although men may or may not have been taking marriage less seriously than they once did, women certainly were. Lois Banner reports, for example, that close to 50 percent of the graduates of eastern women's colleges during the 'teens remained unmarried, and a large proportion of these women were employed in professional capacities (*A Brief History* 48). Such women did not need marriage; they could take care of themselves without it.

Way Down East deals with the issue of exogamy that so troubled Griffith in *Birth of a Nation* and *Broken Blossoms* by replacing the explosive theme of miscegenation with the familiar melodramatic motif of class conflict. Anna Moore, a self-described "ignorant country girl"

(Gish), visits her rich relatives, the Tremonts, in Boston to borrow money for her widowed mother and herself. While in Boston she is seduced by Lennox Sanderson (Lowell Sherman), an upper-class cad who leaves her pregnant after tricking her by means of a false marriage. After the death of her baby, Anna finds work on a farm. She has a romance with the farmer's son, David Bartlett (Richard Barthelmess). Their courtship is thwarted, however, when Anna's past is exposed. Driven out into a blizzard by David's father, Squire Bartlett (Burr McIntosh), Anna is ultimately rescued from an ice-encrusted river by David himself, and harmony reigns. The film ends with not one but three marriages: a marriage between Anna and David; another between David's cousin Kate Brewster (Mary Hay) and Professor Sterling (Creighton Hale), who boards at the farm; and a third between Martha Perkins (Vivia Ogden) and Seth Holcomb (Porter Strong), two comic characters who live in the neighborhood (fig. 2.1). The marriages of these three couples draw together three related motifs centered on the film's conception of romantic love.

Introduced by means of scenes intercut into the continuity early in the action, David is clearly marked as the figure who will merge with Anna in the final scene to create the film's most idealized romantic couple. To further cement David's status as Anna's future husband, a title card assures us before his first appearance that he is "of plain stock" and thus a suitable mate for her.[13] The film's idealization of their romantic pairing is established by the camera's contemplation of their beauty, for both are granted a number of unmotivated close-ups in which the audience is invited to admire their "perfect" features.

In the subplot concerning David's Cousin Kate, the theme of endogamy and exogamy is developed. Kate has been betrothed to David by their parents, and she is also being courted by the exploitative Sanderson. Griffith's opposing perils of marriage within the family and across class lines thus loom before her. David holds the ideal of romantic love up to her when he protests that it wouldn't be right for them to marry "without proper love." Fortunately, Kate herself is in love with the professor, a man who is neither within her family nor outside her class. Thus, like Anna, she is portrayed as freely choosing a man whom Griffith presents as an appropriate marriage partner for her. At the film's conclusion her marital choice is explicitly sanctioned by the social law represented by the film's reigning patriarch, Squire Bartlett, who is shown sharing the couple's postmarital happiness. This depiction stands in striking contrast to Anna's earlier marriage to Sanderson, which occurs in Boston, where her cousin Emma Tremont, a woman (Josephine Bernard), heads the household.

In the case of Martha Perkins, the central role played by beauty in courtship rituals is foregrounded. With her corkscrew curls and large, aging features, Martha is presented as comically plain-looking, in sharp contrast to the beautiful Anna. Yet she still seeks attention from all the available men with whom she comes into contact, even remarking at one point that she "can't keep the men from followin' me." Her jealousy of Anna motivates her to betray the younger woman's secret to the squire, thus providing the immediate cause for Anna's expulsion from the house. As Martha sets out to betray Anna to the squire, Griffith's camera executes its only tracking motion in the film, a rapid movement backward suggesting a strong desire to get out of the way of this unpleasant, unattractive woman (fig. 2.2).

The pairings of David and Anna and of Kate and the professor leave Seth Holcomb as the only remaining eligible male for Martha to marry. That her assent to this marriage is a grudging one is clear from the close-ups of her sour expression during the wedding ceremony. Griffith's celebration of Gish's beauty and her resulting desirability as a marriage partner thus involve the denigration of the less-attractive Martha, who must content herself with a "leftover" man and who is not privileged to share fully in the film's final portrayal of marriage as the culmination of romantic love. Although Martha is denied the possibility of real romance, Griffith's harsh portrayal of her fate is tempered slightly in the film's final shots when Town Constable Rube Whipple (George Neville), intending to kiss the bride, mistakenly kisses Seth instead (fig. 2.3). By thus suggesting a romantic possibility that is, in the terms that the film has set up, unthinkable, Griffith uses this farcically homoerotic shot to suggest that by marrying Seth Martha is at least conforming to acceptable social practice if not to the highest ideals of romantic love.

By portraying the patriarchal family as the only valid social institution, Griffith left himself without an appropriate mechanism for punishing the seducer Sanderson. The family unit, headed by Squire Bartlett, functions as the film's center of justice. The squire, however, has no jurisdiction over Sanderson. Although Constable Whipple is dispatched in one of the final scenes to administer an appropriate punishment to the upper-class cad, this threat of punishment, entrusted to a figure characterized as ridiculous and ineffective, is a notably empty one. That Griffith is forced to suggest a comic solution to the problem posed by a character who had previously been seen as a serious threat to the old-fashioned values espoused by the film suggests that he had reached a moral impasse. Although *Way Down East* depicts the triumph of romantic love and the patriarchal family, it also reflects the limitation of a vision that sees the family in isolation from other social institutions.[14]

Way Down East: *Biology and Birth*

All Gish's great scenes in *Way Down East* focus on suffering—Anna's reactions to Sanderson's betrayal and her baby's death, her denunciation of Sanderson, and, most spectacularly, her ordeal on the ice. What is remarkable about Gish's suffering in this film, however, is the way its sources ultimately emanate from within her body as physical pain. The reality of her distress was attested to by the documentary quality of the film's famous rescue-on-the-ice sequence.[15] Yet, as I have argued, Griffith's crosscutting technique gives sequences like this a nightmarish quality. Gish's pain and danger are returned to again and again, and at times the same moment appears to be repeated in successive cuts. Thus, what is a physical trauma for the film's heroine becomes an emotional trauma for the spectator, a moment of obsessive fixation on an image packed with unacknowledged meanings. The film's climactic focus on Gish's inert form is the culmination of the central role that her body plays in the narrative as a whole, where it is repeatedly invoked to dramatize the folly of her attempt to choose a marriage partner freely. After Anna's attempt to choose a man out of her class, her ability to choose any mate is foreclosed by the increasing domination of her body.

In his book *American Film Melodrama* Robert Lang has rightly pointed out that the ideological underpinnings of *Way Down East* concern the "loss and restoration of the father" (67). But Lang goes on to argue that this motif operates primarily through the film's depiction of the Oedipal struggle that David Bartlett undergoes. However, the film's visual strategies address the theme of the restoration of the patriarchal family in relation not to David's psyche but to Anna's physiology. The "body" of the text enacts a residual discourse focused on the body of the heroine and its suffering. As Elaine Scarry has shown in *The Body in Pain*, the infliction of pain is closely associated with the violation of established hierarchies. Pain reduces its victims to an emotional space within their own bodies. In Scarry's words, "The violation of the hierarchies necessitates reaffirmation by intensifying the bodily experience of the inferior" (211). During the rescue sequence of *Way Down East* Anna's exposed body is conspicuously vulnerable to the elements while the body of her male rescuer is largely concealed by a shapeless overcoat (figs. 2.4 and 2.5).[16]

The film positions Anna's body in relation first to culture and then to nature. Culture is identified with Boston, a center of suffragette activity and the place where Anna's sexual indiscretions occur. The household of her cousins, the Tremonts, is matriarchal; and their female friends are notably modern in their dress, favoring the bobbed hair and loose-fitting gowns first adopted in the dress-reform movement advocated by the suffragettes of the mid-nineteenth century and made popular again by the flappers of the 1920s. They also smoke, a practice only newly acceptable for women.

Anna is brought to the attention of the man who seduces her through the influence of an aunt (Florence Short) whose masculine attire identifies her with the emerging "new woman" type that was seen by many as aspiring to compete with males (fig. 2.6). As a "mannish woman," this aunt is a highly charged figure. During the period when *Way Down East* was made, the feminist movement was fragmenting as a growing impasse developed between an older group that was committed to a wide variety of social issues and a younger one that, influenced by an ongoing male discourse that positioned women as prisoners of their bodies, narrowed their concerns to focus solely on sexuality (Smith-Rosenberg, "The New Woman as Androgyne"). Griffith's portrayal of the Tremonts' aunt, whose costuming represents her as "unfeminine," can be read as alluding to this emergent strand of contemporary feminism. Significantly, the influence of this aunt on Anna's life is presented not in terms of a sermon on women's rights but rather in terms of a gift of a revealing gown. "Oh, Auntie!" cries Anna on receiving this present. "Where's the top?" Thus a "feminist" character that putatively rejects the sexual objectification of women is blamed for promoting exactly that.

During Anna's subsequent relationship with Lennox Sanderson, her body's erotic power is defined as a cultural construction dependent on fashionable attire and sophisticated allusions to art and literature. Gish expresses this phase of her character's development by means of a performance strategy that Richard de Cordova calls "posing" (*Picture Personalities*). Like a model, she remains motionless in a position calculated to show off alluring costumes to their best advantage. Anna first catches Sanderson's eye as she stands at the foot of the Tremonts' staircase wearing the stylish gown that her aunt has given her (fig. 2.7). Sanderson praises her beauty by comparing her to the legendary medieval maid Elaine, at which point Griffith inserts a *tableau vivant* of Anna in yet another costume posing as the Elaine she imagines herself to be (fig. 2.8). Following their elopement Sanderson presents his bride with an elaborate negligé, in which she also poses, thereby arousing his lust to the point at which it overcomes his remaining moral scruples (fig. 2.9). These images associate the eroticism inherent in Anna's body with the trappings of a modern world in which sexual stimulation has taken on the status of a playful diversion available to a decadent upper-class culture. Further, the static quality of Gish's posing technique, in which Anna's figure is presented as a frame to show off provocative clothes, portrays the young girl as a passive figure in this milieu whose actions are easily manipulated by others.[17]

The danger represented by the urban world of Boston is ultimately seen as the threat posed by a society that has relinquished its sense of responsibility for women's welfare. Anna's helplessness when she is cast out on her own is a function of her inability to control the consequences of her sexuality. Earlier her position of helplessness had been visually signaled by representing her body's erotic power as a power created by men. At crucial moments during the Boston section of the story Griffith employs strongly marked point-of-view techniques to depict the film's two major male characters in terms of the visual—and by implication formative—power that they are able to exercise over Anna's sexuality. Both Sanderson and David appear to create the girl's seductive image through their imaginative gazes. The *tableau vivant* is a product of Sanderson's imagination, and Anna's bewitching negligee is his gift. When the false marriage takes place, Sanderson's gaze is replaced by David's. At the point when Sanderson drops the ring a confusing cut disrupts the scene's spatial continuity, and David suddenly appears in the midst of the wedding as he starts up from his bed on the farm (figs. 2.10, 2.11, and 2.12). The marriage scene is thereby reconfigured as a dream vision of the young farmer. Through this unorthodox strategy the director positions this new male character as yet another source of power over Anna.

The threat represented by Anna's sexual allure is undermined not only because it is presented as a function of the male gaze but also because it is incresingly associated with the film's humor. The comedy in the second half of *Way Down East* is focused on characters who surround the Bartlett family: their neighbors Martha and Seth, the professor, Constable Whipple, and the hired hand, Hi Holler (Edgar Nelson). Although the homespun humor that they represent is commonly regarded as the least-successful aspect of the film, it serves a significant function by defusing the erotic charge invested in the body during the early sequences. Vignettes such as the professor awkwardly dancing, Hi Holler being poked in the backside by a pitchfork, Constable Whipple snoring, and the ungainly walks affected by all these rustics depict the body as an object of detached amusement rather than erotic attraction. By surrounding Anna with such characters, the film positions her own body as one less-susceptible to sexual interpretation.[18]

In more particular terms, a sequence of shots involving women's legs de-eroticizes Anna's body by transforming what was previously seen as the source of her female sexual potency into an object of condescending jocularity. As social historians have frequently pointed out, Victorian conventions dictated that women's legs remain hidden beneath long skirts because the image of bifurcation was considered lascivious. "Women's legs . . . were not perceived as an anatomical arrangement for supporting the body and for walking but as blatant arrows that pointed the way to the seat of sex and other functions," Susan Brownmiller states. "The only way to avoid bifurcation was to wear a long skirt that brushed the floor" (83). A shot of some of the fashionable women of Boston taken as they are entering the Tremont house shows that they do not conform to the Victorian standard; instead, they exploit the newly provocative ploy of revealing glimpses of the female ankle (fig. 2.13). Later, when Sanderson is in the process of seducing Anna, an intertitle suggests that his conscience may still get the better of him. A shot taken from Sanderson's point of view of Anna's legs partially draped in her fashionable negligee, however, argues that it is the display of this part of the female anatomy that finally overcomes his attempt at self-control (fig. 2.14). The temptation to lechery represented by the exposure of a woman's legs is shown in a more unambiguously negative light after Anna's departure from Boston when Sanderson attends a party during which his attention is captured by an exhibition of the legs of a woman "entertainer" (fig. 2.15).

Later at the farm, however, the prurient overtones that have been attached to the sight of women's legs are recreated as comedy. A shot of Cousin Kate's legs from the point of view of the enamored professor repeats the suggestions of the sexually enticing nature of women's bodies (figs. 2.16 and 2.17). However, erotic attraction is here associated with the perspective of a character whose ridiculous antics have placed him at a distance from the audience. Thus, what the spectator previously identified as erotic becomes merely comic.[19] Finally, Griffith includes an unmotivated shot from a presumably authorial point of view of Martha's legs decked out in an absurd pair of patterned stockings (fig. 2.18). This shot asks us to share the narrator's view of women's bodies as harmless objects of humor rather than as sites of threatening erotic stimulation.

The problematic dimension of the "modern" female eroticism that Griffith depicts in the first part of *Way Down East* lies in its subversion of the patriarchal family unit. The film reifies this traditional family structure by associating it with nature and by positioning the woman's body as a part of this "natural" configuration. In the restored version of the film, David woos Anna by pointing out the way in which two branches of the river flow together into one. By contrast, Sanderson's continuing association with a culturally constructed eroticism that is "against" nature is suggested later by his gift to Kate of roses in winter, the unnatural quality of which Martha pointedly comments on. Whereas Sanderson's fanciful images of Anna's body make use of artful literary metaphors, David's imaginative visions represent his love as natural and "right."[20] The connection that Griffith makes here between the woman's body and nature builds on traditional cultural constructs in which, as anthropologist Michelle Zimbalist Rosaldo has noted, "notions of the female form often revolve around natural or biological characteristics: fertility, maternity, sex, and menstrual blood" (31). This view argues that although men can approach sexuality as recreation, women must approach it as procreation.[21]

The emphasis on birth in *Way Down East* coincided with a major social controversy over birth control. As Linda Gordon has shown, this controversy intensified during the years from 1910 to 1920, spurred by the suffrage debate and the related feminist issues surrounding it. Although the suffering of childbirth was an argument frequently invoked by contemporary advocates of women's right to birth control, its depiction in *Way Down East* creates quite a different effect. The scene showing the birth of Anna's baby portrays a woman who is driven by her bodily functions (fig. 2.19). The scene is introduced by the intertitle "Maternity: Woman's Gethsemane." The woman represented here, however, is victimized not like Christ by society but rather by her own biology. Childbirth in this representation involves women's betrayal by their bodies. Given this formulation of the issue, the ideal of sexual self-determination espoused by modern women must necessarily founder. The solution to the problem as the film presents it is not birth control but patriarchal marriage.

In presenting birth as he does in *Way Down East* Griffith follows well-worn theories about the nature of women's bodies. Birth lies at the center of long-established scientific conceptions of the female life cycle, for the male-dominated medical profession has traditionally viewed the female body as a site of production. As Carroll Smith-Rosenberg points out in her essay "Puberty to Menopause: The Cycle of Femininity in Nineteenth-Century America," "[T]he central concern of [standard nineteenth-century medical] formulations, central both emotionally and in content, pictures the female as driven by the tidal currents of her cyclical reproductive system, a cycle bounded by the pivotal crises of puberty and menopause and reinforced each month by her recurrent menstrual flow" (24). Emily Martin's analysis of more recent medical discourse about women's bodies shows that this approach has persisted to the present day. According to this wisdom women's capacity to give birth is their defining feature; thus the onset of menstruation is seen as a crucial dividing line between childhood and womanhood, and menopause is understood as the end of a woman's "productive" years.

In *Way Down East* the line between childhood and womanhood is defined by an abrupt shift in Gish's acting technique. In the film's early scenes, Gish signals Anna's status as a child by means of a histrionic performance style that relies on the broad pantomime that was by 1920 associated primarily with slapstick comedy. This performance mode is most evident in the scene in which Anna greets her cousin Emma Tremont (fig. 2.20). Gish's exaggerated gestures and expressions here draw attention to the young girl's childlike innocence, making her appear slightly ridiculous. This portrait is reinforced by other details such as the gloves that are secured by a cord strung around Anna's neck and her diminutive stature set against the lofty grandeur of the doors of the Boston mansion (figs. 2.21 and 2.22).

After Anna's eccentric aunt dresses her up and takes her to the ball, Gish changes her performance technique. Rather than indulging in broad pantomime, she now uses her body to strike self-conscious poses, as we have seen, presenting herself as an object for Sanderson to admire. That her altered sense of her body is related to a newly acquired sense of womanliness is signaled in the vignette in which she practices walking in the high-heeled shoes that she has been given to wear (fig. 2.23). This moment—in which Anna as a girl begins to adopt the techniques of bodily expression associated with mature women—is the last time that Gish uses the techniques of broad pantomime. To portray Anna as a woman Gish not only poses but also introduces subtle changes in her facial expressions, which Griffith underscores by giving the character an increased number of close-ups. Thus Anna's maturity is delineated in terms of a decisive change in her physical presence. She does not gradually grow into womanhood; she suddenly emerges as a woman. The nature of this transformation suggests a maturity defined by a single physical event rather than by slowly developing psychological changes.[22]

If Anna's passage into womanhood is depicted as the sudden emergence of her fertility, the eventual waning of this fertility is emphasized in Griffith's portrayal of her relations with an older, postmenopausal female. In particular, the playful tussle between Anna and David's mother, Mrs. Bartlett, over who should churn the milk into butter suggests a deeper struggle over the childbearing role within the Bartlett family, for it alludes to the nurturing function of the female body, which can both churn milk and create it (fig. 2.24). On the Bartlett farm Anna's ultimate role is as a vessel for the preservation of a patriarchal line, and this role is passed on from one generation of women to the next. The significance of an orderly succession of female childbearers who can assure family continuity is again asserted at the end of the film when Anna kisses David's mother following the wedding (fig. 2.25).[23]

The capacity of Anna's body to create life not only makes her indispensable to the preservation of the patriarchal family but also endows her with a threatening power over it, for she may choose to bear and raise children outside of it. The last part of *Way Down East* mitigates this power, however, by displacing it onto the film's male hero-rescuer. Griffith's desire to appropriate the female capacity to bear children had already been suggested by the title of *Birth of a Nation*, which, as Michael Rogin has observed, can be taken as indicating that the nation is being born in Griffith's film. *Way Down East* depicts birth not as the province of the creative auteur behind the camera but as the right of a heroic male within the fictional world, a male who bears the same first name as the director himself. In the figure of David, Griffith had envisioned a Godlike masculine power that could author not simply works of art but life itself.[24]

This masculine appropriation of the power to give birth is increasingly apparent in the progress of Anna and David's relationship. In the forefront of their courtship is the image of the well, which has traditionally connoted women's role as the bearers of children. In *Way Down East*, however, this symbol is not identified solely with Anna but is shared between her and David. As David is first introduced, he is standing next to a well, and we later see Anna pause beside this same well. Both young people are depicted in these scenes in affectionate rapport with doves, suggesting their suitability for parental roles (figs. 2.26, 2.27, and 2.28). Later Anna draws water from the well—an image suggestive of childbirth (fig. 2.29). Significantly, she is prevented from taking the pail into the house by the arrival of Sanderson, who almost persuades her to leave the family group that she has become part of (fig. 2.30). She is subsequently dissuaded from this course by David, who helps her to carry the pail inside (fig. 2.31).

The portrayal of David as a full participant in Anna's activities at the well is a prelude to his later role as the film's most powerful creator of life. Anna's "sin" has raised the possibility that all children need not be positioned within society as the heirs of men; in a society based on the principle of gender parity, women could control the disposition of future generations. In order to obliterate the implications of this possibility and to redeem her transgression, Anna must herself be born again. Unconscious on the ice, she appears as though dead. Her sexual "fall" has indeed transformed her body into one that is filled with erotic meaning, and she must appear to die in order to reclaim her innocent status. The male who presides over her rebirth appears able to bring about this miracle by virtue of his association with the symbol of the well.[25]

As perhaps Griffith's most celebrated rescue montage, the ice sequence in *Way Down East* fully exploits Hollywood conventions of editing and mise-en-scène to construct an argument about the power and limitations of the female body. In this scene, which was hailed by contemporary reviewers as the greatest climax ever filmed, sadism is disclaimed in the name of spectacle. The almost unbearable attenuation brought about by the director's parallel editing is disavowed by the palpable verisimilitude of his spectacular mise-en-scène, and the violence enacted against a victimized woman is undercut by the "truth" of an actor's virtuoso performance. Audiences are thus led to marvel at the "realism" of a scene in which a woman's power is suppressed in the most forceful possible terms. If he almost literally killed Lillian Gish in the process, Griffith nonetheless managed to use her frail body to demonstrate how desperately women needed men to rescue them from the travails of independence and to keep them secure—if powerless—within the male-dominated world of the traditional family.

The figurative death that Anna experiences on the ice is represented in part through Griffith's awe-inspiring natural mise-en-scène, which emphasizes the coldness and passivity of her exposed body. Pudovkin has singled out the ice sequence in *Way Down East* as a *locus classicus* of the way in which landscape can become character, suggesting that the roaring river and the falls personify Anna's despair (*Film Technique* 129). Yet these images may imply not despair but rather the destructive quality of Anna's sexuality. The "sexual storm" that forms the climax of *Way Down East* is the culmination of an aquatic metaphor earlier developed in the image of the well and given an explicitly sexual turn by the pairing of a traditional symbol of female sexuality, Anna's hair cascading around her head and shoulders, with an image of the mighty river (figs. 2.32 and 2.33). In this context, the scene of Anna lying unconscious on the ice with her hair trailing in the river can be read as the picture of a woman helplessly enthralled by the torrential power of her own sexual urges (fig. 2.34). It is this power that is destroyed by her "death."

Of course, Anna does not remain moribund; she is revived. The agent of her seemingly miraculous rebirth is the man who will marry her (fig. 2.35). By a superhuman act of heroism, he overcomes the crushing forces of nature and Old Testament justice to assume the feminine function of creating life. By bringing Anna back as if from the dead, David not only saves her so that he can marry her but also appropriates her procreative power. Thus Griffith's rescue scenario functions to deny the woman control over the creation of life by revealing her as helplessly passive, awaiting the male to whom she owes her own life. David's rescue operation reenacts the involvement with the protection and nurturance of the human body that he has committed himself to in his work as a farmer. His heroism during the rescue is connected with his role as a worker in specific imagery related to the body itself. Here the emphasis on women's legs that had earlier been associated with erotic attraction gives way to an emphasis on hands. Before David carries Anna's inert body into the cabin to revive her, he blows on her hands and rubs them (fig. 2.36). These gestures precisely echo those of Anna herself when she attempts to revive her dead baby (fig. 2.37). But where Anna fails, David succeeds. As the parts of the body that perform manual labor, his hands are used for running the farm, and they are here celebrated as instruments that can ensure the most basic bodily needs.[26]

Thus, in an era dominated by women's struggle for independence, *Way Down East* constructs a residual discourse around the body of its star to argue that women desperately need men to keep them secure within the traditional family. It limits the contemporary debate over women's ability to make choices to the issue of marriage choices, and then disclaims even this possibility by depicting its heroine as a prisoner of her biology. In a sense Anna's body chooses David, for she owes her life to him. Ultimately even the authority that she derives from her body's ability to give birth is appropriated by the man who eventually marries her. She is fulfilled by being rendered powerless.

Way Down East was a great hit, the last big money-maker that Griffith was to enjoy. Its popularity suggests that at some level the film spoke to the suffragette generation at the moment of its greatest triumph. But the story's verbal brief against the sexual double standard was subtended by a more subtle discourse in which women's rights were wholly denied. As I have argued, this discourse is expressed in the film's visual design and in particular in its representation of the body of Lillian Gish. However, it was not Griffith but rather his powerful star, whom he was about to release from his employ, who garnered the lion's share of the accolades that the film received. From this time forward it was Gish far more than Griffith that the public recognized as the author of a coherent group of films. Her aura of terrorized vulnerability had become her signature.

Orphans of the Storm: *Patriarchy Reconsidered*

If Griffith's characterization of Lillian Gish as an archetypal victim culminated in *Way Down East*, however, this film was not to be his final vision of her. In 1921 Gish returned to Griffith to make one last film, *Orphans of the Storm*, in which she starred with her sister, Dorothy. Set in the period of the French Revolution, *Orphans of the Storm* was based on a property that Gish herself had recommended to her former mentor. Working on a new, more egalitarian basis with his star, Griffith was now in a position of more limited power. In addition, the passage of the amendment granting women suffrage had resolved much of the public controversy surrounding women's roles. The final Griffith-Gish collaboration resulted in a more utopian vision of womanly power—even as the film gave vent to a form of political conservatism by denouncing revolution in its opening intertitle and portraying the people of Paris not as triumphant liberators but as a threatening mob. However, here for the first time the issue of choosing an acceptable marriage partner that had so obsessed Griffith in his previous productions with Gish recedes into the background. Instead, this film considers a wider range of human interconnectedness in which marriage is not a central issue.

Previous Griffith projects in which both Gish sisters were featured, including *The Unseen Enemy*, *Home Sweet Home*, and *Hearts of the World*, all contain the theme of sororal bonding. But in *Orphans of the Storm* this bonding dominates the action. Lillian Gish plays Henriette, foster sister and primary caretaker of the blind Louise, played by Dorothy Gish. Although both sisters have male suitors, these men are given relatively unimportant roles. Henriette vows to Louise that she will never marry without her sister's permission, and this vow is taken very seriously. The film's final scene, which might have emphasized the reunion of the lovers, instead focuses on Henriette asking for Louise's permission to marry.

Orphans of the Storm emphasizes Lillian Gish's strength and determination rather than her vulnerability, as earlier Griffith films had done.[27] Henriette repeatedly fights off soldiers and would-be abductors, often in the presence of men who stand by helpless or unconcerned. Although at the film's climax she is saved from the guillotine by Danton (Monte Blue), it is a rescue performed as an act of reciprocity, for Henriette has previously rescued her rescuer. Moreover, Danton's power over Henriette's life is solely political; he is not her lover, nor her father, nor her older brother. The film's conclusion features a family group that includes men but is dominated by the famous Gish sisters, stars Griffith had created but who had by then developed an independence and authority quite apart from him. Their preeminence is here recognized within the filmic world (figs. 2.38 and 2.39).

In *Orphans of the Storm* the issue of marriage becomes secondary to the devotion between the two sisters, and the metaphoric implications of the film's representation of the female body suggests an emergent discourse in which the heterosexual couple is no longer seen as the only meaningful option for effecting narrative closure.

As Henriette is being led off to the guillotine, she and Louise exchange a long and intensely romantic embrace. In close-up we see Henriette bend down from the cart in which she is riding. Louise caresses her sister's face and hair and kisses her (fig. 2.40). This embrace may be the most passionate moment in all Griffith's oeuvre.[28] Within the Victorian traditions in which Griffith was working, however, such an embrace would have had connotations different from those brought to it by today's viewers. In an essay on female friendships in the nineteenth century, Carroll Smith-Rosenberg comments on "an undeniably romantic and even sensual note" that frequently marked such relationships ("Female World" 276). Smith-Rosenberg explains this phenomenon by noting the gender-segregated nature of nineteenth-century society, which isolated women in a world of their own. In such a context, romantic attraction between women became an acceptable mode of expressing the human need for warmth and closeness to others. In *Orphans of the Storm* Griffith draws on this Victorian tradition to reformulate the range of romantic possibilities, depicting romantic love as a powerful affinity between two people that does not necessarily imply marriage or even sexual union. Instead, it is seen as a passionate attachment that need not be bound to a family-centered unit. *Way Down East* ends with a kiss between two men that is seen as a comic error, defining the narrow boundaries of erotic behavior allowed by a conception of romantic love that achieves its proper closure in monogamous marriage. By contrast, the Gish sisters' kiss in *Orphans of the Storm* signals a moment in which the Hollywood cinema embraces an alternative image of passion that American women of 1921 had open to them.

Lillian Gish enjoyed a long and distinguished career following this, her last film with Griffith, while the cultural power attached to her former mentor's position as a producer/director declined. Gish herself had once attempted directing; she later claimed that it was "no job for a lady." If the job of being a movie star was more to her taste, as was apparently the case, it was perhaps in part because it offered lavish rewards seldom available to women of the time—whether they thought of themselves as ladies or not. Among these rewards was the aura of engaging in creative, expressive work; in a word of being regarded as authors. As Timothy Corrigan has pointed out, directors were later to reemerge as stars whose creative contributions were widely recognized by the public, especially in the discourses that arose around international cinema. But Griffith was not to witness this development. Like the old-fashioned view of the patriarchal family that his cinema championed, Hollywood relegated the discourse on the director as author to a marginalized place among the legends it disseminated.

STAR AND GENRE: JOHN WAYNE, THE WESTERN, AND THE AMERICAN DREAM OF THE FAMILY ON THE LAND

This is a place where people can come and raise a family.
—VAN HEFLIN *in* Shane

If Hollywood wanted to capture the emotional center of Western history, its movies would be about real estate. John Wayne would have been neither a gunfighter nor a sheriff, but a surveyor, speculator, or claims lawyer.
—PATRICIA LIMERICK, The Legacy of Conquest

The true soldier who is the official, instituted go-between, the spokesman of the settler and his rule of oppression . . . speaks the language of pure force. . . . He is the bringer of violence into the home and into the mind of the native.
—FRANTZ FANON, The Wretched of the Earth

HOLLYWOOD has long favored the practice of identifying stars with particular genres, thereby combining two of its favorite marketing strategies. Boris Karloff and Vincent Price have become icons of the horror story, Marlene Dietrich is identified with exotic tales of romance, and Edward G. Robinson and James Cagney represent Hollywood's version of the gangster. There is probably no more famous identification between star and genre than the one between John Wayne, the world's best-known movie actor, and the Western, Hollywood's most enduring formula. Wayne has appeared on the list of Hollywood's ten most popular actors twenty-five times—almost twice as often as any other star (Steinberg 57). His persona was developed during the 1930s while he starred in a series of Western programmers. In keeping with this image, publicity shots almost always show him in Western gear, and he carried "signature" Western accoutrements from film to film: a double-breasted, military-looking shirt, a favorite belt buckle, and a rifle with a large ring level (McDonald 122). This identification of the star with the genre is supported by box-office figures: of the thirty top money-making Westerns made before 1981, eleven starred Wayne (Steinberg 12).

The association between Wayne and the Western thus presents perhaps the clearest case of a star image that can both reinforce and extend meanings inherent in the structure and iconography of a generic formula. Although many studies of the Western (for example, those by Kitses and Tuska) focus on the interaction between the genre and its major directors, the association between genre and star reveals more about the movies as a social practice because both generic identification and the star system constitute major strategies by which Hollywood creates audiences for its products. Emmanuel Levy has suggested that a subgenre exists that could be called "the John Wayne Western," and Michael Budd has shown that Western director John Ford assigned characteristic and distinguishable roles to favorite stars such as Wayne, James Stewart, Richard Widmark, and Henry Fonda. In a larger sense, however, the image that Wayne developed pervaded the Western genre as a whole. The aura that he carried with him from film to film coupled with publicity surrounding his private life could create generically coded meanings even when there were no other elements in a particular cinematic text to support them. The Western genre, in turn, endowed Wayne with significations that he would not otherwise have had: it surrounded his image with a story. To some extent this ability to create and absorb generic meaning is shared by all well-known Western stars and circulates among them. But because Wayne's persona was the most well developed of any Western actor's, a consideration of the meaning he embodied in relation to the formula allows for an analysis that most fully explores the interaction between star and genre.[1]

The Western's concern with women and romantic love is a matter of some debate. Raymond Bellour's widely cited assertion about Hollywood cinema's obsession with the formation of the couple was made in relation to the Western genre specifically. Bellour argues that "the Western is subtended from one end to the other by the problematic of marriage" ("Alternation" 187). Anthony Mann has expressed similar sentiments, claiming that "without a woman, the story wouldn't work" (Qtd. in Bellour, "Alternation" 187). On the other hand, both Robert

Warshow and André Bazin have commented on the genre's lack of emphasis on "love interest." On the surface, at least, Warshow and Bazin would seem to be born out by the evidence of the films: in most, women are relegated to minor roles, and in some, like *The Magnificent Seven* (1960), *The Wild Bunch* (1969), and *Ulzana's Raid* (1972), they scarcely figure at all. Women did not even make up a significant part of the audience for Westerns in their heyday, for according to a survey conducted in 1950, Westerns were ranked by women as their least favorite genre (Handel 124). Unlike other popular Hollywood formulas, the Western has not traditionally been seen as having been significantly shaped by motifs relating to romantic love and marriage. By contrast, Rick Altman has identified the musical as a formula that "fashions a myth out of the American courtship ritual" (27), and Stanley Cavell has labeled an important Hollywood genre as "the comedy of remarriage." Numerous other scholars have accounted for the appeal of genres such as the woman's film, the horror film, and *film noir* as a function of conflicts over socially unsanctioned expressions of sexual passion.[2]

Like the genre itself, Western actors are not customarily identified as ladies' men. As Ed Buscombe has commented, Western stars are not notable for their good looks ("The Idea of Genre" 16). Although actors like Gary Cooper and Randolph Scott were by any measure among the handsomest men in Hollywood in their early days, their careers as heroes of Western dramas blossomed as their youthful allure faded. Similarly, Wayne's persona was not identified with the kind of erotic charge that characterized most Hollywood leading men. When he became a major star in Ford's 1939 Western *Stagecoach*, he was thirty-two, and he enjoyed his greatest successes during the 1950s when he was approaching middle age. In his most memorable films he rarely "got the girl," and the Western characters he created tended to treat women with either clumsy embarrassment or chilly respect when they didn't avoid them altogether.[3] As Andrew Sarris has commented, "Wayne clearly lacked finesse, subtlety, and patience, the indispensable tools of womanizing on the screen" ("John Wayne's Strange Legacy" 35). Wayne was not the first Western star to embody this reticence with women, but he did the most to make it a fundamental feature of the genre. Ultimately, the identification of the Western hero as a man's man became so firmly established that it became a taken-for-granted aspect of virtually all Westerns. Despite the pronounced avoidance of love interest that characterized both the persona of the

Western actor and the genre of which he was a part, however, at a deep level women—and in particular, marriage—formed the core of the Western hero that Wayne created, and women and marriage were central to the genre itself.

Wayne, the Western, and the Ideology of Nationalism

The themes most commonly cited as central to the Western formula reflect the heritage of Frederick Jackson Turner, who in 1893 pointed to the settling of the West as an experience that, more than any other, defined American identity. In Turner's formulation, the adventure of western expansionism pitted civilization against wilderness to create a crucible for the formation of American virtues such as self-reliance and ingenuity. Most commentators on the Western genre work from Turner's basic thesis. Even when such studies deal with Westerns that are critical of this perspective on American history, they accept the conceptual framework that Turner passed down, which is centered on his opposition between civilization and wilderness. This basic opposition is thought to be mediated by the concept of the frontier and its representative, the cowboy hero. Not surprisingly, the civilization/wilderness opposition has engendered a number of structuralist readings of the genre, most notably by Will Wright and Thomas Schatz. Such readings typically recognize the fundamental contradiction as one between a wilderness that fosters a noble individualism and the advent of a desired civilization that is nonetheless accompanied by a less-heroic regime of socialization and domestication. Depending on the critic, this contradiction may be expressed in terms either of abstract moral values or of a gender-related struggle in which a feminized civilization replaces a more primitive world of masculine virtue.[4]

However, scholars of American history such as Patricia Limerick and Richard White have begun to question the Eurocentric values represented by the traditional Turneresque reading of American westward expansion. These critics have observed that the opposition between civility and wilderness reflects a European perspective. Such histories typically portray indigenous Others as savages, thereby equating them with the wilderness and opposing them to the ideals of "civilization" and "progress." Limerick proposes a revised conception of the central term *frontier* whereby the concept is understood not as the last outpost of civilization, as in Turner's formulation, but as a line of demarcation between different cultures, as it has traditionally been used in relation to the borders between European countries.

In the absence of a historiography that revises the value judgments inherent in the traditional opposition between civilization and wilderness posed by the Turneresque thesis, debates over the accuracy with which Western films have rendered the "facts" of Western history, which form the core of the latest book on the genre by Jon Tuska, have limited value. If the writers and directors of Western films have been prone to distortions and omissions, so has the historical record.[5] Earlier studies of the Western by Will Wright and John Lenihan have been more concerned with the ideological significance of the genre, but they have related this significance to the particular periods in which the films under discussion were produced. What remains to be explored, then, is the way in which this venerable Hollywood formula articulates a view of America that has dominated the popular imagination throughout the greater part of the twentieth century. The classic Western—defined in part by its association with the images of John Wayne and stars like him—participates in a particular kind of discourse on American history and American identity that uses the myth of the frontier to contain a central inconsistency in American nationalist ideology. This contradiction is focused on the issue of race, for, as Etienne Balibar has observed, "In many respects, racism has provided nationalism with the only theory it has" (283).

Nationalism, which has been called the most successful political ideology in human history, was largely a creation of the nineteenth century and has continued to flourish in our own time.[6] Its function is to ratify the claims of the state to impose its will on individuals within its sphere. A nationalist movement seeks to bind together people in a particular territory as an endeavor to gain and use state power. The concept of nationhood involves the creation of what Benedict Anderson has referred to as "an imagined political community—and imagined both as inherently limited and sovereign" (15). Citizens are expected to feel themselves part of this community and to develop loyalty toward it. Thus, "regardless of the actual inequality and exploitation that may prevail in each, the nation is always conceived as a deep, horizontal comradeship" (Cashmore 16). In developing this spirit of imagined community, the modern mass media—including cinema—has been central, for the media can make what are in effect national symbols part of the life of every individual and thus break down the divisions between the private and local spheres in which most citizens normally live, and the public and national one.

At the center of the myth of imagined community that the media promulgate is a contradiction, for nationhood is conceived not only as an imagined community characterized by "deep horizontal comradeship" but also as a hierarchy of group identities. "The ideology of nationalism," Robert Miles states, "asserts the existence of a natural division within the world's population, a division between collectivities each with a distinct cultural profile and therefore a distinct capacity for constituting a self-governing nation within a given geographical space" (89). This "distinct cultural profile" is invariably that of the nation's dominant group. Charles Wagley and Marvin Harris have described the discourse by which this dominance is articulated as follows: "the cultural tradition, the language, and physical types of one of the groups of a state's society are proposed as the national language, the national culture, and the national physical type. . . . In the United States, the national ideal is English-speaking, Protestant, northern European in descent, and light Caucasoid in physical appearance" (243).[7]

In the United States this contradiction is a particularly troublesome one, for the tension between the ideal of a community of equals and the drive for domination by groups within the culture has been pronounced. The ideology of American nationalism has attempted to contain this contradiction through a series of metaphors and catchphrases, including "the melting pot," "the salad bowl," and "separate but equal." The fact that none of these phrases has met with universal acceptance over a period of time attests to the continuing struggle in the United States over the conflicting demands of identifying a dominant national type within an imagined community characterized by deep horizontal comradeship.

A fundamental feature of nationalist discourse is the active creation of myths of historical origin. In the twentieth century the most widely disseminated American myth of national origin is embodied in fictions about the settlement of the western states. Why this particular myth? Most obviously, the end of the nineteenth century can be viewed nostalgically as a time when the country was united under a single value system that, at least in theory, viewed all people as equal. Slavery had been dispensed with. Thus the period is well suited to express the "deep, horizontal comradeship" that Cashmore poses as a necessary part of such myths. But the myth of the settlement of the West also raises problems, for the westward expansion brought into focus confrontations with indigenous racial others whose value systems were fundamentally at odds with those of the European settlers and who were not easily accommodated into the ideal of comradeship. The period of westward expansion can also be celebrated nostalgically as one in which individual enterprise flourished. But again, the myth brings contradictions; for the triumphal advent of the railroad and the automobile at the beginning of the twentieth century is associated with technological complexity and the attendant hierarchization and alienation of the labor force. Thus, the moment at which the railroad arrives in the West is typically viewed as representing the climax and the end of the mythic period.[8]

According to a principle enunciated by Florian Znaniecki, the spread of nationalist ideology requires that it be promulgated by popular, charismatic advocates. Znaniecki writes:

> It originates with independent individual *leaders* in various realms of cultural activity, who gradually create a national culture in which a plurality of traditional regional cultures becomes partly synthesized. We call them leaders because and insofar as they attract circles of voluntary followers. They frequently gain also the support of socially powerful sponsors or patrons—princes, magnates, church dignitaries, men of wealth, statesmen, military commanders, heads of political parties (25).

In America John Wayne was for many years seen as such a leader. Wayne assumed a privileged position in relation to this leadership role because of his highly visible public presence as a spokesperson for American pride. Moreover, his image as a former college football hero at the University of Southern California identified him with a sport that is strongly associated with American life.[9] In addition, the sixteen war films that he starred in characterized him as a defender of America against threats from abroad.

The conflation of Wayne's filmic characters and his offscreen persona gave his fictional characters the status of a popular hero who, as Tony Bennett and Janet Woollacott have claimed, is "granted a quasi-real status" (13). Although popular heroes usually have their origins in a particular work or body of fiction, Bennett and Woollacott argue,

> they break free from the originating textual conditions of their existence, functioning as an established point of cultural reference that is capable of working—of producing meanings—even for those who are not directly familiar with the original texts in which they first made their appearance. . . . Functioning as focal points of cultural reference, they condense and connect, serve as shorthand expressions for, a number of deeply implanted cultural and ideological concerns (14).

Wayne was probably more successful than any other actor in history in creating an aura of realism surrounding his performances that allowed his fictional characters to be widely identified with his own life. Joan Didion's essay on Wayne, for example, stresses the congruity between the roles that he played and his personal behavior. But this conflation between performer and character is largely based on fiction. In 1971, for example, the American Marine Corps League named the actor "the man who best exemplifies the word 'American'" (Halliwell 717). Yet Wayne, unlike most other men of his age, did not enter military service during World War II; instead he spent the war years establishing his image as a fictional war hero.[10] More generally, Wayne has been repeatedly praised as an exemplary American by a number of prominent public figures, including six United States presidents (Levy 297). Yet the record of his personal life reveals him as someone who frequently indulged in flagrant adulteries, drunk and disorderly conduct, and physical abuse of women and coworkers. Richard Grenier's evaluation of Wayne, written shortly after the actor's death, aptly begins with the reminder that that star "was after all not a hero but an actor who played heroes" (79).

By this measure, Wayne was a consummate performer who succeeded in investing his characters with an aura of cultural verisimilitude unmatched by any other Hollywood star—a verisimilitude that complemented the generic verisimilitude cultivated by the Western formula. However, Wayne's strategy of "playing himself" on-screen did not always find favor with critics. Although he received an Academy Award in 1970 for *True Grit*, his acting abilities have long been hotly debated; disagreement arises because of the varying criteria that commentators use to evaluate his style. As I argued in chapter 1, the way critics judge performances is a function of the principles that they apply; thus, if demonstrated mastery of bravura expressive technique is the standard, actors like Wayne, who always played the same role and did so using a minimum of technical gimmicks, will come up short. John Belton ("John Wayne"), Richard Dyer (*Stars*), and Andrew Sarris ("John Wayne's Strange Legacy") have all attempted to dissect various of the star's specific performance techniques, but their observations carry limited weight because they provide only fragmentary views of a persona that drew on the accumulated significations of offscreen behavior, personal appearance, and generically coded ideologies far more heavily than on "acting" to carry its meaning. Wayne may not have been a versatile actor, but he was most assuredly a credible one.

On the other hand, most studies of Wayne's image, notably those by Allan Eyles (*John Wayne*), Emmanuel Levy, Richard McGee, and Andrew Sinclair ("Man on Horseback"), have confined themselves to pointing out similarities in the characters he plays while neglecting to explore the nature of the cultural verisimilitude that he brings to these roles. Wayne's impact as a performer is best understood by examining the transtextual persona that he constructed rather than by analyzing the characters that he played or his histrionic technique *per se*.

Because Wayne's career flourished during the Second World War and afterward, and because this period is generally regarded a the "rebirth" of the Western following a period of decline during the 1930s, the examples that I will cite as evidence for my argument will for the most part be taken from Westerns made during the 1940s and afterward. Because of the cross-fertilizing effect of Wayne's image and the conventions of the Western itself, however, the method that I will follow will be to consider features of the genre in general, relating these characteristics at appropriate points in the argument to the enrichment and extension of meaning granted by the formula's association with the Wayne persona. I will give special attention to visual tropes such as landscape and shoot-outs that are salient features of virtually all movie Westerns.[11]

As I have indicated, the governing thrust of my argument centers on Wayne's association with the American mythology of nationalism. I am concerned with the contradiction between egalitarian ideals and the will to domination on the part of the Northern European settlers as played out in the Western genre in terms of the recurring trope of the family on the land. This trope engaged not only the race-centered contradiction at the center of the American value system but also the ideal of the nuclear family which represented a bourgeois ideal of sexual respectability that nationalist discourse appropriated and disseminated among all citizens. The patriarchal presence of John Wayne stands at the center of this system.

The Land as Property and the Ideal of Dynastic Marriage

What is most conspicuously at issue in Westerns is not the right to possess women but the right to possess the land. However, these questions are intimately related. In chapter 1 I outlined Friedrich Engels's argument that female subjugation within the family is a function of the ownership of private property. According to Engels the system of land ownership led to a definition of gender roles whereby men could exercise the right of property ownership while women bore and nurtured the children who would inherit this property. "The transition to full private property is gradually accomplished parallel with the transition of the pairing marriage into monogamy," Engels states. "The family is becoming the economic unit of society" (223). The land thus came to represent the patriarch-father's "real estate." This system implies a social organization that privileges kinship relations. In the case of state-dominated civilizations, group similarity based on principles derived from kinship relations becomes the operative force, for "'kinship' and 'blood' have obvious advantages in bonding together members of a group and excluding outsiders, and are therefore central to ethnic nationalism" (Hobshawm 63).

I will call the form of traditional patriarchal marriage associated with land acquisition and conservation "dynastic marriage." Traditional agrarian cultures are largely organized around this system of marriage. In his study *The Making of the Modern Family* Edward Shorter has observed, "Popular marriage in former centuries was usually affectionless, held together by considerations of property and lineage" (55). Historically, marriage had been a practical arrangement to meet mutual needs, as it provided for procreation and helped build family lands and wealth. Patricia Limerick sees such a pattern of property allocation through marriage alliances operating in nineteenth-century America. She states, "Western history has been an ongoing competition for legitimacy—for the right to claim for oneself and sometimes for one's group the status of legitimate beneficiary of Western resources. This intersection of ethnic diversity with property allocation unified Western history" (27).

The concept of dynastic marriage lies at the heart of Western formula entertainments and of the Western hero whom John Wayne and others embodied.[12] Both the genre and the images of its major stars articulate this thematic through a rhetorical strategy that defines land in terms of property and cultural dominance in terms of racial privilege. Values and traditions that challenge this ideal are seen as illegitimate. It is thus necessary to understand the significance of the genre's emphasis on the land and on the related motif of racial difference before the image of the Western hero and the Wayne persona in particular can be properly appreciated.

Land held a central position in the thinking of the Northern European settlers in America. Most came with the ideal of land ownership in mind. As Patricia Limerick has stated, "White Americans saw the acquisition of property as a cultural imperative, manifestly the right way to go about things" (55). The ideal of property has long persisted in the rhetoric of American values and, indeed, forms the ideological foundation that allows America to claim a unique national identity. Walter Lippmann, for example, claimed, "The only dependable foundation of personal liberty is the economic security of private property" (quoted in Seigan 330). In 1977 C.B. Macpherson commented, "We have made property so central to our society that anything and any rights that are not property are very apt to take second place" (quoted in Nedelsky, "American Constitutionalism" 242). Legal scholar Jennifer Nedelsky has traced the history of property as an ideal in American thought. By the time the Constitution was written, property "had an impressive philosophical tradition behind it: both Locke and republican thinkers such as Harrington stressed the importance and value of property. . . . It was a right with which most Americans had some immediate personal connection, and it had a concrete quality which made it an ideal symbol for the barrier between individual rights and legitimate government power" ("American Constitutionalism" 269).

In Westerns the conflict over land typically involves pioneers against Indians or small farmers against cattle barons with property as the prize that goes to the victors. Often the conflict is explicitly posed in terms of the right of private property as when the concept of the open range is opposed to the right to fence in fields or pastures in Westerns like *Abilene Town* (1946) and *Man Without a Star* (1955). The significance of land is also suggested by the titles of many of these films, which frequently refer to towns or places. In addition, the state most prominently identified with the genre, Texas, has a notable history as a contested territory.

Even Westerns in which land is not overtly at issue almost invariably refer to its central place in the genre by setting an inordinate number of scenes against the grandeur of the natural landscape. Westerns typically open with such scenes and often conclude with them. Ed Buscombe has documented the debt that these images owe to prior traditions of landscape painting, especially the work of Frederic Remington ("Painting the Legend"). More generally, such images identify the nation with nature, drawing on the tradition of associating nationalism with landscape most famously asserted by Spengler. In nationalist discourse "nature [is] perceived as the native landscape, its mountains and valleys inspiring the members of one particular nation" (Mosse 83).

The Western's descriptive interludes centered on landscapes are customarily represented in high-angle long shots, a representational strategy that renders them analogous to what Mary Louise Pratt has spoken of as the "master of all I survey" scene in nineteenth-century European colonialist discourse on Africa in which "a speaker-protagonist stands upon a high place of some kind and describes the panorama below" ("Conventions" 145). In such scenes, the landscape is rendered as an object of discovery by the seer, who is placed in a position of dominance over what is displayed.

Modern versions of this trope may also involve what Pratt calls an "ideology of negation" in which the emptiness of the landscape is represented as prehistoric ("Conventions" 151). "One hardly need comment on the ideological significance of representing parts of the world as having no history and therefore in need of being given one by us," Pratt goes on to observe. "What is of interest here is the association of the prehistoric with the absence of differentiation. One of the most conspicuous hallmarks of high technology, industrial societies, especially capitalist ones, is precisely the endless creation of differentiations, specializations, subdivision" ("Conventions" 152). The Western convention which depicts the landscape as open and free participates in this mode of imperialist discourse and functions to position the land as "wilderness," that is, as empty space in need of occupation.[13] The very title of Henry Nash Smith's influential book on the mythology of the American West, *The Virgin Land*, constitutes a dramatic instance of this descriptive mode. America's "virgin" land appears conspicuously unbounded. Seemingly limitless views function as a prelude to the imperialist mission of defining territories and scanning perimeters. This spirit of imperialist appropriation is apparent in the titles of many Westerns, which frequently point to the function of landscape elements as boundaries, in particular rivers, which both mark perimeters and testify to the arable potential of the land. (Hawks's *Red River* [1948], *Rio Bravo* [1959], and *Rio Lobo* [1970] are well-known examples of this strategy.) The idyllic Western landscape setting is typically animated by the placid movements of horses, wagon trains, or cattle being driven to market. Invariably the presence of domestic animals ties the figures of the European intruders into the landscape in a bucolic portrait of people whose activites are harmoniously integrated with nature. By such strategies the empty landscape is personified; it becomes the metaphorical "'face of the country'—a more tractable face that returns the European's gaze, echoes his words, and accepts his caress" (Pratt, "Scratches" 126–27).

The Western's trope of the garden which the pioneers are charged with creating specifies further meanings attached to the landscape that related it to an ideology of the family home. As Smith states, "The myth of the garden affirmed that the dominant force in the future society of the Mississippi Valley would be agriculture" (139). This emphasis on agriculture was understood in terms of the family farm, which split up the land into one-hundred-and-sixty-acre tracts, each of which could be cultivated by a single family. The New World settlers could hold up the ideal of the family farm as a more egalitarian system than the feudalistic landholding systems tied to entrenched traditions of aristocratic privilege which continued to dominate the landholding patterns of the European cultures that they were rejecting. Patricia Limerick states, "The success of the American experiment rested in the property-holding success of many individuals. Property, widely distributed among the people, would hold the line against pernicious concentrations of power" (58). Dolores Hayden's study of the evolution of the single-family home as a uniquely American ideal connects it to this heritage. "For the first time in history," she states, "a civilization has created a utopian ideal based on the house rather than the city or the nation" (18). She traces this ideal back to the earliest days of the republic:

> Thomas Jefferson, the first mainstream American political theorist to attempt a schematic spatial representation of a national ideal of democracy, favored the model family farm over the model village. The Declaration of Independence and the National Survey that Jefferson produced are the crucial statements of the rights of all men to life, liberty, and the puruit of happiness in a landscape divided into small farms, where every man can own the means of agricultural production. As Jefferson's survey grid appeared on the American landscape west of the Alleghenies, in the late 1780s, this powerful theoretical statement of agrarian life became the framework for a national ideal of home ownership. (19)

Like Engels, the Western understands possession of the land as an integral part of its theme of dynastic progression, for land is seen both as a place that binds the family together as a physical unit and a source of wealth that binds them together as an economic unit. Significantly, the production of Westerns languished during the 1930s, when the ideal of the family on the land was seriously endangered by the economic hardship to farmers brought about by the Depression. By contrast the heyday of the sound Western occurred during the 1950s, when the development of suburbia was fed by the nostalgic fantasy of the family on the land that the Western promoted. Hayden stresses the centrality of this suburban ideal to Americans' sense of themselves as a nation. "Single family suburban homes have become inseparable from the American dream of economic success and upward mobility," she writes. "Their presence pervades every aspect of economic life, social life, and political life in the United States because the main production of these homes beginning in the late 1940s was an economic activity of overwhelming importance that has transformed the American landscape" (114–15). Sociologist Bennett Berger states this issue more succinctly when he asserts that "suburbia . . . is America" (160). [14]

In addition to its connotations of privately held land, the garden ideal, which by the 1950s was expressed primarily in the image of the suburban lawn, implied a familial space that was constructed rather than natural—and one whose character was imposed by the force of a dominant human power rather than one that evolved through a harmonious interaction between people and the environment. The arid, inhospitable aspect of the typical Western landscape disavows the value of the raw land that the settlers are engaged in appropriating; rather, its value is understood as inhering in the labor that the pioneers perform in recreating this landscape as a garden.

Richard White's study of the pattern of land use among European settlers in the state of Washington stresses the destructive ecological imbalances that these homesteaders engendered through their introduction of alien flora and methods of cultivation. The image of the garden with its Edenic overtones effaces such infelicitous aspects of Northern European westward expansion and presents the project of ecological tampering with the land as an unproblematic ideal. The tough Western hero played by William Holden in Sturges's 1953 *Escape From Fort Bravo*, for example, is made sympathetic when he confesses to growing roses brought from the east in the desert scrub behind his military quarters. "My old man had a dream about this place," Holden states by way of explanation. "He dreamed about finding water, growing crops and raising cattle. That's why I do this."

Although the ideal of the family farm is paid homage to in Western films, farmland rarely appears; instead, vast tracts of rocky or desert landscape are most frequently featured. Such land is not readily adaptable to the project of family farming; accordingly, the primary enterprise portrayed in these films is ranching, an undertaking that involves a division of labor spearheaded by a capitalist entrepreneur. Patricia Limerick notes this inconsistancy when she comments, "The events of Western history represent, not a simple process of territorial expansion, but an array of efforts to wrap the concept of property around unwieldy objects" (71).

The intractable quality of the Western landscape as it relates to the enterprise of family farming gives rise to a contradiction in American values that the cowboy hero, in one form or another, embodies. As has often been noted, he typically occupies the position of an outsider to the community. Although he supports the rights of farmers, he is not one of them for he never owns a farm. He may, however, own a ranch, in which case he is seen in grandiose terms as a successful capitalist entrepeneur, commanding panoramic expanses of property.[15] If, as is more commonly the case, he roams freely over the countryside, he becomes a man who is "at home" in the as-yet uncharted wilderness, thereby assuming the position of a kind of "natural" proprietor of the land. In either case, his deep affection for the landscape is seen as granting him a moral right to it, and he is often contrasted to crass speculators in land who appear as villains in Westerns like *Dakota* (1945), *Arizona* (1941), and *The Sons of Katie Elder* (1965). The allegiance of the idealized cowboy figure to the rights of the homesteaders ratifies the more egalitarian but less heroic dream of the family farm, of property widely distributed among all the people.[16] Many Western stars reinforced their fictional characterizations as men who loved the land by purchasing working ranches and spending a good deal of their time on them. Again, John Wayne was the best-known example of this trend.

The Western's ideal of the family farm gives rise to the genre's nostalgia for the dynastic model of marriage which understands the marriage relationship not in terms of individual emotional fulfillment but as an economic partnership, the object of which is to make use of land to build a patrimony for future generations. Stevens's 1953 *Shane*, which Will Wright has labeled "the classic of the classic Westerns" (34), presents its central woman character, Marian Starrett (Jean Arthur), as someone caught between the powerful pull of sexual passion and her obligation as part of a family on the land. Genre convention dictates her choice of remaining with the family despite her personal feeling, and it codes this decision as the "correct" one. The importance of marriage as an economic rather than an erotic union is also emphasized in a scene in Peckinpah's 1962 *Ride the High Country* in which Steve Judd (Joel McRae) and Gil Westrum (Randolph Scott) discuss the subject. Westrum reminds Judd that the woman Judd once loved chose the security of marriage to a prosperous rancher rather than the impecunious, uncertain existance of the wife of a hired gun. The implication is that she, too, has made the "correct" decision.

In marriages defined as economic partnerships, the rituals of romance are beside the point. Thus courtships in Westerns are notably brief and uncomplicated. For example, in Wesley Ruggles's *Arizona* William Holden decides to marry Jean Arthur on first seeing her, and Arthur, who needs someone to help run her ranch, makes up her mind about Holden almost as quickly. "Pioneer" Westerns such as *Cimarron* (1930) and *Drums Along the Mohawk* (1939) also downplay the issues of courtship in order to focus on the economic struggles involved in establishing the presence of the family on the land. In these films issues of inheritance often assume particular importance as happens, for instance, in *Red River*, *The Searchers* (1956), and innumerable similar narratives. Many Westerns stress the mutual interests of—or rivalries among—brothers, (among many examples, *The Younger Brothers* [1945], *Broken Lance* [1954], *The Sons of Katie Elder* [1965], and in a highly overdetermined configuration, *The Long Riders* [1980], a film in which the character-brothers are played by actor-brothers [Stacey and James Keach; and David, Keith, and Robert Carradine]). In *Abilene Town* Randolph Scott, who acts as a champion of the immigrant farmers, is asked at one point: "What do you want out of this deal?" "A little security for my children," he replies. When it is pointed out that he has no children, he counters, "Some day I might" and goes on to specify what the "security" he wants for these fictional beings consists of. "I want what my father didn't have," he says. "Land."

The dynastic model of marriage was strongly associated with the notion of separate spheres for men and women. Edward Shorter describes the roles of husbands and wives in traditional agrarian cultures as follows: "Each had his or her own tasks to perform in this world, and each would be judged by the community on the basis of how well these work assignments were carried out. Each had his or her own roles to act out before the opposite sex; the men were to be domineering, overawing in their patriarchal authority, selfish, brutal, and unsentimental; the women were to be loyal, self-effacing and submissive" (78). The major task of the woman was to produce heirs, for it was women's ability to give birth that instituted the cycle of dynastic progression. Thus, if romantic love is marginal to the Western, marriage is central. A conversation between Tom Dunson (John Wayne) and Tess Millay (Joanne Dru) in Hawks's *Red River* highlights this association between marriage and dynastic progression. Dunson speculates that Matthew (Montgomery Clift) has asked Tess to marry him because "he wanted a strong woman who would bear him sons." Then Dunson proposes to marry Tess himself by promising, "I'll offer you half of everything I've got if you'll have my son." In the more recent Western *Comes a Horseman* (1978) Jason Robards enunciates a similar rationale for marriage to Jane Fonda, who plays a neighboring rancher. "Our son would own the whole valley," he states.

Because of their importance as the bearers and nurturers of children, women are almost invariably seen in Westerns as mothers or potential mothers. The protagonists of these films rarely have fathers, but they frequently have mothers, and "Ma" is a revered figure. The schoolmarm character, who often becomes identified as an ideal marriage partner, is seen as fit for this role largely because of her identification with children and nurturance. Because of the value placed on women as mothers, their chastity and, more generally, their loyalty in sexual matters is of paramount importance. In a study of women in Westerns Sandra Myers has observed that "if a man deports himself properly, in a word if he *performs* as he is expected to perform, his reward will be a beautiful, virginal female" (234). By contrast, the "wrong" kind of women are represented by the prostitutes and dance-hall girls who are not in a position to guarantee the male that he is indeed the sire of his children. In Peckinpah's 1969 *The Wild Bunch*, for example, the social corruption promulgated by the renegade Mexican general Mapache is largely represented in terms of the debasement of women, who are exploited as prostitutes and concubines rather than being granted respectable positions as wives and mothers.

The role of the husband in such a relationship was primarily that of a caretaker and protector of the family. Sociolgical studies of the male role emphasize the connection among property ownership, agrarian culture, and traditional masculinity (Plech, Pugh, Sherrod, Stearns). The cowboy hero is seen as eminently capable of filling this traditional male role, for the Western shares with other male genres like the hard-boiled detective story a preoccupation with what is often called "professionalism." But in the Western this quality is understood in a context that specifies the care of the family unit as the most significant male duty. The Western hero portrayed by Wayne and other Western stars is seen as highly skilled; he shoots and rides better than anyone else. Although he is not customarily a "family man," he stands as a larger-than-life embodiment of the ideal candidate for the roles of husband and father in a hostile world in which struggle, self-protection, and hard physical labor are central realities.

The hero's role as a model of the male who can function as a capable provider is further specified by the nature of his costume, which suggests vocational calling rather than individual taste. Such outfits contain a myriad of occupational connotations: boots, spurs, and chaps for riding; leather vest and neckerchief to keep out the wind; large-brimmed hat to shield the wearer from sun and rain; and a gun for protection against aggressors, both human and nonhuman. In an age when men's clothing has lost the associations that it had earlier had with particular trades and occupations, the cowboy's attire recalls a time when such was not the case. The clothing that he wears serves the needs of professional duty and announces his commitment to a life-style devoted to developing skill and competence.[17]

This image of professional competence is closely tied to a convention in which the heroic male serves as a model for young boys. Again, this role expresses a nostalgia for an agrarian culture in which the father participates in the education of sons who will eventually inherit the patrimony that he has won for them. One of the semiparodic elements in Lawrence Kasden's 1985 *Silverado* concerns this aspect of the cowboy hero, for Kevin Costner is cast in a role that calls for him to ride and shoot with conspicuous virtuosity. (Costner's preparation for this role was clearly extensive; it is obvious in a number of the bravura riding and shooting sequences that no double was used.) Although the Costner character is not married, he functions as a model of male behavior for his young nephew.

More than any other actor John Wayne cultivated this aspect of the Western hero. Thus, as is frequently observed, he is often cast in paternal roles. In the 1972 *The Cowboys*, one of the last films that he made, for example, he calls his wife "Mother," and the story is built around his attempts to save his ranch and provide for his wife's future through a cattle drive involving a group of boys who come to stand as replacements for the sons he has lost. Even when he plays rootless wanderers, Wayne often acts as a father figure to younger characters. Like his ties to the land, this parental image ratifies the rights of other characters to acquire acreage for the purpose of inaugurating a dynasty. Wayne cultivated his patriarchal image offscreen as well by fathering five children, one of whom (Patrick Wayne) appeared with him in some of his films while a second (Michael Wayne) managed his production company, Batjac.

Paradoxically, even though the Western hero is depicted as an ideal candidate for a dynastic marriage, he is rarely married himself.[18] The grandiose image of patriarchal authority that he represents is in conflict with the ideal of companionate marriage which has dominated twentieth-century cultural mores and is understood as a residual discourse; thus married men in Westerns are likely to follow the companionate model but are characterized as possessing a more diminished masculine presence. Films like Ford's *Drums Along the Mohawk* and Troell's 1970 *The Emigrants* focus on this companionate model among the settlers. But the husband figures in these films lack the heroic stature of the cowboy.[19]

In place of a woman, the traditional male type represented by the Western hero often seeks out the company of other men: glamorous masculine adventure takes precedence over quotidian domesticity. The existence of such male groups further reinforces the premodern ethic of separate spheres for men and women, which reflects the values surrounding the system of dynastic marriage. Further, the idealization of male friendships arises from agrarian nostalgia, for opportunities to cultivate male intimacy declined following the industrial revolution, which turned male labor into a competitive market commodity (Sherrod 233). An attachment to the male sphere also symbolizes a resistance to the "feminizing" influence of the city. In contrast to the frontier, the city represents civilization, confinement, and female efforts to domesticate the world (Pugh 150).

If the hero belongs to a group, it is likely to be a group of socially marginal figures like himself. Though these groups are typically all male, membership is defined by the acceptance of a set of shared machismo-identified mores rather than by masculine gender per se. In Westerns like Lang's *Rancho Notorious* (1952), Ray's *Johnny Guitar* (1953), and Fuller's *Forty Guns* (1957), the male groups are led by powerful, tough women. By contrast, men who do not conform to the group's values are often subjected to ridicule and scorn by being associated with a devalued femininity, as happens, for example, in *Destry Rides Again* (1939) and *The Man Who Shot Liberty Valance* (1962). Eve Kosofsky Sedgwick's term *homosociality* aptly describes these male cadres, whose claim to dominance is based on their ability to exercise raw power; to be part of such a cadre is to share in this power. As Sedgwick has argued, the bonds that hold such partnerships together are often articulated in relation to women who function as objects of desire and exchange. In keeping with this spirit of using women to cement the bonds between men, a common Western plot involves a competition of two men over a woman which is resolved as the men begin to know each other and find that the shared values created by their allegiance to the same male-oriented life-style constitute a stronger tie than their desire for the woman. Examples of such plots include *Western Union* (1941), *The Desperadoes* (1943), *Little Big Horn* (1951), *The Big Sky* (1952), *Butch Cassidy and the Sundance Kid* (1969), and *Silverado* (1985).

The mythic quality of these male friendships in Westerns has been explored by Dorothy Hammond and Alta Jablow, who argue that such relationships have played a significant role in social myths since Gilagamesh. "Confrontation with extreme danger heightens and proves the essential quality of friendship," they state (248). It is this preoccupation with testing the bonds of friendship through trials and danger that in Westerns often makes relationships between males appear stronger than those between men and women. Such trials also emphasize the role of males both individually and as a group as able protectors of families. George Mosse's study of nationalism and sexuality explores the role of such asexual male bonding in creating a spirit of nationhood insofar as it echoed the nationalist ideal of deep horizontal comradship.

In the twentieth century this all-male realm has been most conspicuously preserved in warfare and in team sports. As I have noted, John Wayne was identified with both of these activities. His war films repeat the emphasis in many Westerns on the bonds between men created through heroic male adventure. His identification with football, as well, furthered this characterization, for, as Michael Messner has pointed out, "sports have become one of the 'last bastions' of traditional male ideas of success, male power and superiority over—and separations from—the perceived 'feminization' of society. It is likely that the rise of football as 'America's number-one game' is largely the result of the comforting *clarity* it provides between the polarities of traditional male power, strength and violence and the contemporary fears of social feminization" (196).

The Western's focus on male bonding has been perceived by critics like Paul Willemen, Robin Wood, and Stephen Neale (*Genre* 56–62) as evidence of repressed homoeroticism. Perhaps more than any other, the Western genre readily lends itself to the development of a homoerotic subtext. Most Westerns participate in the kind of adolescent male bonding that Leslie Fiedler traced through the history of American culture. The hero and his sidekick in Western programmers is the most obvious instance of this tendency, which John Cawelti has identified as an adolescent ambivalence about heterosexual adulthood. More pointed references to homoeroticism also occur in many Westerns. Such implications are joked about in *The Westerner* (1940), where Walter Brennen tries to sleep in the same bed with a very suspicious Gary Cooper, and in *Little Big Horn* (1951) and *The Train Robbers* (1973), where homosexuality becomes a topic of some debate among members of the male group. An early John Wayne programmer, *The Sagebrush Trail* (1933), appears to take a similar pleasure in poking fun at suggestions of homoeroticism by including a running joke about two male "buddies" who like to break eggs contained in grocery bags carried by the other. (A close-up of raw egg whites oozing out of the bottom of one of the bags is at one point intercut into the action.)

However, insofar as such a homoerotic subtext is invoked, the larger question becomes: To what use is it put in the genre's larger narrative and thematic patterns? To begin to answer this question it is useful to consider one of the most erotically charged of all Westerns—Howard Hughes's notorious 1943 production of *The Outlaw*, which is one of the most explicit examples in the generic corpus of the powerful pull of homosexual attraction. In *The Outlaw*, Thomas Mitchell as Pat Garrett shoots down his friend Doc Holliday (Walter Huston), because Holliday has abandoned him for the younger and handsomer Billy the Kid (Jack Beutel) after complaining that Garrett is growing fat.[20] Significantly, however, the action concludes with Beutel and Jane Russell, the film's leading lady, riding off together into the sunset.

The avalanche of publicity surrounding the film's initial release, which celebrated Russell as an archetypal object of male desire and trumpeted her romance with the film's producer/director Howard Hughes, reinforced the contemporary audience's sense that *The Outlaw*'s male characters were engaged in a misdirected deferral of their participation in the tradition of heterosexual coupling.

Most Westerns that raise the issue of homosexual desire similarly situate it in the context of a larger narrative structure that is centered on the process of heterosexual coupling. Like *The Outlaw*, the narratives of Hawks's *Red River* and *The Big Sky* present their homoerotic subtext as a developmental interlude in the life of a young man that eventually gives way to a narrative resolution in which these characters are paired off with a woman.[21] A similar process of subordination of homosexuality to heterosexuality characterizes *Pony Express* (1953). The film's two leading characters, Buffalo Bill and Wild Bill Hickock (Charlton Heston and Forrest Tucker), express their pleasure at seeing each other by shooting each other's hats off and shooting the guns out of each other's hands. This playful and even sensual camaraderie is given a suggestive edge when Hickock is later described as a man who "doesn't like women." But the film, like the others I have mentioned, makes nothing more of the men's relationship, and early in the action Buffalo Bill is placed at the center of a heterosexual triangle. Thus, although such depictions may acknowledge a homoerotic component in the phenomenon of male bonding, their more fundamental significance is to position homosexuality as a contrasting tendency that can be used to highlight the sexual propriety associated with the Western's valorization of dynastic marriage. In this sense, the homosexual motif figures far differently in Westerns than in films that take other attitudes toward the marriage relationship, as I will discuss in later chapters on Method acting and on the Second City tradition.

In addition to raising the issue of homoerotic attachment, the Western's male groups suggest other concerns surrounding relationships among men having to do with aging and death. The age differences that often exist among various members of the Western's male groups constitute a further expression of the genre's larger concern with the benefits conferred by the system of dynastic marriage, for these generational differences invite a reading that sees them in the context of the immortalizing quality of the tradition of dynastic succession. The figure of the "green kid" who is often featured in these stories suggests the process of generational evolution. On the other end of the spectrum, the Western abounds with grizzled veterans played by actors strongly identified with the genre like Walter Brennan and Gabby Hayes. The comic antics of the veteran, along with the naïveté and ineptitude of the kid, set off the mature dignity of the protagonist. The presence of these figures reminds the audience of the diminished stature of the old man without children, on the one hand, and of the need of young men for father figures on the other.

The genre's pervasive emphasis on violence and killing as well as on the vicissitudes of old age means that death is omnipresent. However, the Western's mythological motifs counter this inevitability through its motif of dynastic progression and the connection of this motif with the land, for this marriage system preserves the father's name if not his body, and it attaches this name to the ownership of a tangible entity: property. That this property is also represented in Westerns as part of nature further connects the pioneers with the natural cycle of death followed by rebirth which casts their lives into the form of an enduring continuum in which the land is the source of a progressive augmentation of familial prosperity. Westerns hold up this value system as the essence of what makes America both distinct and praiseworthy as a nation.

Racial Difference and the Threat of Miscegenation

The central difficulty created by the Western's idyllic portrait of land conceived as property that can confer a kind of eternal life on the families who own it is that to fulfill the dream, one has to acquire land. And the land that the European New World settlers wanted was already occupied. However, the concept of the family farm could be used to rationalize not only the Anglo pioneers' abandonment of the aristocratic heritage of Europe but also their seizure of land from other, competing groups in the New World. This latter attitude was made to seem plausible both because the discourse of the land as property exculpated the pioneers' expansionist ambitions and also because a complementary discourse on racial difference allowed them to perceive the indigenous peoples with whom they came in contact as inherently inferior. This discourse supported the ideal of dynastic marriage by further elaborating on the corollary value of the family on the land.

As Robert Miles has argued, "The effectivity of racism and racialism is to be measured less in their simple presence or absence than in their articulation within the totality of relations within historically specific social formations" (99). Western fictions have appropriated a particular discourse on racial difference that flourished from the nineteenth to the mid-twentieth century and was commonly known as scientific racism. The terminology of scientific racism is thus relevant to any attempt to situate the discursive formation of the Western within a particular historical matrix.

Scientific racism divided the world's peoples into three "races": Caucasian, Negroid, and Mongoloid, based on perceived phenotypical and/or genetic features. This model supplanted earlier discourses of Otherness that attributed difference to religious or environmental factors. A transitional discourse that enjoyed considerable authority, especially in the United States, used evidence derived from the then-popular "science" of craniology to characterize Indians as a distinct race (ironically, a race referred to as "American"). This tradition was superseded in the mid-nineteenth century by a consensus around the "three races" theory.[22]

The significance of the tradition of scientific racism is that the sense of difference embodied in earlier European representations of the Other became interpreted as a primarily *biological* and *natural* difference that is inherent and unalterable. Moreover, a difference so formulated can be presented as scientific (that is, objective) fact. Thus, the authority of science can be invoked to argue that race, in contrast to the more malleable concept of ethnicity, constitutes a difference among peoples that is ineluctable. This discourse was incorporated into the doctrine of social Darwinism, which asserts that as the different races struggle for survival the less "civilized" ones will eventually disappear; their elimination is taken as evidence of their natural inability to evolve. This discourse functions to repress the operation of economic concerns. As Henry Louis Gates, Jr., has stated, "Race has become a trope of ultimate, irreducible difference between cultures, linguistic groups, or adherents of specific belief systems which—more often than not—also have fundamentally opposed economic interests" (5).[23] The Western draws on this racist discourse by invoking a common fallacy in which "[t]he distinction between 'black' and 'white' is superimposed upon the distinction 'savage' and 'civilized'" (Brittain and Maynard 195); thus, American civilization can be equated with Anglo privilege. In this spirit, Western films customarily pit Caucasian heroes like John Wayne against Indian peoples who are popularly thought of as Mongoloid.

Mexicans, as they are conventionally portrayed in Western films, are understood as mestizos, or part Indian, rather than as Castilian Spanish. The identification of Mexicans as Mongoloid in popular discourses of the mid-twentieth century is documented in Mauricio Mazón's book *The Zoot Suit Riots*. Mazón quotes from the testimony offered by an official from the Los Angeles sheriff's department during the widely publicized 1943 "Sleepy Lagoon" murder trial. The sheriff's deputy identified the Mexican defendants as Indian and went on to state that "'the Indian, from Alaska to Patagonia, is evidently oriental in background—at least he shows many of the oriental characteristics, especially so in his utter disregard for the value of life.'" He concluded that such qualities were "'biological—one cannot change the spots of a leopard'" (23).[24]

As the prime instance of the American nationalist myth, the Western appropriates these popular discourses on racial difference to support its conception of the family farm as a social ideal. The European tradition of the family farm could be held up as superior to the patterns established by Indian societies, where land was held communally. Where Western civilization has tended to regard land as an important economic resource that may be bought and sold, Indians commonly regard land as a sacred gift of the creator to be held in common for both present and future generations (Coulter and Tullberg 208). The Mexican claim to the land could also be disregarded through a similar rationalization. Patricia Limerick comments that the reasoning for the invasion of Mexican territories "resembled the persistent way of thinking about Indians—that they were not using the land productively and properly and that, therefore, dispossession would not only be easy but also right" (232). A further distinction between Mexico and the United States could be invoked by pointing to Mexico's Spanish New World heritage, which was characterized by vast feudalistic rancheros and ambitious mining projects, both of which endeavors relied on small groups of owners and large groups of disenfranchised laborers.

At times Westerns openly acknowledge the presence of this ideological conflict over the land. *MacKenna's Gold* (1969), for example, begins with a meditation on the sacred quality that the land held for the Indians who inhabited it, and Ford's last Western, *Cheyenne Autumn* (1964), treats the cultural trauma of removing Indian tribes from their ancestral homeland. *Red River* includes an early scene in which John Wayne confronts a representative of the Hispanic landowner Don Diego, who lays claim to vast acreage in what is now northern Mexico and southern Texas. "That's too much land for one man to own," Wayne states by way of justifying his seizure of the land north of the Rio Grande.

The land that forms the primary setting for the Western was wrested away from the groups who had previously controlled it through both force and negotiation. As the figure positioned at the center of this struggle, the Western hero is constructed to embody both qualities: he possesses unequaled strength and superior negotiating capabilities. His power to use force is typically perceived as virtually limitless. "I'm the law around here," John Wayne asserted in his first major Western role in *The Big Trail* (1930). "And law is justice. Frontier justice."

This militant air is associated with the Wayne persona more than with that of any other actor. It was enhanced by the militaristic aura that he acquired as the star of numerous war films. His earlier identification as a USC football star, which I have explored in relation to his image of patriotism and masculinity, also added to his identification with militarism. Christian Messenger's study of the importance of the school sports hero in American public life explores the implications of this role in terms of its connotations of warlike aggression. "The school sports hero is, on the whole, a pious, upright moralist born out of Civil War aggression and American society's need to find continuity in peacetime preparedness for further organized activity," Messenger states (131). He goes on to observe, "Both individual courage and mass carnage were well served by football images" (135).

The Western hero's power is expressed most pervasively as physical dominance. The imposing stature of Wayne and other Western actors like Gary Cooper, Clint Eastwood, Burt Lancaster, Gregory Peck, and Randolph Scott identifies them as men for whom size constitutes power. John Belton's essay on Wayne rightly stresses this aspect of his image, for the star's towering presence invariably dominates any film in which he appears. A striking instance of the emphasis on Wayne's size occurs in Hawks's 1966 *El Dorado*, in which the first line of the film is spoken by Robert Mitchum about Wayne. Mitchum enters a saloon and inquires of a bartender, "Did a man about six-foot-four just walk in here?" And in *The Sons of Katie Elder* a discussion of Wayne's fearsomeness culminates in the comment, "He's six-foot-four. About 200 pounds."[25]

This dominant position is in turn legitimized in Western films by means of a rhetoric that associates height with moral superiority, as witness the titles of such films as the 1944 *Tall in the Saddle* (which starred Wayne), *The Tall Texan* (1949), *Tall Men Riding* (1955), *The Tall Stranger* (1957), and *The Tall T* (1957). At one point, a character in *Tall in the Saddle* praises another by saying, "He was a good man. Rode tall in the saddle." And in *Escape From Fort Bravo* William Holden speaks admiringly of his father by observing that "he was a big man. Bigger than anything he did." Wayne himself once commented that "my fans expect me to be tall in the saddle" (Eyles, *John Wayne* 18). The motif of height in the Western contains complicated meanings, for in addition to moral uprightness it also symbolizes the nostalgia for a vigilante society in which some benefit at the expense of others. The genre's ambivalent attitude toward this equation of size with power is announced in Walsh's 1955 *The Tall Men* when Clark Gable identifies himself as a man committed to "small dreams," while Jane Russell, whom he eventually marries, sings, "I want a tall man/Don't want a small man." The ethical overtones conveyed by such sentiments are grounded not so much in a universalized discourse of patriarchal power as in a more particularlized ideology of colonialism.

As negotiators, heroes like Wayne also possess noteworthy qualities, for these men embody contradictory characteristics that allow them to be perceived as representing both sides of race-centered negotiations. On one hand, they are closely identified with the disenfranchized groups with whom they have dealings. Their comfortable, freewheeling presence on the land is frequently attributed to their familiarity with nature lore learned from the Indians, and they are often pictured in the company of Indian guides. Their clothing typically features Mexican-style embroidery or fringe associated with Indian attire. Wayne's first major role in Raoul Walsh's 1932 Western epic *The Big Trail* emphatically identified him in these terms: he wears a fringed, embroidered shirt and at one point declares, "The Indians taught me all I know about the wilderness." In *The Tall Men* Clark Gable is characterized as one-quarter Indian, and he leads a fanatically loyal group of Mexican trail hands on the arduous cattle drive that constitutes the primary action of the film. Such details attest to the Western hero's affinities with the communities of racial others that populate Western films and position him as a fair judge of competing interests: he is characterized as someone capable of understanding all sides of racially motivated controversies. At a deeper level, however, the Western hero's affiliation with the cause of the European homesteaders is far more compelling than his ties to racial others, for the actors who play such roles are strongly identified as Anglos. Because this Anglo identification plays a significant role in the way that the American national ideal of egalitarianism is countered by the claim of the dominant group to superior status, it is worth exploring in some detail.

Throughout Hollywood's history the Western has been the genre in which the issue of race figures most prominently; thus my argument takes this issue as a central determining factor in the construction of the images of John Wayne and other Western stars.[26] The discourse on racial difference surrounding these figures has a significant bearing on the shape of the myth of national origin that the Western formula promulgates. Wayne is often identified with Americanism, but this Americanism is more properly viewed as Anglo-Americanism for, as I have argued, he stood for the hegemonic claims of Anglos over the more aboriginal cultures of Native Americans and Chicanos. As Leslie Fiedler has observed, "At the moment of looking into the eyes of the Indian, the European becomes the 'American,' as well as the Westerner" (*The Return* 24–25).

Wayne's stage name was chosen by Raoul Walsh and Edward Goulding.[27] "John" was selected because it "sounded American," but it would be more correct to say that it sounded Anglo. His last name was intended as an homage to the American general Mad Anthony Wayne. By overcoming the Ohio Indians who had been co-opted by the British during the Revolutionary War, General Wayne stood as a symbol for the justification of Indian genocide in the name of Anglo-American freedom from Old World class-based oppression. By appropriating the general's surname, John Wayne positioned himself as a descendent of the tradition of Northern European supremacy in the New World that this Revolutionary War hero represented.

The actor's Northern European appearance (including light brown hair and ruggedly chiseled features) was typically contrasted to the caricatured portrayal of other, competing groups.[28] Most significantly, his unusual height was associated with Anglo superiority. In contrast to the image of masculinity represented by the Method actors of the 1950s, which, as I will argue in chapter 5, is governed by an Oedipal struggle over gender identity, the bodies of cowboy stars like Wayne, despite their notable size, do not function primarily in terms of gender-related phallic symbology. In these films height connotes racial rather than gender privilege: what is significant is that the Anglo-identified hero towers over racial others who are thereby marked as moral inferiors. Thus, like virtually all successful Western stars from Gary Cooper to Joel McRae, Wayne could stand as an idealized symbol of the great wave of North European immigration in the nineteenth century. By contrast, stars such as John Garfield and Al Pacino, whose images carried more ethnic associations, rarely attempted Western roles. The one Western that Humphrey Bogart starred in, *The Oklahoma Kid* (1939), is memorable chiefly for the powerful impression of miscasting it creates.

The actual racial and ethnic origins of Western stars were subject to radical rewritings by Hollywood. For example, Roy Rogers, popularly known during the forties and fifties as "The King of the Cowboys," was, according to the 1983 entry in *Current Biography*, one-eighth Cherokee Indian, although this fact was effectively concealed in the construction of his public persona during the period of his greatest popularity. Rogers began his film career by forming a singing group called The Sons of the Pioneers, and he was later conspicuously identified as a devout Christian, which further cemented his association with a European heritage. Rogers's image was so successful in effacing his racial origins that most studies of media stereotypes of Indians specifically identify the star as an Anglo (see, for example, Friar and Friar [260], Goggy [224–25], Donald Kauffmann [31], and Rainey [291–311]). Needless to say, had Rogers's racial heritage become widely known earlier in his career, he might have personified a very different type of Western hero.

In the case of John Wayne, the Anglo aura surrounding his image was explicitly tied to a discourse on national purpose by means of his identification with war films in which the star fought against other countries for "the American way of life." Wayne's war films allied him with American imperialist interests abroad as well as at home. These imperialist claims were often represented in opposition to the claims of Asians, whose Otherness could also be readily coded as racial difference. The two films that Wayne directed, *The Alamo* (1960) and *The Green Berets* (1968), dramatized the claim to racial dominance that his image represented in unambiguous terms and presented this claim as American patriotism, for he delivers long speeches in both of these productions celebrating American republican values.[29] Wayne's offscreen reputation as a right-wing ideologue cemented his claim to represent the cause of Anglo-American dominance. "I believe in white supremacy," he told an interviewer in 1970, "until the blacks are educated to a point of responsibility" (Riggin 42). Like other aspects of his offscreen persona, Wayne's ideological pronouncements gained credibility through the aura of verisimilitude surrounding his performances in Westerns and the association of this genre with American values.

The cowboy hero's role as a vigilante power and an adjudicator of land values which are associated with racial difference is typically understood in Westerns as a prelude to the more highly mediated mode of cultural domination over the land made possible through the law. The law represents the interests of the state, which the ideology of nationalism is designed to support, and it reflects the contradiction at the heart of the American nationalist myth that I have already defined. The American citizen is part of a "dual societal system: one whose legal normative code reflected that he was part of a people and another whose legal normative code reflected that he was the ruler of racially 'inferior' subjects or things" (Ringer and Lawless 120). This latter use of the law is an instance of what is sometimes referred to as "institutional racism."[30]

In Western films the law is importantly associated with land rights and more broadly with the way in which land is conceptualized in relation to human society. In the Western only one law exists—European law—and it reifies a Eurocentric vision of land as property to be passed down among family members. Limerick states, "Especially in matters of property, law took the primal contest of ownership—the basic reciprocal dialogue of 'Mine, not yours'—and channeled it into the ritualized, rhetorical combat of the courtroom" (63). Jennifer Nedelsky has explored the role played by property in defining the American judicial system. She states, "Property was seen as a specific, identifiable, knowable entity which held a special place in law, republican theory, and 'society'" ("American Constitutionalism" 252). Thus, in America in particular, "the law of the land" is in a significant sense exactly that.[31]

In the case of Indians—certainly the racial Other with whom the Western is most preoccupied—a deep and meaningful tradition has been obliterated by this process. Vine de Loria has observed that "in treating for lands, right of way, and minerals, commissioners negotiating for the government insisted on applying foreign political concepts to the tribes they were confronting" (26). Thus the Indian principle of sharing the land communally was superseded by a European concept of land as privately held property. The law was a major tool in this ideological battle over the land. The failure to resolve Indian land conflicts has its origin in the courts. At root is "the belief that Indian peoples, their property and affairs, are properly subject to the control of a superior white civilization" (Coulter and Tullberg 208).[32]

In our own century Westerns perpetuate the myth that the aboriginal people of America were displaced from the land because it played no significant role in their cultural values. The proper and lawful use of the land is identified in these films with the image of the family homestead, which is validated by a long European tradition. By contrast, racially devalued groups who claim land rights are typically characterized as lawless, specifically in terms of their relation to the land. Indians are frequently seen rampaging pell-mell over the plains in images connoting anarchic barbarity. Mexicans may be portrayed taking siestas on dusty streets or gathering in run-down cantinas, thereby suggesting an equally unacceptable cultural condition of passive degeneracy. Moreover, the genre characterizes the Mexican border as the gateway to the land of lawless anarchy, a haven for criminals and *verboten* to lawmen.[33] Such depictions undermine the pretentions of these groups to represent a coherent and worthy societal posture with respect to the land.[34]

The law in turn is related to language and writing, conforming to what Henry Louis Gates, Jr., has seen as "Western culture's use of writing as a commodity to define and delimit a culture of color" (6). Levi-Strauss has attested to the significance of such delimitation in his comments on the relationship between written language and the hegemony of family—and by extension group—interests: "It is now known, thanks to unquestionable and abundant information, that the birth of writing (in the colloquial sense) was nearly everywhere and most often linked to generational anxiety" (quoted in Derrida, *Of Grammatology* 124). Language is a central element by which national cultures have historically defined themselves. In the United States, the national language is English.[35] The drive to standardize and purify the national language has historically been associated with patriotism (Shafer 52). Westerns acknowledge this fact by identifying the sophisticated use of language—the English language, in particular—with civilized society and, by extension, with civilized law. The Western's preoccupation with the law is closely tied to its respect for education, which the genre identifies with literacy: to be able to read and write is to be able to understand the rules of civilized, lawful behavior. By contrast, the clumsy locutions and halting syntax that characterize the utterances of non-English-speaking groups such as Indians and Mexicans are seen as aspects of their primitivism, resulting in what Gayatri Spivak has called "perceiving a language as subordinate" (524); thus the advent of Northern European culture is associated with social progress. Further, the savage war whoops of the Indians and the pervasive musical motifs that invariably accompany the depiction of Mexican culture in these films connect both groups to a libidinous emotional anarchism at odds with the rational mode of linguistic discourse that is associated with the institution of European law. [36]

Even Westerns that treat disenfranchized groups sympathetically rarely come to terms with the ideological implications of Anglo-European language and law, and thus perpetuate the rhetorical marginalization of victimized Others. A film with the liberal pretentions of the 1950 *Broken Arrow*, for example, does not seriously engage this issue, for the Apache language that it renders as English is presented as halting, rudimentary utterances even after the cowboy hero has presumably learned to speak it fluently. Moreover, when a negotiation occurs between the Indians and the group of Northern European colonists over the violation of a treaty, it is clear that the culprit, who is present and who does not speak Apache, understands every word that is spoken. The audience is thus invited to conclude that the Apache language is nothing more than a crude form of English. Even Arthur Penn's *Little Big Man*, otherwise a scathing satire on the hypocrisy that characterized the Anglo's New World aspirations, treats the unconventional locutions of Chief Dan George, its major Indian character, as the source of gentle, yet still condescending humor. By contrast, Robert M. Young's *The Ballad of Gregorio Cortez* dramatizes the relationship between the law and the English language. Here language difference defines who has access to the law, and the European settlers view the Mexican community with contempt and mistrust because they do not have equal access to the rules and customs of Anglo-European culture that are embodied in its English-language laws.

In conformance with his role as a mediating figure between the European settlers and their racial Others, the Western hero does not abide by the homesteaders' law. He does, however, follow a code. For such men, straightforward dicta such as "A man's gotta do what a man's gotta do" exemplify the uncomplicated idea of vigilante justice to which they adhere. Wayne himself articulated a code in most of his Westerns. In Siegel's 1976 *The Shootist*, for example, he categorially states, "I won't be wronged. I won't be insulted. I won't be laid a hand on. I don't do these things to other people, and I require they do the same for me." As is true of his footloose ways, the Western hero's code sets him apart from the homesteaders, whose complex system of legal writing masks its relationship to structures of cultural domination.

In contrast to the law, which is written, the cowboy's code is an expression of a simple oral culture. Because it is spoken, it possesses what Derrida has termed "self presence," and the hero's association with it endows him with a superior status.[37] Jack Goody and Ian Watt have characterized such oral cultures as homeostatic: "The language [of an oral culture] is developed in intimate association with the experience of the community, and it is learned by the individual in face-to-face contact with the other members. What continues to be of social relevance is stored in the memory while the rest is usually forgotten" (31). Further, in oral cultures, words take on particular connotations in the context of individual situations. Goody and Watt write: "The meaning of each word is ratified by a succession of concrete situations, accompanied by vocal inflections and physical gestures, all of which combine to particularize both its specific denotations and its accepted connotative uses" (29).[38]

That the Western hero is especially sensitive to nonverbal cues is emphasized in his much admired ability to judge the moment when his opponent is likely to draw a gun. Further, he often functions as an interpreter not only because he understands Spanish or Indian languages, but also because he is better able to "read" the characterological and gestural language that accompanies speech. He understands not only what people say but what they mean. In addition, his oral code is more adaptable to individual situations than the written laws of the townspeople, partaking in what Goody and Watt call the "dialectical" quality that characterizes oral cultures. The constant renegotiations that the cowboy's code is prone to are dramatized in *The Wild Bunch* (1969), when Pike (William Holden) and Dutch (Ernest Borgnine) debate the specifics of one of their rules. The question concerns whether Thornton (Robert Ryan), who has promised the railroad that he would track the two men down, is justified in his actions. "He gave his word," says Pike. "That doesn't matter," Dutch responds vehemently. "It's who you give your word to." This exchange illustrates the code's relationship with face-to-face communication as well as its susceptibility to renewal and renegotiation. The virtues possessed by the cowboy heroes associated with such a code arise from the oral culture with which it is associated, and these qualities specify his potential skill as a negotiator.

The simple nature of these oral codes is associated with the cowboy's reliance on simple utterances. The much-parodied closemouthed style of Western stars like Gary Cooper and Wayne himself reinforces the sense of their ambivalent relation to the civilized townspeople and the "primitive" savages. On one hand, the rudimentary vocabulary and simple syntactical patterns that mark their speech define them as men who are ill at ease with the intricate linguistic structures that characterize legal systems designed to deal with complex social orders. The measured tones in which such men speak, however, also set them apart from the libidinous anarchic tendencies attributed to the Indian and Mexican cultures. Wayne, in particular, cultivated a notably flat, deliberate style of delivering dialogue. Like his name, his speech customarily consisted of monosyllabic words put together into succinct utterances. In *The Comancheros* (1961) Wayne genially parodies his down-home Anglo speech by repeatedly referring to the New Orleans gentleman played by Stuart Whitman as "Mon Sewer." The distinctive manner with which Wayne customarily handled dialogue helped to construct a character who, although he lacked intellectual sophistication, lived by a simple, rational code to which emotional expression was totally subordinated.[39]

If the cowboy's code is in many ways admirable, it is also crude, for its relation to the law corresponds to what A. J. Greimas, in his essay "On Anger," describes as the difference between revenge and justice. As Greimas defines the difference, justice is based on the principles of delegation and intellectualization whereas revenge is personal and passionate. Thus, what the Western hero's simple rules of personal vengeance threaten to make obvious is what the law's appeal to "justice" more effectively conceals: that his actions, like those of the homesteaders, represent a self-interested commitment to a particular group within the larger culture. In the case of the Western hero, the nature of the group interest that he represents is typically unambiguous—indeed, it is often defined as the family itself.

The violent shoot-outs that form the climax of virtually all Western films can be understood in this context as an attempt to rationalize the closing down of alternative cultures that took place during the conquest and settlement of the Western states. In these scenes the repressed contradictions that lie beneath the Western's preoccupation with the law and lawlessness come to the fore, for such episodes are invariably constructed on the premise that morality is on the side of the more powerful opponent, the hero with his code, and the issues are typically understood as familial or group centered rather than as abstract questions of law and morality. The outcome of these encounters is portrayed as dependent on skill with firearms rather than on proficiency in the manipulation of legalistic discourse. Further, although most Westerns depict a villain who is Anglo rather than Indian or mestizo, the repressed issues of racial disenfranchisement that permeate the genre are invariably hinted at by his association with a tradition of savagery represented as alien to European values, and even by such clichéd conventions as his swarthy coloring and black hat. The issue of racially motivated struggle that lies at the heart of these scenes is also alluded to by the recurring image of the land, and by the presence of actor-heroes like John Wayne who are strongly identified as Anglos.[40]

The shoot-out thus represents both a resolution and an admission. The use of force by the Anglo-identified hero lays bare the will to domination that underlies the European settlers' repeated invocations of the law with its pretentions to representing a universalized ideal of

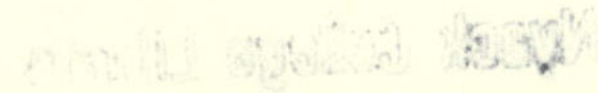

imagined community characterized by deep horizontal comradeship. Conveniently in these films, might makes right, but "right" also makes might. Thus, because he tends to reduce the law, with its lofty aura of impartiality, to an issue of raw power, the Western hero and his code continually threaten to expose the group self-interest on which the law is largely based. It is finally this threat of exposure that leads to the depiction of this figure as something of an embarrassment to the community and situates him as an outsider.

If racial difference plays a significant role in the conceptualization and administration of the law, it is also a significant factor in the genre's depiction of sexual mores. Westerns are preoccupied with miscegenation, for insofar as the land is thought of as the property of a privileged group, that group is tacitly understood as Caucasian. Whereas the tradition of dynastic marriage functions to conserve this patrimony within the group, miscegenation threatens to disperse it. The significance of the tie between group intermarriage and group self-interest is suggested by Jean-Louis Flandrin's observation that during the seventeenth and eighteenth centuries "family" and "race" were commonly deployed synonymously. Within the discourse of scientific racism miscegenation carries quite a different meaning than it does in a discourse of ethnicity, for biological reproduction is central to the task of reproducing races (Miles 88).

In Westerns the miscegenistic threat is viewed differently in relation to the different groups that the genre portrays. As historians of colonialism have pointed out, two of the fates most common to groups who become objects of colonialist domination are subordination or extermination. During the colonization of the western United States, Mexicans met the former of these fates whereas Indians suffered the latter. Western films respond to this difference in their representations of various aspects of these two groups, especially with respect to sexuality. Although the "primitivism" of both is seen in terms of unrestrained libidinous activity, Indians typically manifest this type of behavior as aggression, whereas the lack of restraint that characterizes Mexicans is often seen in specifically sexual terms. Thus, Indians are portrayed as people who stridently provoke their own destruction whereas Mexicans (in particular Mexican women) are seen as courting their subordination by making themselves into sexual victims.

The horror of miscegenation arises most terrifyingly in the Western genre in connection to the danger posed by the hostile Indians to "our women." In Boetticher's *Comanche Station* (1960) this threat is openly discussed when the woman whom Randolph Scott rescues from Indian captivity questions him anxiously about whether her husband will want her back again. Significantly, when Indians rape or sexually appropriate white women, these actions are customarily portrayed as acts of violent aggression rather than sexual desire.

When the Western hero asserts his commitment to equality for all by consorting with a woman of another race, this action takes on quite different meanings depending on which group is concerned. If he marries an Indian woman, as happens, for example, in *Broken Arrow*, *Ulzana's Raid* (1972), and *The Man Who Loved Cat Dancing* (1973), the relationship is seen as a noble but futile gesture toward a vanishing people. Often the woman dies. Should she remain alive, she is more often spoken of than seen; and the relationship is understood as symbolizing a quixotic tie to a doomed group. Mexican women, by contrast, more often appear as mistresses than as wives (for example, in *My Darling Clementine* [1946], *High Noon* [1952], and *Tribute to a Bad Man* [1956]). The position of mistress connotes subordination, for women who assume roles that are understood as primarily sexual are more readily seen as lesser "natural" beings (Ortner). In this realm as well, Wayne's offscreen image managed to accommodate both sides of the contradiction between equality and European dominance, for his Caucasian identification and racist statements were balanced by the more egalitarian image of a man who had married three Latino women.

The Western genre's ambivalent attitude toward racial intermarriage is dramatized in films that equivocate about the racial identity of major characters so that the race issue can be read in a number of different ways. In *Broken Lance*, for example, an Indian woman married to the film's patriarch hero is referred to as "senora" in order to minimize the social opprobrium attached to his act of miscegenation. However, in order that the audience, like the townspeople, may be spared from fully acknowledging such transgressive behavior, the Indian "señora" is played by the Chicano actress Katy Jurado. A similarly double-edged strategy of depicting miscegenation is followed in numerous other Westerns, where the sexually desired racial Other is played by a well-known Caucasian actor (Debra Paget in *Broken Arrow*, Robert Wagner in *Broken Lance*). The presence of these popular stars functions to make the portrayal of transgressive sexuality less "real" and thus more palatable to squeamish audiences. All these strategies are brought into play in Vidor's *Duel in the Sun* (1946), where

Pearl, the sexually desired racial Other, is identified as half Indian, characterized and costumed as Mexican, and embodied by an Anglo actress (Jennifer Jones). In this, as in the other cases I have mentioned, the presence of mixed messages allows the film to sustain the paradox of egalitarianism and Northern European dominance that lies at the crux of the American myth of nationhood.

A striking instance of the Western's treatment of miscegenation occurs in Budd Boetticher's 1958 *Buchanan Rides Alone*. The title of the film announces the hero's lack of interest in marriage, yet paradoxically this disclaimer allows for a fuller treatment of the miscegenation motif than would otherwise be acceptable. The film's opening shot shows the Mexican-American border, and the story is built around the clash of the two cultures. The plot is put in motion when Juan Pedro, a young Mexican (Manuel Rojas), enters a California border town and murders an Anglo who has raped his sister. Later it is revealed that the murdered man's father, who runs the town, keeps a Mexican mistress. Buchanan (Randolph Scott) is drawn into the conflict and is distinguished from the rest of the townspeople as the only Anglo capable of understanding the Mexican youth's motives. Although Juan Pedro's sister never appears, her place in the narrative is occupied by the young Mexican's horse. Juan Pedro is shown to be as highly possessive of this horse as he is of his sister. And the horse, like his sister who has scratched the face of her assailant, strenuously resists the attempts of an unfamiliar Anglo to "tame" it. Buchanan is rewarded for his efforts in behalf of the young Mexican when Juan Pedro ceremoniously presents him with this horse. At the film's conclusion, Buchanan rides off on the horse to West Texas, where he plans to purchase a "spread."

The film's substitution of a horse for a woman allows it to participate in a mediated celebration of the principle of cultural intermingling because Buchanan does not seize the animal by force but is given it by its Mexican owner. Yet this strategy also allows for the assertion of the contrary ideal of Anglo supremacy because the horse is seen as a high-spirited creature which, like a Mexican (or a woman, for that matter), must be brought to heel by a "superior" master, as Buchanan proves he is by riding it away at the end. Further, the horse, which is described as the product of superior breeding, is a palomino. As it appears in the final scene, it conspicuously matches Buchanan's buff-colored cowboy shirt and fair Anglo coloring. Significantly, the expository passages carefully define Juan Pedro himself as a descendant of the Spanish aristocracy rather than as a mestizo. Thus the film is able to affirm the nationalist principle of an egalitarian community at one level while it asserts the propriety of Anglo supremacy at another.

Buchanan Rides Alone offers a notably inventive solution to the paradox of race relations inherent in American nationalist ideology, but the inconsistencies that it struggles to mediate surface in some form in most Westerns. As the obverse of dynastic marriage, miscegenation figures as one of the genre's central preoccupations. However, with the passage of time, the meaning of miscegenation, like the meanings of other of the genre's major motifs, has been altered.

The waning popularity of the Western and of the Wayne hero and its replacement in the fantasy lives of many Americans by genres such as science fiction has been associated by Lane Roth with "the rapid diffusion of technological innovations," which makes the naturalistic Western setting seem outdated (115). This shift, in turn, reflects a changing sense of national identity. Today the symbolism of technology expresses concerns about America's image in the context of a larger sphere of world power relations. Recent science-fiction films may utilize traditional Hollywood formulas of romantic love and marriage, but these elements do not bear the ideological weight that they carried in earlier genres such as the Western. And Westerns themselves are now often constructed in ways that render them susceptible to readings that emphasize internationalism rather than nationalism. Kevin Costner's 1990 hit *Dances with Wolves*, for example, features not two antagonists, as was common in past versions of the formula, but three. The film's two warring Indian tribes, the Sioux and the Pawnee, participate in a bloody encounter that the movie's voice-over characterizes in approving terms; it is the encroachment of the alien Anglo forces into such local disputes that is perceived as a travesty. Such a representation calls to mind American imperialist interference in disputes among the indigenous peoples of Korea, Vietnam, and the Middle East more powerfully than it refers to issues related to the settling of the American West. At the same time, the venerable Western trope of the family farm is alluded to only nostalgically in Costner's film; in its place is a newly environmentalist awareness of the delicate ecological balance of the western landscape, which is related to the land's possession by an idyllic aboriginal society.

Thus as American society has evolved, so have cinematic portrayals of the Northern European settlement of the western states. In an age in which fewer Americans expect to be able to own homes, fewer marry, and fewer remain untouched by their country's role in world affairs, the dream of the family on the land that the Western promoted has had to give way to other dreams and other formulas. The ideal of dynastic marriage that was part of an earlier nationalist fantasy is now perceived by many Americans not as a symbol of a nobler past but rather as merely quaint. John Wayne's image as an Anglo-identified patriarch who could deal effectively with racial Others also appears hopelessly naive in a world culture where power is no longer perceived as the sole province of white males.

The Body and the Land as Earth Mother

The Western's message about the value of dynastic marriage is carried not only by the ideological implications of its narrative but also by the psychological implications of its stylistic tropes. Unlike genres such as the woman's film or the horror formula, the Western has attracted almost no psychoanalytic analysis. Yet the ideological motifs outlined above would lack the power to affect audiences around the world were they not anchored by issues of a compelling psychological nature. A psychoanalytic analysis of a cultural phenomenon that raises issues similar to those posed by the Western has recently been undertaken by the German writer Klaus Theweleit. Theweleit focuses on the body image of a group of prefascist "soldier males" who belonged to one of the German "Freikorps," volunteer military units that sprang up after the First World War to quell revolutionary activity in their homeland.[41]

Theweleit refers to soldier males as the "not yet fully born," and he sees the central psychic issue facing them as the necessity of separating from the mother and preserving their bodily integrity in the face of fears of dissolution. According to Theweleit, these are men who have become fixated at a pre-Oedipal stage of psychic development, when "the child is not able to feel, or perceive, its own psychic boundaries. It perceives itself as united with the body of the mother" (I, 207). For Theweleit, such a fixation leads to the creation of a "body armor" which protects against the threat of dissolution. By creating a body armor these "men of steel" were reacting against the soft, "feminine" interior of their bodies. Such men cultivate an image of soldierly professionalism analogous to that represented by the Western hero.

In her essay "A Father Is Being Beaten: Male Feminism and the War Film" Tania Modleski has questioned Theweleit's dualistic model of the self-Other relationship. She argues that an Oedipal model, which sees the central issue at stake as one of castration, is the only one that can adequately deal with patriarchal oppression, because it foregrounds the authority of the father rather than that of the pre-Oedipal mother. Modleski writes, "Man's alliance with the mothers, formed in order to beat out (or write out) the fathers, is doomed to failure, from a feminist point of view, unless the father is frankly confronted and the entire dialectic of abjection and the law worked through; otherwise . . . the father will always remain in force as the major, if hidden, point of reference—and he may, in fact, be expected at any time to emerge from his hiding place with a vengeance" (71).

Yet despite the fact that it does not place a powerful patriarch at its center, a pre-Oedipal model such as Theweleit employs is still capable of accounting for gender-based oppression. Unlike the Oedipal model, however, it does not construe all modes of domination in gender-related terms; thus it creates a space for other modes of oppression such as those based on racial rather than sexual difference. Such a model also allows for historical variations in the way in which gender-based oppression operates. Although the father may indeed "emerge with a vengeance" at any time in such studies, an exclusive focus on the role played by the father in the Oedipal scenario means that issues like race, which are thereby repressed, may themselves "emerge with a vengeance." In fact, the very centrality of the patriarch figure in the Oedipal model fosters the assumption that a gender-based oppression is not a constructed social circumstance but is rather a psychological given.[42]

Jennifer Nedelsky has associated a Theweleitian preoccupation with building a body armor with the American emphasis on property rights and the attendant concerns about the boundaries between self and Other. She believes that American constitutional law is founded on "a picture of human beings that envisions their freedom and security in terms of bounded spheres" ("Law," 163). Nedelsky goes on to argue:

> What is essential for the development of autonomy is not protection against intrusion but constructive relationship. . . . The boundary metaphor does not direct our attention to this question. Instead it invites us to imagine that the self to be protected is in some crucial sense insular, and that what is most important to the preservation of such a self is drawing boundaries around it that will protect it from invasion ("Law," 168–69).

Nedelsky's opposition between boundedness and relatedness is echoed in Jane Tompkins's reading of the representation of the male body in Westerns: "The male—by remaining 'hermetic' and 'closed up'—maintains the integrity of the boundary that divides him from the world." She associates this image with the Western hero's taciturn nature: "To speak is literally to open the body to penetration by opening an orifice; it is also to mingle the body's substance with the substance of what is outside itself. Finally, it suggests a certain incompleteness, a need to be in relation" (97).

Theweleit suggests that one method of cultivating such a boundary around the self is by wearing a uniform. The German writer Hermann Broch has described the effect of such a uniformed figure as follows: "A uniform provides its wearer with a definite line of demarcation between his person and the world . . . it is the uniform's true function to manifest and ordain order in the world, to arrest the confusion and flux of life, just as it conceals whatever in the human body is solid and flowing, covering up the soldier's underclothes and skin" (Kern 17–18).

The John Wayne hero is strongly identified with the kind of uniforms that suggest such a body armor. Wayne's roles in war films typically involved uniforms, and he often wore cavalry uniforms in his Westerns. His identification as a former football player also characterized him as a man in uniform. More generally, his face expresses the closed quality associated with the psychological type that Theweleit describes: its firm mouth and characteristic squint speak of the necessity of defending oneself against the elements while its lack of expressiveness offers psychological protection against threats more social in nature.

Theweleit sees the bonding of the soldier-male figure with other men like himself as the expression of a regressive narcissism that grows out of his painful need to protect his body armor against the threat represented by woman. The Western's subordination of homoeroticism to heterosexism can thus be understood as part of a preoccupation with male power that understands women as primary objects of domination. This mastery is, in turn, justified in its psychological as well as its ideological construction through its association with the ideals of dynastic marriage and the family on the land.

Theweleit's focus on the soldier-male's drive to domination also provides a psychological underpinning for the Western's preoccupation with race, for if the soldier-male's sense of bodily integrity depends on his identification with a superior gender so also does it depend on his identification with a superior race. Sander Gilman's work on the psychology of racial stereotyping reinforces this conception of the relationship between racial bigotry and an impoverished self-image: "With the split of both the self and the world into 'good' and 'bad' objects, the 'bad' self is distanced and identified with the mental representations of the 'bad' objects. This act of projection saves the self from any confrontation with the contradictions present in the necessary integration of 'bad' and 'good' aspects of the self" (17). The biogenetic connotations of scientific racism play a pivotal role in the Western's concern with miscegenation, for the not-yet-fully-born male is preoccupied with issues of bodily purity. "The man of superior race needs to dominate in order to retain his body intact," Theweleit writes. "Miscegenation would inexorably cause him to disintegrate" (II, 75).

In the inward-looking cultural milieu engendered by the groups of soldier-males that Theweleit studied "frequently quasi-incestuous relationships were constructed" (I, 208), for these men remained significantly tied to their early primary caretakers, who were women; they "never break free of their mothers or react beyond their sisters" (I, 377). The presence of such a fixation on the mother accounts for the odd aura of incest prohibition that hovers around the Western genre. As I have suggested, the hero's sense of all women as mothers often creates a certain awkwardness in heterosexual relations. One of the reasons behind this state of affairs is that courting a woman can have the flavor of violating the incest taboo. Women in these films are often obliquely identified in one way or another as mother substitutes. The presence of widows as potential romantic partners in films like *The Tin Star* (1957), *Rio Bravo*, *The Comancheros* (1961), *Hang 'em High* (1968), and *The Train Robbers* (1973) can be read in this way, as can the motif of the woman who is married or "promised" to another man in Westerns like *Little Big Horn* (1951), *The Naked Spur* (1952), *Comanche Station*, *The Professionals* (1966), and *The Man Who Loved Cat Dancing*.

Theweleit cautions against interpreting this fixation on the mother in terms of an Oedipally based concept of incestuous wishes. "The (threatening) attachment to the mother remains, because, in all likelihood, dissolution of the earlier symbiosis was too abrupt to allow the boy to form an independent ego," he writes. "They want something other than incest, which is a relation involving persons, names and families," he continues. "And if, in spite of everything, they have a desire for incest, it is at the very least, with the earth itself" (I, 277, 205).

This symbiotic longing for "mother earth" is closely related to two Western conventions that I have already alluded to: the lyrical interlude of the figure in the landscape and the climactic shoot-out. Both of these conventions exploit visual techniques that are deeply entrenched strategies of the genre. The lyrical interlude of the figure in the landscape highlights the ability of the filmic mise-en-scène to display expansive visual panoramas. The climactic shoot-out, by contrast, showcases cinema's capacity to fragment space through shot-reverse-shot editing. Virtually all movie Westerns refer to these two tropes in some way, and in the vast majority they figure as the most prominent generic markers.

As I have already observed, Westerns often dwell on wordless images of the landscape. Although such scenes often involve the presence of a number of people and animals, the sense of "Otherness" is suppressed by the strategy of long takes and smooth transitions in which bodies, beasts, and landscape merge into a harmonious whole. These scenic interludes reinforce the spectator's uncritical immersion in the illusion that they create through their emphasis on location photography which has traditionally attested to the genre's preoccupation with verisimilitude even in the heyday of studio-bound filmmaking. The enticing spectacle provided by color and wide screen, which are particularly favored in Western productions, further contributes to the creation of a pleasurable visual display which the spectator is encouraged to accept uncritically.[43]

The American landscape has traditionally had strong associations with the female body, and the pleasure associated with such scenes grows out of the feeling that they convey of a blissful fusion with the mother. Annette Kolodny writes, "The European discovery of an unblemished and fertile continent allowed the projection upon it of a residue of infantile experience in which all needs—physical, erotic, spiritual and emotional—had been met by an entity imaged as quintessentially female" (154).

The sense of oneness generated by the Western's representations of landscape is strongly underscored by the nondiegetic music that invariably replaces dialogue in such interludes. This background music is typically characterized by a rich orchestral fullness and a rhythmical approximation of a horse's lesiurely gait. In her book on film music

Claudia Gorbman notes the connection between music and the presymbolic meaning of the mother's voice: "The underlying pleasure of music can be traced to originary hallucinations of bodily fusion with the mother, of non-separation prior to the Oedipal crisis of language and interdiction. . . . In practical terms this means a deeper sleep, a lowered threshold of belief, a greater predisposition for the subject to accept the film's pseudo-perception as his/her own" (64). Thus music tends to immerse the spectator more fully and less critically in the reality that is being portrayed, because music "lessens awareness of the frame, of discontinuity; it draws the spectator further into the diegetic illusion" (56).

Gorbman describes such scenes as giving rise to what she calls "spectacle bonding," which "punctuates a pause in narrative movement in order to externalize it, make a commentary on it and bond the spectator not to the feelings of the characters but to his/her fellow spectators" (88). In Westerns, this regressive bonding of the group of spectators constructs the as-yet-unsettled landscape as a seductive spectacle that the audience shares in desiring. The landscape's provocative emptiness invites the spectators imaginatively to penetrate and possess it. That the legitimacy of this desire is validated by our sense of the Western landscape as a limitless panorama of unoccupied space is dramatized by the occasional portrayal that does not conform to this pattern, such as the opening of Lang's 1941 *Western Union*, in which the viewer's serene contemplation of the vast expanse of the prairie is abruptly interrupted when a buffalo in the foreground of the frame looks directly at the camera.

At the same time that the landscape invites merging, however, it also reveals itself as harsh and inhospitable. The Western setting is majestic rather than arcadian, characterized by arid deserts and rugged mountains that are notably unaccommodating to the fantasy of a benignly nurturing presence. *Mackenna's Gold* (1969) begins with an extended meditation of this sort in which the camera roams over a spectacular craggy desert landscape as vultures circle overhead. An equally forbidding prospect is presented by Monument Valley, the genre's most famous locale. In such settings, the dream of fusing with the body of the mother celebrated in the lyrical interlude of the figure in the landscape is not unconflicted, for the nature-mother that is so presented is a cold and ungiving one.

This coldness can be seen as engendering the hostility and violence that are so pronounced in the Western genre. Theweleit's soldier-male resorts to violence in order to preserve the integrity of his body, which continually threatens to fragment or dissolve as a result of his inability to separate from the mother. As Theweleit argues, "What seems to hold the masculine-soldierly body together is his compulsion to oppress the body of another. . . . His relation to the bodies he subordinates is one of violence and, in extreme cases, murder" (II, 87).

This inclination toward violence is a prominent feature of the Western hero embodied by Wayne, who, perhaps more than any other star of the period, was identified with violence. If one is to believe his own assessment of his acting abilities, Wayne's major contribution to the art of Hollywood performance was his development of what is called the pass system, a more realistic method of staging fistfights. (Shepherd, Slatzer, and Grayson 161). *The Shootist* (1976), the last film that Wayne made, begins with a montage of his career as a cowboy hero, focusing on scenes of brutality, and the story of that film concerns the character's position in the town as a pariah because of his reputation for violence and mahem.

The Western shoot-out constitutes the most significant violent response to the frustration caused by the vision of the cold mother. The shoot-out most often occurs in the competitive social space of the town rather than in the inviting emptiness of the landscape. This climactic event often involves the protagonist with a villain who is portrayed as a double of himself. The venerable Western convention of white hats and black hats, although hinting at the repressed issue of racial difference at one level, at another level highlights one's sense of the deep similarity between the antagonists that lies beneath their surface differences. The fragmentation of the hero's body that is implied by the presence of the double is reiterated by the fragmentation of the space that the shot-reverse-shot pattern of the shoot-out effects. The triumphant quality conveyed by the resolution of these scenes of violent confrontation is in part created by the camera's reintegration of the space and its positioning of the hero as the single dominating figure.

The Western hero's act of violence fulfills him because it involves the enhancement of his body armor with a gun. In Theweleit's scheme, guns function not primarily as phallic symbols of sexual difference (as an Oedipal model would have it) but rather as objects that allow the pre-Oedipal hero to remake himself as a machine. Quoting from Ernst Jünger's earlier work on the German military mentality, Theweleit writes, "Jünger calls on the machine to take over from the body to perform functions for which the body is inadequate: to function frictionlessly, quickly, powerfully, brilliantly, expressively—perfectly—and to remain whole despite internal explosions" (II, 197). Extrapolating from Jünger, Theweleit goes on to state: "Within the machine 'instinctual life' is controlled and transformed into a dynamic of regularized functions; it is devoid of feeling, powerful; its desiring-intensities take the form of the 'velocity' of 'explosion'" (II, 198). From the perspective offered by Theweleit, the cowboy's reliance on guns is less a matter of demonstrating a power understood as a phallic substitute than of preserving the integrity of the body by associating it with the power and efficiency of a machine of destruction. Guns, in particular, are weapons of choice because their bullets are capable of penetrating the body of another and because "guns have the capacity to do something of which the soldier is normally incapable: they can discharge and still remain *whole*" (II, 179).

By thus "resolving" the psychological dilemma posed by the image of the landscape as a cold mother, the shoot-out provides a temporary respite for the psychic issues that the movie Western addresses. It is, however, a respite rather than a genuine resolution, for the shoot-out does not represent a transcendence of the trauma that gives rise to it but is rather a means of symptomatically assuaging the anxiety generated by the trauma. It is partly due to this impasse that Westerns so often feature endings that are unresolved and ambiguous. The most typical conclusion, in which the hero rides off into the sunset, emphasizes his fundamental isolation from others, his deeply unsociable nature.

Whatever sense of psychological development the narratives of these films achieve arises largely from the presence of a hero in the Wayne image. Although Wayne's association with uniforms and his closed, inexpressive style suggest his similarity to Theweleit's soldier-male type, on a more superficial level his imposing physique and his aura of competence connote calm, controlled maturity. His massive frame is clearly that of a full-grown man, not a boy, and the rifle that he favors over the handguns used by most of those who oppose him accentuates the masterful quality of his presence. Wayne's typically relaxed posture and much-admired sauntering gait as well as his skill at riding, shooting, and fighting further depict him as a man with an easy control of his body. The triumph of such a figure at the end of the Western narrative represents the victory of an image of comfortable adult masculinity at the same time as the less openly acknowledged connotations of Wayne's bodily presence which conform to Theweleit's model deny at another level the validity of the mature image that he so confidently projects.

The contrast between the relaxed maturity connoted by Wayne and the hyperbolically masculinized bodies of more recent he-men stars like Sylvester Stallone and Arnold Schwarzenegger suggests that the repressed anxiety surrounding Hollywood's heroic images of manhood is becoming less readily susceptible to recuperation by the seamless realist containment that Wayne's projected with such seeming ease. In contrast to the naturalness and normalcy associated with Wayne's masculine physique, the bodies of these newer stars are both more exaggerated and constructed; their body armors, marked by the exhibitionistic excesses of exposed overdeveloped musculature, announce themselves as "put on," compensations for a trauma that remains unspecified but is more openly implied. This trauma is characterized in the cinematic formulas with which these actors are associated by a level of violence that Wayne never dreamed of. The new stars typically enact their mayhem not with rifles, as Wayne customarily did, but with automatic weapons or even, in the case of Schwarzenegger in particular, by means of the literal conversion of the actor's constructed body itself into a machine of destruction. The bodies of these stars invite readings that see them as symptoms of a reaction formation in response to a crisis of masculine identity. By contrast, although he may at some level have stood for a similar anxiety, the effortlessly genial male presence of John Wayne could also stand for its repression and containment.

The Wayne Hero Elegized: The Man Who Shot Liberty Valance

Hollywood's preeminent director of Westerns, John Ford, was responsible for making John Wayne a star when he cast the actor in his 1939 *Stagecoach.* Wayne starred in twelve more films for Ford, including several of the director's most highly regarded Westerns. Ford exploited the Wayne image more successfully than any other filmmaker, and he more than anyone else is responsible for its identification with the Western genre.

Ford's interest in dynastic marriage and his corollary concern about miscegenation is evident throughout his oeuvre. *My Darling Clementine*, for example, opposes the degenerate, dying Doc Holliday, who has a Mexican mistress, to the more upstanding protector figure of Wyatt Earp, who appropriates Holliday's former fiancée, an educated European woman from the East. Perhaps the most revealing film in the entire Western canon in terms of miscegenation is *The Searchers*, the penultimate Western that Ford made with Wayne. Its story concerns Ethan Edwards (Wayne), a man whose obsessive fixation on the issue of racially transgressive sexuality excludes him from the more-egalitarian social group. Ethan's politics of racial exclusion are a function of his self-appointed role as the protector of the pioneers' racial hegemony which the settlers, seeing themselves as committed to the contradictory value of deep horizontal comradeship, would prefer to repress. The extremity of the drive for racial purity harbored by Edwards manifests itself not only in the abhorrence that he harbors toward his niece Debbie (Natalie Wood), who is living with the Indian chief Scar (Henry Brandon), but also by his love for his brother's wife, an incestuous longing that expresses his excessive desire to confine sexuality within the limits of the group formed by the family itself. Critics who have faulted *The Searchers* for failing of provide an adequate motivation for Edwards's last-minute change of heart toward Debbie ignore the significance that the film attaches to the issue of inheritance. When Debbie becomes racially "contaminated" by living as the wife of Scar, the wounded and weakened Ethan decides to will his property to Martin Pawley (Jeffrey Hunter), the implication being that Ethan finds it less humiliating to bequeath his patrimony to an heir who is one-eighth Cherokee than to one who could subsequently bequeath it to a child who would be one-half Comanche. He softens his position only after Martin refuses to accept this blatantly race-based principle of inheritance. Martin prefers a more "civilized" view in which the fact of Anglo hegemony is felt to be so secure that it can be transgressed in individual instances and repressed in theory by invoking the contrary principle of horizontal comradeship.

Ford's preoccupation with the male body is similarly evident throughout his oeuvre. The director's famous "stock company" of actors was composed mainly of male performers who projected powerfully individual images, from the earnest timidity of John Qualen to the commanding brashness of Ward Bond. Henry Fonda's body is employed to notable effect in Ford films like *Young Mr. Lincoln* (1939) and *The Grapes of Wrath* (1940), where the actor's lanky frame is silhouetted against the sky during poetic interludes of great lyrical intensity (figs. 3.1 and 3.2). *My Darling Clementine*, in which Fonda plays the legendary Western character Wyatt Earp, opposes the ascetic quality suggested by his reed-thin physique to the fleshy sensuousness of Victor Mature, who plays Doc Holliday. The relationship between Fonda's body and a puritanical sexual morality is specifically emphasized in *Clementine* in the memorable sequence in which he gracefully balances himself on a tilted porch chair only to become comically stiff and awkward a moment later when he is walking and dancing with Clementine Carter (Cathy Downs) (figs. 3.3, 3.4 and 3.5). In *Fort Apache*, Fonda's body is deployed in a different manner, for in this film, as Richard Dyer has observed (*Stars* 165–67), the easy stance of John Wayne's Captain York is played against the ramrod-straight figure of Fonda's Colonel Thursday—a posture that, by 1948, the year the film was made, had acquired unsavory associations with Nazi-style militarism (fig. 3.6).[44]

In *The Man Who Shot Liberty Valance*, Ford's interest in the meanings of dynastic marriage and of various styles of masculine bodily presence is given its most complex and self-conscious expression. It was the last Western that Ford made starring Wayne, and it can be considered his valedictory to the Western hero.[45] The production was not well received on its initial release in 1962, perhaps in part because it denied audiences the colorful scenic splendors that they had come to expect from Westerns—and from Ford's Westerns in particular.[46] *Liberty Valance* was shot in black-and-white, a surprising choice considering its genre and the period in which it was produced. Equally surprising was Ford's decision to confine most of the action to interiors. In place of scenery, the film concerns itself with the nature of the Western hero that John Wayne had created. In particular, it explores in unusual depth the anachronistic qualities of the body image with which this hero had become identified and the character's outdated conception of dynastic marriage. Thus a reading of this film is an apt means by which to give more concrete form to the model of the genre and its hero developed earlier in this chapter.

The focus on the male body in *Liberty Valance* appears initially in its casting. The film features a number of contrasting male characters who are played by actors with highly distinctive and well-known body types and performance styles. Thus Wayne's powerful physique is complemented by James Stewart's supple elegance, Lee Marvin's apelike sinuousness is contrasted to Andy Devine's slovenly portliness, and John Carradine's gothic boniness is set off against Edmond O'Brien's flabby softness. All these actors also have characteristic styles of delivering dialogue, from Wayne's flat deliberation to Stewart's hesistant drawl, Marvin's nasal snarl, Devine's gravel-voiced stutter, Carradine's oratorical mellifluousness, and O'Brien's bombastic verbosity. In *Liberty Valance* each of these performance styles defines a different kind of masculinity, and it is the interaction of these figures—not scenery—that constitutes the core around which the film is built. As Robin Wood has observed ("Shall We Gather?"), the characters function as caricatures rather than as complex individuals, thereby defining various positions that construct the story's ideological thrust.

This discourse on the many meanings inherent in images of the male body is situated within a narrative that centers on the issue of dynastic marriage. By 1962 many Americans were rejecting the fantasy of men who protected the physical and economic well-being of women and women who, in exchange, granted men a sense of immortality by bearing their children. In *Liberty Valance* this is the kind of marriage offered to Hallie Ericson (Vera Miles) by Tom Doniphon (Wayne). The woman declines this arrangement in favor of a more modern form of companionate marriage to the politician Ransom Stoddard (James Stewart).

Virtually every published analysis of *The Man Who Shot Liberty Valance* agrees that the film treats the venerable Western myth of bringing civilization to the frontier. This theme is highlighted through a flashback structure so that the framing story presents Stoddard's mission of transforming the wilderness into a garden as having already been accomplished. The framing story itself concerns Stoddard and Hallie's appearance at Doniphon's wake. In order to explain his presence at the wake to the editor of the town newspaper, Stoddard recalls his debt to Doniphon. Doniphon murdered Liberty Valance (Lee Marvin), a man who once terrorized the town at the behest of ruthless cattle barons, and allowed Stoddard to take credit for his heroic deed. Thus, in the classic manner of the Western protagonist, Doniphon has created a space for the growth of a civilized society in which he himself is unable to participate.

What critics of the film have not addressed is the way in which its construction of "civilization" is predicated on the obliteration of a legacy of racial stuggle. To uncover the traces of this struggle and chart its relationship to representations of marriage and the male body, it is helpful to break down the story's opposition between savagery and civilization into a tripartite division among its male characters. Some, notably Valance and Link Appleyard, the town marshal (Andy Devine), represent a state of libidinous anarchy understood as the expression of a residual discourse centered on the issue of racial difference. Others like Stoddard and Dutton Peabody, editor of the *Shinbone Star* (Edmond O'Brien), represent a more Europeanized discourse on republican egalitarianism which the film codes as emergent. Standing between these two groups is Doniphon, who is committed to a "civilized" ideal of social order but understands this order in hierarchical rather than egalitarian terms. His position, in turn, is connected with his commitment to the ideal of dynastic marriage. The values that Doniphon represents are understood as the dominant ones in the town of Shinbone during the time of the film's major events. The distinctions among these three groups of characters and among their various members can be further specified by referring to differences in their relationship to the land and to language and the law.

Despite the film's almost exclusive use of interior settings, land plays a significant role in *The Man Who Shot Liberty Valance*. The debate over statehood for the territory surrounding Shinbone hinges on the right of the "sodbusters" to fence cropland in the face of the cattlemen's desire for an open range. Further, their relationship with the land distinguishes the more "primitive" characters, who live lives of anarchic freedom, from more "civilized" figures, for whom the land has become a significant, though abstract, value. Doniphon's position in the middle of these two groups, I will argue, is defined by his identification with land.

The "primitive" characters, Valance and Appleyard, represent a regime of self-indulgent excess in which the discipline associated with the life of the family on the land is not in evidence. Valance lives "wherever I hang my hat," while Appleyard, the film's comic buffoon, sleeps in the town jail and eats at the restaurant even though he is married and has a number of children. The unsettled life-styles of these two figures is in turn associated with their ties to the Mexican community, which the film creates as a structuring absence. Early in the film Mexican culture is characterized by its aura of unrestraint when a survey of the town's nightly activities includes a look at a Mexican man picking up a willing senorita who is lounging outside of the cantina (fig. 3.7). Later, Peabody's self-indulgent lapse into drunken oblivion occurs in the same cantina. Appleyard's ties to Mexican culture are established by his marriage to a Chicano woman. His participation in the incontinent behavior which is understood to characterize this culture is hinted at by his bevy of half-breed children and his numerous relatives, both of which suggest a propensity for unrestrained procreation, and by his gargantuan appetite, which speaks of another kind of undisciplined self-indulgence. Valance's relation to the town's minority community is suggested by the Mexican motif of his costume and in particular his silver-handled whip. This mode of attire recalls the Mexican bandido figures that figured prominently in early Westerns (fig. 3.8). The sexual overtones in Valance's out-of-control sadism suggest a darker area of unrepressed libidinous activity, one that is here associated with a perversely "hot-blooded" Latin disposition. Significantly, insofar as Valance's destructive behavior is sexualized, it is also personalized, thereby obscuring the political issues that motivate his activities: the audience is encouraged to understand him simply as psychopathic rather than as a figure marked by racial difference or as an employeee paid by the cattle ranchers to preserve the open range.

The cultured Stoddard represents yet another relation to the land and to racial and sexual mores. Stoddard is a "delegate," not himself a vitally interested party to the changes that the film chronicles in jurisdiction over the land. Stoddard works with the law of the land, not the land itself. Though he uses the law to bring statehood to the territory, he does this in the name of an abstract concept of American republican ideals, not to found a personal dynasty. Nonetheless, his allegiance to the dynastic aspirations of the Northern European townspeople is never in doubt. Although the schoolroom in which he preaches equality under the law is racially diverse, he is most closely associated not with the racially disenfranchised but with a Caucasian woman. For Stoddard, the ideal of the family on the land may not represent his own family, but it is a family that is assumed to be Northern European.

In a marriage consonant with Stoddard's egalitarian legal values, gender roles lose much of their significance. Stoddard's commitment to the emergent companionate ideal in which male and female roles are fluid is suggested by his willingness to perform "women's work" in the restaurant. The difference between Stoddard and Doniphon on this score is suggested by the contrast between Stoddard's feminized body and Doniphon's virile one: Stoddard is often seen in an apron whereas Doniphon is depicted in terms of a heroic masculinity as "the toughest man south of the Picketwire."[47] This distinction plays on the accumulated meanings by then attached to Wayne and Stewart: the former, as quintessentially masculine; the latter, as known from films like *Destry Rides Again*, *Rear Window*, and *Vertigo*, as feminine or impotent.

Doniphon's own attachment to the land is predicated on a concept of dynastic marriage in which the family works toward the well-being of future generations. Wayne thus plays the character most closely associated with the Western trope of the landscape. With the exception of the opening scene of the stagecoach robbery, in which the outdoors is given the quality of a stage set, Doniphon's horse farm is the only nature that we see in the film. He is building a new room on his homestead to welcome Hallie; when she rejects his offer of marriage, he burns it down, for without a wife and children, he is bereft of a rationale for acquiring personal wealth. Wayne's long-established image as a patriarch ensures that the film's audience will accept his character's identification with this concept of marriage with very little expository justification, just as his well-known image as an outdoorsman allows Doniphon to be strongly identified with a love of the land once this association is hinted at in the film. Ford builds on this image by contrasting Wayne's imposing presence and its associations with outdoor living with Stewart's more urbane slenderness.

Positioned between Appleyard and Valance on one hand and Stoddard on the other, Doniphon is associated both with the Mexican community and with the European townspeople. He raises neither wheat nor cattle but horses. He enters and leaves the action of the film to the accompaniment of Mexican music, and under the sign of the cantina (figs. 3.9 and 3.10). Yet the strong Anglo connotations of the John Wayne persona separate the character of Doniphon from the Mexican community. Doniphon may be seen as in some ways *like* the Mexicans, but he is never perceived as one of them. This distinction is also based on the character's commitment to a social order based on hierarchical rather than egalitarian principles. The nature of Doniphon's value system is evident in the presence of his "boy" Pompey (Woody Strode), whose position suggests Doniphon's loyalty to Southern principles of slavery and a chivalric masculine code. His condescending nickname for Stoddard, "Pilgrim," further defines him in opposition to the more "progressive" values of the New England settlers. That Doniphon's value system occupies a dominant position in the Shinbone community is clear from the fact that the town organizes its social space according to similarly hierarchical principles. Pompey, for example, cannot be served in the local saloon. Gender distinctions are enforced less overtly, but equally rigidly. The town is made up of men's spaces (the saloon, the political meeting hall) and women's spaces (the restaurant kitchen, where the women may even order the men to put their pants on).

Doniphon aspires to the ideal of the Northern European family dynasty that a marriage with Hallie represents. Unlike the more egalitarian-minded Stoddard, he sees this partnership in terms of complementary roles played by men and women with men occupying a place at the head of the family unit. Doniphon's high-handed treatment of Hallie grows out of this hierarchical system of values and from his notion of separate spheres for men and women. The contemptuousness with which he shuts the door on a group of women who are hovering outside the meeting hall at the state convention betrays a similar attitude (fig. 3.11).[48]

The powerful aura of masculinity that the character projects is constructed in large part through the film's emphasis on his size and through the imagery of his hat. In this film, in contrast to most of his other Westerns, Wayne's massive physique is for the most part confined to the constricting spaces of the town with its low ceilings and narrow doorways rather than the expansive vistas of the wilderness. Moreover, as Peter Lehman and William Luhr have observed, his body is often framed by doorways that barely clear the top of his head. An early scene shows Wayne seated in a restaurant at a table far too small to allow him to get his knees underneath it; to accommodate his substantial frame he is forced to turn his chair sideways (fig. 3.12). In addition, Ford often shoots the character from a low angle, thereby further accentuating his stature.

The film develops these problematic implications of Wayne's height through imagery related to his hat. The old-fashioned peaked Stetson that Wayne wears in this film adds to the nostalgic portrayal of a hero from another era.[49] In addition, the hat's size suggests the character's dominating masculinity. A number of jokes throughout the film are built around Doniphon's contemptuous treatment of the more modestly scaled hats of others and reveal his sense of superiority to men less virile than he. At one point he tosses Appleyard's battered hat onto the floor of the restaurant kitchen where it is subsequently kicked aside by Hallie (figs. 3.13 and 3.14). Later he flattens Dutton Peabody's small bowler as he wields a gavel to call for order at a town meeting (fig. 3.15). And after Doniphon kills Valance, the latter's hat is thrown carelessly on top of the corpse as it is being carted away (fig. 3.16). Complicating the comic deflation implied in these contemptuous gestures is the film's emphasis on the civilized propriety associated with the removal of hats: Peabody takes his off in the restaurant just before instructing Hallie on the decorum involved in correct table settings, and Stoddard instructs the rustic Appleyard to remove his hat in the schoolroom (figs. 3.17 and 3.18). Like hats, heroic virility may readily be doffed to accommodate the requirements of an emerging genteel culture in which conventions of equality for all disallow overt displays of masculine dominance.

Doniphon's association with this fading ideal of heroic domination is related to the Western trope of the family on the land by means of its connection with the image of the garden, which specifies the nature of the marriage alliance that the narrative raises. Hallie grows the only garden in the film, thereby positioning herself as the representative of land claimed through cultivation. Doniphon makes himself part of this image and its related motif of fertility when he brings Hallie a cactus rose to plant in her garden as part of his courtship (fig. 3.19). Stoddard responds to Doniphon's gesture by asking Hallie if she has ever seen a "real" rose. Stoddard's reference to exotic as opposed to indiginous flora in this scene is not probed, but it marks the values of the future senator as alien. Hallie's subsequent praise of her husband's ability to use the law to make the western wilderness into a garden thus assumes an overtone of slight irony, for what Stoddard has actually done is to reshape the western landscape so that it conforms to Northern European values.

Once he has abrogated his right to establish a dynasty, Doniphon quickly deteriorates. Nonetheless, *Liberty Valance* sees a value in the self-styled American hero and the ideal of the family on the land that Wayne stands for. The cactus rose that Hallie puts into the empty hatbox she so conspicuously carries about with her in the film's framing story can be read as a nostalgic gesture directed toward the lost myths represented by the Western's connected ideals of dynastic marriage and masculine strength (fig. 3.20). Given the connotations of virility and fertility that the film attaches to the images of the hat and the cactus rose, her gesture must be read as a highly symbolic one. Hallie here acknowledges Doniphon as the man who could have fathered her children—children that, so far as we know, she has not borne as the wife of Stoddard.

Whereas Doniphon's image of potent masculinity is expressed through his association with the land, Stoddard's position as a civilized "delegate" of powerful group interests is expressed through his association with the more mediated phenomena of the law and language. Discussions of *Liberty Valance* by critics like Tag Gallagher (*John Ford*) and Peter Lehman and William Luhr have included extensive analyses of this aspect of the film, but they have concentrated their attention on the relation between language and the law without noting the variety of uses to which language is put during the course of the narrative. Undeniably the place at which the association of language and the law is most strongly emphasized is in Stoddard's schoolroom, where the U.S. Constitution is the primary object of study and English grammar is taught as a corollary subject. The credo that the self-styled schoolteacher writes on the blackboard is: "Education is the basis of law and order." Stoddard promotes the ideal of a literate electorate capable of comprehending the written arguments that spell out the terms under which law and order is established and maintained. But Stoddard's idealistic view of the intimate connection between language and the law is countered by the alternative conception of language held by Peabody, who approaches speech as poetry. The editor typically uses words to express emotional rather than rational needs. He quotes Shakespeare to give himself courage, and he uses heavy irony to ridicule the pretentions of Stoddard after the latter has been humiliated by Valance.

In Shinbone these two uses of language, the legalistic and the poetic, remain discrete and complementary. In Capital City, however, their respective functions are confused by the foregrounding of a third kind of discourse: the political rhetoric of Major Cassius Starbuckle (John Carradine). Starbuckle's oratorical bombast marries a corrupt form of poetic utterance to a corrupt discourse on the law. Significantly, this discourse is marshaled in the service of land rights: the cattle barons' open range opposed to the fenced farmland of the "little men." Starbuckle's speech reveals the law as ambiguous and contingent, a system couched in language capable of being manipulated by the rhetorically proficient. Such oratory demonstrates the fact that the sacred truth of legal argument may be manufactured from the imaginative tropes of poetry; it thereby hints at the treacherous quality inherent in all authority based on lingistic utterance.

The debilitating effect of Starbuckle's contamination of both poetry and the law manifests itself in this scene visually through the depiction of the bodies of Peabody and Stoddard, the characters who have previously been portrayed as the personifications of the two opposing linguistic styles. Initially both men appear as cripples (Stoddard has his arm in a sling and Peabody leans on a cane) (figs. 3.21 and 3.22). The aura of weakness and vulnerability that they exude is reflected in the scene's dialogue as well. When Peabody uses Starbuckle-style political rhetoric to claim that Stoddard is qualified to lead the group because of his adherence to a code of vigilante justice, the major ridicules his boast as a mockery of the law. At this point, Ford cuts to a shot which reveals that the space occupied by Stoddard is empty: his body has literally disappeared (fig. 3.23). We do not see Stoddard after he walks back into the room to accept the nomination which he now knows to be based on a fiction. In the later framing story, however, his dress and demeanor appear ominously like those of the man with whom he shares the first two letters of his name (figs. 3.24 and 3.25). The budding-statesman role that he assumed on first coming to Shinbone has been compromised by this point by the suggestion that he may have become something of a pompous politician in the style of Starbuckle.

The shoot-out further emphasizes the compromised quality of Stoddard's claim to leadership. His authority can be undermined because of a significant contradiction in his position with regard to the law. Stoddard sees the law as an ideal, not as a system that can be used to rationalize the power of the dominant group. Yet his own actions throughout the film fail to justify this claim. Although the schoolroom in which he preaches the law is racially diverse, it is still his schoolroom, and it is his law that is taught. The murder of Valance exposes what the law conceals: the forceful imposition of one system of values on another. Valance's association with the cattle barons and the Mexican community suggests that this other system of values has ties to the film's repressed issues of land values and racial difference.

The law of Stoddard, the delegate, operates at the behest of an interest in land appropriation that is not dissimilar to the motives of Valance, but it does so more obliquely. Although the convention in Capital City poses the cattlemen of the north as antagonists, one never sees them. Instead, through the absent figure of Valance, the film is able to hint at an opposition between the principle of land ownership held up by the Northern European settlers and the rootless, degenerate Mexicans. When Stoddard recreates the wilderness as a garden, he does not do so for the benefit of Valance or Appleyard or the Mexican community, who do not appear to subscribe to the principle of private property underlying his effort; he acts for the benefit of

Anglo landowners. Thus, finally, the principle of "equality under the law" disguises the presence of a less palatable principle of might makes right.

The anachronistic position to which Wayne's plain-speaking Western hero is reduced by this point is burlesqued by the figure of the sideshow cowboy who rides his horse into the convention hall and disrupts the orderly proceedings of the law by lassoing Custus "Buck" Langhorn, "the cattlemen's mouthpiece," to the strains of "Home on the Range" (fig. 3.26). The depiction of Wayne as a figure whose image is too expansive to fit into the constricting spaces in which social negotiations are practiced is here dramatized in the absurd image of the cowboy in the political arena. Doniphon himself appears shortly after this display, disheveled and apparently hung over, the power of his imposing masculine presence now dissipated by the advent of the more abstract emergent values held forth in the context of a world where political negotiation rather than physical intimidation reigns.

Yet Doniphon's comments in this scene are not irrelevant, for they point to another aspect of the underlying nature of the issues involved in the shoot-out. Although Stoddard initially believes that he has been "wrong" in killing Valance for motives of personal revenge, he also believes, along with the townspeople, that he has acted in the interests of "the community" against the scourge represented by a psychopathic villain. When he meets Doniphon at the convention, however, the latter poses the issue in more personal terms. He tells Stoddard that the latter must accept responsibility for Valance's murder so that he may marry Hallie, whom Doniphon explicitly relinquishes to him. Doniphon's concluding remarks to Stoddard are "Hallie's your girl now. Go on back in there and take that nomination. You taught her to read and write. Now give her something to read and write about." This formulation of the issue places not an abstract notion of justice or even the welfare of the town as the crucial motivating factor in the murder of Valance, but rather the possession of a Northern European woman who has been made literate and who now must be provided with laws to protect the group interests that she represents. By extension, it can be inferred that a similar drive toward perpetuating racial purity has given rise to the social organization of the town of Shinbone itself.

Wayne speaks his simple phrases in a characteristically forceful and deliberate manner, uttering the rare multisyllabic word like *nomination* with a careful articulation of each part. By contrast, Stewart's more tentative and querulous delivery, characterized by a slight stutter and frequent questioning inflection, has by this point in the action become inextricably associated with the treacherousness of "civilized" discourse. Doniphon's statement thus not only gives him the last word on what the murder of Valance means but also carries the authority that by now is associated with a more straightforward and less-glib use of language. Although Doniphon's style places him as part of an irrecoverable past, it is a past that is seen as enjoying a less-compromised relation to both language and power than the emergent style represented by Stoddard.

The contrasting stagings of the convention-scene showdown and the earlier confrontation between Doniphon and Valance at the restaurant comment on this difference. Both scenes occur in a space defined as male. The restaurant scene, however, concerns itself with raw male power, expressed here by a motif of vertical dominance. To assert his authority Wayne simply rises to his full height, and the debate turns on who will be forced to bend over to retrieve the fallen steak. As I have already noted, Wayne's commanding presence, with its powerful Anglo overtones, associates his physical dominance with Northern European supremacy. Later in the convention scene, authority is asserted through negotiation; hence the debate is carried on by characters who are constantly in motion, walking among their listeners, gauging reactions, and building consensus through slippery rhetorical ploys rather than asserting power through sheer physical intimidation, as Doniphon does. Yet the verbal give-and-take of the latter scene ultimately serves only to obfuscate what the restaurant scene makes clear: the issues involved are power and self-interest.

The motif of obfuscation emerges even more strongly in the staging of the gunfight scene. By repeating this scene from two different perspectives, the film underlines the uneasy quality of its narrative resolution. The initial portrayal of the incident is handled in the classic shot-reverse-shot mode which ends with Stoddard, the town's anointed hero, dominating the space both physically and morally (figs. 3.27, 3.28, and 3.29). However, as Robert Ray has pointed out, the later flashback violates the spectator's sense of complete disclosure which Hollywood shot-reverse-shot editing fosters to reveal the scenario as having been observed and controlled by another. The flashback begins and ends with Wayne's massive form blocking the light from the camera lens, and it emphasizes the large rifle tossed to him by Pompey. By contrast, the figures of both Stoddard and Valance are significantly diminished when seen from Doniphon's more distant perspective, and their much-smaller handguns are scarcely discernible (fig. 3.30). Wayne emerges in this retelling as a shadowy yet dominating presence that will prevent Stoddard from achieving an uncompromised heroic stature. The scene thus plays on the regressive implications of the shoot-out by altering Stoddard's relation to the space; in the first version he presides over its reintegration, but in the second, he is shown as merely a puppet who is manipulated by a far more potent force.

The shadowy quality of Doniphon's presence in this scene, like the shadows associated with most of his other appearances in the film, further suggests his connection with repressed issues in the narrative having to do with racial difference. The film's contrast between a mythic, shadowy past and a brightly lit present has often been commented on (most notably by J. A. Place in *The Western Films of John Ford*). However, these shadows most often appear in the form of silhouettes, which associates them with issues centered on the human body. The film's references to these silhouettes suggest that it is not simply "the past" that is obliterated by the advent of law and order but more specifically the struggle for racial dominance that occurred in the past. Shadows are associated most strongly with the Mexican community, and Doniphon's shadow appears as he is withdrawing from Hallie into the more "primitive" world of the cantina and inebriation (figs. 3.31 and 3.32).[50]

The film's most striking use of silhouetted figures occurs in the scene in which Peabody quotes a portion of *Henry V*'s St. Crispin's Day speech. This speech constitutes perhaps the most celebrated instance in Anglo-American culture of the virtuoso use of language as rhetoric in the service of territorial acquisition. Like Henry, Peabody makes a flowery speech to fortify himself as he looks toward an impending battle in which the stakes are land control. But the silhouette to whom Peabody addresses this oration, like the other shadows in the film, hints at darker implications of this moment having to do with the submerged issue of racial difference (fig. 3.33). Peabody's misspelled headline ("Liberty Valance Defeeted") suggests that his use of language to announce the downfall of an opponent is less masterful than Henry's untroubled assertion of nationalist sentiment. (In *Henry V* it is the French rather than the Mexicans who are seen as having an inferior culture.) Later a shadow of the offending letter *E* falls on Stoddard as he enters Peabody's office, thereby implicating him in Peabody's less-than-competent partisan rhetoric. This striking image hints at the role played by the future senator in the project of using the power of the English language and its law to justify his claim to govern the disposition of the land (fig. 3.34). By associating Stoddard's project with a spelling error the film also associates it with a view of linguistic practices as arbitrary conventions like removing one's hat in the schoolroom, rather than with a view of language as a privileged mode of expression that reveals the "truth" of the law. In *Liberty Valance*, unlike *Henry V*, the principle of closemouthed force represented by Doniphon is not capable of being entirely rationalized by rhetoric. Peabody and Stoddard are less rhetorically proficient than Shakespeare's Henry, and 1962 America appears as a society less ideologically secure than that of Elizabethan England.

The pledge of the new editor of the *Shinbone Star* to "print the legend" can thus be read as the culmination of a progressive erosion of the authority of English writing. This erosion begins with Valance's attack on Stoddard's law book, in this reading an act of colonialist resistance. It continues as the pretensions to universal truth represented by this book are gradually unmasked as strategies of domination by Starbuckle's self-serving oratory and Peabody's sub-Shakespearean bombast. By the end of *The Man Who Shot Liberty Valance*, legends have replaced ideals as the foundation on which the adventure of European westward expansion rests.

Sam Rodhie has argued that *Liberty Valance* lacks a sense of ideological closure that could have taken place if the narrative voice of the film itself had been foregrounded. It is arguable, however, that such a sense is indeed present. The film's suggestions about the constructed nature of linguistic discourse on the law is ultimately related to its suggestions about the constructed nature of cinematic discourse on American myths of national origin. Like the editor of the *Shinbone Star*, John Ford is committed to perpetuating the legends of the Old West. The nature of this project is dramatized in the second flashback of the shoot-out, which is dominated by the character played by John Wayne. The name of this character was changed to Doniphon from Barricune as it was in Dorothy Johnson's original story, and thus shares the Irish heritage of the director.[51] In this rare, self-reflexive moment in Ford's oeuvre, the role of a behind-the-scenes manipulator which is enacted on-screen by Wayne may be seen as an analogue of the role of the director himself. Ford's construction of the gunfight-scene flashback comes close to revealing that it is is ultimately he whom Wayne represents as the behind-the-scenes manipulator of events. Thus it is Wayne-as-Ford who is responsible for the death of Valance. To create a myth of American origins that reifies Northern European hegemony even as it promulgates the opposing ideal of equality for all, Ford, like other Western directors, is engaged in both creating and erasing the traces of the racial Others whose presence exposes this fundamental contradiction in American nationalist ideology.

These associations conveyed by the character of Doniphon apply equally to the patriarchal figure of Wayne himself, who stood for a constellation of values that, by 1962, many Americans perceived as anachronistic. With the emergence of the civil-rights movement and alternative life-styles during the decade of the sixties, conflicts over race and equality assumed new forms. At the same time, as we have seen, the dream of the family on the land and the ideal of dynastic marriage that it implied were becoming less viable. For many Americans affected by these changes, the figure of John Wayne, the quintessential patriarch who could address racial Others from a position of power and strength, could no longer serve as a symbol of their nation.

Following Wayne, the most popular actor in Hollywood history has been Clint Eastwood, who has also been known primarily—at least in the early years of his career—as a star of Westerns. However, the Westerns with which Eastwood has been most famously associated were directed by Sergio Leone, an Italian, and were shot in Spain; thus Eastwood has never been associated with American nationalism in the way that Wayne was. And when Eastwood began to produce and direct as well as act in his films, he did not choose to cast himself in roles in which he could pontificate on themes of American patriotism, as Wayne did in *The Alamo* and *The Green Berets*; instead, in productions like *Play Misty for Me* (1971) and *Tightrope* (1984), he explored the contradictions and vulnerabilities that lay beneath the patriarchal male image so confidently established by Wayne. As Dennis Bingham has observed, "Rather than personify 'the good' or 'justice,' Eastwood's heroes represent nothing but the ego; they expose the extent to which the moral grandeur and 'Americanness' of previous Western heroes had been based on a glorification of self in which subjectivity translates, probably by definition, to 'good'" ("Men with No Names" 39).

To be sure, Eastwood's 1980 Western *Bronco Billy* alludes to the spirit of American nationalism that has become inextricably associated with the genre, but in this film the American ideal of the self-made man is represented by a former shoe salesman who has become the proprietor of a fly-by-night wild West show. Billy's announcement that "I'm who I want to be" is thus a statement that represents a radically diminished sense of the possibilities of American free enterprise compared to the outsized heroic project that Wayne stood for. Although the film's final scene in a circus tent made of American flags pays tribute to the nationalistic association of Westerns, the flags envelop the movie's hero within an enclosed space in which the myths associated with the American West are reenacted as performance; the realistic rendering of the American landscape and the values attached to it are absent.

Companionate Marriage and Changing Constructions of Gender and Sexuality

THE LOVE GODDESS: CONTRADICTIONS IN THE MYTH OF GLAMOUR

The actor is the opposite of a scarecrow—it is his function to attract. The easiest way to attract is to be beautiful.

—Josef von Sternberg

Filmmaking is pointing the camera at beautiful women.

—François Truffaut

The "aesthetic sex" is the subordinate sex because beauty, like truth, is one of those empty terms, filled by the value of a particular society at a given historical moment. So when a woman is upheld by society as beautiful, we can be sure she expresses with her body the values currently surrounding women's sexual behavior.

—Rosalind Coward

Commentators on the star phenomenon like Barry King and Danae Clark have noted that the traditional emphasis on actors as images masks the work that contributes to the production of such images. Of course, as is well known, the "images" approach has been applied most consistently—and most tellingly—to women. Similarly, traditional Hollywood discourses surrounding movie performers have tended to naturalize the acting abilities of women to a far greater extent than those of men, who have more commonly been positioned as workers.[1]

The representation of actresses as images has masked a contradiction inherent in the existence of female stars: on the one hand, they have been held up as ideals of heterosexual romantic attraction under a regime in which the woman is understood to play a subordinate and dependent role; yet, on the other hand, their very success in embodying this ideal of feminine dependence on men has elevated them to positions of power that other women have rarely managed to attain. In this sense the woman star can be said to represent a subversive force that continually threatens to erupt as an emergent discourse of female potency. My discussion of the relationship betwen Griffith and Gish in chapter 2 was predicated on the supposition that Gish embodied this kind of threat at a time when it was as yet unclear how and whether it could be contained.[2]

Although the male-dominated movie industry has been forced to grant power to the female stars who embody the models of romantic desirability on which their productions are so importantly based, traditional Hollywood practice called for an elaborate discourse surrrounding these women that would radically negate the public perception of this power. This discourse—less prevelant today than formerly and always associated with the personas of some women stars more than with others—has repositioned highly motivated and ambitious actresses as passive, frivolous images. Thus, as a general rule, popular lore has depicted male stars as having been trained to master a craft in educational institutions or apprenticeship situations. Female stars, by contrast, have been spoken of as having been "discovered," most frequently as a result of having exhibited themselves or their photographs in public places; alternatively, their success has been attributed to the "casting couch" method. Similarly, actresses are more likely than actors to be looked upon as having risen in their profession by means of an intangible attribute termed "star quality." Writing in the 1950s, anthropologist Hortense Powdermaker (although herself falling prey to prevailing stereotypes of the day) took note of this distinction. "[T]he male actors in Hollywood seem to have more ability and experience than the females," she wrote. "Looks, being photogenic and sexy, count for them too, and they need the same perseverance and faith in themselves as do the girls. But there appears to be no equivalent of arriving in Hollywood through winning some contest, real or fictitious" (274).

Popular biographies of movie performers commonly discriminate between men and women in this way, emphasizing the training and working habits of men while focusing on the romantic adventures and pampered irresponsibility of the women. For example, Larry Swindell's book on Charles Boyer, a male romantic idol of the thirties and forties, stresses the star's early theatrical ambitions and his disciplined approach to his craft. Swindell writes that Boyer's acting training "was a time of intellectual ferment for him" and praises the "admirable high mindedness" with which Boyer approached his theatrical education (23–24). On the other hand, Roland Flamini's book on Ava Gardner, a female romantic idol of the forties and fifties, emphasizes her sexual escapades, her temperament, and her lack of professional responsibility and training. Flamini writes of his subject at age fifteen, "Ava was a beautiful leggy brunette with a fully developed woman's figure" (32).[3]

Once they have achieved success, male stars have at times become directors or producers, generally to the accompaniment of popular approbation. The rare female star like Barbra Streisand who has attempted a similar transition is, by contrast, frequently typed as difficult and headstrong, interfering in matters better left to more competent males. Far more acceptable have been Galatea figures such as Lillian Gish, Marlene Dietrich, and Lauren Bacall, whose careers could be understood as having been launched by powerful male directors—a career path rarely if ever associated with actors who are men. In short, venerable Hollywood practice positions male actors as professionals while females are relegated to the status of icons.

Nowhere is this gender distinction more apparent than in the conventions surrounding performance itself. In chapter 2 I explored some of the implications surrounding the height of stars like John Wayne, and I argued that an aura of physical dominance carried considerable weight. This discourse of height as dominance has an obvious application to the construction of gender relations. Anyone who has attempted to trace the editing continuity of a number of Hollywood films is inevitably struck by the movies' widespread reliance on trenches and crates to ensure that tall actresses would never appear to dominate short actors. It is even plausible to speculate that the popularity of the so-called "American shot" originated at least in part because it could reveal most of the actors' bodies while allowing for the ubiquitous trenches and crates. In any event, it is clear that Hollywood regards the visual domination of men by their women partners as "wrong," and that they have developed conventions to "correct" this imbalance.

Moreover, actors are more likely than actresses to play roles that emphasize their skill as performers. For example, many more play two or more parts in a single film. According to statistics compiled by Leslie Halliwell, ninety-eight male actors have undertaken this feat whereas only sixteen actresses have. (No actress has attempted more than four parts in one film, whereas twelve actors have.) When women have appeared in dual roles, their parts may be constructed so that the film builds to a revelation of the "true" woman behind the "false" actress. For example, *The Dark Mirror*, a 1946 vehicle for Olivia de Havilland in which the actress plays a dual role as good and bad twins, concludes with a close-up of the good twin, who is seen by the audience as representing the "real" de Havilland, whom Hollywood consistently characterized as the epitome of sweetness and nobility offscreen as well as on. Such an ending performs an "unmasking" function, reinforcing the audience's predilection to read de Havilland's "acting" as a minor aberration in a career primarily devoted to being herself.

The actor's ability to shape her or his appearance as part of the project of shaping a character is not commonly regarded as acting in part because it is most commonly identified with female stars. When Robert DeNiro gained weight for his role in *Raging Bull* he was celebrated as a consummate craftsman, but when Marlene Dietrich lost weight for *Morocco*, the change was taken for granted as part of her "magic." When Lon Chaney altered his appearance with makeup it was taken as part of his mastery of his art, but when Greta Garbo used makeup to create an aura of glamorous elegance, she was merely spoken of as "divine"—even by Roland Barthes (*Mythologies*). In fact, however, as I have argued in chapter 1, the art of actors is based not only on what they do but also on how they look. And the standards of appearance for women performers have traditionally been much more rigorous than those for men. To cite just a few of some of the best-known examples of beauty regimens associated with the careers of Hollywood actresses: Rita Hayworth had her hairline raised so that she could be hired by Columbia Pictures; Judy Garland had her teeth capped and her nose restructured at the behest of MGM; Mariel Hemingway endured breast implants to appear in *Star 80*. To speak of the results of such efforts as "images of women" collaborates in the standard Hollywood practice that denigrates the work that goes into the creation of female stars.

To grasp fully the nature of the contradiction that is masked by the gender stereotypes surrounding Hollywood's discourses on stardom and performance it is necessary to explore the relationship between the movies' conventions for representing the human body, the ideologies of romantic love that motivate these conventions, and the discourses on feminine beauty and fashion that circulate in the culture at large.

At the center of this contradiction lies a paradox surrounding modern constructions of the woman as consumer, a paradox that the female star threatens to expose.

Beauty, Consumerism, and Hollywood

In her 1981 book *American Beauty* Lois Banner observes that beauty has become such a profound force in the lives of contemporary American females that it has created a vast industry in which more money is spent than on education and social services. Other historians of vestiture such as James Laver and Quentin Bell have traced the process by which women evolved into such avid consumers of fashion and beauty products. Interestingly enough, two crucial moments in this evolution were both accompanied by major developments in the technology by which images of women's bodies were mass produced. The first of these moments occurred in the latter half of the eighteenth century, when male dress styles became more subdued and less differentiated in terms of class position. This shift is generally understood as one that expressed the growing hegemony of a bourgeoisie that valued male achievement in the marketplace above inherited privilege. Not only fashion but also the discourse on male appearance generally reflected this new emphasis on men's work. As Rita Freedman points out in her book *Beauty Bound*, the modern word describing male beauty, *handsome* has *hand* as its root, thereby associating male attractiveness with the idea of productive labor.[4] This association is furthered by the widely repeated homily "Handsome is as handsome does." Thus by the beginning of the nineteenth century fashion had been largely relegated to the realm of the feminine and was thenceforth more firmly associated with gender rather than class difference. It was perhaps not merely coincidental that this shift was accompanied by the introduction of the mass-produced "fashion plate."

The second important historical moment occurred at the beginning of the twentieth century just as the movies developed the ability to showcase women's bodies to even greater effect than the fashion plate could do. Kathy Peiss has argued that the cinema's close-up photography combined with the popularity of movie actresses helped to provide cosmetics, which had theretofore been associated with prostitutes and decadent aristocrats, with an aura of bourgeois respectability. At the same time, the fashion industry introduced seasonal and yearly changes in its offerings, taking full advantage of not only the seductive images of women's bodies disseminated in the cinema but also the proliferation of mass-media periodicals that could both introduce the new styles and code the old ones as outdated. Film scholars like Charles Eckert ("The Carole Lombard in Macy's Window") and Christine Gledhill ("Developments in Feminist Film Criticism") have pointed out the ways in which Hollywood's discourses on beauty interact with other media images to construct constantly changing standards of attractiveness and up-to-date-ness based on the capitalist principle of planned obsolescence. Gledhill writes, "Women are crucially created in this consumerist culture and its utopian elaboration in entertainment, both in terms of their social and economic role and in terms of their image, which is used to materialize their appeal" (21). Thus, through popular discourses centered on beauty (with cinema prominent among them), women have been positioned as insatiable consumers of capitalism's endless stream of commodities.[5]

The images of fashion and beauty that code men as producers and women as consumers have persisted to the present day despite the larger movement of the culture as a whole toward greater consumerism. Leo Lowenthal's landmark study of celebrity biographies in popular magazines documents the general shift from an emphasis on production to one on consumption in the first half of the century. More recently, Lawrence Birken has argued that the American capitalist culture of abundance has fostered a growing climate of genderless sexual desire that is expressed in terms of an eroticized consumerism for both men and women. Nonetheless, while acknowledging the trend toward a unisex consumer society that Lowenthal and Birkin describe, one has only to witness one of Hollywood's televised Academy Awards ceremonies to be convinced that even in the 1990s the fashion and beauty dimensions of consumer culture at least remain largely centered on the bodies of women.[6]

Although these and other changes in the practices of the fashion industry are related to larger social issues, the increasing ubiquity of fashion images has functioned to remove the popular understanding of the past from the realm of historicity and reposition it as nostalgia. The visual records that dominate the twentieth century typically render experiences of past events and trends most conspicuously in terms of outmoded signifiers related to women's appearance. Fashion thus becomes the chief mark of historical difference. In this way the past is removed to the realm of the "merely" personal and is further trivialized by its association with an inferiorized femininity. Moreover, these marks of difference represent the past as separated from the present by an emptily aestheticized discourse of "style," which appears unmotivated and thus unfathomable; the continuity between past and present is thus obscured. As Roland Barthes observed in his book *The Fashion System*, "Fashion dogmatically rejects the fashion which preceeded it, its own past; every new fashion is a refusal to inherit, a subversion against the oppression of the preceeding fashion" (273). The predominance of fashion imagery in popular understandings of history thus strips the past of its politics.

Hollywood, especially through its female stars, has played a major role in this process of dehistoricization. Many films, including such well-known examples as *Now Voyager* (1942), *Letter from an Unknown Woman* (1949), and *The Way We Were* (1973), use changes in the dress, makeup, and hairstyles of their central women characters—which are notably *not* accompanied by visible signs of aging—to signal the passing of time, thereby diverting the spectator's attention from the evolving political realities that necessarily accompany such changes. A film like the 1974 *Chinatown* also plays on this paradoxical denial of historical continuity and change by offering up its elegant evocations of the coiffures, makeup, and fashion of another era as signs of a contradiction in which the processes of historical change are denied. On one hand, the film constructs past and present as identical (if it is "only" style that separates then and now, viewers in 1974 are free to accept *Chinatown*'s portrayal of the Owens River Valley scandal as an unproblematic analogue to Watergate). At the same time, such fashion-oriented details may also be read a signs of a radical discontinuity between past and present (one cannot imagine oneself as part of a culture that held up such "odd" standards of feminine appearance as expressions of beauty).

The continuing dominance of a gender-coded discourse in the realm of fashion and beauty relates not only to politics of the past but also to those of the present. By constructing hierarchically organized modes of discrimination in a society that overtly proclaims its commitment to ideals of egalitarianism, reified images of fashion and beauty express the culture's political unconscious. The hierarchies that such images establish function in the realm of romantic love and marriage. Most obviously, as social commentators since Thorstein Veblen have pointed out, in a culture where men appear similar to one another, their relative success must be signaled by other means—for example, by the appearance of their wives, whose patterns of conspicuous consumption center on their access to the benefits provided by the beauty industry. As Lois Banner states, "When a wife could spend her day pursuing beauty, it indicated leisure and thereby proclaimed her husband's success" (*American Beauty* 63). Furthermore, women are pressed to utilize the products and services of the beauty industry even while they remain single so that they may cultivate an aura of romantic desirability and thus attract a successful mate, for money and status are still more readily available to women through advantageous marriages than through their participation in the workplace. Beautiful women are marriageable women. As Jeffrey Weeks writes, "[Women's] sexuality could be utilized, stimulated, reshaped as an adjunct to the demands of mass marketing, but it was a sexuality designed to capture the man—cosmetics, clothes, personal accoutrements were big business and essential parts of the reconstructed 'feminine mystique'" (*Sex, Politics and Society* 258).

Like the idealization of romantic love itself the idealization of female beauty masks its function as a discourse on class and ethnic difference, as Susan Sontag, Kathy Peiss, and others have argued. Thus, when the rich could distinguish themselves from the poor merely by appearing to be well fed and adequately sheltered, obesity and pallor were admired. Today, however, the rich must distinguish themselves through expensive diets high in protein and fresh produce as well as through leisure-related fitness activities; accordingly, slender, tanned women have until very recently, been the ideal. Further, social-science studies have shown that "for lower- and middle-class women, ratings of beauty are good predictors of marriage to a higher status male" (Freedman 12).

Beauty is also a function of Anglo hegemony. Herman Buchtman notes that the standards for Hollywood makeup are based on a Greek ideal of the oval face (29). Sociologist Dale Leathers similarly reports that plastic surgeons "generally agree on a very specific ideal of facial beauty" which is derived from a chart devised by the nineteenth-century sculptor Schadow (91); Schadow, in turn, was influenced by the Greek ideal. This desired ideal is what causes Chinese women to undergo operations to widen their eyes and black women routinely to straighten their hair. Hollywood's notorious practice of casting Caucasian actors in the roles of ethnic and racial Others, discussed in chapter 3, frequently functions, especially in the case of women stars, to endow "forbidden" romantic partners with traditional Eurocentric attributes of physical attractiveness so that they can be accepted as objects of male desire.

The socially constructed standards by which the appearance of women is judged and the associations of class and ethnic difference attached to these judgments are tellingly exemplified in a Japanese production that comments ironically on some of Hollywood's most cherished practices, Kenji Mizoguchi's 1952 film *The Life of Oharu*. The story begins as the emissary of a powerful nobleman is dispatched to find a beautiful young woman to become his master's concubine. The list of qualifications for this position is long and, in relation to Western standards, absurd. The woman sought must have a round face, small feet, no moles on her body, and so on. Oharu, the winner of this competition, has previously disgraced herself by eloping with a lower-class man who had been violently attracted by her fetching appearance; now this same attribute allows her to better herself. Later, when age and poverty deprive her of her beauty and force her into a life of prostitution, she is cruelly ridiculed by the men she solicits. "Take a look at this old witch," one remarks to another as Oharu listens. "Still think you'd like to lie down next to a woman?" Thus, her appearance is her fate, the single feature that determines all the major events in her life. Mizoguchi's exposé of the arbitrary and oppressive nature of the aesthetics of female beauty is even more poignant to a Western reader, who is inevitably struck by the ethnic as well as the class discriminations involved in the creation of such standards. The modern ideal of egalitarianism positions the economic agenda that grows out of this discourse on class and ethnic difference as unfortunate, incidental, and unintended. For this reason, the labor that women expend as part of their participation in the beauty culture must be denied. Although a number of theorists explain the fashion system as a discourse centered on sexuality, it is more productively viewed as a discourse that exploits a reified conception of sexuality in order to mask an agenda ultimately based on economic interests. As Rosalind Coward states, "New areas [of the female body] constructed as sensitive and sexual, capable of stimulation and excitation, capable of attracting attention, are new areas requiring *work* and *products*" (81). Naomi Wolfe similarly states, "Inexhaustible but ephemeral beauty work took over from inexhausible but ephemeral housework" (6).

In an attempt to acknowledge this work while at the same time denying its existence, a double-voiced discourse has emerged: beauty is understood as at once "glamorous" and "natural"—in other words, as both constructed and unconstructed. This contradiction grows out of the dual role assigned to women: as consumers they are urged to expend money and work in their pursuit of beauty (i.e., to construct their appearance), yet as objects of sexual desire, they are encouraged to deny this expenditure (i.e., to present the results as unconstructed). In short, women are placed in the position of transforming their bodies into commodities and then denying that they have done so.[7] As both Diane Waldman ("From Midnight Shows to Marriage Vows") and Gaylyn Studlar ("The Perils of Pleasure") have shown, Hollywood's institution of fandom, importantly aimed at women, contributes significantly to this process by presenting the stars as models of "natural" beauty which the inferiorized fan may emulate by buying products and laboring on her appearance. Women are lured into participating in this self-denigrating project by a discourse surrounding beauty that both elevates and demeans them. As Sandra Lee Bartky puts it: "[O]vertly, the fashion-beauty complex seeks to glorify the female body and to provide opportunities for narcissistic indulgence. More important than this is its *covert* aim, which is to depreciate woman's body and deal a blow to her narcissism" (132).[8]

Women are thus both the major consumers for the products and services of the beauty industry and the major symbols of a pattern of social differentiation that the culture overtly disavows. Their work as participants in the manufacture of glamour is denied by depicting the results as a beauty produced by nature and by associating this beauty with the unworldly transcendance of romantic love. Hollywood love goddesses stand at the center of this mystification, and the work that they perform in the production of these discourses is especially conspicuous; accordingly, as I have argued, their personas are constructed to counteract the leading role that they play by representing them as passive "images." The very term *star*, with its connotations of naturalness and imperviousness to time and change, implies this quality.

The Companionate Couple and Hollywood's Construction of Female Performance

As I noted in chapter 1, the ideal of romantic love that Hollywood stars stand for has assumed a variety of particular forms throughout history. Because the model of the companionate couple, which has predominated throughout most of the century, has been defined as monogamous and heterosexual, female sexual allure has largely continued to be tied to displays of gender difference. Although the companionate model posited marriage as a partnership, it continued to present men and women in complementary economic roles: men were the providers and women the consumers. As social historian Beth Bailey has observed, these roles were also emphasized in the courtship conventions that emerged at the beginning of the century: "Money—men's money—became the basis of the dating system and, thus, of courtship. "This new dating system, as it shifted courtship from the private to the public sphere and increasingly centered around money, fundamentally altered the balance of power betweeen men and women in courtship" (13–14). At the same time, however, the model of romance as companionship dictated that women present themselves to men not only as lovers but also as friends. Thus some of the extreme differentiation of gendered fashion that characterized the Victorian era was abandoned.

In the movies, the positioning of female stars has conformed to this new emphasis on women as companionable consumers both in terms of the characters that they have played and the performance techniques called for by such roles. The character types that have traditionally been associated with Hollywood's love goddesses have often been dancers or singers. As Laura Mulvey points out in her essay "Visual Pleasure and Narrative Cinema," such roles can be understood as part of a representational strategy that positions the woman as spectacle. Moreover, as the argument advanced by Claudia Gorbman which I have outlined in chapter 3 claims, the regressive character of the music that is associated with these activities means that the audience is less likely to question their status as realism.

When viewed in relation to the construction of the female role within history, the implications of Hollywood's creation of major women characters as dancers or singers can be specified more precisely. In keeping with the modern ideal of egalitarianism, these "jobs" of dancer and singer allow characters who are unmarried women to be constructed as self-supporting; yet, except in rare instances like the backstage musicals of the 1930s, such jobs do not appear to involve any activity that the audience could construe as work. Thus, young marriageable women could be presented as financially independent while not actually taking part in productive labor. In romantic situations, they might thus be seen as on an equal footing with the man—that is, as potential romantic partners—while their status as passive images remained intact.

This disavowal of labor is also articulated in the construction of the offscreen personas of the female stars who play these roles. Thus, although women actors are more likely than men to sing and dance on-screen, their roles are less likely to "spill over" in a way that could endow their offscreen personas with the status of musical professionals. Thus, Fred Astaire is known primarily as a dancer-star of the movies, Ginger Rogers as a movie star who danced with Astaire. Further, female performers are often positioned as images whose skill in these areas must be manufactured by technological sleights of hand: for example, there is no male equivalent for Marni Nixon, who is widely known to have dubbed the singing voices of a number of female stars in major musicals; and the publicity that surrounded the stand-in who danced for Jennifer Beals in 1983 hit *Flashdance* was not repeated when Patrick Swayze performed similar dances in the 1987 spin-off *Dirty Dancing*. Such denials of women's labor and expertise, which Hollywood discourses have always favored, grow out of the contradiction surrounding the beauty culture, which is seen at once as constructed and yet "natural."

Dancing and singing also perform particular functions in the creation of gendered models of companionate romantic ideals. Dancing allows actresses to demonstrate the qualities of movement associated with modern women's fashions. As Anne Hollander observes in *Seeing Through Clothes*, "It was naturally the movies that confirmed women's visual locomotion" (45). Hollander goes on to describe the characteristic of these clothes and the women who wear them: "Innocence, energy, languor, and menace were transmitted through the behavior, movement, and visual feel of fabrics instead of through color; and this condensed range of feminine clothing signals, dependent largely on surface motion, lent itself very well to the new cool, self-sufficient female image" (46). This new self-sufficient woman appeared well adapted to function as an active companion for her mate; she was no longer seen as encumbered by a wardrobe that imprisoned her as an "angel in the house." [9]

Female stars who play singers are even more prevelant in Hollywood films. Such roles allow for a wealth of close-ups which the constraints of realist plotting could not readily accommodate. These shots offer extended views of the woman's face and hair, thereby foregrounding the star's position as an ideal of beauty and sexual desirability. In addition, they feature the woman's capacity for melodramatic displays of emotional expressiveness. Within the conventions of Hollywood narrative, such displays are likely to be read as evidence of the woman's desirability as a romantic companion for a number of reasons. First, these shots are read in the context of a storytelling tradition in which the close-up most typically functions as a reaction shot, emphasizing one character's response to the actions of another; the audience is thus predisposed to read them in terms of responsiveness. Second, the woman's song itself is most often understood as having been called forth by the desire for an imaginary lover. Last, as Mulvey herself points out, the setting of the performance is frequently constructed as one in which an on-screen audience made up in part of appreciative males reacts to the song as a romantic gesture.[10]

Thus, by representing its leading actresses as singers and dancers, Hollywood has been able to focus on aspects of their bodies and faces that expressed their desirability as romantic companions. At the same time, by surrounding the skills associated with these roles with a discourse of artifice and falsity, the movies have also managed to deny that these representations involved meaningful labor. The companionate model called for women who were independent but not competitive. Hollywood solved this dilemma by creating both character types and discourses around performance through which its female stars could be credible as models of heterosexual companionship while retaining their status as passive images of beauty and romantic desirability.

Sunset Boulevard: ***The Transgressive Female Star and the Companionate Model***

Hollywood's fascination with the woman as performer has at times found expression in fictionalized representations of the movie actress herself. In her book *Shot/Countershot* Lucy Fischer has noted the frequency with which films have taken actresses as their subject. Fischer argues that this trend expresses a larger social reality: the actress occupies a privileged place in regimes of representation because she can be seen as standing for the role-playing that all women must inevitably perform within a patriarchal system in which their chief function is to please dominant males. Drawing on Rosamond Gilder's book *Enter the Actress* Fischer further contends that throughout history, the actress's role has centered on her sexual functions in relation to men: "The actress-woman must role play in life. As ever, her status as performer is tied to her fecundity and her sexual relations with men" (74–75). In the context of the specific concerns of Hollywood cinema in twentieth-century American culture that I am exploring here, the fact of women's sexual subordination, which Fischer sees as a continuing issue throughout history ("as ever"), can be construed in more specific terms related to the contradictions surrounding the star's economic and cultural power and her position as a focus for the cult of female beauty.

The power of the woman star is invariably compromised in such films. Usually she is depicted in a childlike relation to a dominant male who guides her career, for example, in films like *What Price Hollywood?* (1932), *The Bad and the Beautiful* (1954), *The Barefoot Contessa* (1954), *Inside Daisy Clover* (1965), *The Legend of Lylah Clare* (1968), and all three versions of *A Star Is Born* (1937, 1954, 1976). Alternatively, she may self-destructively resist such guidance, as happens, for instance, in *Bombshell* (1933), *Singin' in the Rain* (1952), *The Goddess* (1958), *Imitation of Life* (1959), *Frances* (1982), and *Postcards from the Edge* (1990). This scenario is typically played out in variations that emphasize the relationship between career and romantic interests: when the woman becomes too successful to take second place to a man, she forgoes her chance at love and marriage—and happiness as well.

The beauty of the woman star that makes her an object of erotic desire despite her unseemly position of power is also undermined in such films, which continually threaten to expose the constructedness of Hollywood glamour. In part this quality emerges from the more general tendency toward self-reflexivity generated by the subject of filmmaking itself: in such productions Hollywood revels in exposing its inner workings. As it is manifested in relation to the female star, however, this self-reflexivity typically focuses on her beauty, which begins to assume the form of *beautification*.

In *The Goddess*, for example, the eponymous heroine states early in the narrative, "I daydream about being a movie star sometimes. Not that I think I'm so pretty. But it's all cosmetics." A more subtle allusion to the cinema's role in creating an artifice of beautification occurs in *The Morning After* (1989), which features a scene in which movie actress Viveca Van Loren changes her hair color from blond to its "true" brown. For the character this change signals a transformation from "movie star" to "ordinary person." But because the character is played by the well-known Jane Fonda, this change is read by the audience as one that transforms the character into a far more credible movie star than the one represented by the fictional figure of Viveca Van Loren. Yet at the same time the scene raises questions about the naturalness of the brown hair of Fonda herself: if Viveca dyes her hair, perhaps Fonda does as well. A similar effect occurs in *The Barefoot Contessa* when Humphrey Bogart, who plays a director, coaches Ava Gardner, who plays a newly discovered star, about her future as an image. "Any woman who uses the moon as a key light can't miss," he tells her admiringly. When Gardner inquires what a key light is, he replies, "A key light is your own special light. You have to learn to use it to light you up. It shines on your eyes, your lips, your hair." This speech attempts to position Hollywood glamour as an effect of nature with which a woman with "star quality" is at one. However, the intent of Bogart's statements is contradicted insofar as his words may remind the audience that, at this moment, the "moon" that is casting such a flattering light on Gardner actually *is* a key light. Thus the scene at once asserts and calls into question its invocation of beauty as a gift that is divinely bestowed on a few fortunate women.

This process of demystifying the naturalness of the love goddess's beauty is taken to its furthest extreme in films about aging stars, which have proven to be an especially popular Hollywood subject. *Whatever Happened to Baby Jane?* (1962) mocks the presention to glamour of its has-been actress-protagonist (played by Bette Davis) in large part by emphasizing the grotesque amount of makeup she wears. Similarly the 1990 *Postcards from the Edge* features as its climactic scene a vignette in which the actress-daughter of an aging star expertly applies the cosmetics that transform her mother from an unsightly old woman to a glamorous movie queen. And, as Richard Dyer has shown ("LANA"), the 1959 version of *Imitation of Life* presents Lana Turner's appearance and manner as increasingly artificial as she becomes more mature.

The religious associations attached to Hollywood's discourses on the love goddess are made explicit in the 1978 *Fedora*, yet another film about an aging actress. Here the male narrator makes a confident statement about the unconstructed nature of the female star. "Acting—that's for the Old Vic," he asserts. "But every so often there comes a face that the camera loves. Such faces are born." Subsequently, however, the unproblematic nature of this statement is brought into question when the aging actress to whom he refers is given a chance to speak for herself. She reveals her extreme reliance on the plastic surgery that allowed her to maintain a face "that the camera loves," and she associates this dependence with a religious mission. "I went to the clinic the way the afflicted go to Lourdes," she confesses. In this film, as in many others that deal with this subject, the action builds to a revelation of the ravaged, "unbeautiful" face behind the constructed image of the star.

The figure of the aging star lends itself especially well to a Hollywood-style exposé of beauty because it allows an emergent discourse (the power of women represented by the female star) to be depicted as a residual discourse (the anachronized "constructedness" of the mature actress's appearance and style). Even the sobriquets applied to this figure ("over the hill," "has been") suggest that her historical moment occurred in the past, whereas the cultural authority that the woman star represents actually anticipates a more gender-equal future.

Probably the most celebrated Hollywood film about an actress is Billy Wilder's *Sunset Boulevard*, which features Gloria Swanson as a former movie queen. The film discredits the power of this figure by focusing on her love affair with a younger man, a romance coded as transgressive not only because of the difference in their ages but also because, as Stephen Farber and Sylvia Harvey have noted, it is overlaid with suggestions of incestuous attachment.[11] Further, Swanson's Norma Desmond wields an unseemly power not only over her younger lover Joe Gillis (William Holden) but also over her butler Max (Erich von Stroheim), who was formerly her director and husband as well as the man who "discovered" her. (Max is depicted as having been humiliatingly deposed from his rightful Svengali-like position of dominance over the star and is presented as sustaining at all costs his self-assigned role as a benign caretaker figure.) Norma's "proper" place is briefly alluded to by Cecil B. De Mille who, playing himself in the film, recalls the time when the now-arrogant star was "a little girl" and safely under the control of the men who ran the industry.

Swanson's performance derives much of its effect from the parallels between Norma's career and her own.[12] Much of the publicity surrounding the film's release (including a *Newsweek* cover story) focused on the courage with which she satirized her earlier identification with the myths of Hollywood glamour. (One widely circulated anecdote had Barbara Stanwyck kneeling to kiss the hem of Swanson's dress after viewing a preview of the production.) Swanson's history as an icon of movie glamour was established early in her career. In an article that appeared in *Photoplay* in 1922, director Marshall Neilan enumerated six essential qualities for women stars: beauty, personality, charm, temperament, style, and the ability to wear clothes. He cited Gloria Swanson as Hollywood's premiere example of the last-named quality

(Mordden 52). Alice Williamson's 1927 book on Hollywood stars described her similarly:

> She used to think herself positively plain. She hated her features. She fancied that her rather large, perfect teeth were too big for her face, and she was afraid to smile. But she learned, without ever believing herself a beauty, that her features had a certain effectiveness, and she learned, too, how to make the very best of them. Now all her "possibilities" have become realities.

Sunset Boulevard's many self-reflexive features are centered on Norma.[13] Following conventional practice, the film equates Norma's artificiality with her outdatedness (she is introduced as "an old-time star"), thereby characterizing the female power that she represents as a residual discourse rather than an emergent one. Her depiction as an anachronism is initially emphasized by the word that *sunset* in the film's title and is identified in terms of a histrionic manner associated with the hyperbolic performance style of nineteenth-century melodrama (figs. 4.1 and 4.2). The performances that she concocts to position herself as a spectacle for Joe's admiration are likewise represented as styles of a bygone era: rather than seductive interludes accompanied by romantic music her antics as a Mack Sennett bathing beauty and a Charlie Chaplin look-alike foreground disguise and comic distanciation (figs. 4.3 and 4.4). Her hair, makeup, and clothes are also portrayed as outdated and "unnatural." Critics like J. A. Place and Lucy Fischer have noted Wilder's use of stylized motifs taken from German Expressionism and *film noir*—perceived by 1950 as themselves passé and therefore "constructed"—to represent Norma as an entangling snake, a spider woman and a vampire figure (figs 4.5, 4.6, and 4.7). Most tellingly, the labor that Norma engages in to manufacture an aura of glamour is rendered in excruciating detail and is contrasted with the "naturalness" of the film's 'good'—and romantically desirable—character Betty Schaefer (Nancy Olson) (figs. 4.8, 4.9, 4.10, 4.11, and 4.12).

Not only Norma herself but also her surroundings are invested with an aura of anachronized artificiality. The film's introduction of her identifies her with her decrepit mansion, as she first appears gazing at Joe through its windows (fig. 4.13). This identification is strengthened as the action proceeds by shots that equate her tile floor with a spider web and her rat-infested empty swimming pool with her decaying career (figs 4.14 and 4.15). Wilder's decision to shoot the film in harsh black-and-white, which associated it with the outdated "noir" conventions of the previous decade, adds to the aura of outdated stylization associated with Norma and her phantasmagoric retreat. The film contrasts this aura with the down-to-earth realism of its scenes of present-day Hollywood, which feature the even lighting, unobtrusive mise-en-scène, and eye-level medium shots suggestive of low-key documentary in place of the chiaroscuro, gothic bric-a-brac, and looming close-ups with which Norma's world is portrayed.

Wilder's hyperbolic rendering of Norma's anachronistic world is constituted as an uneasy melange of modernist distanciation and melodramatic excess.[14] Like the Griffith rescue montage that I explore in chapter 2, this overstated technique can be taken as evidence of a "hysterical" symptom that masks an underlying problem. In *Sunset Boulevard*, as in *Way Down East*, the problem is the emerging discourse of women's power, here symbolized by the character of the female star and by her position as the producer of her glamorous image. The film attempts to repress the implications of this power by presenting it as a residual and artificial discourse, but the values that Norma stands for subvert and ultimately subsume the text's valorization of "realism."

In an earlier essay on Jackie Gleason and television acting, I drew on formulations advanced by Rick Altman ("Dickens, Griffith, and Film Theory Today") and Peter Brooks (*Reading for the Plot*) to distinguish between what Altman calls the spatial as opposed to the temporal dimensions of a given narrative and Brooks labels its metaphoric as opposed to metonymic dimension. Brooks argues that the metaphoric dimension represents a hysterical response to trauma insofar as it expresses a need to return to the same material repeatedly (typically through image patterns and other forms of repetition), often in an exaggerated or "excessive" manner. Narratives play this regressive mode against a more mature and realistic one which progresses by means of temporally oriented cause-effect linkages to a conclusion. My analysis of Gleason's *The Honeymooners* identifies this metaphoric excess with an insecurity about the male's continued position of dominance during the 1950s. In *Sunset Boulevard*, however, excess is associated with the woman not the man, pinpointing a different but related anxiety about gender relations focused on the figure of the female star. In *Sunset Boulevard* the interplay between the text's hyperbolized metaphoric dimension and its realistic cause-effect one is embodied in the opposition between Norma, the star, and Joe, the writer. As W.J.T. Mitchell has noted, the contrast between Norma's world and the "real" one that Joe longs to live in is related to an opposition between images and words, the former associated with Norma and with the feminine, the latter with Joe and with his sense of male potency.

The film's representation of writing is rendered in terms of this opposition. Unlike the Western genre in which, as I argue in chapter 3, writing is related to codified law and contrasted with more "primitive" oral cultures, in Wilder's film writing relates to gender difference. Writing is seen as a commodity that symbolizes the man's ability to produce. But Norma's position as a star and a producer of her own image ultimately subverts the assumptions of gender complementarity on which the models of companionate romance are based and which the film codes as an opposition between the words that represent men as producers and the images that represent women as consumers. This subversion occurs as a result of the film's attempt to connect its themes of writing and romance through the motif of collaboration.[15]

In the "realistic" world that Wilder opposes to Norma's constructed one, writing is initially posed as evidence of masculinity. Joe is himself a writer. His subjects include baseball and torpedo boats. His work is discussed on the golf course or between puffs on cigars. To insult Joe about the unworthiness of his writing, the producer Sheldrake (Fred Clark) has only to feminize it by suggesting that Gillis's script might be more suitable as the basis for a film starring Betty Hutton than for one starring Alan Ladd.

The failure of Gillis's writing has denied him a place within a world of commerce in which men's worth is measured by the value of the writing they produce. Gillis tells us early on that he doesn't know what's wrong with the stories he writes; all he knows is "They didn't sell." To be valid, writing must be "worth" something; it must be commodifiable. For Gillis, the relationship between this commercial world and his sense of male potency is symbolized by his car, the keys to which fall out of his pants pocket and the loss of which he likens to "cutting off my legs." Because of his inability to turn his writing into a commodity worth $300, Gillis runs afoul of the law, and to save his now-crippled automobile, he must hide it—and himself.

To reenter the male world that he has left, Gillis needs to produce commodifiable writing. After failing in his attempts to write by himself, he collaborates on two movie scripts, one with Norma and the other with Betty Schaefer, an ambitious young Paramount story editor.

The nature of these collaborations reflects the kinds of romantic partnership that each of these women represents.

Betty Schaefer turns to Joe as a collaborator because she isn't "good enough" to produce a script on her own. Although her name is forgotten by her employer, Sheldrake, she remembers Gillis's name, informing him that "I knew your name. I'd always heard that you had talent." By so doing she suggests her suitability as a romantic partner who is both companionable and subservient. Significantly, they label the script that they are working on together "Untitled Love Story."[16]

Betty's ability to reestablish Joe's sense of himself both as a writer and as a man is signaled by a curious scene in which she confesses to having paid $300 to have her nose straightened—coincidentally, the same amount Joe himself had gone in search of earlier in the film so that he could keep his car. Although Betty's nose straightening has been carried out in the service of her earlier aspirations to movie stardom, she has since relinquished such ambitions, content to remain behind the camera and behind the man she has chosen as her mate. Following Betty's confession, Joe requests permission to kiss her straightened nose, permission that Betty immediately grants. It is at this moment, charged with its implications of phallic exchange, that Betty's desirability as a romantic partner for Joe is confirmed (fig. 4.16).

By opposing Betty's self-effacing naturalness to the artificial glamour represented by the grandiose Norma, the film attempts to oppose the collaboration between Betty and Joe as a model of romantic companionship in "the real world" to the unsuitability of the "false" relationship between Joe and Norma. But because the excessive manner with which Norma is depicted assumes metaphoric significance, the film is led to confront symbolically the contradictions inherent in its portrayal of the female star. This is true because writing is posed not only as a commodifiable representation of the male capacity for productive activity but also as narrative. And the "realism" claimed for such narrative productions is increasingly exposed as false. Although Joe's stories claim to reveal "truth," they are increasingly exposed as fictions. At the same time, an opposite movement occurs: the glamour embodied by Norma, initially characterized as constructed and excessive, gradually reveals the historical reality of the power of the female star.

The masculine potency conferred by writing is initially identified with its relation to realism. Thus Joe's "good" writing is represented simply as writing that expresses his life. When Betty praises an anecdote about a teacher in one of his stories, he replies, "I used to have a teacher like that once!" Betty responds, "That's why it's good! It's true! It's moving!"

This attempt to establish an unproblematic connection between writing and reality, however, is challenged throughout the film by comments that imply just the opposite: that "reality" is nothing more than a kind of fiction. On more than one occasion the film's dialogue plays on the ambiguity between Hollywood fantasies and the "real" lives of its characters. When Joe tells us how it is to read the "hodgepodge of plots" Norma has created for her comeback script, he also confesses that he is, at the same time, "concocting a little plot of my own," referring to his "plot" to become her ghostwriter. When Betty Schaefer releases Joe from admitting the facts about his relationship with Norma by imagining a story about his gold cigarette case that is more or less true, Joe replies, "That's the trouble with you story editors: you know all the plots." And at Artie Green's party, the host takes it upon himself to explain Gillis's formal attire by announcing, "I get it! You're in the pay of a foreign government!" as if connecting Joe's mode of dress with a familiar movie formula. This construction of people's lives out of the myths generated by Hollywood also surfaces in Gillis's romance with Betty, a romance that begins with some playful banter based on the clichés of Hollywood melodrama and culminates in a Hollywood studio, where the lovers wander down a street that is, "all cardboard, all hollow, all phony, all done with mirrors."

The underlying instability of the relation between narrative and reality, which becomes so pronounced as the action progresses, is prefigured in the film's initial credit sequence in which Gillis's voice-over promises to tell "the real story" of his relationship with Norma. However, this pledge is undercut by an image track that presents the action as from the bumper of a car. This car—and the camera—veer suddenly back on themselves to follow a police car to Norma's house—a shot that is later repeated when the men employed by the car-finance company pursue the financially insolvent Gillis along the same road to the same house (figs. 4.17, 4.18, and 4.19). The credit sequence, built around the film's image of the car as a symbol of male potency, concludes its backtracking motion with a striking underwater shot of Joe's corpse that makes it appear as though in the womb (fig. 4.20). This visual discourse, characterized by an aura of regression and dreamlike fantasy, enacts a specular drama of male impotence that is only superficially masked by the discursive dominance represented by the voice-over narration of a male who claims to be providing the spectator with a privileged access to a documentary-like reality. The constructed and arbitrary nature of even the words he speaks is also signaled in this sequence when the credits, which initially render the film's title as a street sign painted on a curb, break free from this realistic context to announce the names of the individuals who produced the artificial product that the film represents (figs. 4.21 and 4.22).[17]

Like all writing, and like the film itself, Joe and Betty's romance is ultimately revealed not as a fact of nature but as a social construction that poses the companionate couple as an ideal. By contrast, the less-harmonious collaboration between Joe and Norma on yet another script is undermined for the opposite reason: the fiction that they are producing cannot accommodate the historical reality of the female star, who cannot readily be subordinated to a male partner and who represents not an anachronism but an emerging discourse of female power.

Unlike Betty, Norma has a name that is more recognizable than Joe's. The power associated with this name is depicted in specifically phallic terms. She brags to Joe that she owns oil wells that are "pumping, pumping," and she insists that he use her car rather than his own. The nature of Norma's power is further specified by the terms of her collaboration with Joe. The two clash because they hold irreconcilable views about film scripts. Norma's writing is not based on the principle of narrative, as Joe's is, but on images. She wants simply to get herself up on the screen. Her idea of a good script is one that never cuts away from her. She also distrusts words, believing in the power of faces. "I can say whatever I want to with my eyes," she asserts at one point. To her the world of movies is not one of fictions but one of glamorous bodies. Where Betty seeks to win Joe's approval by responding to his identification with his stories, Norma tries to please him by buying him clothes. To prepare for her film, she doesn't memorize dialogue; she beautifies herself. When she returns to her old studio, the primary activity that she engages in is basking in the spotlight (fig. 4.23).

Yet Norma is aware that her image alone is insufficient. Because her preoccupation with this image is a function of narrative space rather than narrative time, she needs men to provide this image with a narrative context. The "hodge-podge of plots" that she has concocted needs a writer to give it coherence and a director to provide a mise-en-scène. In the film's final sequence, her butler, Max, pretending to be her director, must set the scene, instructing her that "This is the stairway of the palace," before she can perform. Even then, without a writer to "move things along," her big scene plays in a slow and unrealistic manner (fig. 4.24).

Lacking the sense of passing time provided by narrative, Norma also lacks a sense of history, specifically of a history connected to her own life. In place of Joe's sense of his life as a collection of stories, she cherishes a notion of herself as a star in the heavens, eternal and unchanging. Thus she puts her faith in astrology and covers herself with stars for her "greatest" role as Salome.

If the stars in the heavens are natural and ageless, however, the stars manufactured by Hollywood are not. The constructed nature of Norma's image and the visible effort required to produce it become more pronounced as the action progresses. Ironically, as her preoccupation with her body becomes more and more intense, its capacity to express her sense of herself seems less and less adequate. At first she appears estranged merely from her voice, which expresses her thoughts in the stagey, declamatory manner commonly associated with acting—and with actors themselves. Later, she struggles with the configurations of her body itself as she speaks of a woman who has "done wonders" with the line on her throat and struggles with steam baths and masseuses to lose half a pound.

Such contortions betray the contradiction between Norma's sense of herself as an ideal image of beauty and the labor called forth by such an ambition. Reacting to this contradiction, she tells Joe at one point, "I don't want you to see me; I don't look very attractive." Norma's failure to recreate her body into a form commensurate with her glamorous image of herself is what ultimately leads her to vanish into her role as Salome—and thereby into insanity. The final dissolve on her as she advances toward the camera acknowledges the relationship between Norma's dilemma and that of the Hollywood star system as a whole as it is applied to women, for the the blurring of Norma's image parodies Hollywood's practice of using soft-focus close-ups to disguise the gap between the physical deterioration of aging actresses and the "timeless" idealized identities that have been created for them as stars (fig. 4.25).

Thus, just as *Sunset Boulevard* deconstructs the realism of Hollywood fictions, so does it deconstruct the "naturalness" of glamour. The myth of female stars who simply "play themselves" on screen is exploded by Norma's painful demonstration of the constructed nature of such a self. Her plight reveals the historical reality of the female body in contemporary culture as a commodity produced by women's labor to be manipulated in the marriage market. The excessive stylization with which Norma's struggle for glamour is represented speaks of its metaphoric function: to reposition the emerging discourse of woman's power that she represents as a female star as a residual discourse read as "outdatedness."

Norma's power over Joe is based on her superior economic resources, and, as I have suggested, it is this economic dominance that *Sunset Boulevard* holds up to ridicule by identifying it with her out-of-date style. For a love affair such as that between Norma and Joe to succeed would expose a basic contradiction within the historical reality of the Hollywood star system. As I have argued, the sexual hierarchy proposed by the Hollywood mythmaking machinery connects a male's potency with his ability to dominate women, as Joe's relationship with Betty makes abundantly clear. Yet the power wielded by the female stars created by Hollywood to promote this myth calls this hierarchy into question. Women like Norma Desmond challenge the inevitability of the companionate ideal that Betty Schaefer represents. Because of the money, fame, and erotic desirability with which the industry has endowed them, female stars can become more powerful than the men who created them. Although stars are controlled by the mythmaking machinery of a male-dominated industry, it is the glamour represented by the stars that the public pays to see. Although the stars may participate in the stories of male dominance that Hollywood promulgates as "realism," their power and independence place them outside of this regime. The glamour of love goddesses carries with it the right to romantic domination. Unlike Betty Schaefer, women who are stars are not relegated to the fate of molding themselves to suit the pleasure of males. Secure in the erotic potency with which Hollywood has endowed them, they are free to assert their own sexual desire independent of patriarchal control. The historical reality of such female potency shatters the myth so vigorously promoted by Hollywood of romance as a process whereby companionship is defined by the "natural" domination of men over women.

Despite her preoccupation with herself as a pure image, it is not wholly accurate to say that Norma is unable to conceive of her life in terms of stories. At one point she does tell a story: she relates the story of her romance with Joe to Betty Schaefer. It is a scandalous story, which tells of the unconventional configuration of power relations represented by her love affair with Joe. It thus reveals a reality that

Joe's narratives never did: the reality of cultural taboos. By giving voice to this subversive possibility, Norma gives the lie to the myth of the inevitability of the companionate couple and thus precipitates the film's tragic denouement.

It is this scandal, trivialized as "gossip," that another of Hollywood's powerful women, Hedda Hopper, communicates to still other women through the institutions of fandom. Like Norma, Hedda Hopper is empowered to spread scandal about Hollywood because she is a woman whose glamour is perceptibly constructed and anachronized rather than "natural": there can be no mistaking the fact that she produces her own appearance. Hopper's persona parodies the reified glamour of the stars by participating in an outdatedness akin to the style of Norma herself. Hopper's glamour is symbolized by her penchant for wearing elaborate, somewhat ridiculous hats. (Her gossip column was, in fact, titled "Under Hedda's Hat.") In the scene in which Hopper appears, she wears just such a hat (fig. 4.26).[18]

Unlike Norma, Hedda Hopper is not a star but a writer. And unlike Betty, she requires no male collaborator to help her produce this narrative of cultural taboo framed as Hollywood scandal. "Take it direct!" she instructs her editor over the telephone. "Don't bother with a rewrite man." The death of the film's male writer-protagonist has thus left the production of story-commodities in the hands of a woman whose anachronistic and constructed appearance functions metaphorically to deny the emergent historical reality of female power that she represents. To purvey her "trivial" gossip, this female usurper of the male power of writing even asserts her privilege over society's male guardians of law and order, for she claims a right to use the telephone to dictate her scandal to a fan magazine over the right of the police to report their crime to the civic authorities. This conflict, along with others in the film, suggests that *Sunset Boulevard*'s exposé of the historical realities of the power of the movie love goddess and the role of women as producers of glamour is constantly at odds with its more conservative project of asserting the validity of Hollywood's myth about the naturalness of beauty and the inevitablity of the companionate couple.

Such contradictions are avoided in a non-Hollywood film in which a woman writer/director demonstrably acts as the producer of her own image. Like *Sunset Boulevard* Chantal Akerman's *Je tu il elle* features a voice-over narrator, a motif of writing, and a plot involving sexual desire. In this film, however, the image on display is that of the filmmaker herself, as is the voice-over narration. Thus the constructedness of the fiction is always foregrounded, and the image of the woman is read as a matter-of-fact self-representation, not a hyperbolized fantasy. As a "model" cinematic image, Akerman does not conform to contemporary ideals of beauty, yet rather than depicting her body in inferiorized terms because of this she appears throughout as utterly oblivious to its effect on others. She shows no self-consciousness, even when she senses that she is being observed while naked by a passerby (fig. 4.27).

Akerman's self-constructed image of her body is similar to the images put forward by a number of contemporary video performance artists whose creative strategies have been explored by Chris Straayer. "In performance art, the artist's sustained occupation with his/her body prohibits processes of theatrical identification on the part of the viewer, maintaining the viewer in an I-you discourse that foregrounds the communicative process at work in the videotext," Straayer writes. "More importantly, the performance artist, with the presence of his or her body, enacts a process of subjectivity outside/against verbal language" (155). This use of the body as a means of direct address in which artist and audience enter into an I-you relationship denies the metaphoric significance that a Hollywood film like *Sunset Boulevard* attaches to the representation of the female. For Akerman, the body is a fact, not a sign.

By contrast, writing, in Akerman's hands, is posed as *merely* a sign. *Je tu il elle* addresses itself not only to conventions of representing women's bodies but also to the authority claimed by verbal language, representing writing not as a commodity or a truth but as an arbitrary construct. At one point Akerman claims that she is writing a letter. "I wrote three pages," she says. "Then I tore them up and wrote twelve pages which said the same thing." Subsequently we watch as she lays these pages out in a somewhat sloppy sequence on the floor in front of the camera, displaying writing not as intangible truth but as visible artifact (fig. 4.28).

Akerman's film does not attempt to integrate its portrayal of sexual escapades into palatable romantic fictions that conform to conventional Hollywood expectations.[19] The first such scene is an emotionally empty encounter between the director-protagonist and a married truck driver in which she masturbates him. (The onanistic quality of this episode is emphasized by the fact that Akerman is offscreen as it occurs [fig. 4.29].) Similarly, the film's "climactic" love scene occurs between two women. Although passionate, it is bereft of any romantic context (fig. 4.30).

Most significantly, in *Je tu il elle* spectators are constantly aware of the discrepancy between their own experience of what is being portrayed and that of the participants. The love scenes in particular go on far longer than conventional Hollywood practice would condone; their rhythm is dictated not by the audience's desire for a boy-gets-girl narrative closure but by the participants' desire for heterogeneous and socially unsanctioned sensual pleasures. In this way *Je tu il elle* matches its portrait of transgressive sexuality with a transgressive manner of presentation to create a kind of realism far different from that represented by the conventions of Hollywood love stories employed in *Sunset Boulevard.* Such an experiment, however, demands a great deal of its audiences, most of whom are undoubtedly far more attuned to the pleasures offered by the constructions and contradictions involved in Hollywood's reified mythology of glamour and romance.

MASCULINITY IN CRISIS: METHOD ACTING IN HOLLYWOOD

The imagery of libidinal revolution and bodily transfiguration once again becomes a figure for the perfected community.

—Fredric Jameson

Masculinity is not something one is born with but something one gains . . . in American life, there is a certain built-in tendency to destroy masculinity in American men.

—Norman Mailer

Marlon was a tortured man in the early days, and he was great on screen.

—Sam Spiegel

In an often-repeated story, Sir Laurence Olivier, playing opposite Dustin Hoffman in the 1976 *Marathon Man*, is said to have been astonished at the American actor's lengthy and exhausting Method-inspired preparation activities. Finally, Olivier decided to offer Hoffmann some advice. "Why don't you try acting?" he suggested. This story directs us to the Method's version of itself as so realistic that the term *acting* cannot properly be applied to it. In fact, however, the Method is not different from acting; it is simply a special style of acting. Method performances in such popular films from the 1950s as *A Streetcar Named Desire* (1951) and *Baby Doll* (1956) today seem as artificial as any other historically dated performance technique. When advocates of the Method argue that this style is more "real" than "acted," they are in fact adapting a rhetoric routinely applied to all acting styles in the realist tradition. Changes in courtship conventions entail changes in the fashions of Hollywood performance styles, which can then lay claim to superior status by virtue of their putative ability to achieve greater realism than the style that preceded them. The movies' appropriation of Method acting during the 1950s was yet another strategy by which Hollywood could lay claim to a "realist effect" because of the style's emphasis on a close fit between actor and character and because Method techniques were peculiarly suited to delineate a new type of male romantic hero.

Method Acting and Cinema

The special quality of Stanislavskian Method acting can be most readily understood by comparing it to the British tradition, the other school of performance best known to American film- and theatergoers. Where the British school focuses on external technique, emphasizing makeup, costume, and verbal dexterity, the Method relies on understatement and what it calls "inner truth," cultivating an aura of mood and emotion derived from the actor's own persona rather than stressing the interpretation of the language in the written script. The British system encourages audiences to appreciate the actor's craft from an intellectual distance. The Method, by contrast, seeks to maximize the audience's identification with the performer.

Inspired by realist playwrights like Chekhov and Ibsen, Stanislavsky developed his own interpretation of realism at the Moscow Art Theatre. His concept focused on the psychology of the actor rather than on the social milieu of the character. This he termed "living the part." In *An Actor Prepares* he wrote, "Always and forever, when you are on the stage, you must play yourself" (167). The audience identifies with Stanislavskian actors in part because these performers ignore the audience, even going so far, at times, as turning their backs to the front of the stage.[1] Instead of interacting with the spectators, actors merge their own psyches with those of the characters they play. Through what Stanislavsky termed "affective memory" the actors recreate their roles in relation to aspects of their own personal histories.[2] By emphasizing the subtle processes associated with the performer/character's inner life, such actors position themselves as creative forces who collaborate with the playwright. As Timothy Wiles has observed, "Stanislavsky was the first to sense . . . that what is essentially 'real' about theatrical realism lies as much in the reality of the performance itself as in the true-to-life quality of the play's details" (14). In this sense

Stanislavsky's method foregrounds the actor in the same way that the nineteenth-century concept of the virtuoso foregrounded the musical performer. Like virtuosos, Stanislavsky's actors emphasize the difficulty of performance. The painful struggle that such actors subject themselves to in order to reach buried feelings is often manifest in the tortured quality identified with Method style.

As some critics have observed, such a performance strategy is analogous in many ways to the experience of psychoanalysis—not least because of its emphasis on releasing the power of the unconscious. "The fundamental objective of our psycho-technique," Stanislavsky wrote, "is to put us in a creative state in which our subconscious will function naturally" (266). This approach gave Stanislavsky's system affinities to modernism as much as to realism, for, like the stream-of-consciousness prose of Virginia Woolf and James Joyce, the style of Stanislavskian actors is designed to allow glimpses of their characters' unconscious inner conflicts.

The specific techniques used in Method performance—improvisation, relaxation, the cultivation of psychologically meaningful pauses, and the use of emotionally charged objects—are designed to reveal psychic conflict. The first three of these techniques create characters who appear to be speaking as if from a psychoanalyst's couch. The use of objects is a device used in all realist performance. In his book on Hollywood cinema Gilles Deleuze comments on the significance of this technique for the creation of what he calls the action image: "[T]he emotional handling of an object, an act of emotion in relation to the object, can have more effect than a close-up in the action image. It simultaneously brings together, in a strange way, the unconscious of the actor, the personal guilt of the director, the hysteria of the image" (159). Method actors are specifically trained to use objects as a means of revealing feelings that have been repressed by the character's conscious mind. In the words of Stanislavsky, "Only your subconscious can tell you why [a] particular object [comes] into the foreground of your mind" (292).

Although Stanislavsky's theories were developed for the theater, they are readily adaptable to film performance.[3] The absence of a live audience gives an obvious advantage to actors who are specifically trained to ignore spectators. Further, Stanislavsky's preoccupation with expressing inner conflict rather than cultivating external effects is well suited to the cinema's use of close-ups. Long takes allow for the expression of subtle changes in the character's feelings. The Method actor's concentration on the emotional texture of individual scenes ("pieces" or "units") is also readily adaptable to the moviemaking process, where individual scenes are shot separately and there is always ample time to prepare each one. Finally, the Method actor's reliance on emotional freshness rather than on outward technical mastery may in some ways be better served by a recorded medium than by the theater, where a role might have to be repeated more or less verbatim every night over a period of many months. Film can preserve the best, the freshest, of a varied series of performances of a single scene.

Despite its adaptability to film, however, Stanislavsky's Method failed to influence movie performance styles significantly until it was taken up by Hollywood in the 1950s. In the USSR film directors were wedded to a cinematic formalism that stressed the primacy of the director's editing function and thus had little interest in this new acting style. "The Moscow Art Theatre is my deadly enemy," Eisenstein wrote. "It is the exact antithesis of all I am trying to do. They string their emotions together to give a continuous illusion of reality. I take photographs of reality and then cut them up so as to produce emotions" (Wollen 65).

In his classic study of cinematic performance, *Film Acting*, V. I. Pudovkin attempted without success to negotiate a rapprochement between Stanislavskian technique and the reliance on editing that stood at the center of Soviet filmmaking.[4] His earlier *Film Technique* had advocated the Eisensteinian concept of actors as physical types ("typage") and had reported on the famous "Kuleshov effect," wherein the same close-up of an actor was read by different audiences as expressing widely divergent emotions depending on whether it was followed by a shot of a child playing, a bowl of soup, or a dead woman (168).[5] Both typage and the Kuleshov effect implicitly denigrated the contributions that Method-trained performers could make to the creation of complex and individuated filmic characters.

Kuleshov himself advocated a modified version of the older Delsarte method of performance in which emotions were conveyed through broad, conventionalized gestures. Such an approach, which communicated strong, simple emotions quickly, was much more in keeping with the aesthetics of Soviet montage than was Stanislavskian acting technique. Kuleshov specifically dismisses the expressive potential of Stanislavsky's Method when he states, "One must construct the work of film actors so that it comprises the sum of organized movement, with 'reliving' held to a minimum" (100). In *Film Acting*, however, Pudovkin denies the Kuleshov experiment's implicit valorization of the power of editing over the artistry of acting. He speaks of "the pseudo-theory of the *montage* (edited) image (a theory for which no single individual is responsible). This theory deduces, from the fact that an impression of acting can be composed mechanically by sticking pieces together, the illegitimate assumption that separate pieces, not connected inwardly within the actor, will necessarily give an optimum result" (273).

Pudovkin had begun his film career as an actor and continued to perform roles in his own films and those of others throughout his life. Because of his concern with actors, his work was sometimes labeled "theatrical" by other members of the Soviet film movement (Leyda 222). By advocating a collaboration between actor and director during the editing process Pudovkin's *Film Acting* attempts to retain the Soviet aesthetic of film as montage and at the same time rehabilitate the status of the actor as a center of creative expressivity rather than a passive tool of the director. Through their participation in editing, Pudovkin argues, actors could overcome the fragmentation brought about by having their scenes cut up into pieces and recreate their performances into a larger emotional unity. Tellingly, Pudovkin's single extended example of how this larger emotional unity could be created does not involve acting at all but instead focuses on the juxtaposition of music and image in the climactic sequence of his 1933 film *Deserter*. After describing the sequence, he concludes somewhat apologetically:

> Though the example we have dealt with here does not relate directly to the actor's work, it yet is important for him, for he is one of those who must understand particularly clearly the significance of the treatment of sound and image[in the editing process], not in their primitive *naturalistic* association, but in a more profound—I should term it *realistic*—association enabling the creative worker in the cinema to portray any given event, not merely simply in direct representation, but in its deepest degree of generalization (313–14). [Emphasis added.]

Despite Pudovkin's lavish praise of Stanislavsky and his repeated protests against the misapplication of the notion of typage to describe the characteristic Soviet approach to cinematic performance, the argument put forward in *Film Acting* cannot surmount the inconsistency that is apparent in the above passage, where "realism" is opposed to "naturalism" and signifies the utopian social vision that lay at the heart of Russian formalist film theory's concept of dialectical montage editing. Stanislavskian realism, focused as it is on the inner feelings of the actor and the development of subtle emotional states made possible by long takes, represents a radically different quality. Pudovkin's fundamental commitment to editing over acting is evident when he writes, "I must confess that during my work I have admitted actors to creative collaboration only grudgingly and to a miserly extent" (354–55).[6]

Hollywood's Appropriation of the Method

In Hollywood, Stanislavskian theory at first exercised a similarly negligible influence. Despite the immigration of members of the Moscow Art Theatre like Alla Nazimova, Richard Boleslavsky, and Maria Ouspenskaya during the 1920s and 1930s, the Hollywood studios' story-centered view of actors as script readers precluded the intense actor involvement in the creation of character advocated by the Method.[7] The emergence of Stanislavskian techniques as a major force in film performance was not to occur until historical conditions were propitious and the theories themselves had undergone considerable revision.

For Stanislavsky's Moscow Art Theatre, as for the American Group Theatre of the 1930s which modeled itself on Stanislavsky's theories, the Method approach had political implications. Both the Moscow Art Theatre and the Group focused on contemporary social problems and used improvisation to build an ensemble performance that challenged the older, hierarchically organized "star-centered" theater. For example, a filmed rehearsal for a production of *The Three Sisters* staged by the Moscow Art Theatre includes a sequence in which Stanislavsky asks his players, "Did you try to adjust to each other, to feel each other out?" (Nash). In the American Group Theatre the ensemble ideal extended to the playwright as well; its most characteristic productions, such as *Waiting for Lefty* and *Awake and Sing*, were written by Clifford Odets, one of the Group's own members. Odets's plays for the Group were contemporary dramas of working-class frustration, conforming to Stanislavsky's ideal of an indigenous theater of social protest.

The early political and group-centered orientation of Stanislavskian practice, however, had eroded by the 1950s when Lee Strasberg promulgated his own version of the Method at the Actors Studio. As has frequently been noted, Strasberg emphasized the individuated psychoanalytic dimension of Stanislavsky's program by supplementing the

Method's affective memory techniques with new exercises. The most famous of these required performers to stage reenactments of "private moments" using material from their own lives. Although these exercises enhanced the actor's ability to portray powerful emotional states, Strasberg's training techniques also encouraged his students to substitute their own feelings for those of the characters they played rather than to merge the two together as Stanislavsky had envisioned.[8]

Under Strasberg, Method acting became more confessional than communal.[9] Such an emphasis on the actor in isolation undermined the ensemble-oriented aspect of Stanislavsky's system, producing actors like James Dean, whose on-screen aura of alienation from those around him was enhanced by a solipsistic acting technique that could lead him to step on the speeches of his fellow performers with line readings of his own that were often inaudible. At the Actors Studio Stanislavsky's conception of improvisation as a way to develop a sense of community among actors was replaced by an approach to improvisation that largely celebrated the neurosis of the individual performer.[10]

Because of their tendency to substitute their personal feelings for those of the characters they were playing, Actors Studio performers were well suited to become Hollywood stars.[11] In Hollywood, star types were defined through their participation in specially tailored films ("star vehicles") and through publicity surrounding their offscreen activities. Thus, the closer the fit between the roles that actors could play and their "real" personalities, the more easily promotable they were as stars. In the case of performers from the Actors Studio, who were oriented toward submerging the characters they played into their own psyches, this fit was especially close. In short, Lee Strasberg transformed a socialistic, egalitarian theory of acting into a celebrity-making machine.

Movie stars spawned by Strasberg's Actors Studio were of a new type which is often labeled the rebel hero (Houston, Kael, Morella and Epstein, Spoto, and Zaretsky). The three actors who epitomized the new rebel type associated with the Method were Marlon Brando, James Dean, and Montgomery Clift. In fact, none of these stars was trained primarily at the Actors Studio. Clift never attended at all. Dean took only a few classes there, virtually abandoning his training after the first time that Strasberg criticized him. Brando was trained primarily by Stella Adler, a former member of the Group Theatre who had had a falling-out with Strasberg over his interpretation of Stanislavsky's ideas.[12] By contrast, other equally talented actors of the 1950s with far closer ties to the Studio, such as Julie Harris and Eli Wallach, did not fit Hollywood's image of the male rebel hero and thus never achieved an appreciable degree of Hollywood success.

In part because of the confusion generated by these popular associations of Method acting with stars not trained at the Actors Studio, the two major studies of film acting published to date, Richard Dyer's *Stars* and James Naremore's *Acting in the Cinema*, both question the distinctiveness of Method performance (Dyer 154, Naremore 197–98). However, whether directly influenced by Strasberg or not, the new male stars all to some degree or other adapted Method techniques to support their identification as rebels, transforming Stanislavsky's emphasis on relaxation into the "Method slouch," his interest in improvisation into libidinous temper tantrums, and his concept of inwardness into mumbling, tortured pauses and sloppy grooming. Although these histrionic affectations quickly assumed the status of clichés, it is important to bear in mind that they represented a clear application of Stanislavsky's theories. Such strategies decisively shaped the kinds of characters that these actors portrayed and the manner in which they portrayed them.

Male Gender Identity and Changing Courtship Patterns in 1950s America

The three new rebel stars were seen as a new breed of neurotic, alienated men, reckless and nonconforming both on-screen and off. The cause of their alienation centered on their sense of themselves as male.[13] Clift, Dean, and Brando were the first male stars whose legends encompassed public speculation regarding homosexual activity.[14] Such speculation foregrounded the tenuousness of their commitment to a heterosexual regime in which a male's sexual identity was based on his ability to dominate and provide for a woman. The traditional view of heterosexual male identity involves the cultivation of male-identified characteristics that clearly delineate gender difference. The demeanor of the new rebel stars, by contrast, was marked by such "neurotic" qualities as emotional confusion, irrationality, and violent behavior, suggesting the conflicted nature of their gender identifications.

This conflict was related to contradictions in the culture of 1950s America concerning male roles. As much modern historical and sociological research is making clear, the picture of the 1950s as a time in which women cultivated domesticity while their husbands fulfilled the traditional male roles of household providers masks deep strains that existed in gender relations. As John D'Emilio and Estelle Freedman have recently shown, the companionate concept of marriage, which by the beginning of the century had largely replaced the older concept of separate spheres, came in for renewed attention during this period. Barbara Ehrenreich explores the special problems that men faced as a result of such scrutiny in her book *The Flight from Commitment*. Definitions of appropriate male roles became increasingly amorphous. Middle-class men who had recently returned from the heroic enterprise of World War II found themselves caught up in a corporate world in which traditional masculine qualities like competitive individualism and physical prowess were not highly valued. Further, work itself no longer defined distinct gender roles. By 1950 52 percent of women worked outside the home, part of a large-scale trend that was to continue as the century progressed. As a result, relations between the sexes became newly charged with issues of competition and dominance. The threat to the traditional gender hierarchy posed by such changes was expressed in the new Method stars' sadomasochistic personas, which focused on an ambivalent obsession with male power.

In the realm of sexuality especially, insecurities loomed during the fifties. Most notably, sex was becoming more important. Jeffrey Weeks has commented on "the growing emphasis on sexuality in married love, an emphasis which has its roots in the nineteenth century and its real efflorescence in the 1950s" (200). Weeks further contends that this period saw "the sexual element as increasingly the essential element in the choice of a partner" (*Sex, Politics and Society* 210). In addition, sex was understood in more problematic terms. Popular Freudianism defined monogamous heterosexual behavior as the culmination of a process of maturation rather than as a biological given. And the much-publicized Kinsey reports documented a wide variety of sexual practices among Americans. As social historian Beth L. Bailey has observed, masculinity and femininity "came to be seen not as natural traits, proceeding causally, masculinity from maleness, femininity from femaleness, but as identities that must be acquired, earned and constantly demonstrated" (98). These developments were accompanied by a greater emphasis on sexual behavior and attitudes in general as sex came more and more to be perceived as a central aspect of personality.

Homosexuality in particular underwent a redefinition during this period. Homosexual subcultures began to emerge. In addition, popular Freudianism fostered the view that homosexual behavior expressed impulses that everyone to some extent shared. Hollywood's output reflected these shifts. As Richard Dyer has shown, the emphasis on sexual perversity in the film noir cycle of a decade earlier included allusions to homosexuality in films such as *The Maltese Falcon* and *Gilda*. In fifties films, however, homosexuality was typically not seen as part of a universe of perverse sexuality but was rather sympathetically depicted as a normal phase of maturation—for example, in Westerns such as *The Big Sky* discussed in chapter 3. A confused gender identity was no longer understood as a symbol of ineradicable moral decay but rather elaborated as a developmental problem of a divided protagonist.

Such shifts in conceptions surrounding gender roles were often embodied in popular discourses expressing the conflict in terms of a division between youth and age. Since the beginning of the century factors such as urbanization and the automobile had contributed to the development of a youth culture separate from the traditional family. Philippe Ariés states, "After the Second World War [adolescence] was extended and generalized so that now adolescence has swollen into a huge, unstructured age group that people enter early and leave with some difficulty" (68). Ariés further suggests that the development of this culture of prolonged adolescence, coupled with an increasing emphasis on sexuality divorced from reproduction, played a significant role in the acceptance of homosexual behavior as one of the possible channels of sexual expression that is part of a normal developmental cycle. This view is echoed by David Greenberg in his book *The Construction of Homosexuality*. "The acceptance of some forms of sexual experience whose sole purpose is pleasure, sociability, or the expression of love makes it hard, in the absence of rational grounds, to reject others that are equally harmless and consensual," Greenberg writes. "Thus, there occurred a redirection in hostility toward homosexuality alongside a relaxation of attitudes toward divorce, premarital sex, contraception, abortion, and pornography" (462).

The phenomenon of the youth culture had further repercussions as well. As Thomas Doherty has noted in his book *Teenagers and Teenpics*, this group had long centered their activities on moviegoing, and Hollywood now began to look to youth as its primary market (3). Hollywood's rebel heroes, who dramatized the new concept of the juvenile delinquent, played a significant role in this marketing strategy. As represented in the films of the rebel stars, the new concept of adolescence was frequently associated with a new concern for juvenile delinquency.[15] As James Gilbert has noted, "The accusation that mass culture caused delinquency—especially the 'new delinquency'of the postwar period—was the focus of much contemporary attention" (178).

More generally, as Barbara Ehrenreich, Elizabeth Hess, and Gloria Jacobs note in their book *ReMaking Love*, the youth culture defined itself largely through newly developed courtship patterns that emphasized consumerism: specifically, the older system of "calling" was replaced by the "date," and dating in the 1950s came to be characterized by the custom of going steady. As a result, dates were seen less as simply an opportunity for economic display on the part of men who by lavishly entertaining a variety of women could thereby advertise their capacities as providers. Instead, going steady created a context in which men were expected to demonstrate their suitability as companions for women indoctrinated into the new ideal of companionate marriage. It was in the context of such changing needs and attitudes as these that the love stories and star images of 1950s Hollywood were fabricated.

The neurotic conflicts represented in the Method acting techniques identified with the new rebel heroes redefined romance. Traditionally, Hollywood love stories had focused on a *courtship* which must declare its romantic ideals in the face of *external* obstacles. In the films of these new stars, however, love came to be seen as a *relationship* in which the woman ministered to the *internal* conflicts of a neurotic male who was unsure of his masculine identity. Women who had formerly thought of romance as a means by which they could be taken care of by a competent and chivalrous provider now began to see it as a way to participate in the drama of the male personality.

The Cinematic Method Text: On the Waterfront

In the three films of the 1950s most often cited in connection with Method performance—*On the Waterfront* (1954), *East of Eden* (1955), and *Rebel Without a Cause* (1955)—the central conflict concerns the rebel hero's difficulty defining himself in relation to a father figure. This conflict is depicted in each film by means of climactic, highly charged scenes in which a young man attempts to assert a model of virility different from that of his elder. Such scenes call forth the Method actor's ability to indulge in the kind of emotional outpouring traditionally associated with feminine behavior. James Dean's anguished cry in *Rebel Without a Cause*, "You're tearing me apart!" highlights the rebel hero's conflict over his masculine role. The most acclaimed of these films, *On the Waterfront*, is also the one that makes the most extensive use of Method techniques. Directed by Elia Kazan, a man with close ties to the Actors Studio, it features a performance by Marlon Brando that has come to be regarded as the preeminent example of Method acting in film (Hirsch 299; Kazan, Interview, 8).[16] When the film was made, Brando was not only a movie actor but also a Hollywood leading man, and his performance in Kazan's film won him not only an Academy Award but also a place on the list of the top ten Hollywood stars of 1954 and 1955, a place that he would not regain until the release of *The Godfather* in 1971 assured his rebirth as a preeminent character actor (Steinberg).

Brando's performance in *On the Waterfront* uses Method techniques to define a new type of male movie star and a new concept of romantic love. But the nature of his achievement was not consciously appreciated by those most intimately involved with creating this vehicle for him. In recalling the process of writing and selling the screenplay, both Kazan and writer Budd Schulberg have repeatedly referred to the film's romantic element as a concession to the commercialism of Hollywood. As they saw it, they had attempted to write a story of labor struggle, drawing on the experiences of Father John Corridan, the "Waterfront Priest," and on Malcolm Johnson's *New York Sun* series "Crime on the Labor Front." Terry Malloy, the film's protagonist, was based on Anthony De Vincenzo, a key witness in the New York State Crime Commission's investigation of the docks in 1952. "We had taken real characters and put them through a struggle that was still being waged," wrote Schulberg. "Was it too somber, too real for the Hollywood Dream Machine?" (145). Evidently it was, for Hollywood executives like Spiros Skouras and Daryl F. Zanuck, to whom the pair attempted to sell the screenplay, repeatedly urged them to "'make it a beautiful love story'" (147). The disdain for the boy-meets-girl formula evident in Schulberg's reminiscences has been echoed by critics, who for the most part treat *On the Waterfront* as a "social problem film" with a love story that is peripheral to its central concerns.[17] Such a conception of the film misses how essential the love story is to its articulation of the male hero. Kazan's and Schulberg's enterprise in fact takes its vocabulary from a commercial language in which the love story sets the terms by which manhood is understood and evaluated.

The hero's name, Terry, immediately presents him as a figure of ambiguous gender possibilities. These possibilities are articulated in relation to a class discourse that defines two different modes of masculinity. Terry's developing sense of himself eventually leads him to affirm his male identity in relation to a middle-class mode of social organization different from the working-class values with which he has grown up. This mode involves a companionate relation with a woman in the course of which the issues of gender confusion that he is struggling with are enacted.

Initially Terry sees himself as part of a society that the film codes as one constituted in terms of a residual discourse. This world is made up of competing constellations of male power held by localized groups of longshoremen and union officers who define their masculinity through the exclusion of women. Terry's primary loyalty is to the all-male gang of union officials led by the corrupt boss Johnny Friendly (Lee J. Cobb) and his dandified second-in-command, Terry's brother Charlie the Gent (Rod Steiger). Terry's unquestioning participation in this male-identified system begins to break down, however, when Friendly orders him to set up the murder of Joey Doyle, one of the dockers who is about to violate the accepted intergroup loyalties by giving information to a federal commission that is investigating corruption in Friendly's union. Prodded by Father Barry (Karl Malden) and by Edie Doyle (Eva Marie Saint), the sister of the man he has helped to kill, and despite Friendly's effort to dissuade him by killing his brother, Charlie, Terry cooperates with the federal investigation. He also falls in love with Edie. Terry decides to obey the impersonal law of the land rather than the tough-guy code of the docks, and he chooses the companionship of a potential marriage partner over that of his male cronies. His new roles, constituted in terms of the emerging discourses of bourgeois citizen and companionate husband require a radical change in his sense of himself as a man. Brando dramatizes this change by drawing on the classic techniques of Method performance: improvisation, pauses, the use of objects, and relaxation.

Brando's improvisations are delivered in the context of a rigid structure of oppositional languages that define self-enclosed and irreconcilable groups. The middle-class government officials speak in the most stilted manner, making statements that sound artificial and scripted, such as "You have the right to remain silent if that is what you choose to do." At the other extreme, the working-class dockers and union men speak more informally; yet, sensing their isolation from the more-official forms of bourgeois utterance used to intimidate them, they have developed an ethic of silence in relation to outsiders. As Kayo Dugan (Pat Henning) says, "Down on the docks, we've always been

D and D," betraying even by this locution an argot that must be translated for the benefit of those who are not initiates (Dugan must explain to Father Barry that D and D means "deaf and dumb").

If the speech of the officials conveys itself as an artificial script and that of the dockers as a muted vernacular code, the speech of the women in the film aspires to be a form of personal expression that will bridge the communication impasse. Early in the film Edie Doyle and her female neighbor make strenuous efforts to "speak the truth" about the dockers' victimization and to encourage others to do so. To the men who surround them, however, their efforts appear naive and they are summarily silenced. The men are determined to keep their women mute—even if this involves sending them away. If meaningful communication is to occur, a more potent spokesperson is needed.

This role is assumed by Terry Malloy. His special position is signaled by his manner of speaking. Brando's improvisations set his dialogue apart from that of the other characters.[18] The unrehearsed quality of his speech is conspicuous to anyone watching the film in statements such as "Never's gonna be much too much too soon for me, Shorty," an utterance impossible to imagine as scripted in the form in which Brando delivers it.[19] Similarly, Terry's exchange with Edie during the much-praised scene in which he appropriates her glove contains statements that invite the spectator to construe the character's words as beyond the scriptwriter's control. When Edie tells him she is going to a college run by the Sisters of St. Anne, he asks, "Where's that?" When she responds, "Tarrytown," he says again, "Where's that . . . uh . . . where's that?" When this question, too, is answered, he goes on, "What do you do there, just . . . what . . . ? Study?" Further, when Edie drops her glove, Brando mumbles, "Wait a second," suggesting a motivation having to do more with a command from an actor who has decided to depart from the script than with anything preplanned for the character of Terry.

As these last examples suggest, Terry's moments of improvised speech set him apart not only from the other characters but from the screenplay as well. It is worth noting that Budd Schulberg's script for *On the Waterfront* contains an extraordinary number of repeated phrases (for example—Father Barry: "Don't you see that? Now don't you see that?" Edie: "No wonder people call you a bum. No wonder."). In the taxicab scene, surely one of the best known in all cinema, Terry himself speaks many of his lines twice ("Before we get to where, Charlie? Before we get to where?"; "There's a lot more to this than I thought, Charlie; I'm telling you, there's a lot more"; and, in one of the most famous lines of all, "It was you, Charlie; it was you"). Such a use of language has a quality of obsessive return that presents the characters as part of an inflexible social and psychological milieu in which they feel trapped and helpless.[20]

When Brando improvises broken utterances against such a background, his clumsy syntax suggests a freewheeling actor's intermittent attempts at revolt against a constraining structure that relies on shrilly defensive patterns of repetition to assert its authority. In place of Stanislavsky's ideal of actors as *collaborators* in the process of creating a text, merging their psyches with the script that they are performing, *On the Waterfront* uses Stanislavskian improvisation to depict an actor who often appears to be *competing* with a text that sets itself against him by its adherence to rote patterns of repetition. The rebellion of Marlon Brando the star against a traditional cinema of overly scripted performances can thus be read as an analogue to that of Terry Malloy the character against traditional patterns of masculine behavior. Both actor and character appear as isolated figures, Terry in the context of the world depicted in the film and Brando in the context of the circumstances of its production. Each seeks to define his identity in opposition to rigid, empty systems of authority.

The view that sees *On the Waterfront* as a rationalization of Kazan and Schulberg's friendly testimony before the House Un-American Activities Committee cannot account for the fact that it plays down its "great moment" of informing. Terry's explosive testimony is almost thrown away; Kazan even cuts away from it at a climactic moment to show "Mr. Upstairs" switching off his television set. The courtroom scene cannot become the site where the film's issues are resolved because it focuses only on words; but *On the Waterfront* is at least as concerned with images, which are part of a visual texture that masks their psychological significance. The bleak black-and-white photography and gritty location shooting that give the film its distinctive visual feel identify it with a tradition of documentary realism. But many of the images, especially those of Brando's face and the objects that he interacts with, also convey the inward struggle that marks the character of Terry Malloy. Like its words, the images of the films are gender identified.

Brando's performance must define masculinity against a visual background that represents the male body as diminutive and vulnerable. Boris Kaufmann's bleak black-and-white photography overpowers the film's male groups with a superhumanly scaled and menacing urban landscape: great loading docks, tall iron fences, vast desolate tracts of rubble, and buildings with endless colonnades. In the film's first shot the figures of Johnny Friendly and his group are dwarfed by the looming shape of a docked freighter (fig. 5.1), and the whistle blast from another freighter obliterates Terry's first attempt to speak what he knows to Edie. The threatening quality of this landscape is emphasized by wide-angle shots in which people and things move backwards and forwards in the frame with disconcerting rapidity: a truck chasing Terry and Edie down an alley, Johnny Friendly's henchmen scurrying out of the bar when Father Barry momentarily distracts Terry's attention (figs. 5.2 and 5.3). Most ominously, this world of overscaled structures and precipitous movement involves the threat of falling. We see Joey Doyle fall off the roof of his apartment building and later watch a cargo of whiskey cartons drop on Kayo Doogan, another would-be informer (figs. 5.4, 5.5, and 5.6).

As the film's primary representative of femininity, Edie thinks only of escaping from this environment back to the country where she goes to college or to the older way of living represented in her fantasy of a farm. Terry, in turn, tries to escape through his pigeons, with which he is more than once identified. He releases one of these pigeons into the air just before Joey Doyle's fatal fall (fig. 5.7). The bird's ability to counteract the gravitational pull that ensures Joey's destruction is underscored by Friendly's bodyguard Tillio (Tami Mauriello), who compares Joey to a bird who could sing, "but he couldn't fly."

As if in response to this threatening visual context, Brando's Method techniques depict a character who is cautious and uncertain. The anguished pauses that mark his performance are dramatized by high-key lighting and by Leonard Bernstein's overwrought musical score. At such moments the film's long close-ups of the character of Terry Malloy suggest a level of experience that is verbally inexpressible (fig. 5.8). Like the silences that occur on the psychoanalyst's couch, these pauses convey inner confusion and blockage. Terry cannot articulate what is going on inside of him because he does not consciously understand it.

Brando also draws on a Method-inspired use of objects to represent his character's repressed gender-related insecurities. As I have indicated, one of Brando's most celebrated scenes in this film involves his appropriation of a woman's glove. When Terry first meets Edie, he takes up a glove that she has accidentally dropped and refuses to return it to her, playing with it and eventually putting his hand into it as he engages her in conversation (fig. 5.9). As James Naremore has noted, "Few virile male leads before him . . . would so effortlessly have slipped on a woman's glove" (*Acting in the Cinema* 194). A further motif that brings out Terry's "feminine" side involves his pigeons. In a curious scene on the roof he tenderly holds a pigeon erroneously referred to as "she" by Edie, then clearly identified as a male by Tommy, the young Golden Warrior ("She's a he. His name is Swifty"). Immediately following Tommy's statement, however, the pigeon lays an egg in Terry's hand. This hermaphroditic creature, to which Terry refers approvingly on more than one occasion, can be taken as a model for Terry's own confused identity, which effects a complicated mediation between masculinity and femininity.

In keeping with the Method's psychoanalytically oriented preoccupations, Brando also interacts with objects in such a way as to bring out psychologically coded meanings having to do with enclosure, which Freud identified with femininity, or thrusting and penetration, which he identified as male. Terry's habit of chewing gum, which involves the body's enclosing properties, has overtones of femininity. These overtones are further played upon when Terry offers gum to Edie to comfort her during the wedding scene (fig. 5.10). His gesture of exchange here contrasts to some of the film's instances of male bonding, which are marked by exchanges of cigarettes—objects with more phallic overtones. A cigarette is exchanged between Father Barry (Karl Malden) and one of the dockers as the priest is being hauled up out of the hold, for example. Women may also be included in this ritual of male bonding: the snatches of dialogue we overhear among members of the wedding party indicate that, like the men, the tough-talking bride smokes, a further sign of her accommodation to a traditional male world.

The film's major example of a male-coded object is the gun given to Terry by his older brother, Charlie. Despite the scenario implied by Charlie's decision to give him this gun, Terry cannot bring himself to use it to carry out the traditional role of the male who acts rather than speaks.[21] The gentleness with which Brando pushes this object away as Steiger begins to brandish it in front of him and the careless way that he holds it in the bar suggest the character's lack of traditional male authority (fig. 5.11). Terry soon abandons the gun and gives testimony at the hearing instead. When the hearing fails to clarify his sense of himself, Terry must find another strategy. At this point Brando engages with yet another object: Joey Doyle's jacket. The feminine associations of enclosure inherent in this jacket are called forth when Father Barry makes a show of zipping it up after Terry's beating (fig. 5.12). Yet the jacket is nonetheless clearly identified as male. It thus constitutes an appropriate image for the androgynous persona that Terry ultimately adopts. In wearing Joey's jacket, Terry affirms his commitment to a sexual identity that can encompass both masculine and feminine traits.

Terry's ambivalent gender identity increasingly centers on the representation of his body, and this representation is complicated by Brando's relaxed Method posture. In an essay entitled "Don't Look Now" Richard Dyer has explored the significance of the aura of hardness surrounding erotic representations of the male body. This aura is typically achieved by means of an emphasis on visible musculature and an association of the body with action, often through the use of an active, upright posture. By contrast, Brando's Method slouch depicts his body as limp rather than upright, and he plays the first love scenes with Eva Marie Saint in a passive position traditionally identified as feminine. At the same time, however, his broken nose and the cut eyebrow that he affects for this role announce the character's association with the prototypically male world of boxing. The body image of the character that emerges has conflicting associations with both pugnacity and weakness. If the film is to rehabilitate his image as a romantic male hero, these contradictions must be addressed. Like his pigeon Swifty, who sits on the highest perch and attacks all who try to displace him, Terry must establish his superiority to women and to other men.

The masculine side of Terry's persona begins to take precedence when he makes love to Edie. Here, in a sequence noteworthy for its eroticization of female surrender to a forced sexual encounter, Terry asserts the traditional male right to dominate women (figs. 5.13, 5.14, 5.15, and 5.16).[22] Brando's rendering of this scene, however, differs from the performance strategy followed by prior male stars in that he exhibits an explosive rage that is perceived as passionate rather than merely controlling; it is the antithesis of the repressed state earlier expressed in his tortured pauses. The character appears to have "unblocked" himself through a brutally physical assertion of masculine privilege vis-à-vis women. Only after this dramatic assertion of male dominance is Terry willing to carry out the femininizing role of speaking out at the hearing.

Even though Terry's violent encounter with Edie has satisfied him regarding the superior capabilities of his body in relation to those of a woman, Friendly's attempt to assault him at the hearing serves as a reminder that he must assert this superiority in relation to the male world as well. Throughout the film his physique is contrasted with that of Friendly. Whereas Cobb's body is massive and his gestures aggressive, Brando's body is flaccid and his gestures indecisive. Although Terry's movements are identifiably those of a former boxer, he demurs when Friendly tries to involve him in a playful sparring match near the beginning of the film. Although he no longer identifies himself as part of an individualistic world of competitive male groups that define their dominance in terms of pure muscle, Terry must prove his masculinity by means of a test of physical prowess. He approaches this test as a bourgeois man who is ruled by the law. His new masculinity is purely symbolic, exemplified by his ability to stand up after being beaten and to thrust himself through the door of the leading dock (figs. 5.17, 5.18, 5.19, and 5.20). This action calls forth associations with a sexual act in which Terry's whole body is deployed as a phallus, and it incorporates him into the visual environment that has previously posed such a threat to the dominance of the male figure. His walk into the loading dock contrasts his body to Friendly's for the last time as the former union boss is dunked in the harbor by Pop Doyle (John Hamilton) in a comic inversion of Friendly's original crime of throwing Doyle's son Joey off the roof (fig. 5.21).[23]

Terry's stoic assertion of bodily supremacy speaks more eloquently to the dockers than any words; but it does move them to words. Here the pattern of repeated utterances that has heretofore prevailed is appropriated in the service of a new commitment to intergroup communication. Now the repetitions are combined with variations that emphasize the relationship between Terry and the other dockers. "If *Terry* don't work, *we* don't work. . . . If *he* walks in, *we* walk in with him." This new sense of community, fragile and tentative, constitutes the film's ultimate resolution, a resolution centered on the battered but still identifiably male body of Terry Malloy.

This choric solidarity is made possible, both thematically and dramatically, by the strong vulnerability of the protagonist. Thematically, the resolution is classic and archetypal; the scapegoat purges and renews the society. But dramatically it is innovative, made possible by the particular ideological potency of the new man that Brando enacts. Brando's performance elaborates a model of male gender insecurity that recreates romance as a drama of male neuroticism. The Stanislavskian techniques that he employs not only lend themselves to the expression of this motif but also invest his characterization with an unprecedented aura of verisimilitude. Brando's acting in *On the Waterfront* is thus designed to persuade movie fans of the 1950s that Hollywood's newest love stories were not only pleasurable but also "realistic."

In recent years the influence of the Method on the creation of male star personas has been to some extent reformulated. In place of the anxiety-fraught romantic relationships suggested by the neurotic male Method stars of the fifties, newer Method stars like Robert de Niro, Dustin Hoffman, and Al Pacino typically project a cold narcissism that suggests that they are beyond romance. These actors represent the self-absorption that Lee Strasberg brought to Method performance not by revealing an anguished inner torment as the stars of the fifties were inclined to do but rather by projecting a truculent incommunicativeness that pointedly excludes the audience.

Many of the most successful films made by these actors, such as *Raging Bull* (1980), *The Godfather* (1972 and 1974), and *Kramer vs. Kramer* (1979), treat the failure of romantic coupling. By contrast, attempts to feature these stars in traditional romantic plots in films like *Bobby Deerfield* (1977), *John and Mary* (1969), and *Falling in Love* (1984) have for the most part been notably unsuccessful. For these performers the drama of identity does not necessarily involve a relationship with a woman. De Niro, for instance, is at his best playing psychotic characters like Travis Bickle in *Taxi Driver* (1976) or Johnny Boy in *Mean Streets* (1973). Pacino has been successful at portraying homosexuals in films like *Dog Day Afternoon* (1975) and *Hustling* (1980). Hoffman plays at transvestitism in *Tootsie* (1982) and autism in *Rain Man* (1988). The identity issues raised by such roles and by these stars' offscreen personas as difficult loners suggest that a pre-Oedipal scenario may have replaced the Oedipally related crises of gender roles acted out by the Method stars of the 1950s. How this shift relates to the changing conventions of romance and marriage is as yet unclear. In the world of commercialized artistry that is Hollywood cinema, however, such changes are always meaningful.

PART IV

Epilogue: Beyond the Couple

THE DESTABILIZATION OF GENDER NORMS AND ACTING AS PERFORMANCE

Theatre is what takes place between spectator and actor.

—Jerzy Grotowski

New ways of modeling or framing social reality may actually be proposed and sometimes legitimated in the very heat of performance, emerging as a sort of artifact or popular creativeness.

—Victor Turner

In recent years acceptable outlets for sexuality have broadened so that the heterosexual couple is no longer seen as the sole norm in American society. Homosexuality, promiscuity, and other nontraditional forms of sexual expression have gained wide currency, aided by the premium that advertisers have put on eroticism in any form. As Estelle Freedman and John D'Emilio have stated: "The logic of consumer capitalism pushed the erotic beyond the boundaries of the monogamous couple as entrepreneurs played with erotic impulses and affluent youth pursued their pleasures outside the marital bond" (324–25). This aggrandizement of sexual satisfaction for its own sake tended to divorce it from intense psychological relationships; instead, the modern view of sex insists "that physical and spiritual passion have little to do with one another" (Robinson 144). In response to these new ways of thinking, ideas about marriage itself have evolved so that the companionate model has come to be viewed less as a lifetime partnership and more as a means to achieve an ephemeral ideal of personal fulfillment. As Jeffrey Weeks observes, "Marriage was an alliance built increasingly along the lines of sexual attraction and emotional compatibility rather than an open-ended commitment for life" (*Sex, Politics and Society* 274).

Hollywood has responded to these changes in more than one way. It has continued to make films in the traditional realistic mode while modifying their content in such a way as to validate the new life-styles (for example, *Looking for Mr. Goodbar* (1977), about promiscuity; *The Boys in the Band* (1970), about homosexuality). The movies have also followed the trend toward instant emotional gratification by placing greater emphasis on sensation-filled momentary thrills and less on carefully plotted character development. But most significantly, in terms of the concerns of the present study, new theories of acting have emerged, for the preoccupation with the self that has led to altered attitudes toward sexuality has also led to altered conceptions of theatrical character.

Recent film theory has sometimes characterized these new approaches as modernist or progressive, but such formalistic definitions are not framed to capture fully the altered interaction between text and audience that most defines these radical acting styles, which actively attempt to involve the spectator in the drama. These new techniques all share an antirealist bias: rather than creating a complete world that the audience shares vicariously by means of a "fourth wall" convention, they approach the film as a performance in which the audience does not witness a representation but participates in a presentation. All the major theorists of modern performance, including Antonin Artaud, Jerzy Grotowski, and their American followers Joseph Chaikin, Richard Schechner, and Herbert Blau, operate from this assumption.[1]

In what follows, I will consider the impact of three of the most influential of these new styles on exemplary Hollywood films that take up the issue of the newly problematic nature of the romantic couple. The first of these styles, associated with Viola Spolin and the Second City Performance Troupe, foregrounds improvisation. Unlike Method acting, however, it uses this technique not to probe the inner depths of the actor/character's psyche in the interests of a more persuasive illusion of realism but to foreground the process of character creation itself in the interests of forging a communal bond between performer and audience. In this approach, the characters become caricatured objects of satiric humor, and the emphasis is placed on the spirit of community that emerges between the actors and spectators who have collaborated in such exposés. *Nashville* is probably the best-known Hollywood film to make use of this style.

Like the Second City approach, the absurdist style also foregrounds the process of character creation, but it does not do so in order to establish a spirit of community between actors and audiences. Rather, it treats the performance event itself as a kind of game between actor, filmmakers, and audiences. Absurdism posits character as a construct constituted from a series of roles. Absurdist actors dramatize the absence of a psychic center to the characters they play by using the occasion of their performance to problematize the relationship between role-playing and identity. The absurdist emphasis on the self as a series of roles parallels poststructuralist notions of fragmented subjectivity. It also has much in common with Erving Goffman's sociological studies of role-playing as a mainstay of all behavior, as well as with recently popular theories of narcissism that posit a syndrome of fragmented, "inauthetic" personality structures. If the Stanislavskian actor typically appears to be caught up in a pattern of Freudian neurosis, the absurdist actor is more commonly understood as schizophrenic, literally a "split" personality. Audiences are placed at the center of this split insofar as the performance event is based on principles of equivocation and ambivalence. A Hollywood film that balances on the edge of realism to create the equivocal, ambivalent effect of absurdist performance is *House of Games*.

Yet another approach to acting that foregrounds the performance event has been put forward by Bertolt Brecht, who advised actors to join together with the audience as observers of the characters they played. Unlike Spolin, however, Brecht did not advocate this strategy for the therapeutic purpose of creating communal ties between actors and audiences but rather for the political purpose of laying bare the characters' ideological motivations. Brechtian "alienation effect" acting is most commonly associated with the films of Jean-Luc Godard, but the style is also exploited in the recent Hollywood production *Do the Right Thing*.

Second City in Hollywood: Nashville

The Second City began staging its improvised comedy reviews in Chicago during the 1950s in a coffee house serving the University of Chicago community. Like Method acting, the Second City approach to performance relied heavily on improvisation, but its premises were quite different. The style was developed through the efforts of early group members Paul Sills and David Shepard, and it has been perpetuated through the years by Del Close, Josephine Forsberg, and Bernard

Sahlins (the group's impresario). Based most directly on the theories of Sills's mother Viola Spolin, who was later to publish her ideas in a book entitled *Improvisation for the Theatre*, the Second City style also drew from the traditions of commedia dell'arte as well as from the theories of Brecht by way of the politically minded David Shepard, whose goal was to create an American people's theater (Sweet 2).

From Brecht came a commitment to social satire and the concept of characters as social types rather than complex individuals. These types were defined by what Brecht called social "gests," a coinage that combined the meanings of *gesture* and *gist*. Brecht sought to separate the identities of the actors from those of the characters they played (the famous "alienation effect"). To further the alienation effect, Brecht advocated short, disjointed scenes rather than a single, flowing narrative, and he introduced music as a way of further cutting off the audience's identification with the characters. Rather than identifying themselves with the characters they portrayed, Brechtian actors were encouraged to identify with the audience as observers of these characters. "The audience identifies itself with the actor as being an observer," Brecht wrote, "and accordingly develops his attitude of observing or looking on" (93). To foster the intimacy between actor and audience, Brecht envisioned a coffee-house atmosphere where people would be exposed to theater while eating and drinking. Thus, he reasoned, theater could position itself as a part of everyday life rather than as a world apart. Second City took up all these suggestions, developing short, satirical scenes in a cabaret setting. The group fostered collaboration between actors and audience by creating its scenes from audience suggestions.

Such Brechtian techniques were combined at Second City with the theories of Viola Spolin, whose "theater games" were originally conceived as therapeutic exercises to free the expressive potential of ordinary people. Spolin's notion of improvisation as a group-oriented game built around a predetermined structure (or story) originated with commedia dell'arte and had little to do with the Method's emphasis on affective memory. While affective memory technique focused on the individual actor, Spolin's theater games involved a group working together. "A healthy group relationship demands a number of individuals working interdependently to complete a given project with full individual participation and personal contribution," she wrote. "There must be group agreement on the rules of the game and individual interaction moving forward the objective of the game if the game is to be played" (9, 5). Unlike Brecht, for whom the theatrical experience ultimately emanated from the author-playwright, Spolin's theater was defined as a spontaneous collaborative enterprise. For her, as Paul Sills was later to put it, theater games were a way of developing "the consciousness of a community" (Sweet 17).

Spolin's concept of improvisation as a structured group activity also encompassed the audience. Unlike Stanislavskian performance, which aimed for an effect of documentarylike realism by ignoring the spectators, Spolin's more theatrically oriented theories encouraged the actor to include the audience in the performance. For her, the audience has to be an active participant in the theater game: "If [the audience is] to be part of this group agreement, they cannot be thought of as a single mass to be pulled hither and yon by the nose, nor should they have to live someone else's life story (even if for one hour), nor identify with the actors and play out tired, handed down emotions through them" (13).[2]

At Second City, characters and scenes are composed by the actors from the audience's suggestions, and the audience's laughter and other responses help to determine the direction that the improvisation takes. Where Method-oriented characters emerge from the depths of the actors' psyches, Second City characters are drawn from the actors' understanding of social types. Whereas the intense audience identification fostered by Method performances is best achieved in the context of complex, melodramatic, realistically drawn plots involving close romantic and familial conflicts that gradually reveal the interior conflicts of one central character, Second City performance styles are best suited to short, satirical skits in which the spectators enjoy recognizing social foibles that a group of actors show them by caricaturing recognizable social types. Where a Method performance seeks emotional "truth," the Second City performance aims for acute social observation.

Second City associates improvisation with cleverness. Bernard Sahlins has stated, "I'd rather have someone with an academic background than a theatrical one, because our actors are also our writers. The man with an academic background uses his head and knows what to say" (McCrohan 75). Interviews with former members of the troupe confirm that Sahlins practiced this principle in his hiring procedures. Alumni from the early years, in particular, recall being intimidated by the quick-wittedness of their fellow performers. "When you're in Second City, you read every paper, every magazine, every book," recalls former Second City actor Jack Burns. "You have to—in order to respond to the improv suggestions." (McCrohan 74) This emphasis on quick-wittedness is evident in the group's audition practices, which include a procedure called "five through the door." In "five through the door" an actor is expected to come onstage as a character, exit, and come back immediately as another five times. Such rapid transformations would be unthinkable in the context of the Actors Studio approach, where a single scene could involve hours of preparation.

The audience's involvement with such cleverness was extremely close in the early years, when University of Chicago students came to see skits about the University and about intellectual life generally. Later, when the group began to broaden its appeal, the close rapport between performer and audience became more problematic. An instance of this breakdown is reported by Second City historian Donna McCrohan:

> The Second City offered satire with a biting edge. It assumed the intelligence of its audience. It addressed people who laughed at references to Dada and Wittgenstein's Vienna. It took on local issues and personalities, such as Loyal Davis, father of future first lady Nancy Reagan. Says Darden: "He was a brilliant surgeon. That's why his reputation was so powerful. He would purposely humiliate not students but doctors who were training with him, in public, frequently. Davis is a fairly common name, so one thing we repeated quite a bit, Barbara would say to me, 'You can't get along with anybody.' And I would say, 'I can get along with Dr. Davis, and nobody can get along with him, he's such a nut.' Invariably five or six doctors in the audience would know exactly who I was talking about. And University of Chicago students were in the audience. When they laughed, the whole audience would laugh with them. They probably thought people were laughing at the way I said *nut*." (57–58)

Despite such occasional lapses in the rapport between audiences and performers, the format of actors responding to audience suggestions ensured that the audience would remain intimately involved with all Second City improvisations. Mike Nichols and Elaine May, perhaps the most brilliant improvisers from the early days of the group, excelled at a characteristic Second City routine in which the audience is asked to supply a first line and a last line and the actors improvise a skit that begins and ends as the audience has directed. This routine encapsulates Spolin's directives regarding the active role assigned to the audience and a structure or goal of the improvisational "game" shared by both actors and the people for whom they are performing.

When Second City actors moved from theater to film and television, the aspect of their performance style that involved interaction with an audience was largely lost, because the audience could no longer be part of the act. Many, like Mike Nichols, Elaine May, Alan Arkin, Paul Mazursky, Larry Tucker, John Belushi, Valerie Harper, and Shelley Long, went on to have relatively conventional careers as comic writers, actors, and directors. Some Second City alumni, who performed on television programs like *SCTV* and *Saturday Night Live*, exploited the less-controlled production procedures of television and the revue format to reproduce in part the group-centered improvisational spirit and the social satire that they had learned at Second City. But they still lacked the active audience participation that made Second City improvisation so compelling as it was practiced in a theater context.

The first major film effort mounted by Second City alumni, Theodore J. Flicker's 1965 *The President's Analyst*, starred, among others, Severn Darden, a founding member of the group and perhaps its single most accomplished improvisational talent. Though *The President's Analyst* carried on the satirical tradition of the troupe by lampooning the telephone company and the Secret Service, it made no attempt at reproducing an improvisational feeling. Elaine May's *Mikey and Nicky* (1976), starring Peter Falk and Method-influenced John Cassevetes, made extensive use of improvisation, but the effect was closer to Stanislavsky than to Second City. Director Henry Jaglom, another Second City alumnus, captured the feeling of Second City–style improvisation more successfully in films like *Sitting Ducks* (1980) and *Someone to Love* (1987), but he too failed to achieve the sense of a cooperative group endeavor made possible by a live audience.

It remained for Robert Altman to assimilate most fully the Second City agenda into commercial Hollywood filmmaking. Though Altman has never himself been associated with Second City, he has employed a number of actors who were trained there, including Roger Bowen, Ann Ryerson, Barbara Harris, and Paul Dooley, evidently finding their approach congenial with his own vision. (In addition, according to Mark Rydell, Second City's Larry Tucker coauthored his characterization of gangster Marty Augustine in Altman's 1973 *The Long Goodbye*

[Wexman, "An Interview with Mark Rydell"].) All Altman's films are characterized by improvisational effects, signaled by ungrammatical sentences, broken-off phrases, unclear diction, and overlapping dialogue. Especially in his comedies, Altman's approach to improvisation closely parallels that of Second City, emphasizing satire, the observation of social types, and group interaction (Cardullo).

Because acting styles figure so centrally in the creation of meaning in many Altman films, a performance-centered model is well suited to describe them. Other conceptual categorizations that have been applied to Altman's work, such as self-reflexive, progressive, and art cinema, are oriented toward descriptions of visual style, and thus have difficulty dealing with the centrality of acting and performance in his oeuvre. Of the critics who have responded to the performance aspect of his films, Maurice Yacowar has detailed the variety of ways in which Altman uses actors, from associating specific character types with particular actors to establish meaning intertextually to exploiting the personas of established stars in unexpected ways; and Robert Self has defined Altman's idiosyncratic presence as an auteur in terms of a spirit of collaboration between director, actors, and crew.

Altman's films begin the process of actively involving the audience in the performance by deconstructing the classical Hollywood model. In most Hollywood films, as is well known, director-authors erase the overt signs of their position as the text's enunciating presence in order to encourage the spectator to become closely involved with a reified point of view in relation to a narrative posed as realistic. As we have seen, such a close, uncritical identification with the image on the screen can be highly erotic; hence, many film stars have found themselves the objects of moviegoers' romantic fantasies. Altman's productions consistently thwart this process of identification between a passive spectator and an invisible, godlike author through references—often joking ones—to the filmmaking process and the people who have taken part in it; partly for this reason, his films are noticeably lacking in erotic charge. Altman's cinema continually reminds its audience that the director is directing and the actors are acting. By thus making the audience members conscious of their position as an audience, these films speak in Brechtian fashion to the spectators' conscious more than to their unconscious. The spectator is thereby "freed," so to speak, from the film's seductive power. In this way, the viewer is transformed from a position of passively spying on the intimate affairs of others to actively participating in a performance event.

As I have suggested, this shift in the audience's role corresponds to the changing cultural climate in which Hollywood films are made. Where the classical Hollywood film has been largely taken up with stories of heterosexual romance, Altman's films, created during a period when the ideal of the heterosexual couple was being radically challenged by the new ethic of sexual freedom, depict a fragmented world in which romantic bonding is no longer seen as providing the core of social stability. When Altman does deal with couples, they do not conform to Hollywood ideals either in appearance or in the nature of their romantic interactions (for example, the gawky, oddly disconnected couples in *Thieves Like Us* [1974], *A Perfect Couple* [1979], and *Beyond Therapy* [1987]). Often, his films analyze the breakdown of the couple while seeking to re-create the ideal of a community by redefining the concept in terms of the bond created between actors, technicians, and audience members in the course of the filmic performance itself—in much the same way as Viola Spolin envisioned the creation of a community in the theater. These celebrations of new configurations of community may have languished during the return to traditional family values during the 1980s, but they flourished in the freewheeling era of the seventies.

The film in which Altman most fully develops the Second City–like principle of a community created between filmmakers and audience is *Nashville*, a production that features Second City actress Barbara Harris and self-consciously casts itself in the form of a genre that has traditionally foregrounded the problematics of performances and their audiences—the Hollywood musical (Feuer, Altman). In *Nashville* a fictional presidential candidate, Hal Phillip Walker, comes to Nashville with his advance man John Triplette (Michael Murphy) to promote his candidacy in the Tennessee primary by staging an extravaganza featuring country-and-western stars. As in most "putting on the show" musicals, the plot of *Nashville* is a slight affair, functioning mainly as a means of introducing performers and songs.

Yet *Nashville*'s story line is even looser than that of most other musicals. The Panavision frame is often filled with activity that creates ambiguity about where the "main" action is located. Moreover, the film includes many scenes that are purely gratuitous in that they do not even lead into a song, such as that of the self-styled BBC reporter Opal (Geraldine Chaplin) apostrophizing wrecked automobiles, or suburban-matron-cum-gospel singer Linnea Reese (Lily Tomlin) describing a friend's injury to an unidentified listener, or the pantomimed performance by Albuquerque (Barbara Harris) at an auto race. Altman is reputed to have shot many more scenes than ultimately appear in the finished work, and he talked at one point about recreating his production as a six- or eight-hour television miniseries. He also favored the idea of creating two *Nashvilles* for theatrical release, which he intended to call *Nashville Red* and *Nashville Blue*, using the same beginning and ending for each but different middles. The two films were to be screened at theaters on alternate nights (Wexman, Interview with Martin Starger).

Not surprisingly, then, *Nashville* projects an arbitrary, aleatory quality that is far removed from the character-centered stories of the classical style. By contrast, *Nashville*'s story appears to be driven by the multifarious skills of actors rather than the "logical" motivation of characters; that is, by a desire to show actors executing clever turns—riffs, or "lazzi" as they are called in the commedia dell'arte—or to show actors confronting what appear to be improvisatory challenges, as when the Panavision composition shows Barnett (Allen Garfield) reacting to an amateur photographer who enters the frame in the midst of a quarrel that he is having with Triplette.

Such an interest in presenting actors *as actors* is consistent with the Second City approach in which the cleverness and social observation that the actor employs in creating a character are what is enjoyed. Altman's foregrounding of actors also speaks to the group orientation of Second City insofar as his decentered narrative and flat Panavision compositions reflect fragments of the stories of many different character types that are not bound together into a tightly knit unity by a director-author but rather respond to strong creative contributions made by a group of performers. The actor as a creator of character is announced in *Nashville* in a variety of ways. The appearances of Elliott Gould and Julie Christie as "themselves" remind the spectator of their roles as actors in other Altman films. The burns on Ronee Blakely's body are made part of the biography of the character that she plays. Karen Black plays a singer called Connie White. Further, the film's publicity stressed that the actors wrote many of their own lines. Ronee Blakely is said to have composed the monologue that marks the onstage emotional breakdown of her character Barbara-Jean. Barbara Baxley has been widely credited with creating the monologue about the Kennedys delivered by her character Lady Pearl. And *Nashville*'s concluding credits announce the role of many of the performers in writing songs for the film. Even the production crew is positioned within the *Nashville* performance as creative contributors: music director Richard Baskin portrays an inept musician called Frog, and the film's publicist Sue Barton "plays" a show business publicist called Sue Barton. The effect of all these authorial presences is to create a work that speaks in multiple voices, as an interacting group rather than as an invisible and indivisible God.

Of course, this group must have a leader to orchestrate its individual performances. As director, Altman performs this function; but here again, he announces his presence openly rather than making his machinations appear as an unseen hand guiding the text. The film's opening credit sequence is pitched at the viewer in the manner of a late-night television commercial, directly addressing the audience in the crassest terms as consumers of the *Nashville* product that Altman has created. The first scenes in the recording studio remind us that we are watching another type of recorded performance. Further, as John Belton has shown, Altman's predilection for zoom shots represents him as a human consciousness rather than as a part of nature.

A more significant aspect of Altman's presence concerns his approach to genre as a game played between author and audience.[3] As in Second City, where the audience sometimes participates in a skit by determining its first and last lines, the audience of *Nashville* is assumed to have, if not created, at least assented to the film's generic presumptions by agreeing to enter the theater. For musicals, these include the following: A show will be mounted in the course of the narrative, perhaps partly as a result of the machinations of a clever servant figure. It is likely that, in the process, an established star will become incapacitated and will be replaced by a new star. A renewed community will be formed around the production. Altman fulfills these generic expectations, but he does so in unexpected ways. In *Nashville* the clever servant is a political advance man and the established star is incapacitated by an assassin rather than a broken leg. In addition, other moments in the film such as the humiliating striptease performed by Sueleen Gay (Gwen Welles) are far darker than is customary in musical comedies. These departures from accepted generic codes signal Altman's willingness to go to extreme lengths to outwit the expectations of his audience in the generic game.

Altman's self-conscious approach to generic narrative is signaled in the presence of two author-surrogate figures within the film. These figures, Opal with her ever-present microphone and the mute Tricycle

Man, split the guiding function of the directorial presence into separate audio and visual components. Opal, like Altman, is an outsider to Nashville, and the glib intrusiveness that characterizes her attempt to capture the city comments ironically on Altman's own "outsider's" interpretation of the country-music scene. Yet Opal addresses Altman's thematic concerns with undeniable insight when she notes that Nashville's characters are "all wrong for Bergman" and when she anticipates the film's climactic assassination by observing, "I believe that Madame Pearl and all these people here in this country who carry guns are the real assassins. Because they stimulate the other innocent people who eventually are the ones who pull the trigger."

Opal's comically offensive loquaciousness contrasts with the muteness of the Tricycle Man, who is a purely visual presence. Altman often uses him as a transition device: the camera tracks in and out of scenes with the movement of the tricycle, thereby substituting a purely formal bridge for a more traditional plot-related one. With his magical powers, the Tricycle Man recalls the trickster figure that appears in many folkloric traditions. The Tricycle Man's ability to transform one object to another has significant similarities to Altman's ability to change one scene into another. Altman's transitions are thus positioned as "tricks" performed by a director-magician rather than part of a "logical" sequence motivated by a director-psychologist.

By identifying himself with the Tricycle Man's magic, Altman signals a more ominous side of his function as storyteller: like the Tricycle Man, part of Altman's skill as an entertainer is his facility at hoodwinking the audience, surprising us about the outcome of his story by tricking us into misplacing our attention. The major surprise of *Nashville* is the assassination of Barbara-Jean. As a responsible storyteller, Altman prefigures this incident a number of times through the narrative: by Opal's comment, by the presence of guns in various scenes, and by Lady Pearl's memories of the Kennedy brothers. This sense of foreboding is initially associated with the soldier, Pvt. Kelly (Scott Glenn). Tom (Keith Carradine) asks Pvt. Kelly at the airport if he's killed anyone lately. Later the soldier steals into Barbara-Jean's hospital room as the guard on duty discusses his gun with the nurse at the desk. But at one point in the film Pvt. Kelly reveals that his obsession with Barbara-Jean is a benign one. At the hospital he tells Mr. Green that "my momma saved her life. They used to live next door to each other. My mama's the one that put out the flames. She always loved Barbara-Jean more 'n anything: she's still keepin' a scrapbook on her. Only thing she said to me when I joined up was 'Son, when you're doin' your travels, I want you to see Barbara-Jean. You don't have to say nothing' about me or nothin' like that. I just want you to see Barbara-Jean.' So that's what I'm doin'." Following this speech the camera cuts to Opal explaining her theory of assassination to Triplette. Then there is another cut to the lonely drifter Kenny (David Hayward) arguing with his mother on the telephone. From this point on, Kenny, the actual assassin, is shown a number of times in close-up obsessively gazing at Barbara-Jean.

Altman is here offering a conventional Oedipally based "explanation" for Kenny's rage against powerful women, contrasting his conflicted relationship with his mother with Pvt. Kelly's harmonious one.[4] However, it is an explanation that few audience members are likely to notice, for when Pvt. Kelly speaks out to Mr. Green (Keenan Wynn), the old man has just heard the news about his wife's death. Empathizing with the shock and sorrow of Mr. Green, the audience, in its role as onlooker, may lose sight of its role as a participant in the game of theatrical plotting. By diverting our attention at a crucial moment, Altman, like a magician, has tricked us into missing the significance of essential information. This is an aspect of game-based theatricality in which the audience is placed in opposition to the director-author. The game exposes the pitfalls implicit in the spectator's tendency to become a passive onlooker in the presence of a drama that it too easily accepts as realistic.

This aggressive attitude toward the audience of the film is echoed by the treatment of audiences within the film. *Nashville*'s audiences are characterized as adoring (at the airport), hostile (at the Opry Belle concert in which Barbara-Jean breaks down), exploitative (at the smoker), and seductive (at the Exit Inn, where Tom performs "I'm Easy"). This ambiguity is foregrounded, for audience members are often also characters, and at times the film seems confused about which is which. On at least two occasions we are told that there is a celebrity in the audience at a moment when the camera is looking at the "wrong" celebrity, evidently misunderstanding which member of the audience is about to be singled out and transformed into a character. Often groups of characters are part of audiences on the stage itself. In the Sunday-morning church montage distinctions between audiences and performers are further dissolved as we see Haven Hamilton as a choir boy and hymn-chanting congregations as part of a religious performance.

This confusion about what it means to be a member of an audience reflects a larger problematic having to do with the corresponding status of characters—and ultimately with the ambiguity of identity itself. The spectator tends to adopt the role of onlooker in relation to realistically drawn characters such as Barbara-Jean. But *Nashville*'s more caricatured portrayals tend to equate characters with social role rather than psychic depth. The distance between actor and character adds to the audience's sense of the character's artificiality, especially in scenes that we take as having been composed by the actors for comic effect, such as Albuquerque's pantomimed performance at the automobile race or Haven Hamilton's songs.

The destabilized relationship between actor and character is at its most ambiguous during the much-praised scene in which Keith Carradine as Tom sings "I'm Easy." This musical performance describes the position of certain of the women in the audience to whom it is addressed far more accurately than it does that of the self-absorbed character who sings it, thereby giving rise to questions about both the character and the actor/performer (figs. 6.1, 6.2, 6.3, 6.4, and 6.5). If seen as composed by Tom, the song is either deeply ironic, deeply cynical, or simply another part of the folk artist's repertoire of seductive clichés put on for the occasion. If seen as composed by Carradine, it is either one of the above or the sincere outpouring of an actor whose material is simultaneously being twisted into unforeseen shapes by the scene's director. Thus the question of what is being expressed is complicated by the question of who is speaking and with what motives. The audience's involvement in these ambiguities is part of Altman's "theater game."

The position of actors as authors is more blatantly stated in the "roles" played by Elliott Gould, Julie Christie, and Sue Barton as "themselves." When Gould is introduced to Linnea Reese's husband, Del (Ned Beatty), Del returns to him moments later to say, "I'm sorry; I didn't know who you were." Gould's reply, "I haven't changed," is at this point perceived as a deeply paradoxical one. Although it is true in one sense, it is false in another. For Del, Gould *has* changed insofar as his social position in the group is now different. At such moments *Nashville* questions how far identity may legitimately be construed as social role.

For many of the film's characters, such as Albuquerque and L.A. Joan, the changing social roles that are constructed by changing one's name or one's costume *are* identity. Lacking a consistent core of selfhood centered on the development of realtionship to others measured over time, such individuals also lack any grounds for commitment to whatever choices they may make. Thus their "freedom" is meaningless. In such a world self-esteem comes not from the perpetuation of one's "good name" but from the self-enhancement that arises from the power inherent in having one's name known by others—for whatever reason. If such yearning after celebrity is the product of a sense of individuality that overrides the claims of community, it is paradoxically an individuality that, by cutting off its surroundings, has deprived itself of any means of cohering.

This confused sense of personhood is associated in *Nashville* with a society where momentary thrill-seeking has replaced disciplined, goal-directed activity. In popular and influential books of social criticism published during the 1970s Richard Sennett and Christopher Lasch described this impasse as cultural narcissism. As Sennett puts it, "The sheer fact of commitment on a person's part seems to him or her to limit the opportunities for enough experience to know who he or she is. Every relationship under the sway of narcissism becomes less fulfilling the longer the partners are together" (9). Sennett sees this principle as operating in the larger world to create what he calls an "intimate vision of society" (5). In such a world the role of audience takes on a special meaning, for "the frustration this audience experiences in their own lives arouses in them a need, and that need they project onto the public actor" (196). In *Nashville* actors respond to this need by demonstrating their ability to render perfectly controlled public personas. They perform themselves, writing and singing their own songs, and singing them in a style that emphasizes not so much the training of a superior voice as the capacity to modulate and pattern the strong emotional content of the subjects that they address, like infidelity and homelessness. As I have elsewhere argued ("The Rhetoric of Cinematic Improvisation"), the performers represented in *Nashville* possess an unparalleled ability to present "canned" intimacy packaged for public consumption. Their remarks to audiences within the film have a smooth, rehearsed quality even when ostensibly given off-the-cuff: Haven Hamilton welcoming a guest to his "lovely home," Connie White telling a small boy in the front row of the Opry that he can "grow up to be the president," Barbara-Jean delivering an "unplanned" but impeccably modulated speech to her fans at the airport. The comical quality of many of Haven's utterances, in particular, arises from his seemingly boundless ability to trivialize every situation by interjecting his controlled nonsequiturs. When introduced to Julie Christie, for instance, he remarks, "Isn't that something! Just today we were talking about the New Christy Minstrels and now here's Julie Christie!"

Even the appearance of these performers reflects their ability to project control: perfectly coiffed "hairdos" and fluffed-up dresses for the women and intricately beaded and fringed jackets for the men. Connie White's skepticism regarding Julie Christie's claim to stardom, based on her observation that Christie "can't even comb her hair," is thus significant; for Connie, being a successful performer necessitates the kind of controlled presentation of the body that she herself practices on her own person. (She does not consider the possibility that Christie may be exercising a similar control over her appearance, but one based on an emerging discourse rather than the residual one to which she herself is committed.)

The rehearsed, lifeless quality of these responses stands in contrast to the performers' private moments, when less-coherent expressive modes come to the fore, breaking out from behind the masks that the stars wear as public figures. Then the chasm between spontaneous feeling and the conventional role-playing demanded by society is painfully apparent, and the characters flounder in their imposed isolation, unable to adapt their personal emotions to the inflexible social structure surrounding them. Such moments give the effect of having been improvised, in contrast to the apparently tightly scripted scenes that are played out in front of audiences. The awkwardly tentative quarrel between Barbara-Jean and her husband, Barnett, in their room at the hospital is one instance of seemingly improvised private behavior; the memories of Lady Pearl about the Kennedy brothers, which she brokenly recounts to the embarrassed Opal, is another. Perhaps the most dramatic instance of this clash between inchoate private feeling and rigid social forms occurs during Barbara-Jean's performance at the Opry Belle, when she falters in the delivery of her rehearsed routine and launches helplessly into improvised personal reminiscences. At this break in the customary procedure, the audience within the film erupts furiously, deeply insulted at this rupture in the established pattern.

The residual discourse to which Nashville still gives lip service is based on an ideal of the nuclear family as the center of communal life. As Thomas Elsaesser has observed, "The film's secret dynamic comes from being structured around the disintegration of the family as a viable emotional unit, and the massive reassertion of the fantasy of the family and togetherness on the level of the spectacle" (37). The family at the level of spectacle is an ideal conspicuously promulgated in Barbara-Jean's song "My Idaho Home" and in Haven's predilection for introducing his son during his performances. In response to the choreographed gun-twirling put on by the young girls of the Tennessee Baton Twirling Institute, Haven remarks, "You'll soon be grown up and be lookin' for a husband." This fatuous prediction is made absurd by what we see of the women of Nashville, none of whom seems at all concerned about finding a husband or with keeping the husband she has. The ideal of the stable heterosexual couple created through the acceptance of an ideology of romantic love—the ideal so vigorously promoted by Hollywood in the past—has disintegrated in *Nashville*. Sexual promiscuity and infidelity are contemplated with equanimity by virtually all the characters. Romantic love itself has been transformed into a cliché by Tom and an exercise in self-indulgence by Mary (Cristina Raines), a member of the trio that Tom performs with and one of his many bed partners. If such depictions foreclose the possibility of the traditional couple as a reified ideal, the Sunday-morning church scenes undercut the ideal of family togetherness that follows from it, for these scenes reveal that many couples, including Linnea and Del Reese and Haven and Lady Pearl, hold differing religious beliefs.

Without a socially sanctioned basis on which to ground their identities, Altman's characters have no clear limits or center. None of *Nashville*'s stars or would-be stars gives evidence of possessing a unified self defined by a cohesive personal history and well-formulated goals. The resulting sense of fragmentation and purposelessness is shared by the *Nashville* community as a whole, which, like the characters, seems to lack any access to a coherent and meaningful past. Like the songwriters who remember "My Idaho Home" and old love affairs, Nashville itself has created a past: the rebuilt Parthenon, a visual reference to a proud historical heritage that functions as an analogue to the vulgarized American history that Haven proposes in his song "We Must Be Doin' Somethin' Right to Last Two Hundred Years." Released in the year preceding America's Bicentennial, Altman's film reveals the way in which changing American values have led to the loss of any sense of personal or communal historical continuity. The indifference of the audience at the Parthenon to the fate of Barbara-Jean is the most dramatic indication of the culture's preoccupation with the excitement of the moment at the expense of the past, even when the past is immediately—and shatteringly—available to them.

Though the film's final scene of performance at the Parthenon suggests the shallowness of modern America, *Nashville*'s portrait of contemporary American culture is not wholly nihilistic. This is true because the scene also offers the audience the possibility of a renewed sense of community, one based not on the voyeuristic participation in an aesthetic of romantic love but on the shared experience of actors and audience in the creation of a socially affirming theatrical spectacle. The scene thus, in one of its aspects at least, exemplifies Victor Turner's observation about "the role of collective, innovatory behavior, of crowds generating new ways of framing and modeling the social reality which presses on them in their daily lives" (Benamou 46). During Albuquerque's final song, all the couples in the film reunite and leave the scene, clearing the way for a new community which is not based on the concept of heterosexually paired individuals. The stage is given over to women and blacks, groups who emerged during the 1960s and early seventies as voices asserting their right to occupy a space in the front and center of American life. The Parthenon audience is made up of anonymous spectators, many of whom are children—a more empathetic group than any other audience yet put forward in the narrative (figs. 6.6 and 6.7). *Nashville*'s final close-up shows a policewoman. Though she functions as a conventional symbol of restored order, she is also a woman, a member of one of the newly emerging groups that is here celebrated (fig. 6.8).[5]

The film has prepared for this celebration by its earlier depiction of issues involving blacks and women. The characters in *Nashville* who are seen as possessing the greatest dignity and integrity are members of these two groups: Tommy Brown and Linea Reese. When Tommy is verbally accosted by the inebriated Wade for being an "Oreo cookie," the discomfort that this challenge engenders arises in part because of the unaccustomed presence of a vital political issue in the midst of Nashville's prevailing atmosphere of saccharine homilies. The earlier humiliation of Wade's co-worker Sueleen at the smoker, where she is forced to strip, focuses on the institutionalized victimization of a woman at the hands of male voyeurs who control the community's money and power (figs. 6.9, 6.10, 6.11, and 6.12). At such moments, Altman's theater games are less playful than satirical, touching on major contemporary social issues. Thus the film's final portrait of a changed society, with blacks and women occupying the center of the frame, appears as a legitimate conception.

In the final shots of the Parthenon, Altman effaces his own enunciative presence and those of his actors, adopting the "invisible" style of classical realism. As a result, the film's audience can momentarily merge with the audience within the fiction and participate vicariously in a communal sing-along. The words of the song are disheartening: "You may say that I ain't free, but it don't worry me." Yet the communal spirit that prevails has been actively invoked throughout the narrative. The community that Viola Spolin envisioned as the product of spontaneous actor-audience collaboration with a theater game has much in common with this cinematic enactment of the performance experience.

The Couple as Cliché: Boy "Gets" Girl in Mamet's House of Games

During the 1970s, the American theater was transformed by such phenomena as Happenings, the Living Theater, and Performance Art. The subsequent years have been viewed as something of a reaction to this period of radical experimentation, and critics like Robert Brustein, Dennis Carroll, and Richard Eder have positioned David Mamet, along with playwrights such as John Guare, Beth Henley, and Marsha Norman, as part of a return to realism. Mamet's work often features elements that lend credence to such a categorization, including *in medias res* openings, quotidian settings, dialogue spiced with the street argots of marginal social groups, and a thematic focus on the social evils of the American capitalist enterprise. Nonetheless, Mamet himself vehemently denies any adherence to realist principles, preferring to situate his oeuvre in the tradition of absurdist drama (his play *Glengarry Glen Ross*, for example, is dedicated to Harold Pinter). The appropriateness of this categorization is borne out by a striking feature that characterizes both his stage and film productions: his self-conscious treatment of actors.[6]

A book on acting written by Melissa Bruder and other former students of Mamet states, "In the theatre, character is an *illusion* created by the words of the playwright and the physical actions of the actor" (74). C.W.E. Bigsby has observed that the characters Mamet creates for the stage are frequently storytellers. The analogy between their roles as tellers of tales and the storytelling role of the playwright himself suggests the characters' own status as part of a story rather than as believable representations of actual people. Moreover, the kind of stories that they tell calls into question the place of authentic inner feelings in relation to self-aggrandizing or manipulative role-playing. In *Sexual Perversity in Chicago*, for instance, Bernie tries to impress his younger friend, Dan, by telling him stories about his past sexual exploits. These anecdotes begin plausibly but gradually become more and more fantastic. The audience is left unsure about how—or if—these narratives relate to any actual experience.

Such stories are closely related to other extended statements which are cast in the form of contemplative ruminations about the characters' beliefs and values. In *Glengarry Glen Ross*, for example, Richard Roma, a real estate salesman, delivers a long, philosophical speech to someone he has just met. "How can I be secure?" Roma asks rhetorically. "Through amassing wealth beyond all measure? No. And what's beyond all measure? That's sickness. That's a trap. There is no measure. Only greed" (48–49). Roma's intelligence and the action of the play as a whole give this statement the force of genuine insight. Later, however, it is seen as part of Roma's sales pitch. Nonetheless, the personal value system articulated in this speech is not rendered entirely irrelevant by the revelation of commercial motives at its end, for it is excessive in terms of this function. The relationship of utterances like this to an "authentic core" of a character's psyche is ultimately as ambiguous as the meaning of the sexual stories that Bernie tells Dan in *Sexual Perversity*. Ambiguities of this order are generated by characters whose identities cannot be sufficiently defined to stabilize the meaning of what they say. Their "integrity" thus remains an irresolvable issue.

Mamet's plays invariably hold up emotional intimacy as an ideal, yet this ideal is never achieved because his characters are constantly slipping from one role into another. In *American Buffalo* Don betrays his relationship with his adopted son, Bobby, in the interest of making some easy money. And in *Speed-the-Plow* Bob Gould, the new head of a Hollywood studio, betrays his relationship with his longtime associate Charlie Fox because he is briefly seduced by the notion that he can make a socially relevant picture. Such betrayals have long been staple components of dramatic action, but in Mamet's plays these moments of peripetia lack the force of decisive reversal, for the characters never quite "reveal" themselves by such acts.[7] The plays fail to distinguish authentic feeling from expedient role-playing in any satisfactory way; nor do they define the value of what is at stake. Just as the actors are condemned to play roles, so are the characters. Although they often seem confused and frustrated by these roles, which change according to their circumstances and whims, the necessity for playing roles remains inescapable. In Mamet's theater, the actors are characters, but the characters are also actors.

Mamet's preoccupation with role-playing works well on the stage, where an aura of artificiality is in keeping with the conventions of the medium. The movies, however, have traditionally been more closely tied to the conventions of realism. Nonetheless, in recent years Hollywood directors like David Lynch have experimented with the semi-parodic performance styles associated with the absurdist sensibility in films and television shows such as *Blue Velvet* and *Twin Peaks*. And Dennis Bingham has argued that the attitude of slight self-mockery identified with the star persona of Jack Nicholson owes a great deal to the absurdist aesthetic. The filmmaking strategy adopted by Mamet as evidenced thus far has been to adapt absurdist conceptions of acting and character to the norms of classical realistic storytelling by yoking them to longstanding Hollywood traditions like the star system and the romantic couple.

Mamet's 1988 film *Things Change* adheres to the Hollywood traditions of realistic representation in most ways, but it self-consciously undercuts the conventions of the star system in the way that it uses Don Ameche. Throughout his long career Ameche has inhabited a varied series of star images or "roles," most notably that of a debonair playboy during the 1930s and as an elder statesman of the acting profession in the publicity surrounding his 1982 hit *Cocoon*. His stature as a venerable mainstay of the system and his reincarnation in recent years as a character actor lend a special presence to any role that he plays. A conventional casting arrangement would exploit this presence by using Ameche to invest a character conceived of as eminent or legendary with an appropriate aura, as Francis Ford Coppola did with Marlon Brando in *The Godfather* and Carol Reed did with Orson Welles in *The Third Man*. In *Things Change*, however, Ameche plays against type as Gino, a shoeshine man, and this casting decision opens a space between actor and role.

Although such incongruity can occur in more traditional Hollywood productions, Mamet's film thematizes the gap. During the course of the story, Gino himself must act a role; and the role he enacts, that of a powerful Mafia Don, calls for a dignity and self-assurance far more in keeping with the persona of the actor who plays him than with the character of Gino himself. To further complicate this already strained relationship between actor and role, Gino's "character" forms a friendship with another Mafia Don, Joseph Vincent (Robert Prosky). This friendship is based on comments that Gino makes about shining shoes, which Vincent mistakes for allegorical nuggets of wisdom. The resulting intimacy between the two men is therefore largely based on "sincere" statements that are misunderstood. Is such a friendship to be read as meaningful? Or is it invalidated by the fact that it is founded on a rapport based on misconceptions? Like the intimacies portrayed in Mamet's plays, the friendship between Gino and Vincent is at once sincere and false, just as the character of Gino strikes the spectator as both a touching figure and a role acted by Don Ameche. The film's title, *Things Change*, thus refers as much to the spectator's relationship to the characters as it does to the actions portrayed in the narrative.

Mamet's first film, *House of Games*, boasts no star presence as charged as the one that Don Ameche brings to *Things Change*.[8] But Mamet again focuses on the ambiguous status of the self as rendered through performance. *House of Games* dramatizes this issue through its aggressive rejection of yet another Hollywood convention: the couple. The film initially appears to be cast in the mold of the conventional thriller formula in which the hero and heroine find time to fall in love while extricating themselves from a perilous situation. But in Mamet's film, the audience's expectations of romantic fulfillment are frustrated. The plot concerns an elaborate con game in which Dr. Margaret Ford (Lindsay Crouse), a female psychiatrist who has authored a best-selling book, is bilked out of $80,000. In the process Mike (Joe Mantegna), the mastermind behind the con, seduces her. The promise of romance thus turns out to be just part of the con. When Dr. Ford discovers the ruse, she does not attempt to create a romantic partnership with Mike; instead, she murders him.[9]

By emphasizing gender separation, the film establishes the expectation that a romantic heterosexual union will resolve rigid sex-role dichotomies. The milieu in which the aborted romance occurs is defined largely in terms of gender difference. Dr. Ford's world is made up almost entirely of females, and the world of the con men is populated solely by males. This emphasis is repeated in the film's use of contrasting settings: Dr. Ford exists in a professional environment that is modern, brightly lit, and antiseptic, whereas the demimonde inhabited by the con men is run-down, shadowy, and cluttered. The failure of these two spheres to come together is a function of a fundamental incompatibility between men and women which the text both represents and enacts.

Mamet's preoccupation in this film with gender separation and with the problem of the heterosexual couple invites two contradictory modes of interpretation. The film's strategy of balancing conflicting interpretations off against one another is suggested during the credits, which are backed by a Bach fugue, in which two different musical lines run in counterpoint, as well as by its first shot, which focuses on a stone wall made up of ambiguous Rorschach-like patterns. The two conflicting interpretative modes can be labeled the psychoanalytic and the absurdist. They are signaled at varying points in the film by the motifs of the dream and the joke. The conflict of the two readings leads to an interpretive crisis that finally prevents the spectator from enjoying the secure perspective and character identification that characterize realist film.

A psychoanalytic reading would position Dr. Ford as a representative of the "phallic woman," enacting a scenario in which she appropriates male power. Such a reading would point out that she adopts many of the accoutrements of traditional male behavior and that she is strongly identified with writing, the masculine significance of which is suggested at various points throughout the film by repeatedly associating the shape of her pen with such blatantly coded phallic objects as a cigar, a pocket knife, and a gun (figs. 6.13, 6.14, and 6.15). Just as her female patient is understood to have murdered her father before the action begins, Dr. Ford herself later performs an act of overthrowing patriarchal domination when she kills Mike. The psychoanalytic reading would conclude that, because she has assumed the position of the man, she is left at the end of the film without any reason to enter into a heterosexual partnership.

The psychoanalytic reading explains the film's rendering of guilt and the law. Ford lives in torment when she believes herself to have murdered an "innocent" police officer. As a penance for her presumed crime, she has destroyed some of her writing as well as the more "official" writing represented by her medical degree, the source of her professional power. She later discovers, however, that her capacity for guilt is simply one of the vulnerabilities that has allowed the con men to exploit her. Like her patricidal patient, she is imprisoned by it. Her state of enthrallment is telegraphed visually by means of rhymed shots that equate the bars of the young woman's prison cell with the blinds of the psychiatrist's home (figs. 6.16 and 6.17).

This reading finds evidence of the heroine's unbridled phallic power in the very moments at which the spectator expects rehabilitation and repentance. Once Dr. Ford comes to understand the arbitrary and exploitative nature of patriarchal law, her guilt vanishes. Near the film's conclusion, she is accosted in the lobby of a restaurant by an offscreen male voice, which initially appears to be that of yet another policeman who has come to punish her in the name of a system of patriarchal authority more legitimate than that represented by the con men. But the voice is soon revealed as that of an autograph seeker, a fan who provides yet another testimony to the authority of Dr. Ford's writing. By writing "forgive yourself" she author-izes a law of her own (fig. 6.18). In the final moments of the film this self-legitimizing woman steals a gold lighter, a phallic object that she has coveted from the beginning. She has attained a position above the law and above conscience, a state of libidinous freedom that exists beyond the reach of patriarchally derived norms.[10]

Although the evidence for such a reading is clearly marked throughout the film, it is also systematically undermined by a concurrent critique that sees psychoanalysis as perpetrating values that are as meretricious and self-serving as those of the con men. On more than one occasion Dr. Ford's therapeutic efforts are described as a con, once by the psychiatrist herself. But the critique is most tellingly set forth in the film's use of language to position psychoanalytic discourse as both fallible and arbitrary.

Mamet is routinely praised for his ability to draw on specialized idioms, which presumably add to the realism of his work. But the use of such specialized languages holds a further significance as well, for they reveal the value systems of various classes and occupational groups. In recalling his early years, the playwright has stated, "Our schoolyard code of honor recognized words as magical and powerful unto themselves. . . . It was the language of games, the language of an endeavor which is, in its essence, make believe—the language of American business" (*Writing in Restaurants* 3–4). Among other things, the title of *House of Games* refers to business as a game. Elsewhere Mamet has elaborated on this characterization of business by observing that "the code of an institution ratifies us in acting amorally, as any guilt which might arise out of our acts would be borne not by ourselves but shared out through the institution" (Bigsby 123). In *House of Games* two occupationally based institutions—or businesses—are set against each other, that of the con artists and that of psychoanalysis. Each institution possesses its own specialized language, which reflects its special mode of interpreting experience. Mamet calls the authority of the more legitimate interpretive mode of psychoanalysis into question by setting it against the street slang of the con men.

This conflict is centered on the interpretation of slips of the tongue. Dr. Ford makes a number of such slips during the course of the film, and they are variously interpreted. Two occur during conversations with her friend Maria and are given conventional Freudian readings by the older woman. In the first instance, Ford substitutes "pressures" for "pleasures," prompting Maria to suggest that she is working too hard. In the second instance, she substitutes "my father" for "her father," leading Maria to imply that she is overidentifying with her patricidal patient. The model for such interpretive schemes is explicitly set forth early in the film when Ford excitedly explains one of her patient's dreams to Maria. Her explanation centers on the the word *lurg*, which she interprets as *girl* spelled backwards. "*She* is the animal," Ford concludes, thereby claiming to have discovered a privileged key with which she can unlock the inner secrets of the young woman's character.

Such an emphasis on understanding the hidden motivation behind linguistic slippages emanates from a psychoanalytic institution that strives to achieve empathic understanding in the name of therapeutic healing. The validity of this approach, which is based on Freudian dream theory, is called into question later in the film, however, when Ford makes a similar slip while talking to Mike in the airport. She refers to her theft of "your" knife—although she is not "supposed" to know to whom the knife belongs. Mike seizes on this error as quickly as a psychoanalyst would, but he accounts for it using a new set of terms. To him it is not a question of Ford's having made a Freudian slip but of her "cracking out of turn," and he is not interested in analyzing the causes of the mistake but rather in calculating its implications in terms of his own designs. It is significant that the film will not permit a conventionally psychoanalytic reading of this slip; there is no way to determine if it is intentional or unconscious. But such a distinction is irrelevant in terms of Mike's system of interpretation—and in terms of the requirements of the film's plot at this point. As is evident in earlier incidents in which Mike reads slips in body language as "tells," he understands moments of self-betrayal not as opportunities for forging an identificatory rapport between two people, but rather as occasions for seizing an advantage in a relationship that is fundamentally adversarial.[11]

The basic discrepancy between these two systems of interpretation is brought home to Dr. Ford when, tormented by guilt, she impatiently waits for her friend Maria to finish a lecture so that she can seek her advice. Maria's lecture uses the vocabulary of psychoanalysis, but it makes an unexpected point. She states: "Compression, conversion, elaboration are devices for transforming the latent into the manifest in the *joke*." [12] As she utters the word *joke* she gestures for emphasis, thereby shocking Dr. Ford into a waking vision that appears as a montage of images relating to the murder of the police officer which she believes she has committed (figs. 6.19, 6.20, 6.21, and 6.22). The word *joke* has jolted her into the realization that in her dealings with Mike she has entered a radically different world in which language and action are interpreted not therapeutically, as they are in dream analysis, but exploitatively, as part of a hostile joke. She had earlier been forewarned of a possible shift of this sort by Billy, who had challenged her with the query, "What do you think this is? Some dream?" The opposite of a dream, it turns out, is not reality but a joke.

In *House of Games* the incompatible modes of the dream and the joke are played out not only in the clash between the psychiatrist and the con men but also in the ambivalent relationship of the spectator to the text. Mamet's rendering of point of view does not conform to the model posed by classical realism in which the spectator is positioned as though she or he were the enunciative site of the discourse. Rather, in *House of Games* the spectator's participation in the fantasy oscillates between an identification with the characters similar to that which occurs in a dream and a more distanced awareness of the cinematic text as a joke or con perpetrated by the director. These opposing modes of participation are respectively associated with the film's two primary characters, Dr. Ford and Mike. Because Dr. Ford is present in virtually every scene and because her perceptions guide the film's point-of-view strategies, the spectator is led to identify closely with her and to consider her perspective authoritative. [13] However, we are also hindered in this identification. The film's point-of-view techniques are deployed with such stilted emphasis, including a conspicuous use of cut-ins and hand-held camerawork, as to seem hyperbolic. In fact, Mamet's highly stylized mise-en-scène, which features striking lighting effects and the absence of naturalistic background imagery and sounds, represents whatever is shown as if in quotation marks. Symbols are carefully positioned as such and are sometimes even subject to a self-conscious treatment that borders on humor, as in the case of the leaking water pistol (fig. 6.23). Such stylization destabilizes our tendency toward a passive dreamlike identification and demands that we assume a more active, critical stance. We are invited to respond to the film as an entertainment rather than an imitation, and to see our role not as one of identifying with the central character but of anticipating the plots perpetrated by a filmmaker who is understood as a con artist or jokester.[14]

This more absurdist reading of the film as a joke places the spectator in a position not of empathizing with the protagonist but of competing with the director. From this perspective, the psychoanalytic "core" of the story appears as part of a puzzle generated by the text, a con comparable to the one carried out by Mike. Mamet's identification with Mike is reinforced by the film's title, which refers both to the pool room where Mike plies his trade and to the movie theater in which Mamet plies his; as well as by its plot, which takes in the audience as Mike takes in the psychiatrist. Such an association between Mamet and Mike recasts the movie's gender conflict in terms of a struggle between a spectator oriented toward an empathic identification with a female protagonist and a filmmaker oriented toward cunning manipulations analogous to those of the male antagonist.

The spectator's oscillation between empathy and distance is controlled by the film's unconventional approach to acting and characterization. Many of the sequences feature the artificial performance styles identified with the absurdist tradition (which caused a number of reviewers to complain about the film's "bad acting"). Most notably in the scene in which Dr. Ford first encounters Mike the dialogue is sprinkled with phrases like, "Cut to the chase," and "Let's talk turkey, pal," which are delivered in a conspicuously stiff manner. This impression of artificiality leads to progressive complications as the action proceeds.

In the case of Dr. Ford the spectator's distanced response is tempered by empathy because we quickly come to understand the psychiatrist as an overcontrolled person. Thus, her stilted, uninflected speech patterns are at times readable as a coherent dimension of her character rather than as a performance mannerism affected by Lindsay Crouse. When a client anxiously inquires why the doctor has canceled her appointment, Ford responds in a flat, emotionless tone with the words, "Didn't I just tell you. What did I just say . . . ?" The spectator reads the tone of these comments as the expression of a highly disciplined person attempting to cover extreme agitation. Later when Ford sees Mike at the airport, she does exhibit agitation, but this time it is an agitation understood as being feigned by the character. "They're following me," she claims. "They're *waiting* for me." As she is about to kill Mike, she feigns yet another pose as she reverts to her more customary flat style of delivery to announce, "I can't help it. 'I'm out of control.'"[15] In this case, the speech comes across as heavy irony on the part of a character who has caught on to the fact that she has been pegged by the con men as someone for whom control is a powerful psychological issue. She has learned from the con men how to play roles—including the role of "herself"—with greater self-awareness. After the murder, yet another transformation is performed on the positioning of the character as she momentarily appears in the restaurant lobby as a femme fatale out of the film noir tradition as imagined by a director-cinephile. Standing in front of a waterfall amid colorful surroundings (fig. 6.24), she seems to have escaped to the tropics as Jane Greer attempted to do in *Out of the Past* and Kathleen Turner did in *Body Heat*. Thus, during the course of the film the figure of Dr. Ford is repeatedly repositioned, sometimes appearing as a construction of Lindsay Crouse's performance, at others as a coherent character, and at others as a conventionalized fantasy created by David Mamet.

Although Dr. Ford's character is fragmented by these techniques, the dominant mode by which it is perceived is increasingly pitched in the direction of coherence. By contrast, the character of Mike, whose demeanor is superficially the more natural of the two, increasingly takes on the qualities of a con, a trick, a joke perpetrated on the audience by the filmmaker. His name calls up associations with Mike Nussbaum, the actor who plays Mike's close associate Joey, just as Joey's name recalls that of Joe Mantegna, who plays Mike. Further, the character himself is depicted as a consummate actor, effortlessly adapting his behavior to the situation at hand. At a Western Union office he attempts to extricate money from a marine by giving a credible performance as a veteran. Later he performs a convincing imitation of dismay when he "realizes" that he and Joey have lost $80,000. His most seemingly "authentic" moment occurs after he has made love to Ford and shares some worldly wisdom with her. "Take something from life," he advises. "I'm not afraid to stand up and assert myself, and I think *you* aren't either." Like the philosophical speeches of other Mamet characters, this pronouncement remains intractably equivocal, neither wholly explicable in terms of the requirements of the con nor completely credible as a revelation of deep personal conviction.

Mike is shown alone only once. Standing against a black background, he is meticulously backlit as he performs a disappearing act with a coin (fig. 6.25). This action, however, grants the spectator no privileged relation to him as a character. Instead, the self-conscious artistry of the shot emphasizes his status as a created construction of the writer-director. The film includes only one other shot of Mike not authorized by the presence of Dr. Ford. As he sits with Joey in the back of a cab waiting for the psychiatrist to appear with her $80,000 he comments, "Funny how things happen sometime." This gnomic pronouncement suggests that Mike is actually bemused by an unexpected turn of events, which, as it turns out, is not the case—we later discover that things are proceeding precisely according to his predictions. Thus, at this moment he appears enough "out of character" for repeat viewers of the film to suspect that Mamet is using the scene as part of his own "con" of the theater audience by leading the spectator to believe that Mike is acting in good faith in relation to Dr. Ford when in fact he is not. At this point, more than any other, the spectator's impulse toward passive identification with a character taken to be "real" is most radically undermined by a heightened subliminal awareness of a presence behind the camera who may himself not be acting in good faith.[16]

It is thus the relationship between the spectator and the cinematic text itself that is ultimately at stake in the reading of Mamet's oppositional systems. The question becomes: should we immerse ourselves in a dreamlike identification with the film's protagonist, or should we adopt a more distanced response to the film as a joke told by the director?

The spectator's dilemma is linked to a principle that can be described in terms of a concept known in the field of quantum mechanics as complementarity. As described by its originator, Niels Bohr, this concept implies that "evidence obtained under different experimental conditions cannot be comprehended within a single picture but must be regarded as *complementary* in the sense that only the totality of the phenomenon exhausts the possible information about the object. Thus two interpretations of a given phenomenon may be mutually exclusive yet at the same time necessary to explain the totality of the phenomenon" (Holton 210).[17] The concept was designed to address the paradox posed by attempts to measure the speed and position of atomic particles and to define light as either waves or matter. The determination of these uncertainties is inevitably skewed one way or another by the perspective taken by the scientist-measurer. Bohr related this problem to "the general difficulty in the formation of human ideas, inherent in the distinction between subject and object" (124). In tracing the origins of Bohr's idea of complementarity, Gerald Holton has stressed the influence of William James, who first used the term. Holton quotes James as follows:

> Let anyone try to cut a thought across the middle and get a look at its section, and he will see how difficult the introspective observation of the transitive tract is. . . . Or if our purpose is nimble enough and we do arrest it, it ceases forthwith to be itself. . . . The attempt at introspective analysis in these cases is in fact like . . . trying to turn up the light quickly enough to see how the darkness looks (124).

Bohr's concept is thus part of a larger intellectual trend often identified with modernism in which the self focuses on the incompatibility between its modes of participation and observation, and thereby becomes split. James explicitly equates this psychic split with the notion of complementarity when he states: "It must be admitted, therefore, that in *certain persons*, at least, *the total possible consciousness may be split into parts which coexist but mutually ignore each other*, and share the objects of knowledge between them. More remarkable still, they are *complementary*. Give an object to one of the consciousnesses, and by that fact you remove it from the other or others" (Holton 125–26).

The absurdist aesthetic of character, in which the self is dissolved into a series of roles, grows out of this awareness of the self as fundamentally split between the subject and the object of thought. It follows that absurdist actors are unable to use the occasion of their performance to reveal an authentic self because the self is not perceived as an integral whole. In *House of Games* a dilemma of this order plagues Dr. Ford, who must attempt to merge her consciousness with that of her troubled patient even as she exercises her power as separate individual in whom the authority of psychoanalytic theory is vested. Dr. Ford's dilemma is shared by the film's spectators, who are continually "split" into incompatible roles as participants in Dr. Ford's problems and observers of Mamet's joke. The participant role, which characterizes the position of the spectator in realistic representation, is thus part of the drama of *House of Games*, but it is heavily qualified. Mamet can therefore be said to use realism without participating in it.

The film's conclusion adds yet a further ambiguity to the spectator's position. The final shot is a long close-up of Dr. Ford, who is wearing a Mona Lisa-like smile. By this point in the film our difficulty in reading the shot lies less in our uncertainty about whether to take the film as a dream or as a joke than in our uncertainty about our relationship to the joke itself. Are we the audience of the joke or its object? Just as Dr. Ford has earlier been tricked into believing that she was the audience for the con when she was in fact its object, so have we repeatedly taken ourselves to be an audience only to discover that the joke is on us as well as on the heroine. Moreover, Mamet's final ploy consists of undermining our identification with Dr. Ford herself. After she murders Mike, her character becomes opaque. One is not certain how to read her; is one to approve or disapprove of what she has done? Though Mike seems deserving of some kind of punishment, Ford's action seems extreme and partakes of vigilantism. Further, her theft of the lighter in the last scene makes her seem as unscrupulous as he. At the same time Mamet's repeated close-ups of Dr. Ford in this scene encourage continued identification with her. The result is a radical destabilization in the relationship between the spectator and the protagonist.

In this way *House of Games* concludes by denying its spectators a position as either the intended audience of Mamet's jokelike entertainment or its butt. To identify with Dr. Ford is to be made into a butt, not only by the filmmaker, but perhaps also by Dr. Ford herself as his newly amoral surrogate—as she herself may be acknowledging by her enigmatic smile in the final shot. However, to reject Ford entirely and take a position with the implied filmmaker is to identify with the gratuitous humiliation of an "innocent" woman analogous to that perpetrated by Mike.

Mamet's refusal to provide a clear resolution can be understood in gender-related terms by referring to Freud's own interpretation of jokes that he called "tendentious." "Generally speaking," Freud wrote, "a tendentious joke calls for three people: in addition to the one who makes the joke, there must be a second who is taken as the object of the hostile or sexual aggressiveness, and a third in whom the joke's aim in producing pleasure is fulfilled" (*Jokes* 100). Freud described such jokes as typically involving two men and a woman. Their aim is to compensate for the sexual frustration occasioned by the male joke teller's anticipation of the woman's sexual rejection by substituting the pleasures of male bonding at the expense of the female, who is now taken as the joke's object. The sexual source of the hostility behind Mamet's joke is alluded to at several points in *House of Games*. As the perpetrator of the joke/con within the diegesis, Mike describes Dr. Ford to his "audience" of male associates as a "broad" and a "bitch." Moreover, when Ford later accuses Mike of raping her ("You took me under false pretensions"), he tacitly acknowledges the validity of her claim ("Is that what I did? Well, then, that's just the way things happened, isn't it."). The seduction scene itself involves a number of disturbing close-ups of hands struggling for possession of the woman's body, thereby depicting the lovemaking itself as a kind of rape (fig. 6.26). Seen in the context of the rigid gender separation that marks the film as a whole, such moments suggest a powerful current of heterosexual hostility underlying the action—a current further complicated by the knowledge of spectators that the object of this hostility, Dr. Ford/Lindsay Crouse, is also the wife of the film's director.[18]

The failure of heterosexual romance within the diegesis is thus echoed in the sexist overtones inherent in the notion of joking represented both in and by the film. In terms of the diegesis boy clearly does not get girl; rather boy "gets" girl, and then girl "gets" boy. In terms of the film itself, the director finally "gets" the spectator because the spectator fails to "get" the director. Because Mamet denies his audience an opportunity of establishing any firm position in relation to his main character, we are unable to enter into a empathic rapport with the filmmaker. With this impasse in mind, one may be inclined to read the movie's final moments as revelatory of the director's deepest affinities with the character of Mike, whose most inexplicable line, "It's funny the way things happen sometime," may now become readable as the voice of the writer-director himself. For in this film, as in few others, the way things happen is, indeed, sometimes "funny."

Performance as Communicative Action: Do the Right Thing

In chapter 2 I suggested that *Orphans of the Storm* can be seen as a film that transcends the cliché that sees the romantic couple as a center around which society is ordered, and I further argued that Lillian Gish's role in the production of that film was a significant factor in its break with Griffith's earlier adherence to more traditional patriarchal ideals. Similarly, my discussion of *Nashville* saw it as an attempt to articulate a new basis for community after the demise of the older couple-centered model. An even more recent film whose concerns encompass yet transcend the ideal of marriage and the romantic couple is Spike Lee's 1989 *Do the Right Thing*. Unlike *Orphans of the Storm* and *Nashville*, the implications of Lee's film are more apocalyptic than utopian. Its story concerns a day in the life of an African-American neighborhood in Bedford-Stuyvesant that culminates in a race riot directed at a local pizza parlor owned by Sal, an Italian-American (Danny Aiello). *Do the Right Thing* follows Hollywood tradition by featuring romantic coupling, but ultimately this motif is subsumed by a performance style oriented toward the investigation of larger social issues.

The film features two couples. The older pair, Da Mayor and Mother-Sister (Ossie Davis and Ruby Dee), are shown together at the end; the younger pair, Mookie and Tina (Lee and Rosie Perez), are not. The relationship between Da Mayor and Mother-Sister proceeds in time-honored fashion with courtly gestures on his part and an initial show of disdain on hers. Eventually, Da Mayor demonstrates his ability to serve as a traditional male protector figure, first by rescuing a child from being run down by a car, then by rescuing Mother-Sister herself from the seizure of hysteria that she succumbs to on witnessing the race riot which forms the film's climax. The understanding ultimately arrived at by these two is conspicuously nonsexual. Tina and Mookie's affair, on the other hand, is marked by both sexual energy and emotional strife. Tina frequently expresses her dissatisfaction with her lot—and with Mookie. For his part, Mookie remains largely passive.

The portrayal of the romantic interactions of each pair reflects their differing political orientations. These opposing attitudes center on the issue of race relations and are overtly stated in printed quotations at the film's conclusion. Da Mayor and Mother-Sister adhere to Martin Luther King's policy of stoic nonviolence. Da Mayor thus tries to stop the riot. By contrast, Mookie, whose job delivering pizza for Sal places him at the center of the conflict, acts in accordance with Malcolm X's strategy of violent confrontation. He tells Sal's son Dino to fight back against the oppression of his older brother. More significantly, in the film's climactic scene it is he who begins the riot by throwing a garbage can through the window of the pizzeria.[19]

The anger and frustration that prevent a harmonious union between Mookie and Tina and that grip the neighborhood as a whole emerge from the sense felt by the inhabitants of the bleakness of their situation. In this neighborhood of African-Americans and Puerto Ricans the businesses are owned by Italians and Koreans, who prosper by bleeding the already bereft African-American residents of the little disposable income that they possess. Although Mookie is constantly cajoled by both his girlfriend and his sister to "get his life together" and "get a real job," it is not clear how he could act on this advice. He is the only African-American in the film who is employed at all and, given the social context in which he is placed, it is difficult to see what better alternatives are open to him. He cannot "be a man" and take responsibility for his young illegitimate son, as he is continually admonished to do by these women, without losing his sense of identification with the community of African-American males who make up his social environment.

Further, the women themselves constitute complementary problems for Mookie. If Tina represents an exogamic liaison that loosens Mookie's ties with his own group (he complains at one point about having a son with the Latin name "Hector"), his sister Jade represents the temptations and dangers of a too-exclusive attachment to loyalties within one's immediate family. Thus, Mookie has found no acceptable middle ground between an incest-oriented attitude that views all outsiders to the family with hostility and a miscegenistic alliance that flies in the face of prevailing group antipathies. The conditions surrounding the breakdown of the institution of marriage and the family within the African-American community are graphically rendered in this portrayal.

As Jerome Christiansen has argued, *Do the Right Thing* has much in common with the Western. Although Christiansen defines the similarities in terms of the appeal to an absolutist code of ethics ("Do the right thing" and John Wayne's "A man's gotta do what a man's gotta do"), the comparison is perhaps more pointed in terms of the dominant motifs of property and race relations shared by both. As Geoffrey Nowell-Smith has observed, property and inheritance are central to Lee's film. Although Sal claims that Mookie is "like a son" to him, Sal has built up his pizza parlor as a modern homestead to pass on to his "real" sons: he retains the fantasies of a family dynasty which the Western has promoted. Part of Mookie's inability to commit himself to family life stems from his lack of a patrimony—or of the prospect of obtaining one. The conflagration of Sal's pizzeria repeats the torching of the encroaching settlers' homesteads that the Indians carried out—but this time the act is seen from the point of view of the disenfranchized racial Others.

Do the Right Thing also takes up the Western's motif of miscegenation, not only by its emphasis on Mookie's hostility in the face of the "outsider" Sal's attentions to his sister Jade but also by playing out the ensuing brother-sister quarrel in front of graffiti that reads "Tawana told the truth" (fig. 6.27). This slogan, which refers to a notorious case in which many in the black community were galvanized by the suggestion (ultimately proven false) that a black woman had been raped by white men, neatly reverses the racial prejudices that surround the Western's treatment of similar events (where it is the Indians' savage treatment of white women that is made into the stuff of legend).

The cacophony of clashing colors and grating noises that characterizes urban ghetto life is made palpable in Lee's film, and the virulent enmity between competing social groups that these clashes often reflect becomes explicit in the scene in which the "ghetto-blaster" of Radio Raheem (Bill Nunn) is pitted against the radio of a group of young Puerto Ricans to see whose music can drown out the other's. Raheem later tries to blast his radio in Sal's pizzeria, filling the room with strains of the theme of the film, Public Enemy's "Fight the Powers that Be," and thereby asserting his right to ownership of the audial space of the establishment.[20] The earlier quarrel over whether the pictures on the pizzeria's walls should be of African-Americans or Italian-Americans focuses on similar claims to the possession of visual space.

That the film's final scene of reconciliation takes place between Mookie and Sal rather than between Mookie and Tina points to its concern with the economic base on which social mores such as romantic love are based. The final tense exchange between employer and employee concerns a dispute over money, but it is a transaction in which mutual understanding plays a role (fig. 6.28). Coming in the wake of the highly acrimonious actions (on both sides) that characterized the activities of the previous night, this negotiation can be read as an example of what Jürgen Habermas has referred to as "communicative action." Communicative action represents the triumph of what Habermas terms the "lifeworld" of actual experience over the abstract systems that societies use to structure this experience. As opposed to the official systems of social organization, the lifeworld reflects the way in which people actually live. It thus represents a kind of excess. Habermas describes exchanges centered on lifeworld-based communicative action as follows:

> a postraditional everyday communication that stands on its own feet, that sets limits to the inner dynamic of independent subsystems, that

> bursts open encapsulated expert cultures—and thus that avoids the dangers both of reification and of desolation" (*Theory* 2:486).

The final communication between Sal and Mookie in *Do the Right Thing* conforms closely to this description, for it lays bare the structure of economic dependency represented by the employer-employee relationship. Moreover, the exchange sets limits on the inner dynamic of this relationship for, by allowing Mookie's salary money to lie on the sidewalk, both Sal and Mookie demonstrate to each other that their emotions transcend purely economic issues. Lee's film is not entirely despairing about the possibility of changing the power relation that it reveals. The result of the exchange between Sal and Mookie is ambiguous; it resists being recuperated into a predetermined system and thus does not provide a classical sense of closure for the film. The subsequent statements by Malcolm X and Martin Luther King recapitulate this feeling of open-endedness.

The unresolved quality of this conclusion conforms to the aims of the film's overall performance strategy, which is based on a politicized, Brechtian "alienation effect" approach to acting. This performance mode aims to open up questions rather than offer the illusion a finished "real world." In *Do the Right Thing* characters are not realistically drawn individuals but historically situated social "gests." They are for the most part presented as members of groups rather than individually. When shown in close-up, their faces are typically subject to the caricaturing effect of wide-angle lenses (fig. 6.29).[21]

Through such Brechtian performance strategies the film attempts to involve its audience in a reenactment of the breakthrough of lifeworld over system. Accordingly, its mode of address is presentational rather than representational. Characters often speak to the camera; even when they talk to one another, their statements are rarely framed by the conventional over-the-shoulder shots favored by traditional realism. They engage the spectator not by their complicated individuation but by their rhythmical speech patterns, which include such motifs as rhyming, list making, and stuttering. Such patterns draw on the conventions of rap music and more generally on the ongoing oral traditions of black culture.[22] Teresa de Lauretis has commented on the use of a similar strategy in Lizzie Borden's *Born in Flames*:

> The use of music and beat in conjunction with spoken language, from rap singing to a variety of subcultural lingos and no-standard speech, serves less the purposes of documentation or cinema verité than those of

> what in another context might be called characterization: they are there to provide a means of identification of and with the characters, though not the kind of psychological identification usually accorded to main characters or privileged "protagonists" (188–89).

The emotions of love and hate that Radio Raheem wears as brass knuckles are invoked willy-nilly in a narrative that is multifocused, episodic, and frequently unmotivated by cause-effect logic.[23] The film's antirationalistic principle of narrative structure demonstrates its sympathy with the disenfranchized characters it portrays, who live similarly unstructured moment-to-moment existences. Habermas sees such a rejection of structure as a response to an excessive social rigidity associated with the effects of mainstream mass media such as cinema. He writes:

> The communicative practice of everyday life is one-sidedly rationalized into a specialist-utilitarianism lifestyle; and this media-induced shift to purposive-rational action orientations calls forth the reaction of a hedonism freed from the pressures of rationality (*Theory* 2:480).

Such an analysis places the formulaic love stories of classical Hollywood, which speak to the interests of society's dominant groups under the guise of benign entertainments, at the center of the social malaise chronicled in *Do the Right Thing*. An application of Habermas's formulation to Lee's characters would read their sexual and aggressive responses as expressions of an antirational hedonism that reacts against the destructive constraints imposed on them by romance-centered "diversions." In this film, the motif of romantic love is seen, in an important sense, as a displacement of the economic issues that are really at stake.

In a quintessentially Brechtian move, the main character in *Do the Right Thing* is played by the director himself. The resulting self-reflexivity invites a double reading of the main character as both Mookie and Lee. The possibility of the latter reading is explicitly raised when the character is initially introduced, for his first words, "Wake up!" repeat the last words uttered in Lee's previous film, *School Daze*. Further, they are spoken to Joie Lee, who is Lee's sister as well as Mookie's. When Mookie ultimately makes a kind of peace with Sal, the scene thus contains overtones that suggest the predicament of an African-American director who makes a film in which violence against the white establishment is presented as a distinct option and then expects his white Hollywood producers to pay for it. Lee's ambivalent relation to Hollywood is hence analogous to the position of his protagonist in relation to the culture of Bedford-Stuyvesant. Both feel caught between serving the dominant group and rebelling against it—and both end up doing a little of each. Thus the film takes up the subject of its own production and makes it into material for historically informed interpretation.

Like *Je tu il elle*, *Do the Right Thing* uses the presence of its director as an actor as part of its rendering of the film itself as a cultural artifact. In such a Brechtian mode of representation the emphasis of classical Hollywood on modeling reified gender roles and romantic attachments is overtaken by a concern with exploring questions involving the structures of social organization that lie behind this project as well as the role of cinema and its audiences in supporting or dismantling such myths. In this study I have tried to suggest some of the complexities inherent in the former project; in closing I can only gesture toward the complexities inherent in the latter one.

ILLUSTRATIONS

THE PETRIFIED FOREST / THE MALTESE FALCON

1.1

1.2

1.3

1.4

1.5

1.6

1.7

1.8

THE MALTESE FALCON

1.9

1.10

1.11

1.12

1.13

1.14

1.15

1.16

1.17

1.18

1.19

1.20

1.21

1.22

1.23

1.24

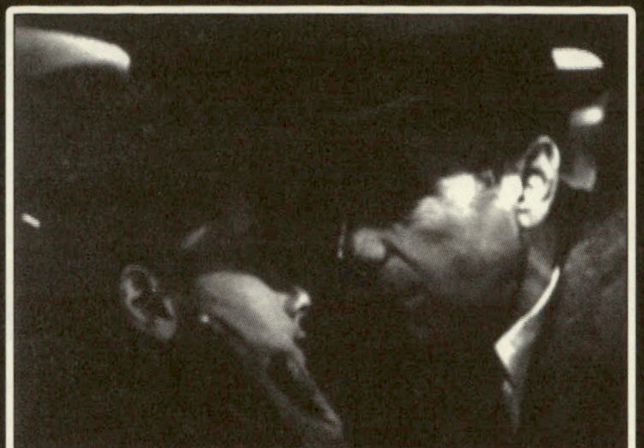
1.25

1.26

1.27

1.28

1.29

1.30

1.31

1.32

THE BIG SLEEP

1.33

1.34

1.35

1.36

1.37

1.38

1.39

2.1

2.2

2.3

2.4

2.5

2.6

2.7

2.8

2.9

2.10

2.11

2.12

2.13

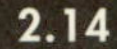

2.14

2.15

2.16

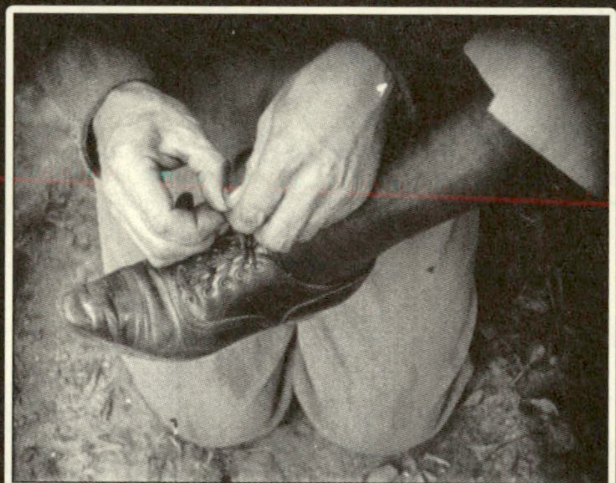

2.17

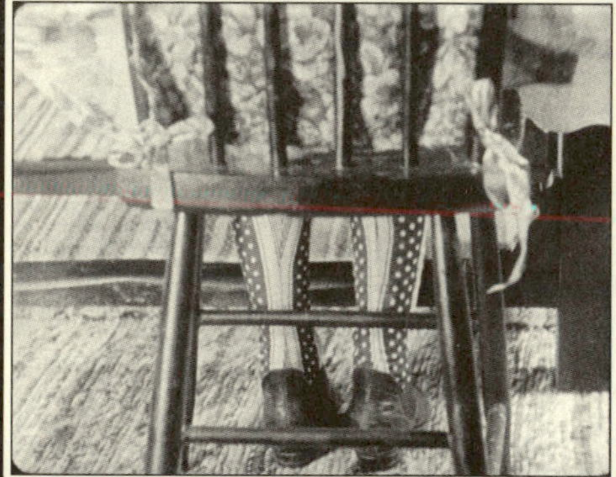

2.18

WAY DOWN EAST

2.19

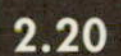

2.20

2.21

2.22

2.23

2.24

WAY DOWN EAST

2.25

2.26

2.27

2.28

2.29

2.30

WAY DOWN EAST

2.31

2.32

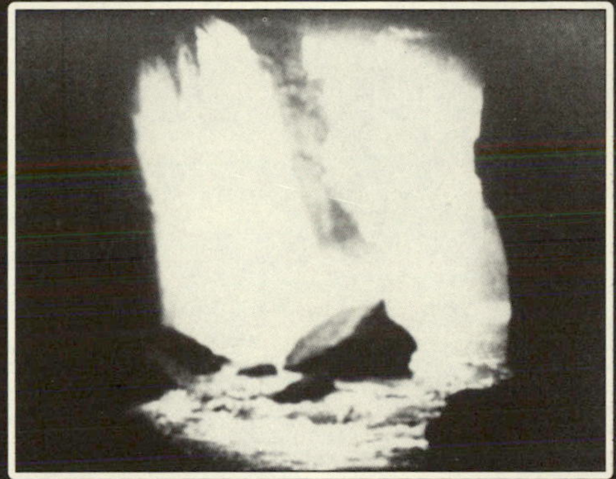

2.33

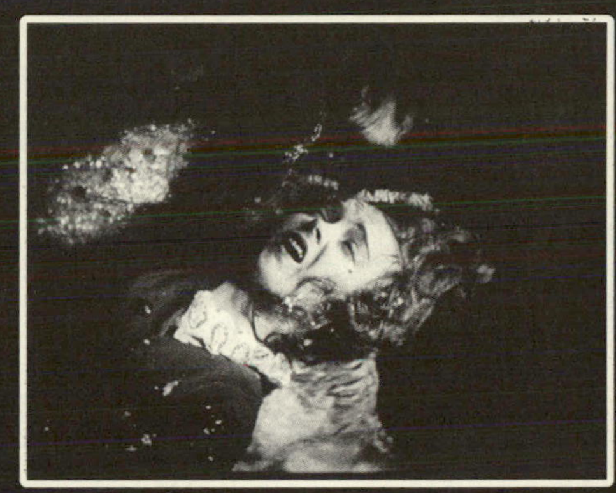

2.34

2.35

2.36

2.37

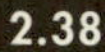

2.38

2.39

2.40

YOUNG MR. LINCOLN / THE GRAPES OF WRATH / MY DARLING CLEMENTINE / FORT APACHE

3.1

3.2

3.3

3.4

3.5

3.6

THE MAN WHO SHOT LIBERTY VALANCE

3.7

3.8

THE MAN WHO SHOT LIBERTY VALANCE

3.9

3.10

3.11

3.12

3.13

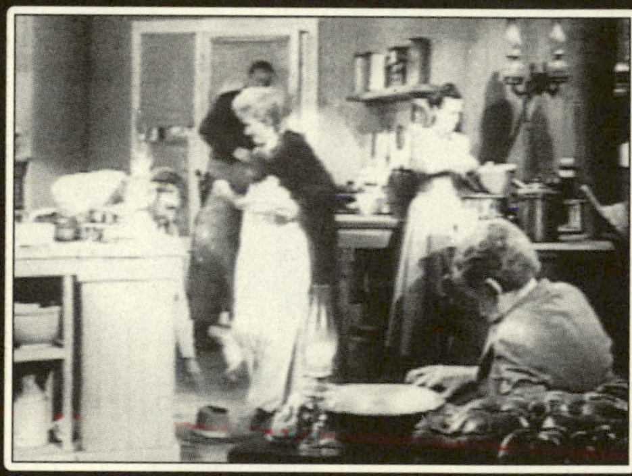
3.14

3.15

3.16

THE MAN WHO SHOT LIBERTY VALANCE

3.17

3.18

3.19

3.20

3.21

3.22

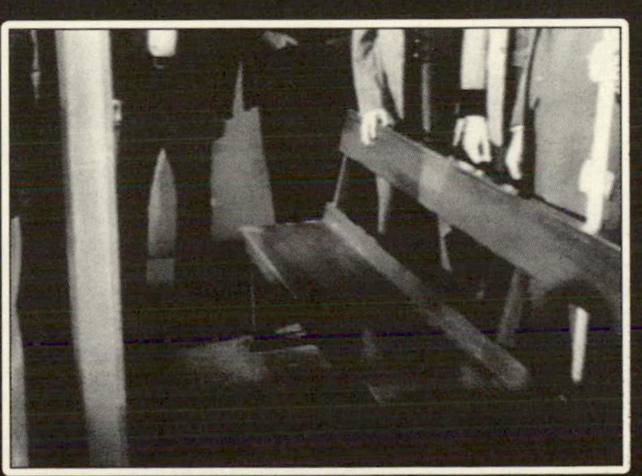

3.23

3.24

THE MAN WHO SHOT LIBERTY VALANCE

3.25

3.26

3.27

3.28

3.29

3.30

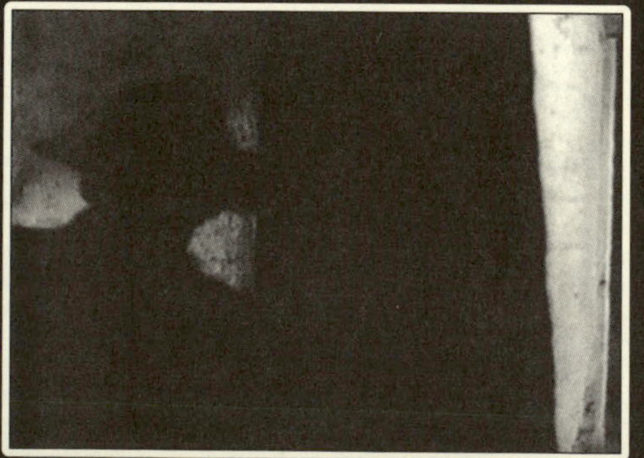

3.31

3.32

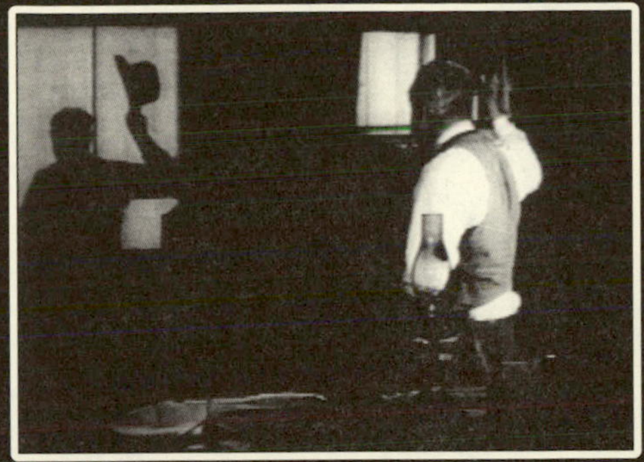

3.33

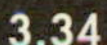

3.34

4.1

4.2

4.3

4.4

SUNSET BOULEVARD

4.5

4.6

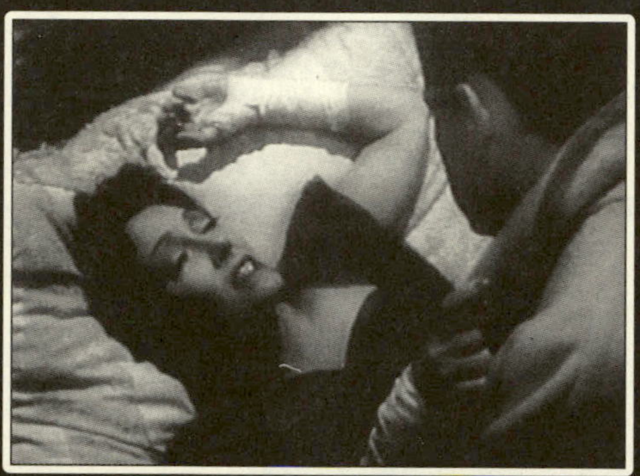
4.7

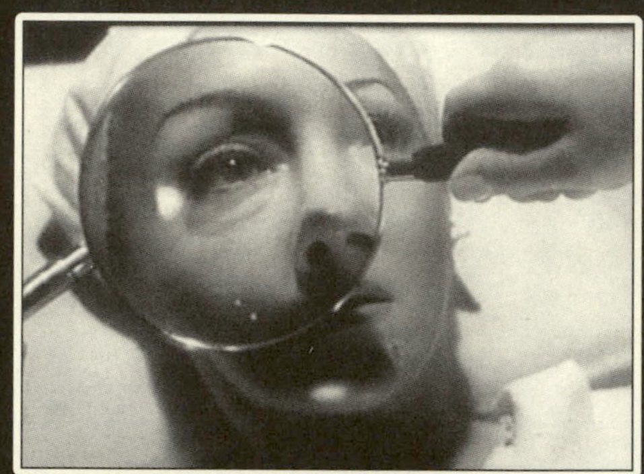
4.8

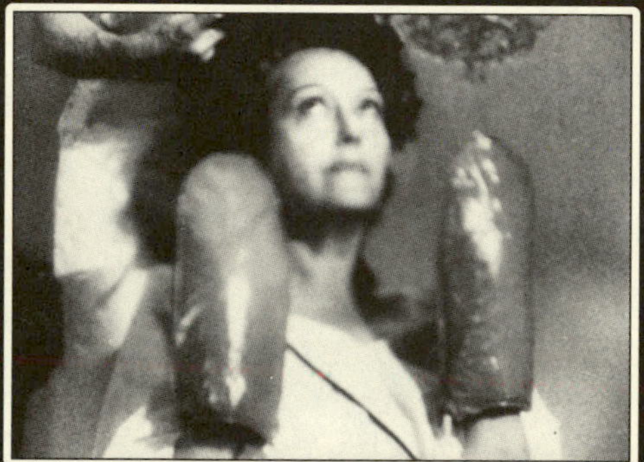
4.9

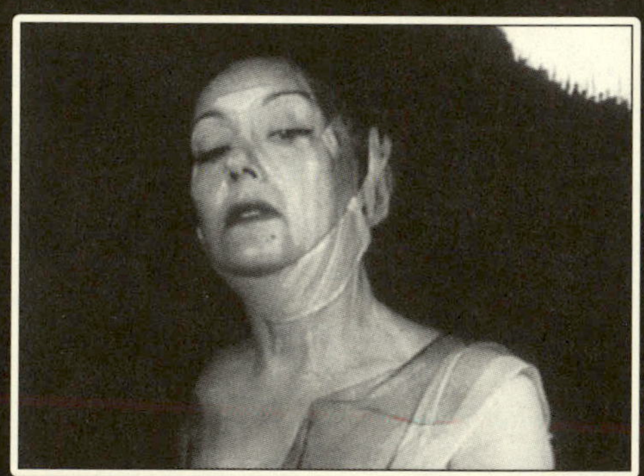
4.10

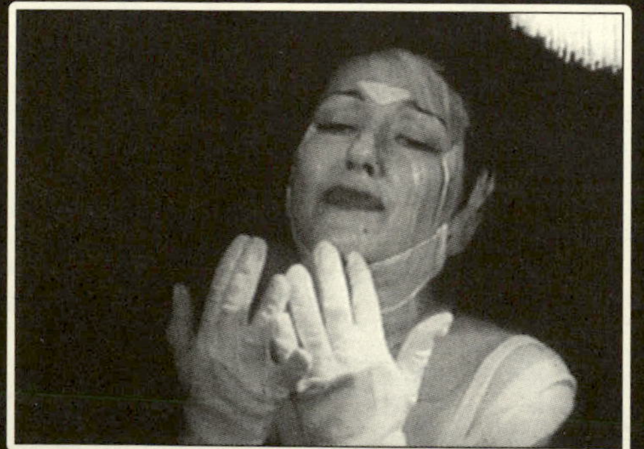
4.11

4.12

SUNSET BOULEVARD

4.13

4.14

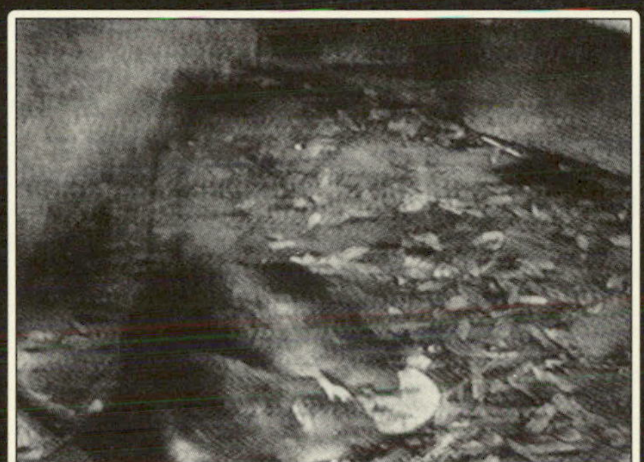
4.15

4.16

4.17

4.18

4.19

4.20

4.21

WRITTEN BY
CHARLES BRACKETT
BILLY WILDER
D. M. MARSHMAN, JR.

4.22

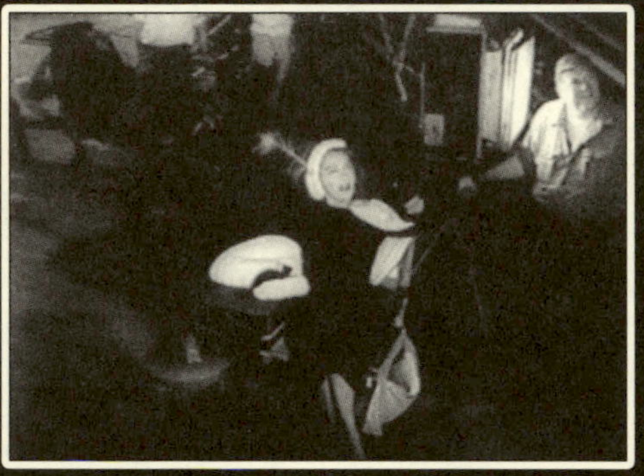

4.23

4.24

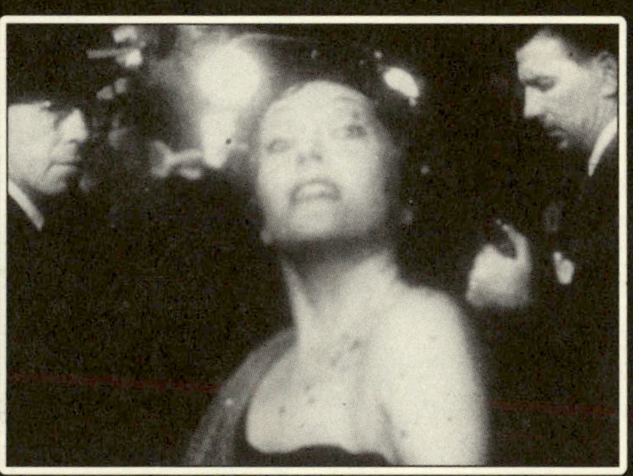

4.25

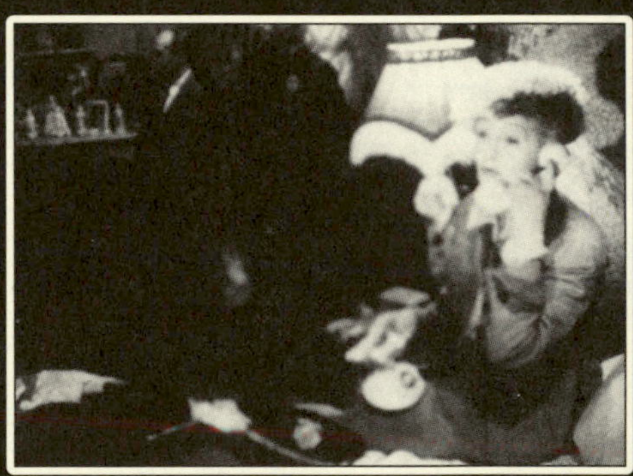

4.26

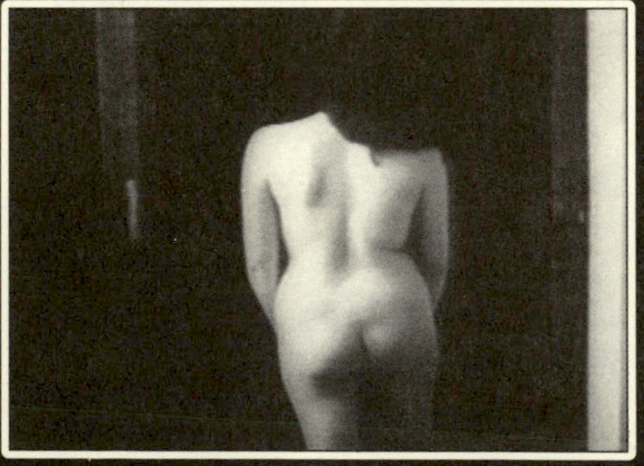

4.27

4.28

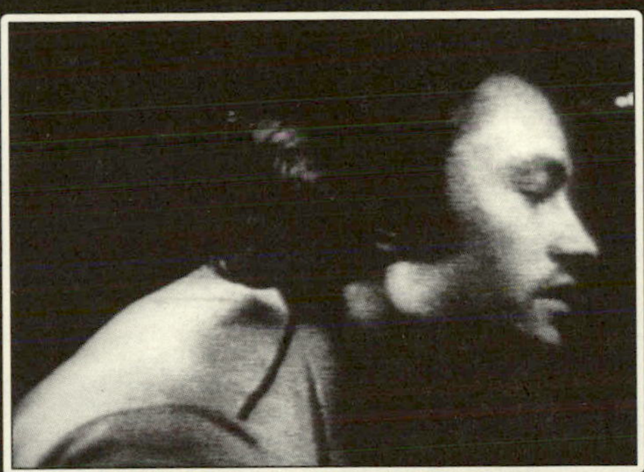

4.29

4.30

5.1

5.2

5.3

5.4

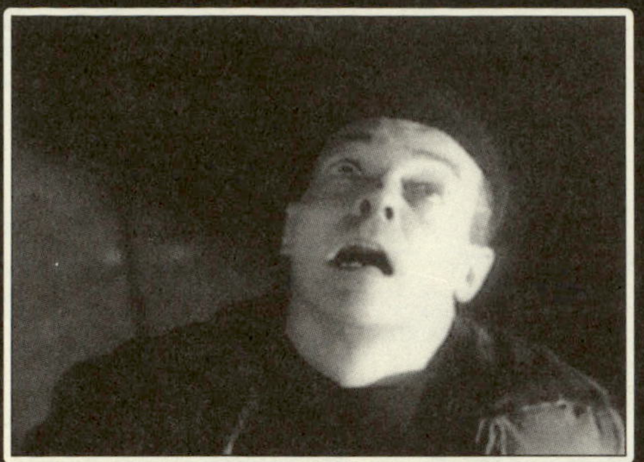
5.5

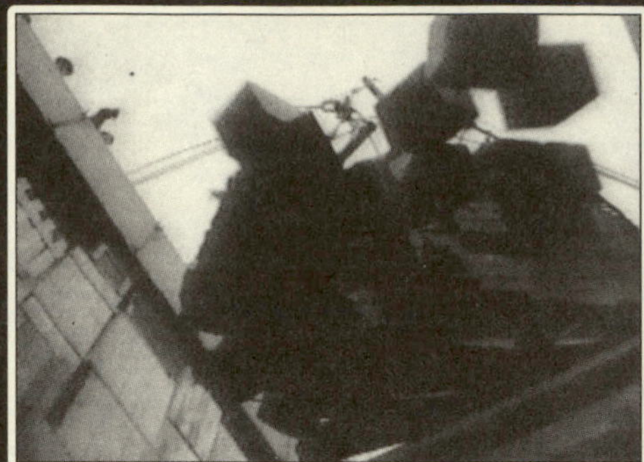
5.6

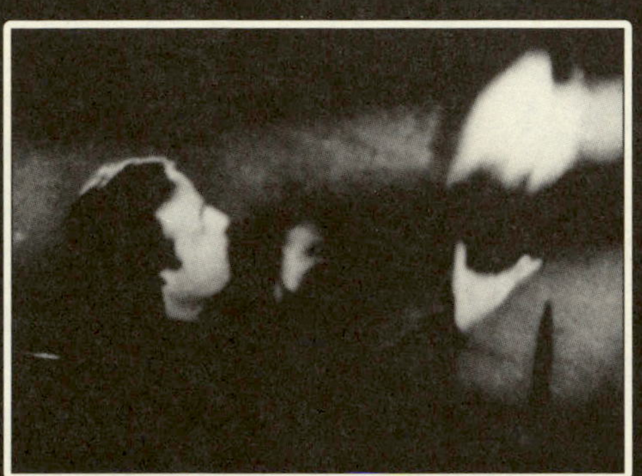
5.7

5.8

5.9

5.10

5.11

5.12

ON THE WATERFRONT

5.13

5.14

5.15

5.16

5.17

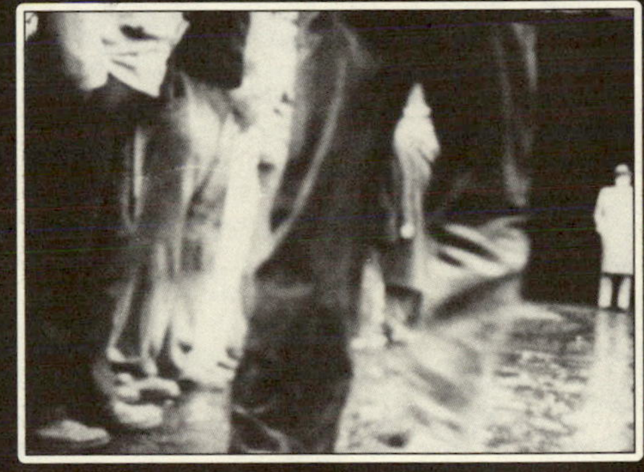

5.18

5.19

5.20

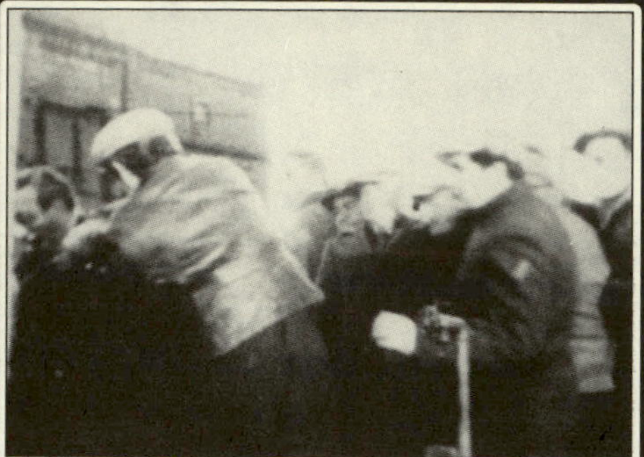

5.21

6.1

6.2

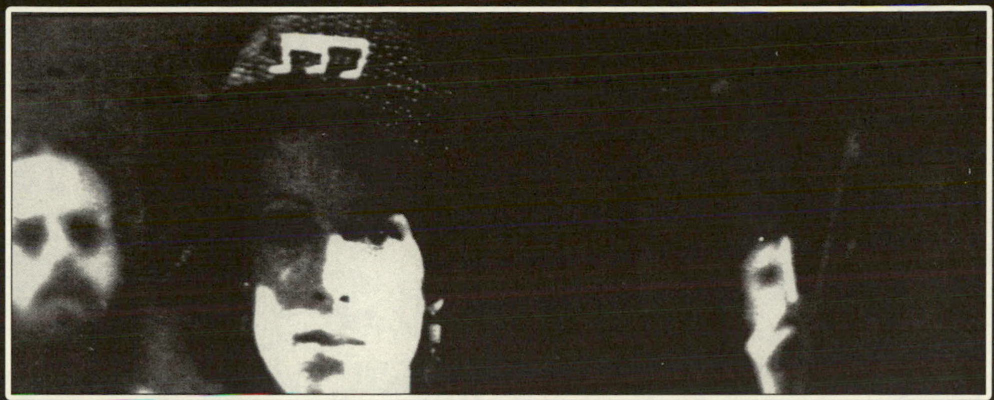

6.3

6.4

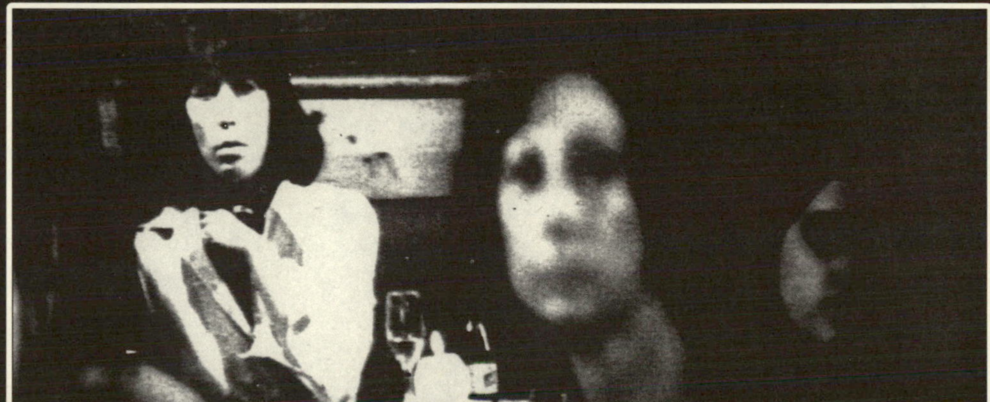

6.5

6.6

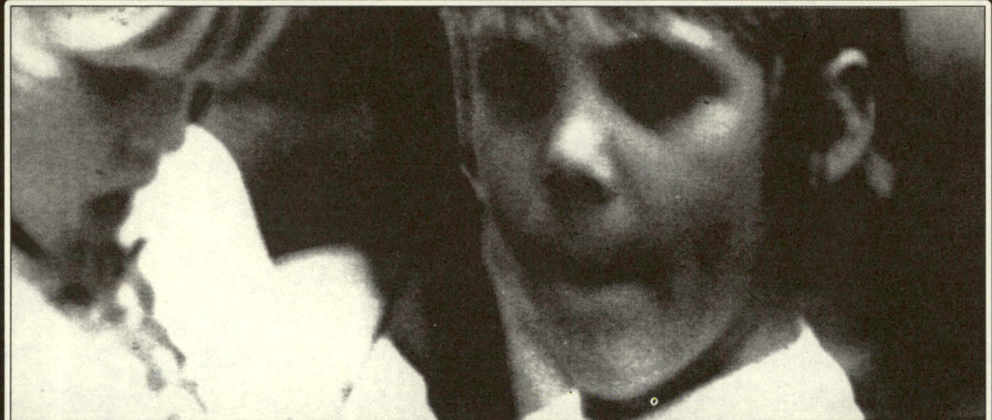

6.7

6.8

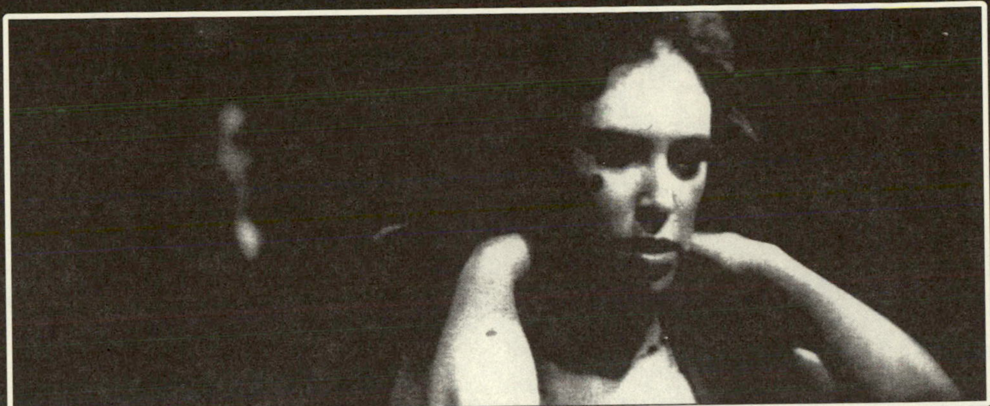

6.9

6.10

6.11

6.12

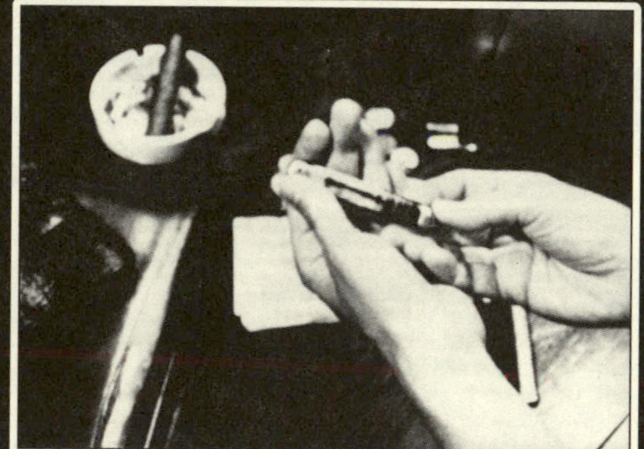

6.13

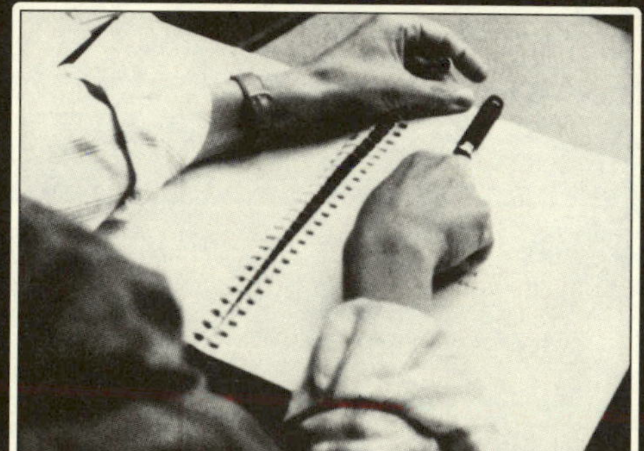

6.14

6.15

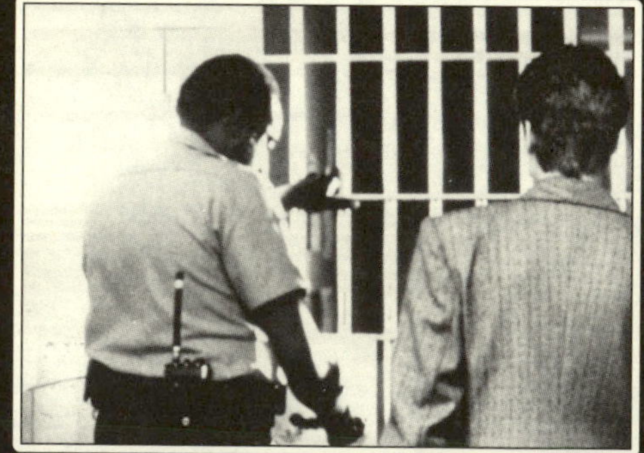

6.16

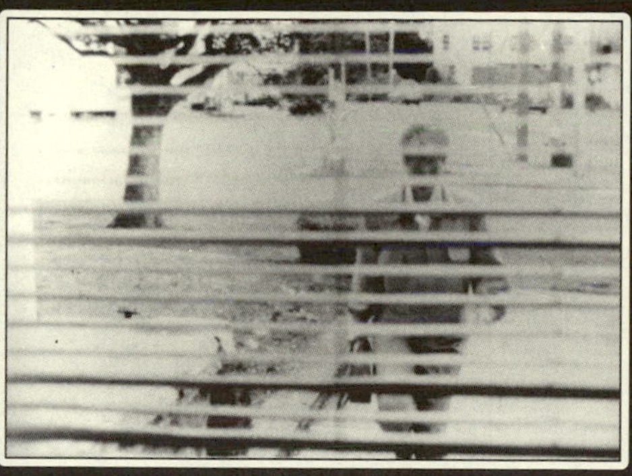

6.17

6.18

6.19

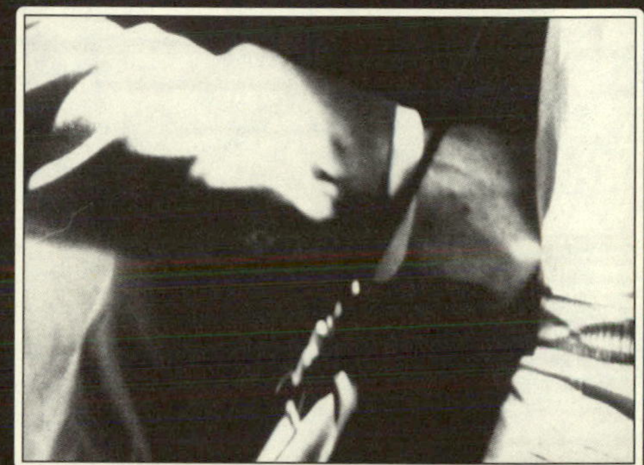

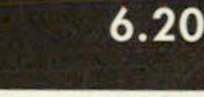

6.20

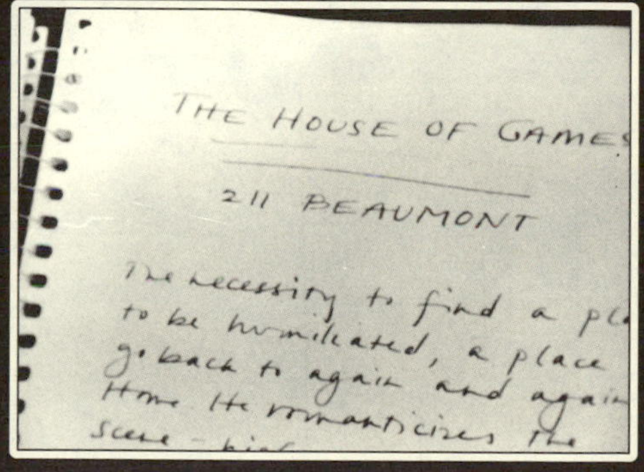

6.21

6.22

6.23

6.24

HOUSE OF GAMES / DO THE RIGHT THING

6.25

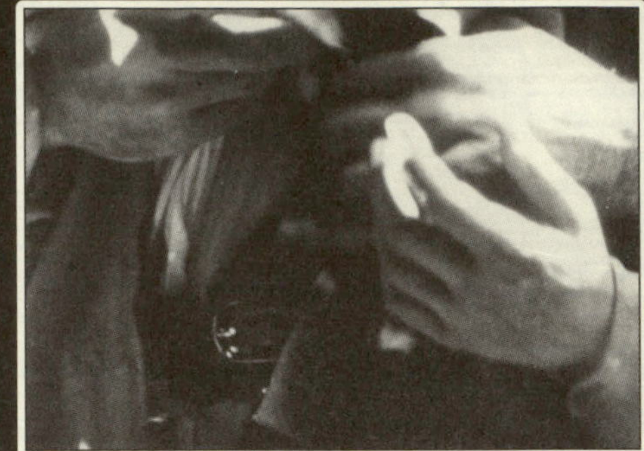

6.26

6.27

6.28

6.29

NOTES

Preface

1. In a critique of an earlier essay of mine ("The Critic as Consumer") Tania Modleski characterized my approach as setting "World Historical Events" in opposition to issues of gender (*The Women Who Knew Too Much* 131). However, I see my aim as one of attempting to relate these questions, not oppose them. I agree with Modleski's argument that the psychic mechanisms that films mobilize in the interests of internalizing gender ideologies deserve exploration; but I question whether a focus on gender in isolation from class, race, and ethnicity, as well as from issues of historical change would be "more feminist," as she suggests.

2. Rorty's emphasis on contingency offers an important corrective to some of the more rigidly doctrinaire and programmatic positions taken by certain Marxist theorists. However, my specific commitment is more to what Fraser terms "democratic-socialist-feminist pragmatism" (106) than to Rorty's separation between the realms of the private-aesthetic and the political-public. For Fraser's critique of Rorty, see her essay "Solidarity or Singularity: Richard Rorty between Romanticism and Technocracy" in her collection *Unruly Practices* (93–112).

Chapter One

1. Examples of the use of this strategy by two prominent Hollywood directors are elaborated in chapter 4's analysis of Elia Kazan's *On the Waterfront* and in my essay "Mastery Through Masterpieces: American Culture, the Male Body, and Huston's *Moulin Rouge*." Also relevant in this context is Mark Langer's comment on a dispute between director Robert Flaherty and his production company: "William Fox wanted to write a love story into a film that Flaherty was shooting on the tribal life of the Pueblo Indians, but Flaherty refused" (44).

2. I do not intend this formulation to be construed as one that advocates a simple deterministic relationship between Hollywood films and their viewers. The movies themselves are obviously influenced by events and trends within the culture and the relationship between the industry, its artists and their audience is a complex and highly mediated one, as I will argue in terms of specific cases in subsequent chapters.

3. In the interview he gave to the *New York Times* on the occasion of publishing this book, Singer said that he had written it by dictating it to his wife, calling the project a "semicollaborative venture." If this description of marital relations is to be taken as following the standard of "proper" romantic love, it is a standard that would be seen by many today as a hopelessly anachronistic one.

Jeffrey Weeks has critiqued Singer's argument by labeling it essentialist: "that is, a method that attempts to explain the properties of a complex whole by reference to a supposed inner truth or essence, the assumption [quoting Singer] 'that in all sexological matters there must be a single, basic, uniform pattern ordained by nature itself'" ("Questions" 16).

4. Freud's distinction between anaclitic and narcissistic object choices can be found in his essay "On Narcissism."

Much recent theory dealing with representations of the human form draws heavily on Freudian theory, focusing primarily on issues of sexuality. An exception to this trend is the work of Elaine Scarry, whose book *The Body in Pain* does not treat the issue of sexuality at all. My own consideration of the relationship between romantic love and marriage and Hollywood performance styles is obviously concerned with issues of sexuality, but I have attempted to approach sexual desire not as a Freudian drive but rather as a cultural construct shaped by a social agenda that is built around material interests and relations of power.

Carol Gilligan and Eve Stern have put forward a pointed critique of the androcentric bias in Freud's theory, which tends to approach romantic love as a male-centered phenomenon. Freud's theories about "normal" female narcissism and its relation to women's romantic relationships as well as his ideas about female sexual development and behavior have long provided targets for feminist attacks and revisions by scholars like Nancy Choderow and Juliet Mitchell. My own appropriation of Freudian theory for the purposes of the present study is generally limited to Freud's concept of the unconscious and the attendant mechanisms of repression and displacement.

5. Philippe Ariés has also put forward influential descriptions of the way in which cultural forms have supported such class separations. To cite one example. Ariés has written:

> Up to the Eighteenth Century, and long after, sex simply meant procreation and the functions of the sexual organs among the vast numbers of common folk in town and country. Poetry and high art bridged the gap between desire and love; but the world of feeling and the world of genesis were kept firmly apart. Popular songs and pictures and bawdy stories never strayed far from the genital. So there was a wholeheartedly sexy side facing a rather refined asexual side("Thoughts on the History of Homosexuality" 68).

6. I have privileged the model put forward by Habermas over the utopian formulations of a number of feminist theorists because it does not give precedence to the experience of one gender over that of another. By contrast, some feminist visions of Utopian harmony are founded on an essentialist view of female sexual development or the female body. Feminist political theorists like Nancy Hartsock have argued that women's capacity to give birth endows them with a unique advantage. Hartsock writes, "The unity of mental and manual labor and the directly sensuous nature of much of woman's work leads to a more pround unity of mental and manual labor, social and natural worlds, than is experienced by the male worker in capitalism. The unity grows from the fact that women's bodies, unlike men's, can be themselves instruments of production. In pregnancy, giving birth, or lactation, arguments about a division of mental from manual labor are fundamentally foreign" (243). Such formulations pose an ideal society in which women would occupy a privileged position rather than advancing a gender-neutral principle in which both women and men could par-

ticipate and which can speak to the oppression of other groups as well as women. (For an extended critique of feminist theories centered on an essentialist view of gender difference, see Brown and Adams.)

7. Some studies of the representation of love in literature see it as acting as a displacement for creativity (DiBattista) or religious faith (Polhemus). My own argument, by contrast, understands love as a significant issue in terms of its function in the regulation of private life.

8. Although much of the data on which Engels based his argument has since been discredited, his conclusions are still accepted by many social scientists (see, for example, Brown, Leacock, Mair, Rubin, and Sayres et al.). It is important to stipulate, however, that Engels's analysis is based on a relationship between people and property that characterizes Western capitalist culture but is not necessarily universal. My discussion in chapter 3 of the relation of Indians to the land, for example, presumes a different model.

9. I have used the term *ethnicity* as opposed to *race* throughout this chapter to avoid the ambiguities and perjorative connotations that surround the latter term. I treat the distinction between these two concepts at some length in chapter 3.

10. At the same time, these formerly deviant patterns can be understood as contributing to an emerging discourse on sexuality as a foundation for personal rather than group identity which became increasingly dominant in the United States following the Second World War. As French historian Michelle Perrot observes, "The pederasts of the Nineteenth Century were the first to develop the model of a strictly hedonistic sexuality cut off from procreation, which was destined to enjoy a brilliant future" (643).

11. Of historians of sexuality and private life, Philippe Ariés in France, Jeffrey Weeks in England, and Lawrence Stone in the United States are among the most authoritative. A number of distinguished anthropologists have also turned their attention to histories of this sort, including Jack Goody and Robin Fox.

12. For histories of romantic love and marriage in the United States, see Bailey, D'Emilio and Freedman, Fass, May, and Rothman.

13. As a result of such prejudices, critics often prefer British actors who receive a classical stage training which emphasizes the effective delivery of dialogue over Hollywood performers who merely "look good." Conversely, Mark Nash and Andrew Higson's documentary "The Acting Tapes," broadcast on Britain's Channel 4, dismisses the stage-oriented British training in favor of American Method technique. Higson later stated: "Once English actors speak, not only do they speak with a class accent, but they are definitely trying to say 'I am speaking'" (2). In truth, these approaches simply represent different performance styles, any of which can be effective when placed in the appropriate context.

14. A useful history of the discourse on acting as it applies to film can be found in Naremore, *Acting in the Cinema*, 46–67.

15. This distinction relates to a larger debate over the status of literary character, which has similarly vacillated between formalist and mimetic principles. The mimetic orientation, which approaches characters as actual living beings, is perhaps most famously identified with Samuel Johnson's praise of Shakespeare's lifelike personages. It is similarly evident in some modern studies such as W. J. Harvey's *Character and the Novel*. "Characterization often overflows the strict necessities of form," Harvey writes.

"A surplus margin of gratuitous life, a sheer excess of material, a fecundity of details and invention, a delightful submergence in experience for its own sake—all of these are observable in the work of the great novelists" (188).

By contrast, the advent of the New Criticism and later semiotics has led to an emphasis on characters as formal constructs, most influentially embodied in recent years in Barthes's treatment of character as code in *S/Z*, Greimas's attempt to conceptualize characters as "actants," and Jameson's notion of the "character-effect." This approach has been applied to film by Robert Burgoyne and by John Frow. Both Jonathan Arac and Ian Hunter have explored some of the theoretical implications involved in the historical shifts in the discursive formations surrounding literary character.

In general postructuralism's disciplined attention to textuality has been accompanied by a diminished interest in the issue of character. This deemphasis is also reflected in the emphasis on abstraction in much radical avant-garde film, as Richard Brender has pointed out. In contemporary cinema studies the neo-formalism of Bordwell and Thompson has emphasized the role played by character in classical Hollywood cinema but has formulated this role in a similarly text-bound manner (in the context of goal-related activity within a cause-and-effect narrative construction).

16. Dyer's concept of structured polysemy has proven extremely useful as a way of explaining the means by which various aspects of a star's image become dominant at different times or in different situations. Dyer's own analysis of the evolution of Jane Fonda's image in *Stars* or the study of Joan Crawford carried out by Robert Allen and Douglas Gomery attest to the value of this approach. My own concern is less with describing the diverse and fragmented qualities of a star's persona than to focus on the ways in which the various strands coalesce in specific cinematic texts around a particular ideology of romantic love and marriage.

Other critics (for example, Boorstein, Braudy [*Fame*], and Kindem ["Hollywood's Movie Star System"]) have stressed the role of stars in promoting the ideal of bourgeois individualism. My own argument supports this formulation but concentrates on a specific aspect of this phenomenon by arguing that in the case of the stars the ideology of individuality is significantly expressed in terms of the "freedom" to engage in conventional activities associated with courtship.

17. Todorov's distinction between various kinds of verisimilitude was recently cited by Steve Neale as a useful frame for the consideration of film genres ("Questions of Genre"). I invoke Todorov again in my own discussion of the Western formula. One could make a further distinction between intertextuality (typecasting) and extratextuality (publicity, promotion, and critical discourse). The reader should also bear in mind the important distinction between issues involved in constructing a realist regime of performance and those connected on the one hand to the mimetic quality of the photographic image as a marker of realism and on the other to character-driven realistic fictional narrative.

Related series of distinctions regarding acting styles are exemplified in James Naremore's concept of the performance frame in *Acting in the Cinema*, Stephen Heath's divisions among agent, character, person, image, and figure, and David Marc's categories of representational, presentational, and documentary performance.

18. For a fuller discussion of such distinctions, see Graham Thompson's essay "Approaches to Performance." Gaylyn Studlar has shown that even as early as the 1920s

some movie fans questioned the veracity of the information on stars that was purveyed in the fan magazines ("The Perils of Pleasure").

19. See, for example, popular biographies of these figures by Kitty Kelly, Roland Flamini, and Joe Hyams. Taylor has presented special problems in relation to this model, for she has had a long career and has married often. Thus, early biographies present Mike Todd as her "great love," while more recent ones cast Burton in this role.

In the case of another of Hollywood's love goddesses, Ingrid Bergman, James Damico has argued that the construction of the star's persona as innocent and asexual contributed to the storm of controversy surrounding her affair with Roberto Rossellini; but it is also arguable that over the long term the publicity resulting from this liaison enhanced Bergman's star image ultimately rendering her as a noble victim of tragic romantic passion. Perhaps the star most successful at structuring her romantic life in such a way as to generate maximum publicity in the greatest range of media forums was Marilyn Monroe, whose marriages to honored national figures from other fields (sports and theater) invited widespread speculation about the nature of the romantic attraction in each case.

20. The best extended study of the development of Bogart's acting style can be found in Allan Eyles's book on the actor, especially pages 7–13. Peter Bogdanovich's essay on Bogart also makes a number of useful observations.

21. Sylvia Harvey has explored the ways in which the *film noir* cycle in general worked to undermine traditional family values. My own argument supports this general assertion but gives it greater historical specificity by reading *The Big Sleep* as an attempt to begin to reassert the traditional value of marriage by investing it with more modern connotations of companionship.

22. These characteristics are most in evidence in the final scene between Spade and Brigid; it is likely that Bogart used lip gloss and possibly also eye drops in this scene to achieve an appropriately adreneline-charged appearance.

23. I discuss the portrayal of homosexuality in *The Maltese Falcon* as it relates to Huston's other films in my essay "Mastery Through Masterpieces: American Culture, the Male Body, and Huston's *Moulin Rouge*."

24. Robin Wood has argued that Bogart's performance style was of minimal importance in the audience's construction of meaning in *The Big Sleep*. Wood writes, "One can question whether it is valid to claim that [Bogart] gives a great performance in *The Big Sleep*, or whether to discuss his performance except in the context the film gives it" ("Acting" 25). My own argument implies the contrary: that Bogart's persona provides the film itself with a context and that his performance carries a narrative that would fall apart without his presence.

25. Hawks was fond of reminiscing about the improvised quality of Bogart's impersonation of a prissy academic in this scene, but in fact it is taken directly from Chandler's novel (McBride, *Hawks on Hawks* 102).

Chapter Two

1. Psychobiographical studies of Griffith agree that women presented a problem for him personally, but they differ in the importance that they attach to his relationship with his father (Merritt, Rogin ["'The Sword Became a Flashing Vision'"], Schickel) as opposed to his sister (Hansen, Linda Williams).

2. The intertitles of Griffith's films, probably including this one, were frequently written by Anita Loos under the director's supervision.

3. Following most other critics of Griffith, I have used "parallel editing" and "crosscutting" interchangeably, although Bordwell et al. distinguish between these terms in order to delineate intercutting that depicts temporally distinct events from intercutting that depicts contemporaneous ones. (André Gaudreault makes a similar distinction but assigns the terms differently.) My discussion of Griffith's rescue montages assumes that shots intercut with one another always refer to contemporaneous events.

4. According to Kristin Thompson, the first known use of parallel editing occurred in the 1906 film *The One Hundred-to-One Shot*. Another early example was Wallace McCutcheon's 1908 film *Her First Adventure*, made at Biograph while Griffith was working there (Bordwell et al. 211).

5. A number of alternative explanations of Griffith's rescue sequences have been put forward over the years. In an essay on *The Lonely Villa* Rick Altman builds on Eisenstein's contention that Griffith's more general strategy of parallel editing grows out of a class-oriented vision that contrasts the haves and the have-nots. More formalistic readings have been offered by others. George Pratt, for example, has claimed that the "little melodramas" Griffith made early in his career provided him with special "impetus to film techniques," in particular the development of the last-minute rescue (78). William Johnson similarly argues that "Griffith's use of the last-minute rescue came from one predilection among several rather than from a dominant obsession" (14); and William Cadbury sees this strategy in somewhat abstract terms as "a reward for moral action" (45). Such accounts do not explain why Griffith came to prefer this device for structuring his climaxes. In *D. W. Griffith and the Origin of American Narrative Film*, the most authoritative study of the director's stylistic development to date, Tom Gunning sees the rescue montage as part of Griffith's move toward a character-centered "narrator system" of storytelling, but he does not address the question of why the filmmaker associated this technique with victimized women in particular. Raymond Bellour comes closest to my own approach in his analysis of Griffith's crosscutting as a device for creating the heterosexual couple, but he does not consider this project in relation to the particular roles assigned to each of the partners or the significance of the temporal attenuation that attends this project.

6. Kristin Thompson points out that the most common distortion in crosscut scenes involves the compression of time rather than its extension: Crosscutting can shorten the time that it takes to tell the story (Bordwell et al. 211). Such distortion is designed to promote narrative efficiency. When this consideration is born in mind, the ideological implications of reversing this practical convention appear even more striking.

The perverse nature of Griffith's strategy was noted early in his career by a reviewer of his 1909 Biograph one-reeler *The Drive to Life*, who wrote, "The thrilling suspense at the finish of the picture is too long drawn out to be fully effective. . . . In alternate scenes we see [the hero] racing through the streets and we see the fiancé and her girl friends about to eat the [poisoned] candy. They have the sweets at their lips for an interminable length of time, so long that we are sure their arms would be paralyzed, while the young man in the automobile is crashing through toll gates, knocking over wagons and whirling around corners. Of course he arrives in time, as we knew he would, but either the chase is too long or the act of eating the candy is commenced too early in the picture" (Quoted in George Pratt 78). Tom Gunning draws on the work of Meier Sternberg to explore the retardatory function of Griffith's parallel editing in terms of its capacity to generate suspense (*D. W. Griffith* 191), but Gunning refrains from speculating on the ideological function(s) that could be served by such a technique.

The misogynistic tendencies inherent in Griffith's rescue montages are taken to an extreme in many slasher films, where threats to women are often prolonged by editing far beyond their actual temporal duration by a relentless use of parallel montage. For further discussion of the use of parallel montage in the slasher film, see Carol Clover's essay, "Her Body/Himself: Gender in the Slasher Film."

7. Even after she left Griffith, the suffering that Gish subjected herself to in the interest of her performances made her legendary. Director King Vidor's autobiography, for example, states that when the star appeared at the MGM studio to shoot the death scene in his 1926 film version of *La Boheme*, she told him that she had managed to achieve the parched lips that the scene called for by not drinking any liquid for three days and sleeping with cotton pads between her lips and her gums (50–51).

8. The soft-focus effects that Sartov devised for close-ups of Gish have since become standard Hollywood practice for photographing aging women stars.

Gish's predilection for Sartov probably accounts for Bitzer's somewhat uncharitable view of her, just as Griffith's predilection for Gish probably accounts for the unflattering portrait of her in Linda Arvidson's memoirs.

9. Griffith's stereotyped portraits of racial others remained prominent features of his films throughout his career; it is important, however, to distinguish his approach to the various groups that he depicted. In the feature-length films, blacks most often appeared as shuffling, superstitious, and not overly honest servants (cf. *A Romance of Happy Valley* [1918], *The Greatest Question* [1919], *One Exciting Night* [1922]). Moreover, Griffith invariably cast white actors in major black roles. By contrast, he often depicted the plight of Native Americans quite sympathetically, especially in his early Biograph shorts.

10. Both Julia Lesage and Michael Rogin ("The Sword") treat miscegenation in their essays on Griffith. Lesage, however, sees it as a displacement of a more fundamental problem with misogyny. Rogin similarly approaches miscegenation as a reaction against the incest fantasy, but he formulates the issue in psychoanalytic rather than social and institutional terms (i.e., as an issue for Griffith, but not for his audience). By invoking the social taboo against miscegenation, however, Griffith is building on a tradition common to virtually all societies by representing marriage partners in terms of patterns of endogamy and exogamy.

The incest/miscegenation theme comes up in other Griffith films, but, to my knowledge, it is only in the films with Gish that miscegenation appears as a clearly defined taboo. In the 1910 *Ramona*, starring Mary Pickford, the Spanish heroine who marries a Native American against her family's wishes subsequently discovers that she herself has Native American blood (Griffith had played the Native American husband in the earlier stage version of Helen Hunt Jackson's popular novel.) Similarly, Clarine Seymour's Mary in *The Idol Dancer* (1920), marries a white man, although the "blood of vivacious France, inscrutable Java, and languorous Samoa mingle [sic] in her veins."

11. Background information on the sources of the film can be found in Stanley Kauffmann, Edmund Kelly, Kozloff, and Vineberg. The title refers to parts of Maine that were east of Boston.

12. Such a theme was especially ironic given the director's personal situation, for he was then in the process of transferring his own affection from Gish to Carol Dempster. Thus, if Gish had cause to suffer at that moment in history, it was Griffith himself who was to blame.

13. The contrast between the corrupt city slicker and the honest rustic was a staple of contemporary melodrama and was an important feature of the original play (Rahill).

14. William Everson sees Sanderson's escape from serious censure as indicating a modern, anti-Victorian tone in *Way Down East*; but it is difficult to reconcile this position with Griffith's painstaking depiction of Sanderson's culpability as well as the strongly disapproving attitudes of all of the film's sympathetically drawn characters (158).

15. The fullest account of the shooting of the ice sequence can be found in Lennig's essay. Gish and Barthelmess themselves appear in most of the footage, but Robert Henderson and Richard Schickel report that Allen Law and Elmer Clifton doubled for Gish in some of the scene's long shots.

Linda Williams has explored Griffith's use of this sequence as a device to punish Gish for her sexual "transgression," although she does not place the issue of birth at the center of her argument.

16. Griffith's attention to the female body as a symbol can be seen as an example of a more general tendency in his work, which Thomas Elsaesser and Adam Barker have referred to as metaphoric as opposed to the more metonymic tendencies of the classical Hollywood style proper. As Elsaessar and Barker observe, Griffith's cinema "relied on the perception of correspondences, of 'sight links,' of empathetic, antithetic relations, of mental and moral parallels" (307). If all Griffith's films exploit the body as a primary metaphor, *Way Down East*, in particular, centers this project on the figure of Gish.

17. Dudley Andrew's discussion of *Broken Blossoms* focuses on Griffith's less-critical presentation of Gish's body as erotic spectacle in the earlier film and the problems that this approach leads to. In part, *Way Down East* can be viewed as the director's attempt to resolve these problems by revising his earlier celebration of his star as an object of erotic contemplation.

18. These characters and the actors who play them were carried over by Griffith from Lotte Blair Parker's original play. Because of negative responses from the reviewers, Griffith cut many of the comic scenes from *Way Down East* after it had opened. For a description of the full version, see Gunning, "Rebirth."

19. This shot recalls a similar insert in Edwin S. Porter's 1903 *The Gay Shoe Clerk*, in which one of the first uses of a close-up shows a woman's foot and ankle as her shoe is being tied. Tom Gunning and others have commented on the exhibitionistic quality of Porter's shot ("The Cinema of Attractions" 65–66). It is tempting to see Griffith's use of a similar strategy in *Way Down East* as a comment on the purient overtones inherent in the developing conventions of cinematic representation as well as in the developing standards of sexual morality.

20. Griffith draws a more general contrast between the formal, forbidding spaces of the Tremont household in Boston and the flowing, hearth-centered domestic environment of the Bartlett farm thereby sharpening his condemnation of the emergent urban aristocracy who, as Lawrence Stone has observed "withdrew to their own world

behind their park walls or inside the grounds of their Palladian villas," largely abandoning "the rich and integrated community life of the past" (*The Family* 684).

21. Other widely cited discussions of this traditional positioning of women's bodies as a part of nature can be found in Griffin and Ortner. In the Victorian ideology to which Griffith subscribed, "sex" was excluded from the list of attributes of respectable women, except when it was associated with procreation and birth (Kern; Smith-Rosenberg, "Puberty to Menopause").

22. Gish's shift from broad pantomime to more subtle effects reflects the more general trend toward minimalism in motion-picture performance conventions of the period which the actress here adapts to a particular ideological purpose. The larger trend is discussed by Naremore (*Acting in the Cinema* 52–57), Pearson, Staiger ("The Eyes . . .") and Thompson (in Bordwell et al.). The pantomime form was associated with the teachings of François Delsarte, and the more subtle style with the new aesthetic of realism.

23. Griffith's depictions of strong affection between mothers and sons, which functions as a central issue in films like *The Greatest Question*, helps to create a narrative tension that leads to resolutions in which exogamy is perceived as a necessary step for the man as well as the woman.

24. The desire of men in general to appropriate women's procreative power is a hypothesis that has been put forward by a number of feminist theorists, including Margaret Mead, Karen Horney, and Simone deBeauvoir. More recently it has served as the focus of arguments by Lucy Fischer, Alette Odin Hill, Nancy Huston, Eva Fetter Kittay, and Adrienne Munich, among others.

25. As Nina Auerbach has noted, the fate of dying is common to many of the fallen women of Victorian melodrama. "Generally the fallen woman must die at the end of her story," Auerbach writes, "perhaps because death rather than marriage is the one implacable human change, the only honorable symbol of her fall's transforming power" (161).

26. In her autobiography, Gish reports that she objected to the look of pristine beauty that Griffith favored for Anna in this scene. Rejecting Griffith's fairy-tale vision of a beautiful heroine magically revived by a handsome hero, Gish believed that the character's appearance should reflect the marks of her ordeal (234).

27. Gish's strength is also emphasized in her most recent films, *A Wedding* (1978) and *The Whales of August* (1987).

28. The passion of this kiss is noted by Marjorie Rosen (51) and Molly Haskell (*From Reverence to Rape* 54–55), although it is not commented on by any of the film's early reviewers. Thus, the charge that Griffith is exploiting this scene for its "perverse" overtones is not borne out by the contemporary critical response. Further, the scene must be considered in relation to the scenario as a whole, which foregrounds and celebrates the power of women.

Chapter Three

1. In 1974 Alan Williams called for further study of the relationship between genres and stars, but thus far little work of this kind has been undertaken. One such discussion is Richard de Cordova's overview essay "Genre and Performance"; another, which explores the influences of two contrasting star types on the thematic motifs of

the musical, is Leo Braudy's chapter "Genre: The Conventions of Connection" in his *The World in a Frame*. Yet a third is Andrew Britton's consideration of the relationship between genres and star vehicles in chapter 6 of his *Katharine Hepburn: The Thirties and After*.

2. See, for example, Mary Ann Doane, *The Desire to Desire* (on the woman's film); Robin Wood, "An Introduction to the American Horror Film"; Linda Williams, "When the Woman Looks" (on the horror film); and various essays in E. Ann Kaplan, ed., *Women in Film Noir*.

3. Wayne's reticence with women does not appear to have been a feature of his private life; in fact, quite the contrary seems to have been the case. Nor was it an aspect of his screen presence in the Western programmers he made during the 1930s (see, for example, *The Trail Beyond* [1934] and *The Desert Trail* [1935]). Rather, it was a quality developed in the later Westerns he made that enhanced certain of the genre's thematic motifs.

4. A recent feminist analysis of the genre by Jane Tompkins advances perhaps the most in-depth gender-based elaboration of the wilderness-civilization opposition, relating these two poles to masculine and feminine principles respectively. My own discussion of the genre's ideological thrust, by contrast, emphasizes the Western's construction of bodily difference in racial rather than gender terms.

5. Tuska's project of "defantasization" distinguishes among three categories of Westerns: formulary, historical reconstructions, and romantic historical. In his view, only the last is shaped by ideological considerations, whereas "historical reconstructions" are characterized by a concern for accuracy, and formulary Westerns are ideologically empty. My own analysis, by contrast, sees all discourse, historical or otherwise, as motivated by ideological concerns. (In fact, Tuska waffles on the nature of the distinction between the formulary Western and the romantic historical reconstructive Western: cf., "What happens in the formulary Western happens because the formular structure demands it. What happens in a romantic historical reconstruction happens for an *ideological* reason" [19]; "not even the formulary Western entirely escapes this charge of possessing an ideology, albeit of a most rudimentary kind. . . . What truly distinguishes the romantic historical reconstruction from the formulary Western is the wide variety of ideologies which can be transmitted by means of it" [37].)

6. My discussion of nationalism draws on the work of a number of political theorists, including Benedict Anderson, Anthony Birch, John Breuilly, Ellis Cashmore, E. J. Hobshawm, Robert Miles, George Mosse, Charles Wagley and Marvin Harris, and Florian Znaniecki. It is important to bear in mind that most of these commentators speak from a European perspective in which racial and ethnic differences conform more closely to national boundaries. However, most scholars agree that the growth of a nationalist ideology in the United States was profoundly influenced by this tradition.

7. Although my subsequent discussion of the Western deals with most of these attributes, it does not explicitly address the issue of Protestantism. However, the Protestant churches that are so conspicuous in many of the towns that form the settings for Western films speak to the genre's association between American values and Northern European religious practices.

8. The United States Census Bureau officially declared the "closing" of the Western frontier in 1890.

9. Although Wayne never made first string at USC and lost his football scholarship after his second year there, Hollywood publicity inflated his particulation in this sport (Shepherd, Slatzer, and Grayson 90–91, 125). The clipping file at the Margaret Herrick Library in Los Angeles, for example, includes a 1942 Republic Pictures biography that states: "At the University, John was a star athlete and was an All American football designation."

E. J. Hobshawm has pointed to the significance of public athletic events in promoting nationalist sentiments: "What has made sport so uniquely effective a medium for inculcating national feelings, at all events for males, is the ease with which even the least political or public individuals can identify with the nation as symbolized by young persons excelling at what every man wants, or at one time in life has wanted, to be good at." (143) In the case of Wayne's identification with college football, it is important to note the sport's strong identification as uniquely American and the role played by the college leagues—especially nationally ranked teams such as USC—in generating widespread interest in activities that link regions and nation.

10. There is some dispute about why Wayne did not serve in the war. Because he had children, he could not be drafted, but he could have enlisted. Some commentators claim that an old football injury made him ineligible, but the most recent biography of the star by Shepherd, Slatzer and Grayson explains the situation by stating that he preferred to "attend to his career" (201).

11. Because I am here concerned with relatively circumscribed issues of characterization and body image in relation to the genre rather than with more general questions pertaining to generic identification and evolution, I have not attempted to address any of the theoretical controversies currently surrounding generic study. Thus I have not explored the factors that make the Western a genre, justified my choice of examples from the generic corpus, examined the relationship between genre and medium, or traced generic cycles. I have drawn most of my examples from films that are well known rather than attempting to select a representative corpus of works as is done by Bordwell, Staiger and Thompson; Huntington; and Wright. Neither have I attempted to trace the cycles of development and decline that characterize the studies of Westerns carried out by Bazin, Cawelti, and Warshow, or tried to distinguish between what Wright terms "classic" Western plots and later "professional" plots, though I have in passing alluded to some changes that the genre went through over the years. The most significant of these changes concerns the Western's treatment of racial difference, which was more blatant in the early years and assumed more disguised forms as criticism and evolving social awareness made filmmakers more sensitive to the potentially offensive nature of their representations. It could also be inferred from my argument that the Western's position as a myth of national origin was the result of a gradual evolution and that the Wayne persona emerged at a point in the genre's development when it was definitively positioning itself in terms of this function.

Similar considerations of economy and simplicity have led me to treat Wayne's image as monolithic, although a number of observers have noted its development over the years. (Levy, for example, distinguishes among five phases of the Wayne persona, while Sinclair distinguishes among seven.) The most obvious sign of evolution was the increasing irony and self-consciousness with which the characters he played were presented as his image grew into a cultural cliché.

12. This formulation of the place of women in the Western genre differs significantly from the conception put forward by Steven Neale, who sees women as necessary for the articulation of sexual difference through the organization of gazes. "The presence of [male and female characters] enables the process of the construction of sexual difference to function all the more effectively," he states. "Hence if the Western, like the war film, predominantly features the male, it also almost always incorporates the direct representation of woman, no matter how 'contrived' or clumsy this may seem in terms of the logic of a given narrative" (*Genre* 59). By contrast, my own conception of Hollywood's project of creating the couple places the narrative at the center of the argument. Thus, I have not postulated women chiefly as visual signifiers of sexual difference but rather as narrative representations of "love interest." Accordingly, I do not see their roles in Western stories as either "contrived" or "clumsy" but rather as central to the concerns of the formula itself.

13. Cf. Christopher Miller: "Africa is conceived of as a void and unformed prior to its investment with shape and being by the Christian or Islamic outside" (13).

14. For a discussion of the development of the concept of the suburb as an American ideal, see Stilgoe. A more particularized discussion which uses Los Angeles as its model can be found in May (49–59).

15. The 1960s cycle of television Westerns like *Bonanza*, *The Big Valley*, *The High Chaparral*, *Lanur*, and *The Man From Shiloh*, in which the heroes own vast ranches, is discussed in Brauer and Brauer (105–37).

16. In his study of the mythology of the American frontier, Richard Slotkin has explored the way in which the figure of the frontiersman who served as the prototype for the cowboy hero was developed in American myth as a hunter rather than a husbandman, a man who roamed freely over the land rather than cultivating and taking possession of it and who was "regenerated" by his violent confrontation with game and with the racial others who opposed the European westward expansion. Slotkin's formulation sees the mythological Western hero as someone who is "purified" by these acts of violence, which articulate his dominance over racial others as an extension of his dominance over nature.

The representation of the cowboy as a hunter rather than a husbandman also involves masculinist overtones that are carried over to his role as a rancher. Anthropologist Marshall Sahlins attributes Americans' heavy consumption of meat to a masculinist valuation of the movable livestock associated with the male ritual of hunting over the more prosaic occupation of husbandry, which produces vegetables and grain. The American preference for beef in particular undoubtedly owes a good deal to the heroic manly images of Western stars like John Wayne, who often portray ranchers engaged in producing this commodity.

17. Richard Sennett's book *The Fall of Public Man* traces the decline of this association between male costume and vocational calling.

18. As critics like Cawelti and Wright have noted, in Westerns made prior to World War II, when there was a less heightened awareness of the injustice perpetrated on indiginous populations in the course of Northern European westward expansion, the cowboy hero was more likely to settle down with the schoolmarm at the conclusion of the story. More recent films, however, have tended to stress the ambivalent relationship between the group of settlers with their aspirations toward ownership of the land and the free-ranging cowboy.

19. These two kinds of male characters conform to the contrasting types of traditional and modern men described by sociologist Joseph Plech. According to Plech, the traditional male is characterized by hyperaggressiveness, lack of emotionality, and a preference for the company of other men; whereas the modern is identified by his concern with economic achievement, bureaucratic power, and a preference for the company of women.

20. For discussions of the film that develop this point, see Pauly, "Howard Hughes," and Westrum.

21. Such a reading calls into questions Robin Wood's argument about Hawks's advocacy of sexual anarchy. ("The logical end of the characterizing tendencies of Hawks's work is bisexuality; the ultimate overthrow of social order, and the essential meaning of the chaos the films both fear and celebrate" ["Responsibilities," 660].) Although such revelations of homoerotic motifs in Hollywood cinema constitute valuable appropriations of mainstream culture in the interest of empowering marginalized discourses, one must read Hawks's films against the grain to justify the claim that their dominant message is one of "sexual anarchy." By contrast, a reading more consonant with the film's larger ideological project (the "preferred" reading) would argue that Hawks presents "aberrations" such as homoeroticism in his Westerns and male transvestitism in his comedies in order to assert more firmly the significance of the patriarchally dominated heterosexual hierarchy. Such departures from traditional gender roles are seen in the Westerns as immature, and in the comedies as humiliating. A sexually conservative position is invariably affirmed at the conclusion of Hawks's narratives by the image of conventional heterosexual coupling. Such endings underline the "fear" represented by the preceding portrayal of gender "chaos" more than they stress its "celebration." My reading thus differs from Wood's in placing greater emphasis on the containment of these tendencies effected by the films' conventional resolutions than on the challenges to the traditional order that precede them.

In addition, I would question Wood's assertion (also advanced by Wollen) that marriage and family are absent in Hawks's Westerns as opposed to Ford's, because Hawks's versions of the formula, like Ford's and for that matter most others, typically end with a suggestion of marriage. Moreover, much of the evidence for a homosexual reading of Hawks's male relationships can also be approached as evidence of his attempts to create quasi-familial structures (John Wayne, Montgomery Clift, and Walter Brennan in *Red River*; Kirk Douglas and Dewey Martin in *The Big Sky*) which are posed as inadequate substitutes for conventional families because these groups lack a woman—a lack remedied by the story's resolution.

A similar argument can be made in relation to Paul Willemen's reading of the homoerotic overtones of the climactic sadomasocistic encounters in Anthony Mann's Westerns with James Stewart. Although Mann presents these moments as perverse rather than immature as Hawks does, he, like Hawks, understands such aberrations as disruptions that the narrative strives to overcome by means of the conventional Hollywood panacea of "the love of a good woman." Here again, I take the meaning of these encounters as determined most fundamentally not by the visual strategies employed in the scenes themselves as they relate to the issue of sexual difference but by their place in a narrative context that seeks to reaffirm the need for traditional gender relations by dramatizing the threat posed by passion that is "misdirected" rather than placed in the service of traditional dynastic marriage.

22. For descriptions of this earlier tradition, see Stanton (32–33 et passim.) and Cashmore (45).

Because my discussion of racial difference in this chapter is based on an analysis of popular discourses surrounding the Western genre, I have followed the genre's convention of referring to the aboriginal people of America as "Indians" rather than using the more currently acceptable term *Native Americans*. (In the 1950 *Broken Arrow*, for example, though it is a film of avowedly pro-Indian sympathies, the Apaches are referred to as "Indians" while the Caucasians are called "Americans.")

23. An excellent recent discussion of the tradition of scientific racism can be found in Stephen J. Gould's *The Mismeasure of Man*.

24. Following the Second World War Cesar Chavez and other Chicano activists appropriated this discourse on race, using the term *La Raza* ("The Race") to refer to Chicano pride in their Mexican heritage (Jacobs and Landau 305–26).

25. The emphasis on Wayne's height is a prominent feature of publicity surrounding his image. Following are some sample comments drawn from the clipping file on Wayne at the Margaret Herrick Library:

> [t]he producers of Western movies like to pick as their stars big, husky he men. —Press Release, Republic Pictures, 1942
>
> It is entirely conceivable that the first films in which John Wayne starred were tailored to his natural acting style and towering height. —Press Release, Paramount Pictures, 1966
>
> On the set, he stands tall, towering above everything except the overhead mikes. —*Los Angeles Times Magazine*, 1967

26. This emphasis on race goes against the trend established in other recent work on cinematic representations of the male body. Following the direction set by Laura Mulvey, whose landmark essay "Visual Pleasure and Narrative Cinema" connected the bodies of women represented in mainstream film with the perverse sexual pleasure inherent in the act of viewing the cinematic image itself, Dyer ("Don't Look Now"), Neale ("Masculinity as Spectacle"), and Lehman ("*American Gigolo*") focus on the eroticism rather than the racial overtones contained in such images. But images of the human body, whether male or female, may contain meanings other than sexual ones. I will return to the issue of sexuality later in this chapter. For the moment, however, it is sufficient to note that Mulvey's own subsequent reading of the meanings contained in the cinematic representation of male bodies uses Vidor's 1946 *Duel in the Sun* as its main example. As Bazin points out in his essay on the Western, the emphasis on sexuality in this film is extremely atypical of the genre.

A study that departs from this pattern of accepting sexual difference as its primary distinction to consider the male body in terms of ethnicity has been carried out by Mark Winokur. Winokur has noted Hollywood's attempts to obliterate the evidence of ethnic difference in its leading men, a tendency more pronounced in the early years than presently. One can view this process as a specialized instance of what studies of the American social formation have identified as the assimilationist ideals envisioned in the American melting-pot metaphor, which has today partly given way to a more pluralistic ideal. It is generally agreed among social scientists that the melting-pot model has historically proved more readily applicable to some groups than to others. Winokur's study focuses on William Powell's identity as a Jew, and Jews constitute a group that, in the United States at least, has largely followed the assimilation model. In the case of minorities like Mestizos and Indians, who are typically characterized in popular American discourse as racial rather than ethnic Others, social scientists have tended to view the assimilationist model as more problematic.

Anthropologist Jack Goody has posed this difference in terms of a distinction between class and caste. "In sociological discussions the major difference tweeen class and caste turns upon the openness or closure of a series of horizontally juxtaposed groups or strata," he states, "that is, upon whether or not mobility is allowed between them" (*Production* 100). In American society those perceived as racial Others function largely in terms of a caste model; thus the mechanisms of social mobility are significantly closed to them. For other discussions of this distinction, see Omi and Winant (47–51), Lambert and Taylor (passim), Birch (230–32), and Ringer and Lawless (141–44). Most recently, Werner Sollors's *Beyond Ethnicity: Consent and Descent in American Culture* has embraced the assimilationist model without distinguishing between ethnicity and race, arguing simply that "an omission of the Afro-American tradition in a discussion of ethnic culture in America would create a very serious gap" (36).

27. At least, this is the story told by McDonald (113). Shepherd, Slatzer, and Grayson claim that the name was invented by Walsh and studio head Winfield Sheehan (111). All agree, however, on the rationale behind the choice. The source of the anecdote is in both cases Walsh, who was at the time planning to star the then-unknown Wayne as a hero who leads a wagon train westward in his 1930 *The Big Trail.*

Wayne's natal name was Marian Mitchell Morrison. He was later to claim that it "didn't sound American enough" for Hollywood's needs (Riggin 43).

28. By the 1940s blondness in males became associated with Nazism, and actors like Richard Widmark, Alan Ladd, and Dan Duryea established themselves as cold-blooded killer types. After the horror of World War II faded in the 1950s, both Widmark and Ladd created new heroic Anglo images in Westerns, though both are primarily remembered for their incarnations as satanic icons of the forties *noir* cycle.

29. Wayne was determined to make *The Green Berets* despite its controversial nature. However, it proved to be enormously popular, Wayne's second biggest moneymaker after *Chisum* (1970).

30. Knowles and Prewitt attribute the term *institutional racism* to Stokely Carmichael (183). For further discussions of this phenomenon, see their essay and also Miles (50–61).

31. Nedelsky and Limerick place different emphases on the relation between property and equality in American political theory. Nedelsky states, "Inequality has been at the center of the traditional American understanding of the relationship between property and liberty. Liberty, according to the tradition, generates unequal property through the free exercise of unequal faculties" ("American Constitutionalism," 260). Limerick, as I have already quoted her, stresses the importance of the principle of "property widely held." For the purposes of my own argument this difference of emphasis is moot, for both agree that contradictory values are involved and it is this contradiction that my argument involves.

32. For a discussion of the legal history of Indian-U.S. government affairs that argues that the Indians have been favorably treated, see Washburn.

33. The concept of the border informs much recent theorizing by Hispanic scholars. For a discussion of the complex meanings attached to the image of the Mexican-

American border in films produced in both countries, see Alex Saragoza's essay "The Border in American and Mexican Cinema."

34. My approach to these racial stereotypes departs from traditional "images of . . ." studies in that it considers the construction of such images in relation to the larger narrative and ideological concerns of the Western formula.

For similar reasons, my argument differs from those of Philip French and Brian Henderson, who have understood the Western's preoccupation with the Indians as a displacement of societal attitudes toward blacks during the fifties. Although this may be a valid enough association, it is important not to lose sight of the specific attributes assigned to particular ethnic groups in the Western formula, because these qualities interact with other elements in these narratives to create genre-specific meaning. In the case of the Western, in particular, I am suggesting that this meaning contributes in a significant way to America's sense of itself as a nation.

The few Westerns like *Broken Arrow* (1950), *Cheyenne Autumn* (1964), *Little Big Man* (1979), *The Ballad of Gregorio Cortez* (1984), and *Dances with Wolves* (1990) that attempt to treat the cause of Indians and Mexicans sympathetically demonize the Anglo population, thereby ultimately posing another form of racial hierarchy that also plays against the nationalist ideal of horizontal comradeship. (For an extended discussion of this tendency toward reverse racism in science fiction, see Huntington.) The Western in which Anglo and Indian cultures are perhaps treated most evenhandedly is Robert Aldrich's 1972 *Ulzana's Raid*, although the film presents a rather bleak view of both societies and certainly does not attempt to promote any vision of horizontal comradeship. For a good discussion of Aldrich's balanced portrayal in this film, see Nachbar.

35. This conception of the role played by language and the law in cinematic discourse differs from the Lacanian model which has enjoyed considerable currency in film studies within the last decade. My anthropologically oriented approach is designed to address more directly issues of racial difference and historical specificity which Lacanian theory has tended to overlook. In particular I have sought to avoid the Lacanian tendency to essentialize discussions of legal issues by referring to *the* law rather than discriminating among the various juridical regimes characteristic of diverse cultures.

The central place of language in the development of a nationalist sense of community is often commented on. See, for example, Benedict Anderson (69), Hobshawm (51–63, 93–100), Lambert and Taylor (15), and Ringer and Lawless (84–85).

36. For a further discussion of the role played by Indian speech patterns in Westerns, see Stedman.

37. For a good recent discussion of Derrida's critique of this concept, see Brunette and Wills (9–11).

38. In a subsequent discussion of this topic Goody expands further on this distinction. Written law, he states, leads to "a sharpened conception of rules and norms," whereas in oral cultures laws "are not so 'fixed'; they generally emerge in context (like proverbs), not in the 'abstracted' way of a code" (*The Logic of Writing* 174). (Note that Goody uses the term *code* differently from the way I do here.)

39. James Grant rewrote most of Wayne's dialogue to conform to the star's idiosyncratic speaking style (Shepherd, Slatzer and Grayson 272–73).

40. Earlier productions were more likely to represent the race issue more openly;

see, for example, the many silent Westerns that featured Chicano "bandidos" as villains. In William S. Hart's 1917 *The Aryan*, which the screen's first major Western star regarded as his finest work, Hart portrayed Rio Jim, an embittered white man who rules over a band of racially mixed outlaws. When a woman from a wagon train appears to beg for water "to save her race," however, Rio Jim abandons his band to assist the Anglos. The film included in its promotional materials a studio-composed synopsis describing its hero as follows: "He is a white man, she can see that, although he lives among half-breeds and Indians, and she knows he will run true to the creed of his race—to protect its women" (Fenin and Everson 92).

In the late 1920s the Mexican government placed an embargo on all Hollywood films that presented derogatory images of Mexicans (Woll 28), thereby helping to drive the race issue in the Western underground.

For an extensive discussion of the prevalence of racially stereotyped villains in early Westerns, see Stanfield.

41. Though Theweleit does not comment on the applicability of his analysis to other groups of males, reviews of *Male Fantasies* published by Paul Robinson and by Chris Turner and Erica Carter have claimed that his findings can indeed be extended to other men.

42. An Oedipally based interpretation of the Western was published by Kenneth Munden in 1958. Munden's analysis is based on a model such as Modleski calls for, in which the father figure plays a central role. But this approach leads to difficulties when Munden attempts to conceptualize the place of this male role in the Western drama. Munden poses the figure of the villain as a symbol both of the father and of the powerless mother because he must resort to "hired guns" to carry out the phallic threat he represents. However, the executive-type villain Munden describes, who represents corrupt tendencies among the civilized settlers, plays a relatively small role in most Western stories. Far more prominent is the villain who represents a savage violence. Even when hired guns work at the behest of an executive-banker type, it is typically one of these, and not the corrupt banker figure, who occupies center stage. In the 1971 *Shootout*, to cite only one of many examples, the banker figure is summarily dispatched by his hired gunman in order to clear dramatic space for the climactic showdown between the hero and the young gunman who has been haranguing him thoughout the action. The fact that the hero and villain are often coded as doubles of one another connects the dynamics of their relationship to those of a fragmented self-image rather than to father-son struggles, as I will argue.

43. For a discussion of the history of the Western's exploitation of spectacular effects, see Buscombe, *The BFI Companion to the Western* (41–42).

44. In his book *Anatomy as Destiny* Stephen Kern describes the changing conventions of male posture which dictated a ramrod stance before World War I and a more drooping appearance afterward.

45. The twenty-five-minute section that Ford directed in *How the West Was Won*, released the same year, featured Wayne in a cameo role as General Willaim T. Sherman. But *Liberty Valance* was Ford's last extended statement on Wayne's relation to the genre.

46. A report in *Variety* announced that the film had grossed 30 percent more abroad than in the United States. "Wayne continues as a hotshot name in faraway places," the author comments. "They like his masculinity."

47. Andrew Sarris has identified the term *Picketwire* as a bastardization of *Purgatoire* and thus places the setting of the film in Colorado, south of the Purgatoire River (*John Ford* 119).

48. The orator Starbuckle addresses his speech to "Ladies and Gentlemen," but no women are in evidence in the convention hall.

49. As George Fenin and William Everson have pointed out, the peaked Stetson had become outmoded for movie cowboys by the 1940s (189). *Man Without a Star* includes a scene in which Kirk Douglas's initiation of a green kid includes showing him how to push down the top of his Stetson to make a flat crown.

50. Doniphon's incipient alcoholism is suggested earlier in the film when Hallie denies him liquor. The character's weakness for liquor, which is only hinted at in Ford's film, is made explicit in the Dorothy M. Johnson short story on which the production is based.

For a discussion of other differences between the story and the film, see Jim Hill (263–65).

51. Ford's identification with the Wayne character in this film is also suggested by his later comments about it, for he has repeatedly insisted that the film is "about" the Wayne character and that this character is the movie's "hero."

For an extensive exploration of Ford's cinematic preoccupation with Irish characters and culture, see Lourdeaux.

Chapter Four

1. In her essay "Costume and Narrative" Jane Gaines notes the way in which similarities in the on-screen and offscreen clothing of major female stars increased the audience's inclination to believe that they were simply being themselves on-screen. Peter Wollheim's essay on Hollywood portraiture documents the way in which one highly elaborated Hollywood institution promoted this identification.

2. For whatever reasons, the power of women stars as box-office draws was far more pronounced in the early years of Hollywood than presently; whereas half of the top stars in the 1930s were women, by the 1970s, just over 10 percent were.

3. One could argue that the distinction between these two ways of speaking merely reflects the respective characters of the two stars; but the Hollywood selection process that favored Boyer on the one hand and Gardner on the other is itself part of the construction of this discourse. Its implications can be dramatized by applying John Thompson's concept of "the commutation test," in which the critic measures the effect of a performer in a given role by imagining another in the same role; this operation would result in Boyer's biographer speaking of him as as a "leggy brunette with a fully developed man's figure" and Gardner's referring to her as intellectual and high-minded.

4. I explore the association between hands and labor in chapter 2.

5. In her essay "Designing Women" Maureen Turim has carried out a case study that examines the ways in which Hollywood movies functioned with other mass-media discourses in the post–World War II era to popularize Christian Dior's "New Look" for women.

6. The consumer patterns of males are influenced more by phenomena such as the sports culture, which is discussed in chapter 3.

7. Hollywood's ideal of a female beauty that is natural yet highly constructed is

emphasized in Steve Neale's analysis of the movies' introduction of color technology. Neale argues that the appearance of female stars was placed at the center of the new ideology surrounding color, and that "the discourse of 'natural beauty' existed alongside, in combination with, the discourse of glamour" (*Cinema and Technology* 154).

8. Although scholars like Elizabeth Wilson, Kaja Silverman, and Maureen Turim ("Fashion Shapes") have construed women's relation to fashion as one of many sites of struggle between oppression and freedom, the freedom that they invoke is highly circumscribed, for women who do not follow fashion may be viewed as eccentric or simply as dowdy if their styles are not read in terms of an emergent fashion discourse, as, for example, Diane Keaton's offbeat attire was in *Annie Hall* (1977).

9. Cf. the comments of anthropologist Marcel Mauss: "I was ill in New York; I wondered where previously I had seen girls walking as my nurses walked. I had the time to think about it. At last I realized that it was in the cinema. Returning to France, I noticed how common this gait was, especially in Paris; the girls were French and they too were walking in this way. In fact, American walking fashions had begun to arrive over here, thanks to the cinema" (100).

10. It should be stressed that close-up photography allows for an intimate rapport between actresss and audience that decisively differentiates such scenes from the conventions of live performance, in which distance functions to present the woman as a body on display rather than as an ideal of desirable emotional intimacy. Thus the forums that feature live performances by women—burlesque and strip shows—privilege the female body in motion over the woman's capacity for facial expressiveness.

11. Another well-known film made in the same year, *All About Eve*, also treats the anomalous balance of power likely to govern a relationship between a younger man and an older, more powerful woman, similarly focusing on the professional insecurity of the latter; however, because the woman in this case is a stage rather than film actress, the subject of beauty *per se* is not emphasized. By contrast, a number of more recent Hollywood films such as *Harold and Maude* (1971), *Moment by Moment* (1979), *Forty Carats* (1973), *Love and Pain and the Whole Damn Thing* (1972), and *White Palace* (1990), treat far more sympathetically the reversal of power positions likely to occur in May-December love affairs in which the woman is the older partner. In the fifties, only Douglas Sirk's *All That Heaven Allows* (1955) explores this issue in any depth, although it attends more to sexual desire and social class than to gender-related power relations. Fassbinder's 1973 remake, *Ali: Fear Eats the Soul*, is more concerned with power relations but complicates them by adding a racial issue.

12. For the Norma Desmond role Wilder originally wanted Mae West, an actress whose constructed aura of overstated glamour was far more pronounced than Swanson's.

13. Earlier scripts of the film contained far more satire of Hollywood producers and studio executives as well as actors. (For example, in the draft at the University of Southern California: NORMA: "Look at them, in the front office—the rug peddlers, the junk dealers, the dance hall bouncers.")

14. Apparently the dark mood of *Sunset Boulevard* was not initially intended. Bob Thomas's biography of William Holden describes the original conception of the film as "a comedy depicting [a fading movie queen's] adventures in the new Hollywood and ending in triumph over her old enemies" (60). Similarly, the working title on record in the Paramount files at the Margaret Herrick Library in Los Angeles, "Can of Worms," suggests a lighter mood than is evident in the finished film.

15. Collaboration and its problems doubtlessly held a special appeal for Wilder during the making of *Sunset Boulevard*, for he was at the time going through a divorce as well as splitting up with his longtime screenwriter partner Charles Brackett. (Previously, Brackett and Wilder had often been referred to as "the happiest couple in Hollywood.") The motif of writing and collaborative writing in particular figures prominently throughout Wilder's oeuvre, but it is most thoroughly explored in *Sunset Boulevard*.

16. The motif of writing has, as I noted in the previous chapter, been one of the major concerns of poststructuralist theory. The poststructuralist group known as the French feminists have devoted particular attention to the relation between women's and men's writing. Of particular relevance in the present context is Hélène Cixous's contention:

> Male writers have needed the loving support of their muses, mistresses, or mothers in order to put them aside, deny them, reject them, idealize them or kill them in their writing, but, in any case, to *ingest* them so as better to evacuate them, purify themselves, and identify with the Father—if only then to kill him like the good sons they are (Jardine 89).

In keeping with the overall thrust of the present study, I have attempted to historicize this general formulation by associating the male writer's appropriation and subordination of the woman in this particular case with the film's advocacy of the ideology of the companionate couple.

17. The credit sequence thus constitutes a highly self-conscious variation on what Leo Charney has termed the "ouside-in" logic of classical credits, which are constructed as transitions into the realistic world of Hollywood narrative.

18. Wilder originally wanted a triumverate of gossip columnists to appear in the film: Hopper, Sidney Sklolsky, and Louella Parsons; but Parsons refused to cooperate. Early credit lists in the Paramount files at the Margaret Herrick Library cite Sklolsky, but his name is crossed out.

19. Some critics have contrasted Akerman's portrayal of explicit sexuality in *Je tu il elle* with the conventions of pornography, and it is true that the film's scenes of sexual adventure play on these expectations also. But the larger project of mainstream cinema's love stories is engaged by the anti-narrative and anti-spectacle thrust of the film as a whole.

Chapter Five

1. In keeping with Stanislavsky's commitment to exploring the limits of realist representation, this manner of playing represented the furthest extension of the "fourth wall" convention first espoused by Diderot as a means of increasing drama's capacity for illusionism. For a discussion of Diderot's influence on the development of theatrical realism, see Arnold Hauser's essay "The Origins of Domestic Drama."

2. For an attack on the efficacy of the technique of affective memory, see Bentley.

3. Stanislavsky himself was not hospitable toward the idea of Method acting in film. As Jay Leyda reports, "Stanislavsky's personal feeling about cinema began in contempt, warmed into antagonism, and never went beyond tolerance in later years" (76).

4. In the films he made as a director, however, Pudovkin's primary identification is with the Soviet tradition. Jay Leyda reports that *Deserter*, for instance, contained

3,000 shots as compared to the average sound film's 800 to 1,000 (297). In such films character is delineated through editing much more than through acting. Pudovkin freely resorted to other nonperformance techniques to portray character as well. In *Mother*, for instance, high-angle shots of the mother designated in the title suggest her helplessness, and the father's self-indulgence is revealed by a close-up of his hand scratching his stomach. In both *Film Technique* and *Film Acting* Pudovkin also proudly recounted his ability to elicit desired reactions from nonperformers. In his 1928 *Storm Over Asia*, for example, he was able to draw an awed and fascinated response from a crowd of Mongolian peasants by presenting them with a show put on by a Chinese conjurer out of range of the camera (170). And in *The Story of a Simple Case* (1932) he evoked a smile from a young boy for a scene in the film through similarly deceptive means (339–41). In such a creative context the controlled and integrated acting techniques cultivated by Method performers are ill served.

5. It is doubtful that the Kuleshov experiment ever actually took place; if it did, it is unclear what form it took. However, the status it is accorded in the writings of various Soviet theorists attests to the significance that they attached to the concept of character depiction through editing rather than acting. For a recent discussion of the problematic status of this well-known experiment see Holland and Kepley.

6. Pudovkin equates realism with the theory of montage even more emphatically later in *Film Acting* when he writes,

> Naturalism, idealism and realism in art stand in the same relation to one another as do mechanism, idealism, and dialectical materialism in philosophy.
>
> Those of the naturalist school, in copying a phenomenon of actuality and not generalizing it, create a mere cold mechanism, without the inner links that exist in actuality within the phenomenon, and without the outer links that bind it to other phenomena as a part to the whole (330).

In a later essay, "Stanislavsky's System in the Cinema," Pudovkin avoided this inconsistency in his discussion of cinematic realism and called upon the director to create unity in the actor's performance. Even here, however, the paradox of how the actor could develop inward feeling in the context of a filmic practice that gave primacy to editing remained unanswered.

7. Hollywood's orientation toward well-crafted stories did not necessarily reflect a valorization of writers over actors. Scripts were often tailored to the talents of specific actors, and important stars could have scripts rewritten to suit their preferences. But the highly polished surfaces of most studio-made films of the period precluded the ragged effect of too much creative participation by actors on the set.

Richard Blum argues that *Theodora Goes Wild*, directed by Boleslavsky in 1936, shows the effects of Method-style improvisation (29). Yet the film plays far more like a polished 1930s comedy than it does like the emotion-charged realistic dramas most associated with the Method school.

8. Useful accounts of this process can be found in Blum, Hirsch, Garfield, Lewis, and Strasberg.

9. Jean Benedetti's recent biography of Stanislavsky blames Richard Boleslavsky for this shift. Boleslavsky was the person primarily responsible for introducing Americans to the principles of Method acting, and he emphasized affective memory. Meanwhile, Stanislavsky himself was developing his theories in another direction which stressed physical action (259).

10. The lack of commitment that Marlon Brando had to the communal ideals of Stanislavskian performance has been attested to by Rod Steiger, who has complained bitterly about Brando's predilection for leaving the set during the production of *On the Waterfront* after his speeches had been filmed so that Steiger was forced to deliver his own lines to an assistant director in scenes such as the famous taxicab tête-à-tête. (Kazan's autobiography excuses Brando's discourtesy by explaining that the star had to leave the set to attend his psychoanalytic sessions [525].)

Published accounts of the group improvisations that Brando participated in at the Actors Studio reveal him as having been competitive and hostile toward his fellow performers, often expressing these feelings through the use of obscenities and physical violence. In part this behavior can be seen as a function of Strasberg's design of the exercises themselves, one of which was labeled "ineluctable force versus immovable object." An example of Brando's interpretation of this exercise is offered by David Garfield:

> Brando was supposed to be returning to his apartment where he had hidden some drugs. Eli Wallach was told he was an FBI agent who had been assigned to find the narcotics in Brando's apartment. He said to Brando, "Give me a minute to walk around the room, then you walk in." When Brando entered he looked at Wallach and said, "Who the fuck are you?" Wallach, shocked at the language—not usual on the stage at that time—said, "What?" Brando repeated the question. Wallach sputtered something about the super having let him in to look at the apartment, which he was interested in renting. Brando's language got cruder and cruder. Wallach said, "Just a minute." Brando pushed him and said, "Just get out." Wallach said, "Don't push, don't push." Brando continued the stream of threat and invective and kept pushing him. Wallach resisted and Brando picked him up and threw him out of the room, slamming the door behind him. Wallach opened the door to get back in; he was furious and really ready to kill Brando. But Marlon was laughing. So was the class—uncontrollably. In the post-scene discussion Wallach was criticized for not finding the narcotics (61–62).

Needless to say, such an approach has little to do with Stanislavsky's ideal of collaboration and ensemble playing.

11. The compatibility of the Method with the Hollywood star system has also been noted by Robert Brustein (*Culture Watch*) and Gordon Gow (*Hollywood in the Fifties*).

12. For Adler's interpretation of the Method, see her book *The Technique of Acting*, which has a foreword by Brando. In it she argues that Stanislavskian actors should attend to matters of style and craft—to the outer as well as the inner aspects of performance. Even in his early career, Brando followed this practice, taking on roles that emphasized accents, costume, and makeup in films like *Viva Zapata* (1952), *Julius Caesar* (1953), and *Teahouse of the August Moon* (1956). Nonetheless, Hollywood typed him as a rebel along with Clift and Dean.

Brando's ease with the techniques of self-exposure that the Method represents was later attested to by Bernardo Bertolucci, who commented on the star's bravura turn in *Last Tango in Paris* (1972). "Instead of entering the character, I asked him to superimpose himself on it," Bertolucci has recalled. "I didn't ask him to become anything but himself. It wasn't like doing a film. It was a kind of psychoanalytic adventure" (Morella and Epstein 139).

13. The personas of each of these performers also reflect the increasingly uncertain

class definitions of the postwar era, not least because their more naturalistic speech patterns invited class-oriented associations. Clift could be seen as the displaced aristocrat trapped in proletarian roles in films such as *A Place in the Sun* (1951) and *From Here to Eternity* (1953). Dean's image was that of a disaffected bourgeois exposing the emptiness of middle-class family life in *East of Eden* (1955) and *Rebel Without a Cause* (1955). Brando, with his ethnic-sounding name and his publicized associations with Third World women, was the proletarian figure caught between stifling bourgeois standards and loyalties toward marginal subgroups in films such as *The Wild One* (1954), *Viva Zapata*, and *On the Waterfront* (1954). For further discussions of these associations, see Biskind and Ehrenreich, and Naremore.

Brando promoted his identification as a lower-class ethnic by means of manufactured information that associated him with the Third World. A publicity release for *I Remember Mama*, his first stage role, claims that he was born in Calcutta. His first wife Anna Kashfi also claimed to be East Indian, though she was actually Irish. His later identification with the cause of American Indians became a significant part of the legend surrounding his star image after he allowed Sasheen Littlefeather to represent him at the Academy Awards ceremony in 1972.

14. Most of the more serious biographies of these stars refer to this issue. See, for example, Bosworth, Downing, Morella and Epstein, and Thomas. Many analyses of the stars and their films also make mention of it, including Biskind and Ehrenreich, and Lippe.

15. For a discussion of the relationship between juvenile delinquency and the mass media of the period, see Gilbert. Although Brando's character in *On the Waterfront* is described as "pushing thirty," the role was immediately identified with the adolescent conflicts represented in the films of the other Hollywood Method stars.

16. Kazan's reputation has suffered because of his identification as an actor's director. (See, for example, Robin Wood's essay "The Kazan Problem.") My own analysis of *On the Waterfront*, by contrast, implies that the integration of a strong performance style into a cinematic text is in itself a considerable directorial achievement.

17. See, for example, Biskind, Christiansen, Hey, Mellen, Murray, Neve, Roffman and Purdy, and Sayre. Most of these discussions see the film as a glorification of the act of informing, and thus as an apologia for Kazan's and Schulberg's friendly testimony before the House Un-American Activities Committee. The fullest statement of this argument can be found in Navasky.

Although persuasive on its own terms, this line of argument has tended to obscure elements of the film that distinguish what happens to its hero from what happened to its authors. The federal investigation in *On the Waterfront* is in no way corrupt or ill advised; it is based on the Kefauver hearings of corruption on the docks, not on HUAC. Thus, Terry's decision to inform is of a different order from the decision made by the filmmakers regarding HUAC. Although this shift may be thought of as placing the actions of Kazan and the others in a more favorable light, its relationship to the central concerns of the film is quite another matter. (I am indebted to Robert Savage for bringing this point to my attention.)

Other readings of the film have argued that its complications are focused on an isolated individual divorced from society as well as from romance. See, for example, Michaels, Kitses ("Elia Kazan"), and Hinson. An exhaustive history of the making of the film and the backgrounds of its various collaborators can be found in Hey.

18. In an analysis of performance in *East of Eden* Joanne LaRue and Carole Zucker have pointed out the way in which James Dean's Method style also functions to set his character apart from the others. However, Larue and Zucker assert that this strategy is wholly attributable to Elia Kazan's direction rather than Dean's acting, claiming that the star's Method-derived style does not contribute to a sense of the character's alienation. My own discussion of Brando in *On the Waterfront* makes a case against such a view by emphasizing the way in which any performer's extensive use of Method techniques associated with inwardness will tend to produce a characterization in which alienation is a central feature.

19. The final shooting script, which was later published, gives this line as, "Never will be much too soon" (26). Almost all Brando's dialogue departs from the published script in a similar manner, although the speeches of the other characters tend to follow Schulberg's written dialogue quite closely.

20. The strategy of repeating lines was to become a central feature of Sanford Meisner's version of the Method. Meisner contends that this technique "is emotional and impulsive, and *gradually*, when the actors I train improvise, what they say—like what the composer writes—comes not from the head but truthfully from the impulses" (36–37). Meisner's very different view of the effect of repeated lines speaks to the usefulness of this strategy in training, not in actual performance.

21. Terry's decision not to stage a climactic shoot-out calls into question Robert Ray's characterization of *On the Waterfront* as a "disguised Western" (145).

22. Here, as in many Hollywood films, the woman's resistance is seen as a function of her misunderstanding of the situation, which the film's authors have constructed to validate the male point of view, and of her own emotions. It is only by subjecting woman to physical force that the man compels her to acknowledge her "true" feelings. Thus the film's rhetoric works to undermine the integrity of the female will and to sanction the use of force in heterosexual relations. For discussions of the conventions governing the cinematic representation of forced sexual encounters, see my *Roman Polanski*.

In an essay on *American Gigolo* Peter Lehman has argued that representations of male passivity during erotic interplay lead to "hysterical" overcompensations in other parts of the narrative. My own reading of *On the Waterfront* supports this view by reading the scene of sexual assault as a compensation for the male's earlier passivity.

23. In an influential article Lindsay Anderson argued that this scene reflects a fascistic world view, for the men who follow Terry behave like "leaderless sheep in search of a new master" (130). By contrast, Michel Ciment and Kenneth Hey see the scene as a crucifixion, with Brando as a Messiah who suffers in order to lead the men into a better world (Ciment 112, Hey 690). But because neither of these positions considers the role played by sexuality in the film, they are unable to account for the scene's extreme emphasis on physicality and its relationship to Brando's distinctive performance style.

Chapter Six

1. My *Roman Polanski* discusses the influence of Grotowskian performance styles on the filmmaking practice of this director.

2. As this discussion implies, improvisation carries complex meanings and can be

used for many different purposes. Stanislavsky envisioned it as a means of expressing what I have elsewhere called "documentary realism," which aims to enhance the fiction's illusion of verisimilitude ("The Rhetoric of Cinematic Improvisation"). But, as I argue in what follows, improvisation can also convey a feeling of "threatrical realism," in which the process of performance itself is foregrounded. This latter effect has become increasingly important in relation to more recent performance styles, including that developed at Second City. In his book on John Cassavetes, Raymond Carney writes, "The films are not interested in displaying the relatively trivial improvisation of actors acting but rather the profound improvisation of characters living" (61). Such a judgment, while providing a valid characterization of Cassavetes's own use of improvisation, implies an unjustified denigration of theatrical improvisation, which is capable of conveying meanings that are equally valid.

3. For a further development of this concept in relation to Altman's oeuvre as a whole, see my "Critical Survey" in Wexman and Bisplinghoff.

4. An early version of the script dated 6/8/74 in the Margaret Herrick Library in Los Angeles provides far stronger motivation for Kenny: his car is trashed by Hal Phillip Walker supporters, and following the shooting he is heard claiming that he intended to kill Walker.

5. The ending of *Nashville* has been the subject of considerable controversy. Robin Wood voices the response of the majority of critics when he writes: "The ending of *Nashville* is a genuine disgrace, either cynical or sentimental or both" ("Hollywood" 106). My own argument contends that the ending is indeed both cynical and sentimental, and that the complex response it evokes is a function of the complicated spectator-text interaction it constructs rather than of the kind of textual and characterological "depth" demonstrated by the realist conventions of the classical style. Wood's essay on Altman puts forward the strongest sustained criticism of his work yet published, yet it is based on the assumption that the director is trying and failing to follow the classical norms I have just described.

6. Mamet's first ambition was to act, and he taught acting for a number of years. Many of the essays in his collections *Writing in Restaurants* and *Some Freaks* focus on acting, and Mamet wrote the introduction to the practical handbook on acting by Melissa Bruder and others, which advocates a system based on his methods.

7. Ambiguities surrounding the existence of a core of authentic values held by various characters are also strongly present in Chekhov's plays, and it is perhaps a sense of this affinity that has led Mamet to prepare adaptations of a number of Chekhov works, including *The Cherry Orchard*, *Uncle Vanya*, and *The Three Sisters*. It also seems plausible to infer that Chekhov's proto-absurdist sense of character lay behind his objection to Stanislavsky's interpretation of his work. According to Stanislavsky, Chekhov claimed that the director took what was intended as comedy and turned it into serious drama (100). This transformation undoubtedly involved treating the characters as Stanislavskian personages who revealed their authentic selves through performance rather than Ckekhovian role-players whose integrity remains an ambiguous issue.

8. Mamet had previously prepared screenplays for *The Verdict* (1982) and *The Untouchables* (1987). According to Carroll's bibliography, *Things Change* was written before *House of Games*, which was at one time called "The Tell."

9. In referring to the film's characters by name, I have followed the usage specified in the published screenplay.

10. The most thoroughgoing analyses of *House of Games*, by Laura Kipnis, Diane Shoos, and William Van Wert, all represent varients of this psychoanalytic reading. All these critics assume that the film's strategies operate under a fundamentally realist regime in which the characters' interiority is the central issue. My own reading, by contrast, argues that the film foregrounds the audience-text interaction in such a way as to render its relation to realism equivocal and its approach to spectator-character identification problematic.

11. Mamet has shown his interest in creating this kind of ambivalent interaction in the following statement:

> When playing poker it is a good idea to determine what cards your opponents might hold. There are two ways to do this. One involves watching their idiosyncrasies. . . . This method of gathering information is called looking for "tells."
>
> The other way to gather information is to analyze your opponent's hand according to what he *bets*.
>
> These two methods are analogous—in the Theater—to a concern with *characterization*, and a concern with *action*; or, to put it a bit differently: a concern with the *way* a character does something and, on the other hand, the actual *thing that he does* (*Writing in Restaurants*).

12. The published script renders the line somewhat differently, juxtaposing "dream" and "joke" ("Compression, inversion, elaboration are devices for transforming the latent into the manifest. In the dream, and also in the . . . ? In the *joke*!").

13. Mamet has claimed that he was heavily influenced in his conception of *House of Games* by Eisensteinian theories of montage editing, which he seems to have interpreted in terms of their ability to render the emotional significance of a character's point of view. For example, the vignette in which Joey demonstrates a brief con for Dr. Ford's benefit was altered during the course of production, presumably to make it more dramatic in terms of its point-of-view implications. (In the final version, the trick is exposed by a shift in the camera's position.) (See *House of Games* vi–vii and 26.) Mamet himself has explained the Eisensteinian influence by claiming that he has learned to use "uninflected" shots and to carry the emotional charge of a scene through editing rather than mise-en-scène. The meaning of this distinction is rather difficult to pin down, but it remains clear that Mamet follows the principles of the continuity editing system rather than those of Eisensteinian montage.

14. In *Frame Analysis*, his study of fabrications and deceptions, Erving Goffman has noted that the most elaborate cons occur as artistic representations rather than in the real world because in fiction the perpetrator is in a better position to control the possible anticipated responses of the victim and thus to create more elaborate "chains" and "sequential containments" (181, 186). Mamet's con is a good example of this difference, because it is constructed to operate effectively in the world that he has created, and not necessarily in the world outside the film.

15. In the published screenplay of the film, the second part of this speech is rendered in quotation marks as I have reproduced it here (69).

16. It is also possible, of course, to read this statement as evidence of a slip-up on the part of a writer-director who does not intend to "cheat" on his audience. One would then judge *House of Games* as an imperfect film.

17. The thematic implications of Bohr's principle of complementarity are provocatively explored in Gerald Holton's *Thematic Origins of Scientific Thought*, from which

the quotations in the present essay are taken. Bohr's conception was later popularized in a book by J. Robert Oppenheimer. Oppenheimer's book, in turn, was invoked by Norman Rabkin to account for the effect of Shakespearean drama. Rabkin's use of the principle, however, differs from my own in that it focuses on opposing thematic currents within texts rather than instabilities in the spectator-text relationship.

18. The attitude toward women displayed in Mamet's published interviews and essays is ambivalent at best. "[I]f you look around the United States of America, you will see that we do have a certain amount of misogynistic men," he has stated. "For example, all of them" (Harriott 84). However, there is also ample evidence that the playwright-filmmaker sees gender difference as a fruitful source for dramatic ideas. He has asserted, for instance, that "the competition of business . . . is most times prosecuted for the benefit of oneself as breadwinner, as provider, as paterfamilias, as vestgial and outmoded as you may feel those roles to be" (*Some Freaks* 90).

19. The meaning of this moment has been much debated. Geoffrey Nowell-Smith calls it "contrived." W.T.J. Mitchell contends that Mookie commits an "ethical" act by which he deflects violence away from people and toward property. This contention has been challenged by both Jerome Christensen and Andrew Ross. Christiansen sees it as merely "stupid" (585), whereas Ross understands it, as I do, as "a response to the economic underdevelopment of the community" (37).

Lee himself has said: "It's a complete lack of faith in the judicial system, a complete lack of faith in justice taking place" (Ebert 891).

20. Before making *Do the Right Thing* Lee directed the video of Public Enemy's "Fight the Power"; Thomas Doherty has noted the influence of music videos generally on the style of the film, especially on its opening credit sequence (19).

21. Some commentators have critized the film's handling of characterization. Murray Kempton, for example, has argued that Mookie is an insufficiently sympathetic protagonist. And Stanley Crouch has objected that the white character, Sal, is portrayed in more complex, realistic terms than the blacks are. However, the film's strategy is designed to complicate the audience's responses, disallowing any single character to be seen simply as a hero or a villain. As Andrew Ross has stated, the film shows "an absence of any clear cut or reductionist picture of racial conflict of the sort that is comfortably valorized in white liberal film which address the topic of race relations" (40).

22. Houston Baker has traced the relationship of this oral tradition to black literature in his book *Blues, Ideology and Afro-American Literature*.

23. Raheem's love-hate speech is a variant of a similar sermon in *The Night of the Hunter*.

BIBLIOGRAPHY

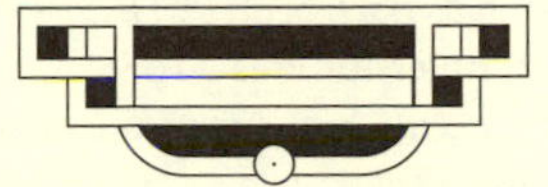

Abrams, M. H. "Literature as a Revelation of Personality." Caughie 17–21.

Adams, Parveen. "Representation and Sexuality." Adams and Cowie 233–52.

———, and Elizabeth Cowie, eds. *The Woman in Question: M/F*. Cambridge, Mass.: MIT Press, 1990.

Adler, Stella. *The Technique of Acting*. New York: Bantam, 1988.

Affron, Charles. *Star Acting: Gish, Garbo, Davis*. New York: Dutton, 1977.

Albertini, Francesco. *Falling in Love*. Translated by Lawrence Venute. New York: Random House, 1983.

Allen, Robert, and Douglas Gomery. *Film History*. New York: Knopf, 1985.

Altman, Rick. *The American Film Musical*. Bloomington, Ind.: Indiana University Press, 1987.

———. "Dickens, Griffith, and Film Theory Today." *South Atlantic Quarterly* 88.2 (1989): 321–59.

———. "*The Lonely Villa* and Griffith's Paradigmatic Style." *Quarterly Review of Film Studies* 6.2 (1981): 123–34.

Amossey, Ruth. "Autobiographies of Movie Stars: Presentation of the Self and Its Strategies." *Poetics Today* 7.4 (1986): 673–703.

Anderson, Benedict. *Imagined Communities: Reflections on the Origin and Spread of Nationalism*. London: Verso, 1983.

Anderson, Lindsay. *About John Ford*. London: Plexus, 1981.

———. "The Last Sequence of *On the Waterfront*." *Sight and Sound* 24 (1955): 127–30.

Andrew, Dudley. "*Broken Blossoms*: The Vulnerable Text and the Marketing of Masochism." *Film in the Aura of Art*. Princeton: Princeton University Press, 1984. 16–27.

Arac, Jonathan. "*Hamlet, Little Dorrit* and the History of Character." *South Atlantic Quarterly* 87.2 (1988): 311–28.

Ariés, Philippe. "Love in Married Life." Ariés and Béjin 130–39.

———. "Thoughts on the History of Homosexuality." Ariés and Béjin 62–75.

———, and André Béjin, eds. *Western Sexuality: Practice and Precept in Past and Present Times*. Translated by Anthony Forster. Oxford, England: Basil Blackwell, 1985.

Artaud, Antonin. *The Theater and Its Double*. Translated by Mary Caroline Richards. New York: Grove Press, 1958.

Arvidson, Linda. *When the Movies Were Young*. 1925. Reprint. New York: Benjamin Blom, 1968.

Auerbach, Nina. *Woman and the Demon: The Life of a Victorian Myth*. Cambridge, Mass.: Harvard University Press, 1982.

Aumont, Jacques. "Griffith—the Frame, the Figure." Translated by Judith Ayling and Thomas Elsaesser. Elsaesser and Barker 348–59.

Babu, B. Ramesh, ed. *Minorities and the American Political System.* New Delhi: South Asian Publishers, 1989.

Bailey, Beth L. *From Front Porch to Back Seat: A History of Courtship in America.* Baltimore, Md.: Johns Hopkins University Press, 1988.

Baker, Houston. *Blues, Ideology and Afro-American Literature: A Vernacular Theory.* Chicago: University of Chicago Press, 1984.

Bakhtin, Mikhail. (V. N. Vološinov). "Discourse in Life and Discourse in Art (Concerning Sociological Poetics)." Davis and Schleiffer 392–410.

———. *Rabelais and His World.* Translated by Hélène Iswolsky. Bloomington: Indiana University Press, 1984.

Balibar, Etienne. "Paradoxes of Universality." Goldberg 283–94.

Balio, Tino, ed. *The Hollywood Film Industry.* Madison, Wis.: University of Wisconsin Press, 1985.

Banner, Lois. *American Beauty.* New York: Knopf, 1983.

———. *Women in Modern America: A Brief History.* New York: Harcourt Brace Jovanovich, 1974.

Barnes, Michael L., and Robert J. Sternberg, eds. *The Psychology of Love.* New Haven: Yale University Press, 1989.

Barry, Iris. *D. W. Griffith: American Film Master.* New York: Museum of Modern Art, 1940.

Barthes, Roland. "The Face of Garbo." *Mythologies.* Translated by Jonathan Cape. New York: Farrar, Straus & Giroux, 1972.

———. *The Fashion System.* Translated by Matthew Ward and Richard Howard. New York: Hill and Wang, 1983.

———. *S/Z.* Translated by Richard Miller. London: Jonathan Cape, 1974.

Bartky, Sandra Lee. "Narcissism, Femininity, and Alienation." *Social Theory and Practice* 8.2 (1982): 127–43.

Bataille, Gretchen M., and Charles L. P. Silet, eds. *The Pretend Indians: Images of Native Americans in the Movies,* 22–34. Ames, Iowa: Iowa State University Press, 1980.

Battcock, Gregory, and Robert Nickas, eds. *The Art of Performance: A Critical Anthology.* New York: Dutton, 1984.

Baxter, John. *The Cinema of John Ford.* New York: J. F. Barnes, 1981.

Bazin, André. *What Is Cinema?* Translated by Hugh Gray. Berkeley: University of California Press, 1971.

Bell, Quentin. *Finery.* New York: Schocken Books, 1976.

Bellour, Raymond. "Alternation, Segmentation, Hypnosis: Interview with Raymond Bellour." Conducted by Janet Bergstrom. Penley 186–95.

———. "The Obvious and the Code." *Screen* 15 (1974): 12–20.

———. "To Alternate, to Narrate." Elsaesser and Barker 360–74.

Belton, John. "John Wayne: As Sure as the Turnin' of the Earth." *Cinema Stylists,* 340–48. Metuchen, N.J.: Scarecrow Press, 1983.

———. "*True Heart Susie.*" *Cinema Stylists,* 161–67. Metuchen, N.J.: Scarecrow Press, 1983.

Benamou, Michel, and Charles Caramello, eds. *Performance in Postmodern Culture.* Madison, Wis.: Coda Press, 1977.

Benedetti, Jean. *Stanislavsky.* New York: Routledge, 1988.

Bennedetti, Robert. *Seeming, Being, and Becoming: Acting in Our Century*. New York: Drama Book Specialists, 1976.

Bennett, Tony, and Janet Woollacott. *Bond and Beyond: The Political Career of a Popular Hero*. New York: Methuen, 1987.

Benthall, Jonathan, and Ted Polhemus, eds. *The Body As a Medium of Expression*. New York: Dutton, 1975.

Bentley, Eric. "Emotional Memory." *Theory of the Modern Stage: An Introduction to Modern Theatre and Drama*, 403–24. Edited by Eric Bentley. New York: Bantam Books, 1976.

Berger, Bennett M. "Suburbia and the American Dream." Yin.

Bhabha, Homi K. "The Other Question." *Screen* 24.6 (1983): 18–36.

———. "Signs Taken for Wonders: Questions of Ambivalence and Authority Under a Tree Outside Delhi, May 1817." *Critical Inquiry* 12.1 (1985): 144–65.

Bigsby, C.W.E. *David Mamet*. London: Methuen, 1985.

Bingham, Dennis. "Men with No Names: Clint Eastwood's 'The Stranger' Persona, Identification, and the Impenetrable Gaze." *Journal of Film and Video* 42.4 (1990): 33–48.

———. "Performance Anxiety: Jack Nicholson and the Art of Masculinity." Paper Delivered at the Society for Cinema Studies Conference, Washington, D.C., 29 May 1990.

Birch, Anthony H. *Nationalism and National Integration*. London: Unwin Hyman, 1989.

Birdwhistle, Ray L. *Kinesics and Context*. Philadelphia: University of Pennsylvania Press, 1970.

Birkin, Lawrence. *Consuming Desire: Sexual Science and the Emergence of a Culture of Abundence 1871–1914*. Ithaca, N.Y.: Cornell University Press, 1988.

Bishop, Sharon, and Marjorie Weinsap, eds. *Philosophy and Women*. Belmont, Calif.: Wadsworth, 1979.

Biskind, Peter. "The Politics of Power in *On the Waterfront*." *Film Quarterly* 29.1 (1975): 25–38. Reprinted in Peter Biskind. *Seeing Is Believing: How Hollywood Taught Us to Stop Worrying and Love the Fifties*, 169–82. New York: Pantheon, 1977).

———, and Barbara Ehrenreich. "Machismo and Hollywood's Working Class." *Socialist Review* 10.2/3 (March–June 1980): 109–30.

Blau, Herbert. *The Eye of Prey: Subversions of the Postmodern*. Bloomington: Indiana University Press, 1987.

Blum, Richard. *American Film Acting: The Stanislavsky Heritage*. Ann Arbor: UMI, 1984.

Bogdanovich, Peter. "Bogie in Excelsis." *Pieces of Time: Peter Bogdanovich on the Movies 1961–85*, 82–99. New York: Arbor House, 1985.

———. "The Duke's Gone West." *New York*, 25 June 1979, 67–70.

———. *John Ford*. London: Studio Vista, 1967.

Boorstein, Daniel. *The Image: A Guide to Pseudo-Events in America*. New York: Atheneum, 1980.

Bordwell, David. "*The Man Who Shot Liberty Valance*." *Film Comment* 7.3 (1971): 18–20.

———. *Narration in the Fiction Film*. Madison, Wis.: University of Wisconsin Press, 1985.

Bordwell, David, Janet Staiger, and Kristin Thompson. *The Classical Hollywood Cinema: Style and Mode of Production to 1960*. New York: Columbia University Press, 1985.

Bosson, Laurel. "Toward a Theory of Marriage: The Economic Anthropology of Marriage Transactions." *Ethnology* 27.2 (1988): 127–44.

Bosworth, Patricia. *Montgomery Clift*. New York: Bantam Books, 1978.

Bourdieu, Pierre. *Distinction*. Translated by Richard Nice. Cambridge, Mass.: Harvard University Press, 1984.

———. "Marriage Strategies as Strategies of Social Reproduction." Forster and Ranam 117–44.

Bowser, Eileen. "Griffith's Film Career before *The Adventures of Dollie*." In *Film Before Griffith*, edited by John L. Fell, 367–74. Berkeley: University of California Press, 1983.

———. *The Transformation of Cinema, 1907–1915*. New York: Scribners, 1990.

Brain, Robert. *The Decorated Body*. London: Hutchinson, 1979.

Braudy, Leo. "Film Acting: Some Critical Problems and Proposals." *Quarterly Review of Film Studies* 1.1 (1976): 1–18.

———. *The Frenzy of Renown: Fame and Its History*. New York: Oxford University Press, 1986.

———. "Genre: The Conventions of Connection." *The World in a Frame: What We See in Film*. New York: Doubleday, 1976.

———, and Morris Dickstein, eds. *Great Film Directors: A Critical Anthology*. New York: Oxford University Press, 1978.

Brauer, Ralph, and Donna Brauer. *The Horse, the Gun, and the Piece of Property: Changing Images of the TV Western*. Bowling Green, Ohio: Bowling Green University Press, 1975.

Brecht, Bertolt. *Brecht on Theater*. Edited and translated by John Willett. New York: Hill and Wang, 1964.

Brender, Richard. "Functions of Film: Léger's Cinema on Paper and on Cellulose, 1913–25." *Cinema Journal* 24.1 (1984): 41–69.

Breuilly, John. *Nationalism and the State*. New York: St. Martin's, 1982.

Brewster, Ben. "A Scene at the 'Movies.'" Elsaesser and Barker 318–25.

Brittain, Andrew, and Margaret Maynard. *Sexism, Racism, and Oppression*. Oxford, England: Basil Blackwell, 1984.

Brittain, Arthur. *Maculinity and Power*. New York: Basil Blackwell, 1989.

Britton, Andrew. "Cary Grant: Comedy and Male Desire." *CineAction* 7 (1986): 36–51.

———. *Katharine Hepburn: The Thirties and After*. Newcastle Upon Tyne: Tyneside Cinema, 1984.

Brod, Harry, ed. *The Making of Masculinities: The New Men's Studies*. Boston: Allen & Unwin, 1987.

Brooks, Peter. "Freud's Masterplot: A Model for Narrative." In *Reading for the Plot: Design and Intention in Narrative*, 90–112. New York: Vintage, 1985.

Brown, Beverley. "Natural and Social Division of Labor: Engels and the Domestic Labor Debate." Adams and Cowie 45–70.

———, and Parveen Adams. "The Feminine Body and Feminist Politics." *m/f* 3 (1979): 35–50.

Browne, Nick. "Griffith's Family Discourse: Griffith and Freud." Gledhill 223–34.

Brownmiller, Susan. *Femininity*. New York: Fawcett Columbine, 1985.

Bruder, Melissa, Lee Michael Cohen, Madeline Olnek, Nathaniel Pollack, Robert Privito, and Scott Ziegler. *A Practical Handbook for the Actor*. New York: Vintage, 1986.

Brunette, Peter, and David Wills. *Screen/Play: Derrida and Film Theory*. Princeton: Princeton University Press, 1989.

Brustein, Robert. *Culture Watch: Essays on Theatre and Society, 1969–1974*. New York: Knopf, 1975.

———. *Who Needs Theatre: Dramatic Opinions*. New York: Atlantic Monthly Press, 1987.

Buchtman, Herman. *Film and Television Make-Up*. New York: Watson-Guphill Publications, 1973.

Buckley, William, Krishna Kumar, and Ruth P. Simms, eds. *Racial Conflict, Discrimination, and Power*. New York: AMS Press, 1976.

Budd, Michael. "Genre, Director and Stars in John Ford's Westerns." *Wide Angle* 2.4 (1978): 52–61.

Burgoyne, Robert. "The Interaction of Text and Semantic Deep Structure in the Production of Filmic Characters." *Iris* 7 (1986): 69–80.

Buscombe, Ed. *The BFI Companion to the Western*. New York: Atheneum, 1988.

———. "The Idea of Genre in the American Cinema." Grant 11–25.

———. "Ideas of Authorship." Caughie 22–34.

———. "Painting the Legend: Frederic Remington and the Western." *Cinema Journal* 23.4 (1984): 12–27.

Byrnes, Heidi, ed. *Contemporary Perceptions of Language: Interdisciplinary Dimensions*. Washington, D.C.: Georgetown University Roundtable in Languages and Linguistics, 1982.

Cadbury, William. "Theme, Felt Life, and the Last-Minute Rescue in Griffith After *Intolerance*." *Film Quarterly* 28.1 (1974): 39–49.

Cadwalader, Sandra L, and Vine de Loria, eds. *The Aggression of Civilization: Federal Indian Policy Since the 1880s*. Philadelphia: Temple University Press, 1984.

Calder, Jenni. *There Must Be a Lone Ranger*. London: Hamish Hamilton, 1974.

Cancian, Francesca M. *Love in America: Gender and Self-Development*. New York: Cambridge University Press, 1987.

Caplan, Pat, ed. *The Cultural Construction of Sexuality*. London: Tavistock, 1987.

Cardullo, Bert. *Indelible Images: New Perspecitves of Classic Films*. Lanham, Md.: University Press of America, 1987.

Carney, Raymond. *American Dreaming: The Films of John Cassavetes and the American Experience*. Berkeley: University of California Press, 1985.

Carroll, Dennis. *David Mamet*. New York: St. Martin's, 1987.

Cary, Diana Serra. *The Hollywood Posse*. Boston: Houghton-Mifflin, 1975.

Cashmore, Ellis. *Dictionary of Race and Race Relations*. London: Routledge, 1984.

Caughie, John, ed. *Theories of Authorship*. London: Routledge & Kegan Paul, 1981.

Cavell, Stanley. *Pursuits of Happiness: The Hollywood Comedy of Remarriage*. Cambridge: Harvard University Press, 1981.

———. *The World Viewed*. Cambridge, Mass.: Harvard University Press, 1979.

Cawelti, John. "Reflections on the New Western Film." Nachbar 113–17.

Cawelti, John. *The Six-Gun Mystique*. Bowling Green: Bowling Green University Press, n.d.

Chaikin, Joesph. "The Context of Performance." In *Actors on Acting*, edited by Toby Cole and Helen Kritch Chinoy, 665–69. New York: Crown Publishers, 1970.

Charney, Leo. "Where to Begin? Paratext, Intertext, and the Viewer's Experience of Classical Credits." Paper delivered at the Society for Cinema Studies Conference, Los Angeles, 25 May 1991.

Chodorow, Nancy. *The Reproduction of Mothering: Psychoanalysis and the Sociology of Gender*. Berkeley: University of California Press, 1978.

Christiansen, Jerome. "Spike Lee: Corporate Populist." *Critical Inquiry* 17.3 (1991): 582–95.

Christiansen, Terry. *Reel Politics*. New York: Basil Blackwell, 1987.

Ciment, Michel. *Kazan on Kazan*. London: British Film Institute, 1973.

Clark, Danae. "Acting in Hollywood's Best Interest: Representations of Actors' Labor During the National Recovery Administration." *Journal of Film and Video* 42.4 (1990): 3–19.

Clover, Carol. "Her Body, Himself: Gender in the Slasher Film." *Representations* 20 (1987): 187–228.

Cohn, Jan. *Romance and the Erotics of Property: Mass-Market Fiction for Women*. Durham, N.C.: Duke University Press, 1988.

Cole, Toby, and Helen Krich Chinoy. *Actors on Acting*. New York: Crown, 1970.

Combs, Richard. "At Play in the Fields of John Ford." *Sight and Sound* 51.1 (1982): 124–29.

Comolli, Jean-Louis. "Historical Fiction: A Body Too Much." Translated by Ben Brewster. *Screen* 19.2 (1978): 41–53.

Cook, Pam, ed. *The Cinema Book: A Complete Guide to Understanding the Movies*. London: British Film Institute, 1985.

———. "Star Signs." *Screen* 20. 3 & 4 (1979–80): 80–88.

Coulter, Robert, and Steven Tullberg. "Indian Land Rights." Cadwalader and de Loria 185–204.

Coursen, David F. "John Ford's Wilderness." *Sight and Sound* 47.4 (1978): 237–41.

Coward, Rosalind. *Female Desires: How They Are Sought, Bought, and Packaged*. New York: Grove Press, 1983.

Crane, Cheryl. *Detour*. New York: William Morrow, 1988.

Cripps, Thomas. "Mexicans, Indians, and Movies: the Need for a History." *Wide Angle* 5.1 (1982): 68–70.

Crofts, Stephen. "Authorship and Hollywood." *Wide Angle* 5.3 (1983): 16–22.

Crouch, Stanley. "Do the Race Thing." *Notes of a Hanging Judge*. New York: Oxford University Press, 1990. 237–44.

Damico, James. "Ingrid from Lorraine to Stromboli: Analyzing the Public's perception of a Film Star." Marsden, Nachbar, and Grogg 66–74.

Daniels, Roger, and Marry H. L. Kitano. *American Racism: Explorations of the Nature of Prejudice*. Englewood Cliffs, N.J.: Prentice-Hall, 1970.

Dargis, Manohla. "Body/Language: On Acting Styles, the Rehearsal Process, and Performance Politics." *The Independent*, May 1990, 28–32.

Davis, Robert Con, and Ronald Schleiffer, eds. *Contemporary Literary Criticism: Literary and Cultural Studies*. 2d ed. New York: Longman, 1989.

DeBouvoir, Simone. *The Second Sex*. Translated by H. M. Parshley. New York: Knopf, 1952.

De Cordova, Richard. "The Emergence of the Star System in America." *Wide Angle* 6.4 (1985): 4–13.

———. "Genre and Performance: An Overview." Grant 129–39.

———. *Picture Personalities: The Emergence of the Star System in America*. Champaign, Ill.: University of Illinois Press, 1990.

de Lauretis, Teresa. "Aesthetic and Feminist Theory: Rethinking Women's Cinema." Pribram 174–95.

Deleuze, Gilles. *Cinema I*. Minneapolis: University of Minnesota Press, 1986.

de Loria, Vine. "The Problem of Indian Leadership." Maynard 21–26.

D'Emilio, John, and Estelle B. Freedman. *Intimate Matters: A History of Sexuality in America*. New York: Harper and Row, 1988.

Derrida, Jacques. *Of Grammatology*. Translated by Gayatri Spivak. Baltimore, Md.: Johns Hopkins University Press, 1974.

Deutelbaum Marshall, ed. *Image: On the Art and Evolution of the Film*. New York: Dover, 1979.

DiBattista, Maria. *First Love: The Affections of Modern Fiction*. Chicago: University of Chicago Press, 1991.

Didion, Joan. "John Wayne: A Love Story." In *Slouching Towards Bethlehem*, 29–41. New York: Simon and Schuster, 1979.

Ditz, Toby L. *Property and Kinship: Inheritance in Early Connecticut*. Princeton: Princeton University Press, 1986.

Doane, Mary Ann. *The Desire to Desire: The Woman's Film of the 1940s*. Bloomington: Indiana University Press, 1987.

———, Patricia Mellencamp, and Linda Williams, eds. *Re-Vision: Essays in Feminist Film Criticism*. Frederick, Md.: University Publications of America, 1984.

Docherty, Thomas. *Reading (Absent) Character: Towards a Theory of Characterization in Fiction*. New York: Oxford University Press, 1983.

Doherty, Thomas. "*Do the Right Thing*." *Film Quarterly* 43.2 (1989/1990): 35–40.

———. *Teenagers and Teenpics: The Juvenilization of American Movies in the 1950s*. Boston: Unwin Hyman, 1988.

Donald, James. "Stars." Cook 50–56.

Douglas, Mary. *Natural Symbols: Explorations in Cosmology*. New York: Pantheon, 1982.

Downing, David. *Marlon Brando*. New York: W. H. Allen, 1984.

Dubois, Ellen Carol. *Feminism and Suffrage: The Emergance of an Independent Women's Movement in America 1848–1869*. Ithaca: Cornell University Press, 1978.

Dyer, Richard. "Don't Look Now." *Screen* 23.4 (1982): 61–73.

———. *Heavenly Bodies: Film Stars and Society*. New York: St. Martin's, 1986.

———. "Homosexuality in Film Noir." *Jump/Cut* 16 (1977): 18–21.

———. "LANA: Four Films of Lana Turner." *Movie* 25 (1977/78): 30–52.

———. "Resistance Through Charisma: Rita Hayworth in *Gilda*." Kaplan 91–99.

———. *Stars*. London: British Film Institute, 1979.

Eagleton, Terry. *The Ideology of the Aesthetic*. Oxford: Basil Blackwell, 1990.

———. *Literary Theory: An Introduction*. Minneapolis: University of Minnesota Press, 1983.

Ebert, Roger. "Spike Lee." In *Roger Ebert's Movie Home Companion*, 889–93. Kansas City, Mo.: Andrews and McMeel, 1989.

Eckert, Charles. "The Carole Lombard in Macy's Window." *Quarterly Review of Film Studies* 3.1 (1978): 1–21.

———. "Shirley Temple and the House of Rockefeller." Steven 35–51.

Eder, Richard. "David Mamet's New Realism." *New York Times Magazine*, 12 March 1978, 40–43.

Editors of *Cahiers Du Cinema*. "John Ford's *Young Mr. Lincoln*." Nichols. vol. 1, 493–528.

Ehrenreich, Barbara. *The Hearts of Men: American Dreams and the Flight From Commitment*. Garden City, N.Y.: Doubleday/Anchor, 1983.

———, Elizabeth Hess, and Gloria Jacobs. *ReMaking Love: The Feminization of Sex*. Garden City, N.Y.: Doubleday/Anchor, 1986.

Eisenstein, Sergei. "Dickens, Griffith and the Film Today." In *Film Form*, edited and translated by Jay Leyda, 195–205. New York: Harcourt Brace Jovanovich, 1949.

Eisler, Benita. *Private Lives: Men and Women of the Fifties*. New York: Franklin Watts, 1986.

Ellis, John. "Stars as a Cinematic Phenomenon." In *Visible Fictions: Cinema, Television, Video*, 91–108. London: Routledge, 1982.

Elsaessar, Thomas. "*Nashville*: Putting on the Show." *Persistence of Vision* (1984): 35–43.

———, and Adam Barker. "The Continuity System: Griffith and Beyond: Introduction." Elsaesser and Barker 293–317.

———, with Adam Barker, eds. *Early Cinema: Space, Frame, Narrative*. London: British Film Institute, 1990.

Elster, Jon, and Rune Slagstad, eds. *Constitutionalism and Democracy*. Cambridge: Cambridge University Press, 1988.

Engels, Friedrich. *The Origin of the Family, Private Property, and the State*, edited by Eleanor Burke Leacock. New York: International Publishers, 1972.

Epstein, Cynthia Fuchs. *Deceptive Distinctions: Sex, Gender and the Social Order*. New Haven: Yale University Press, 1988.

Everson, William. *American Silent Film*. New York: Oxford University Press, 1978.

Eyles, Allan. *Bogart*. London: MacMillan, 1975.

———. *John Wayne and the Movies*. New Jersey: A. S. Barnes, 1976.

Faderman, Lillian. *Surpassing the Love of Men: Romantic Friendship and Love Between Women from the Rennaissance to the Present*. New York: William Morrow, 1981.

Fanon, Frantz. *The Wretched of the Earth*. Translated by Constance Farrington. New York: Grove Press, 1968.

Farber, Stephen. "The Films of Billy Wilder." *Film Comment* 7 (Winter 1971): 8–22.

Fass, Paula S. *The Damned and the Beautiful*. New York: Oxford University Press, 1979.

Fenin, George, and William Everson. *The Western: From Silents to Cinerama*. New York: Grossman, 1973.

Feuer, Jane. "*Nashville*: Altman's Open Surface." *Jump/Cut* 10/11 (1976): 31–32.

Fiedler, Leslie. *Love and Death in the American Novel*. rev. ed. New York: Stein and Day, 1966.

———. *The Return of the Vanishing American*. New York: Stein and Day, 1968.

Fischer, Lucy. *Shot/Countershot: Film Tradition and Women's Cinema*. Princeton: Princeton University Press, 1989.

———. "*Sunset Boulevard*: Fading Stars." In *Women and Film*, edited by Janet Todd, 97–113. New York: Holmes & Meier, 1988.

Flamini, Roland. *Ava*. New York: Coward, McCann and Geoghagan, 1983.

Flandrin, Jean-Louis. *Families of Former Times: Kinship, Household and Sexuality*. Translated by Richard Southern. New York: Cambridge University Press, 1979.

Ford, Dan. *Pappy: The Life of John Ford*. Englewood Cliffs, N.J.: Prentice-Hall, 1979.

Forster, Elborg, and Patricia M. Ranum, trans. and eds. *Family and Society: Selections from the Annales*. Baltimore: Johns Hopkins University Press, 1976.

Foucault, Michel. *The History of Sexuality*. Vol. 1, *An Introduction*. Translated by Robert Hurley. New York: Vintage, 1980.

———. "What Is an Author?" Caughie 282–91.

Fox, Robin. "The Conditions of Sexual Evolution." Ariès and Béjin 1–13.

Fraser, Nancy. *Unruly Practices: Power, Discourse and Gender in Contemporary Social Theory*. Minneapolis: University of Minnesota Press, 1989.

Freedman, Rita. *Beauty Bound*. Lexington, Mass.: C. D. Heath, 1986.

French, Philip. *Westerns: Aspects of a Movie Genre*. New York: Oxford University Press, 1977.

Freud, Sigmund. *Jokes and Their Relation to the Unconscious*. Edited and translated by James Strachy. New York: W. W. Norton, 1960.

———. "Narcissism: an Introduction." Translated by Cecil M. Barnes; revised by Joan Riviere. In *A General Selection from the Work of Sigmund Freud*, edited by John Rickman, 104–23. Garden City, N.Y.: Doubleday Anchor, 1957. (Originally published 1914.)

Friar, Ralph E., and Natasha A. Friar. *The Only Good Indian*. New York: Drama Books Specialists, 1972.

Frow, John. "Spectacle Binding: On Character." *Poetics Today* 7.2 (1986): 227–50.

Fuchs, Cynthia J. "*Sunset Boulevard*: What a Woman! What a Part!" Paper delivered at the Society for Cinema Studies Conference, Iowa City, 15 April 1989.

Gaines, Jane. "Costume and Narrative: How Dress Tells the Woman's Story." Gaines and Herzog 180–211.

———, and Charlotte Herzog, eds. *Costume and the Female Body*. New York: Routledge, 1990.

Gallagher, Tag. *John Ford: The Man and His Films*. Berkeley: University of California Press, 1986.

———. "Shoot-out at the Genre Corral: Problems in the 'Evolution' of the Western." Grant 202–16.

Garfield, David. *A Player's Place: The Story of the Actor's Studio*. New York: Macmillan, 1981.

Gates, Henry-Louis. "Editor's Introduction: Writing 'Race' and the Difference It Makes." *Critical Inquiry* 12.1 (1985): 1–20.

Gaudreault, André. "Detours in Film Narrative: The Development of Cross-Cutting." *Cinema Journal* 19.1 (1979): 39–59.

Gaylin, Willard, M.D., and Ethel Specter Person, M.D., eds. *Passionate Attachments: Thinking About Love*. New York: The Free Press, 1988.

Geduld, Harry M. *Focus on D. W. Griffith*. Englewood Cliffs, N.J.: Prentice-Hall, 1971.

Geertz, Clifford. *The Interpretation of Culture*. New York: Basic Books, 1973.

Gehrig, Wes D., ed. *Handbook of American Genres*. New York: Greenwood Press, 1988.

Gellner, Ernest. *Nations and Nationalism*. Oxford: Basil Blackwell, 1983.

Gilbert, James. *A Cycle of Outrage: America's Reaction to the Juvenile Delinquent in the 1950s*. New York: Oxford, 1988.

Gilder, Rosemond. *Enter the Actress*. Boston and New York: Houghton Mifflin, 1931.

Gilligan, Carol, and Eve Stern. "The Riddle of Femininity and the Psychology of Love." Gaylin and Person 101–21.

Gilman, Sander S. *Difference and Pathology: Stereotypes of Sexuality, Race, and Madness*. Ithaca: Cornell University Press, 1985.

Gilmore, David D. *Manhood in the Making: Cultural Concepts of Masculinity*. New Haven: Yale University Press, 1990.

Gish, Lillian, with Ann Pinchot. *The Movies, Mr. Griffith, and Me*. Englewood Cliffs, N.J.: Prentice-Hall, 1969.

Gledhill, Christine. "Developments in Feminist Film Criticism." Doane, Mellencamp and Williams 18–48.

———, ed. *Home Is Where the Heart Is: Studies in Melodrama and the Woman's Film*. London: British Film Institute, 1987.

———, ed. *Star Signs*. London: British Film Institute.

Goffman, Erving. *Frame Analysis*. Cambridge, Mass.: Harvard University Press, 1974.

———. *The Presentation of the Self in Everyday Life*. Garden City, N.Y.: Doubleday/Anchor, 1959.

Goggy, Gary A. "When Television Wore Six-Guns: Cowboy Heroes on TV." McDonald 218–62.

Goldberg, David Theo, ed. *The Anatomy of Racism*. Minneapolis: University of Minnesota Press, 1990.

Goody, Jack. *Comparative Studies in Kinship*. London: Routledge, 1969.

———. *The Development of the Family and Marriage in Europe*. New York: Cambridge University Press, 1983.

———. *The Logic of Writing and the Organization of Society*. New York: Cambridge University Press, 1986.

———. *Production and Reproduction: A Comparative Study of the Domestic Domain*. New York: Cambridge University Press, 1976.

———, and Ian Watt. "The Consequences of Literacy." *Literacy in Traditional Societies*, 27–68. New York: Cambridge University Press, 1968.

Gorbman, Claudia. *Unheard Melodies*. Bloomington: Indiana University Press, 1990.

Gordon, Linda. *Woman's Body, Woman's Right: A Social History of Birth Control in America*. New York: Grossman, 1976.

Gould, Stephen J. *The Mismeasure of Man*. Harmondsworth: Penguin, 1984.

Gow, Gordon. *Hollywood in the Fifties*. New York: A. S. Barnes, 1971.

Grant, Barry Keith, ed. *Film Genre Reader*. Austin, Tex.: University of Texas Press, 1986.

Greenberg, David. *The Construction of Homosexuality*. Chicago: University of Chicago Press, 1988.

Greene, Gayle, and Coppelia Kahn, eds. *Making a Difference: Feminist Literary Criticism.* New York: Routledge, 1985.

Greimas, Algirdas Julian. "Actants, Actors, and Figures." Greimas 106–20.

———. "On Anger: A Lexical Semantic Study." Greimas 148–64.

———. *On Meaning: Selected Writings in Semiotic Theory.* Translated by Paul J. Perron and Frank H. Collins. Minneapolis: University of Minnesota Press, 1987.

———, and Francois Rastier. "The Interaction of Semiotic Constraints." *Yale French Studies* 41 (1968): 86–105.

Grenier, Richard. "John Wayne's Image." *Commentary*, September 1978, 79–81.

Griffin, Susan. *Woman and Nature: The Roaring Inside Her.* New York: Harper and Row, 1978.

Griffith, Richard. *The Movie Stars.* Garden City, N.Y.: Doubleday, 1970.

Grotowski, Jerzy. *Toward a Poor Theatre.* New York: Touchstone Books, 1968.

Guerrard, Roger-Henri. "Private Spaces." In *A History of Private Life.* Vol. 4, *From the Fires of Revolution to the Great War*, edited by Michele Perrot and translated by Arthur Goldhammer. Cambridge, Mass.: Harvard University Press, 1990.

Gunning, Tom. "The Cinema of Attractions: Early Film, Its Spectator and the Avant-Garde." *Wide Angle* 8. 3–4 (1986): 63–70. Reprinted in Elsaesser and Barker 56–62.

———. *D. W. Griffith and the Origin of American Narrative Film: The Early Years at Biograph.* Urbana: University of Illinois Press, 1991.

———. "Rebirth of a Movie." *American Film* 10, no. 1 (1984): 18–19, 93.

———. "Weaving a Narrative Style and Economic Backgrounds in Griffith's Biograph Films." *Quarterly Review of Film Studies* 6.1 (1981): 11–26. Reprinted in Elsaesser and Barker 336–47.

Gustafson, Gary, and Bangs L. Tapscott. *Body, Mind and Method: Essays in Honor of Virgil C. Aldrich.* Boston: D. Reidel Publishing, 1979.

Habermas, Jürgen. *The Theory of Communicative Action.* Volume 1, *Reason and the Rationalization of Society.* Translated by Thomas McCarthy. Boston: Beacon, 1981.

———. *The Theory of Communicative Action.* Vol. 2, Translated by Thomas McCarthy. Boston: Beacon Press, 1984.

Hall, Edward T. *The Hidden Dimension.* Garden City, N.Y.: Doubleday, 1966.

———. *The Silent Language.* Garden City, N.Y.: Doubleday, 1959.

Halliwell, Leslie. *Halliwell's Filmgoer's Companion.* New York: Scribners, 1984.

Hammond, Dorothy, and Alta Jablow. "Gilgamesh and the Sundance Kid: The Myth of Male Friendship." Brod 241–58.

Handel, Leo. *Hollywood Looks at Its Audience A Report on Film Audience Research.* Champaign: University of Illinois Press, 1950.

Hansen, Miriam. "The Hieroglyph and the Whore: D. W. Griffith's *Intolerance.*" *South Atlantic Quarterly* 88.2 (1989): 361–92.

———. "Pleasure, Ambivalence, Identification: Valentino and Female Spectatorship." *Cinema Journal* 25.4 (1986): 6–32.

Harmetz, Aljean. *The Making of the Wizard of Oz.* New York: Knopf, 1977.

Harriott, Esther. "Interview with David Mamet." *American Voices: Five Contemporary Playwrights in Essays and Interviews* Jefferson, N.C.: McFarland, 1988.

Hartsock, Nancy. *Money, Sex and Power: Toward a Feminist Historical Materialism.* New York: Longman, 1983.

Harvey, Sylvia. "Woman's Place: The Absent Family of Film Noir." Kaplan 22–34.

Harvey, W. J. *Character and the Novel*. Ithaca: Cornell University Press, 1965.

Haskell, Molly. "Can TV Actors Make It in the Movies?" *New York Times*, 4 February 1979, sec. 2, 1+.

———. *From Reverence to Rape: The Treatment of Women in the Movies*. New York: Penguin, 1974.

———. "John Wayne: Straight From the Hip." Peary 505–9.

Hauser, Arnold. "The Origins of Domestic Drama." In *Theory of the Modern Stage: An Introduction to Modern Theatre and Drama*, edited by Eric Bentley, 403–24. New York: Bantam, 1976.

Hayden, Dolores. *Redesigning the American Dream: The Future of Housing, Work, and Family Life*. New York: W. W. Norton, 1986.

Heath, Stephen. "Body, Voice." In *Questions of Cinema*, 176–93. Bloomington: Indiana University Press, 1981.

Henderson, Brian. "*The Searchers*: An American Dilemma." *Film Quarterly* 34.2 (1980/81): 9–23.

Henderson, Robert M. *D. W. Griffith: His Life and Work*. New York: Oxford University Press, 1972.

———. *D. W. Griffith: The Years at Biograph*. New York: Farrar, Straus & Giroux, 1970.

Henley, Nancy. *Body Politics: Power, Sex, and Nonverbal Communication*. Englewood Cliffs, N.J.: Prentice-Hall, 1979.

Hey, Kenneth. "Ambivalence as a Theme in *On the Waterfront*. An Interdisciplinary Approach to Film Studies." *American Quarterly*. 31.5 (1979): 667–96. (Reprinted in *Hollywood as Historian: American Film in a Cultural Context*. Edited by Peter C. Rollins, 159–89. Lexington: University Press of Kentucky, 1983.)

Higson, Andrew. "Acting Taped—An Interview with Mark Nash and James Swinson." *Screen* 26.5 (September–October 1985): 2–25.

Hilger, Michael. *The American Indian in Film*. Metuchen, N.J.: Scarecrow, 1986.

Hill, Alette Olin. *Mother Tongue, Father Time*. Bloomington: University of Indiana Press, 1986.

Hill, Jim. *The American West from Fiction (1823) into Film (1909–1986)*. Jefferson, N.C.: McFarland, 1990.

Hirsch, Foster. *A Method to Their Madness: The History of the Actors Studio*. New York: Da Capo, 1984.

Hobshawm, E. J. *Nations and Nationalism Since 1780*. New York: Cambridge University Press, 1990.

Holland, Norman. "Film Response from Eye to I: The Kuleshov Experiment." *South Atlantic Quarterly* 88.2 (1989): 415–42.

Hollander, Anne. *Seeing Through Clothes*. New York: Viking, 1978.

Holton, Gerald. *Thematic Origins of Scientific Thought: Kepler to Einstein*. rev. ed. Cambridge, Mass.: Harvard University Press, 1974.

Hornby, Richard. "Understanding Acting." *Journal of Aesthetic Education* 17.3 (1983): 19–37.

Horney, Karen. *Feminine Psychology*. New York: W. W. Norton, 1967.

Houston, Penelope. "Rebels Without Cause." *Sight and Sound* 25.4 (1956): 178–81.

Hunter, Ian. "Reading Character." *Southern Review* 16 (1983): 226–43.

Huntington, John. *Rationalizing Genius: Ideological Strategies in the Classic American Science Fiction Short Story*. New Brunswick, N.J.: Rutgers University Press, 1989.

Huston, Nancy. "The Matrix of War: Mothers and Heroes." Suileman 119–38.

Hyams, Joe. *Bogart and Bacall: A Love Story*. New York: David McKay, 1975.

———. *Bogie: The Biography of Humphrey Bogart*. New York: New American Library, 1966.

Hyder, James. "*House of Games*." *Film Quarterly* 44.3 (1991): 61–62.

Jacobs, Paul, and Saul Landau, eds. *To Serve the Devil: Natives and Slaves*. New York: Vintage, 1971.

Jameson, Fredric. *The Political Unconscious*. Ithaca, N.Y.: Cornell University Press, 1981.

Jardine, Alice. "Death Sentences." Suileman 84–98.

Johnson, Dorothy M. "The Man Who Shot Liberty Valance." In *Indian Country*, 89–107. New York: Ballantine Books, 1953.

Johnson, Samuel. *Samuel Johnson on Shakespeare*. Edited by W. K. Wimsatt, Jr. New York: Hill and Wang, 1967.

Johnson, William. "Early Griffith: A Wider View." *Film Quarterly* 19.3 (1976): 2–13.

Kael, Pauline. "Marlon Brando and James Dean." In *The Movie Star*, edited by Elisabeth Weis. New York: Anchor, 1989.

Kaplan, E. Ann. "Mothering, Feminism, and Representation: The Maternal Melodrama and the Woman's Film 1910–40." Gledhill 113–37.

———, ed. *Women in Film Noir*. London: British Film Institute, 1980.

Katzenstein, Mary Fainsod. "Feminism and the Meaning of the Vote." *Signs* 10. 1 (1984): 119–38.

Kauffmann, Donald L. "The Indian As Media Hand-Me-Down." Bataille and Silet 22–34.

Kauffmann, Stanley. "D. W. Griffith's *Way Down East*." *Horizon*, Spring 1972, 51–60.

Kazan, Elia. Interview. *Movie* 19 (1971–72): 8.

———. *A Life*. New York: Anchor, 1989.

Kelly, Edmund. "*Way Down East*: A Popular Play of the 1920s." *Those Were the Days* 2 (April 1972): 28–30+.

Kelly, Joan. *Women, History and Theory*. Chicago: University of Chicago Press, 1984.

Kelly, Kitty. *Elizabeth Taylor: The Last Star*. New York: Simon and Schuster, 1981.

———. *His Way: The Unauthorized Biography of Frank Sinatra*. New York: Bantam Books, 1986.

Kempton, Murray. "The Pizza Is Burning." *The New York Review of Books*, 28 September 1989, 37–38.

Kepley, Vance, Jr. "The Kuleshov Workshop." *Iris* 4.1 (1986): 5–24.

Kern, Steven. *Anatomy as Destiny: A Cultural History of the Human Body*. New York: Bobbs-Merrill, 1975.

Kerr, Paul, ed. *The Hollywood Film Industry*. London: Routledge, 1986.

Kindem, Gorham R., ed. *The American Movie Industry: The Business of Motion Pictures*. Carbondale: Southern Illinois University Press, 1982.

———. "Hollywood's Movie Star System: A Historical Overview." Kindem 79–93.

King, Barry. "Articulating Stardom." *Screen* 26.5 (September–October 1985): 27–50.

———. "The Star and the Commodity: Notes Toward a Performance Theory of Stardom." *Cultural Studies* 1.2 (1987): 145–61.

King, Barry. "Stardom as an Occupation." Kerr 154–84.

Kipnis, Laura. "One Born Every Minute: *House of Games*." *Jump/Cut* 36 (1991): 25–31.

Kirby, Michael. "On Acting and Non-Acting." In *The Art of Performance*, edited by Gregory Battcock and Robert Niklas, 97–117. New York: E. P. Dutton, 1984.

Kitses, Jim. "Elia Kazan: A Structuralist Analysis." *Cinema* [Beverly Hills] 7.3 (n.d.): 26–35.

———. *Horizons West*. Bloomington: Indiana University Press, 1969.

Kittay, Eva Feder. "Womb Envy: An Explanatory Concept." Trebilliot 84–96.

Knowles, Louis L., and Kenneth Prewitt. "Institutional Racism in America and the Ideological Roots of Racism." Buckley, Kumar, and Simms 183–89.

Knox, Alexander. "Acting and Behaving." McCann 62–72.

Kobal, John. *Rita Hayworth: The Time, the Place, the Woman*. London: W. H. Allen, 1977.

Kolker, Robert Phillip. *A Cinema of Loneliness*. New York: Oxford University Press, 1980.

Kolodny, Annette. *The Lay of the Land: Metaphor as Experience and History in American Life and Letters*. Chapel Hill: University of North Carolina Press, 1975.

Kozloff, Sarah R. "Where Wessex Meets New England: Griffith's *Way Down East* and Hardy's *Tess of the d'Urberville's*." *Literature/Film Quarterly* 13.1 (1985): 35–41.

Kristeva, Julia. "In Praise of Love." In *Tales of Love*, translated by Leon S. Roudiez. New York: Columbia University Press, 1987.

Kuhn, Annette. "*The Big Sleep*: Censorship, Film Text and Sexuality." In *The Power of the Image: Essays on Representationn and Sexuality*, 74–95. Boston: Routledge and Kegan Paul, 1985.

Kuleshov, Lev. *Kuleshov on Film*. Translated and edited by Ronald Levaco. Berkeley: University of California Press, 1974.

Kunzle, David. *Fashion and Fetishism: A Social History of the Corset, Tight Lacing, and other Forms of Body Scupture in the West*. Towota, N.J.: Rowan and Littlefield, 1982.

Lakoff, Robin, and Raquel Scherr. *Face Value: The Politics of Beauty*. Boston: Routledge and Kegan Paul, 1984.

Lamb, Blaine P. "The Convenient Villains: The Early Cinema Views of the Mexican American." *Journal of the West* 14 (1975): 75–81.

Lambert, Wallace E., and Donald M. Taylor. *Coping with Cultural and Racial Diversity in Urban America*. New York: Praeger, 1990.

Lang, Robert. *American Film Melodrama: Griffith, Vidor, Minnelli*. Princeton: Princeton University Press, 1989.

———. "Looking for the 'Great Whatzit': *Kiss Me Deadly* and Film Noir." *Cinema Journal* 27.3 (1988): 32–44.

Langer, Mark. "*Tabu*: The Making of a Film." *Cinema Journal* 24.3 (1985): 43–64.

Larue, Johanne, and Carole Zucker. "James Dean: The Pose of Reality? *East of Eden* and the Method Performance." Zucker 295–324.

Lasch, Christopher. *The Culture of Narcissism*. New York: Norton, 1978.

Laver, James. *The Concise History of Costume and Fashion*. New York: Scribners, 1969.

Leacock, Eleanor Burke. "Introduction." Engels 7–66.

Leathers, Dale G. *Non Verbal Communication Systems*. Boston: Allen & Unwin, 1976.

Lehman, Peter. "An Absence Which Becomes a Legendary Presence: John Ford's Structured Use of Off-Screen Space." *Wide Angle* 2.4 (19): 36–43.

———. "*American Gigolo*. The Male Body Makes an Appearance of Sorts." Ruppert 1–9.

———, ed. *Close Viewings*. Tallahassee: Florida State University Press, 1990.

———, and William Luhr. *Authorship and Narrative in the Cinema*. New York: G. P. Putnam's Sons, 1977.

Lenihan, John H. *Showdown: Confronting Modern America in the Western Film*. Urbana, Ill.: University of Illinois Press, 1980.

Lennig, Arthur. "The Birth of *Way Down East*." *Quarterly Review of Film Studies* 6.1 (1981): 105–16.

Lerner, Gerda. *The Woman in American History*. Menlo Park, Calif.: Addison-Wesley, 1971.

Lesage, Julia. "Artful Racism, Artful Rape: Griffith's *Broken Blossoms*." Gledhill 235–54.

Levi-Strauss, Claude. *The Elementary Structures of Kinship*. Translated by Rodney Needham. Boston: Beacon Press. 1949.

Levitan, Jacqueline. "The Western: Any Good Roles for Feminists?" *Film Reader* 5 (1982): 95–108.

Levy, Emmanuel. *John Wayne: Prophet of the American Way of Life*. Metuchen, N.J.: Scarecrow Press, 1988.

Lewis, Robert. *Slings and Arrows: Theater in My Life*. New York: Stein and Day, 1984.

Leyda, Jay. *Kino: A History of the Russian and Soviet Film*. Princeton: Princeton University Press, 1983.

Limerick, Patricia Nelson. *A Legacy of Conquest: The Unbroken Past of the American West*. New York: W. W. Norton, 1988.

Lippe, Richard. "Rock Hudson: His Story." *CineAction!* 10 (October 1987): 46–54.

Lourdeaux, Lee. *Italian and Irish Filmmakers in America: Ford, Capra, Coppola, and Scorsese*. Philadelphia: Temple University Press, 1990.

Lowenthal, Leo. *Literature, Popular Culture, and Society*. Palo Alto, Calif.: Pacific Books, 1968.

Luhmann, Niklas. *Love As Passion: The Codification of Intimacy*. Translated by Jeremy Gaines and Doris L. Jones. Cambridge, Mass.: Harvard University Press, 1986.

Luhr, William. "Tracking *The Maltese Falcon*: Classical Hollywood Narration and Sam Spade." Lehman, *Close Viewings*, 7–22.

Lynn, Kenneth J. "The Torment of D. W. Griffith." *The American Scholar* (Spring 1990): 255–64.

Mair, Lucy. *Marriage*. New York: Pica Press, 1971.

Maland, Charles. *Chaplin and American Culture: The Evolution of a Star Image*. Princeton: Princeton University Press. 1990.

Malone, Michael. *Heroes of Eros: Male Sexuality in the Movies*. New York: E. P. Dutton, 1979.

Mamet, David. *American Buffalo*. London: Methuen, 1984.

———. *Glengarry Glen Ross*. New York: Grove Press, 1987.

———. *House of Games*. New York: Grove Press, 1987.

———. "I Lost It at the Movies." *American Film*, June 1987, 18+. Revised and expanded as the introduction to the published screenplay of *House of Games*.

Mamet, David. *Sexual Perversity in Chicago and the Duck Variations: Two Plays by David Mamet*. New York: Grove Press, 1978.

———. *Some Freaks*. New York: Viking, 1989.

———. *Writing in Restaurants*. New York: Penguin, 1986.

Marc, David. *Demographic Vistas*. Philadelphia: University of Pennsylvania Press, 1984.

Marowitz, Charles. *The Art of Being*. London: Secker & Warburg, 1978.

Marsden, Michael, John G. Nachbar, and Sam L. Grogg, Jr., eds. *Movies as Artifacts: Cultural Criticism of Popular Film*. Chicago: Nelson-Hall, 1982.

Martin, Emily. *The Woman in the Body: A Cultural Analysis of Reproduction*. Boston: Beacon Press, 1987.

Mast, Gerald. *Howard Hawks, Storyteller*. New York: Oxford University Press, 1982.

———, and Marshall Cohen, eds. *Film Theory and Criticism: Introductory Readings*. 3d. ed. New York: Oxford University Press, 1985.

Mauss, Marcel. "Body Techniques." In *Sociology and Psychology*, translated by Ben Brewster, 95–123. London: Routledge and Kegan Paul, 1979.

May, Elaine Tyler. *Great Expectations: Marriage and Divorce in Post-Victorian America*. Chicago: University of Chicago Press, 1980.

Maynard, Michael A., ed. *The American West on Film: Myth and Reality*. Rochelle Park, N.J.: Hayden Book Company, Inc., 1974.

Mayne, Judith. *The Woman at the Keyhole: Feminism and Women's Cinema*. Bloomington, Ind.: Indiana University Press,1990.

Mazón, Mauricio. *The Zoot Suit Riots: The Psychology of Symbolic Annhilation*. Austin, Tex.: University of Texas Press, 1984.

McBride, Joseph. *Hawks on Hawks*. Berkeley: University of California Press, 1982.

———, and Michael Wilmington. *John Ford*. New York: Da Capo, 1975.

McCann, Richard Dyer, ed. *Film: A Montage of Theories*. New York: Dutton, 1966.

McCrohan, Donna. *The Second City: A Backstage History of Comedy's Hottest Troupe*. New York: Perigee Books, 1987.

McDonald, Archie. "John Wayne: Hero of the Western." McDonald 109–25.

———, ed. *Shooting Stars: Heroes and Heroines of Western Film*. Bloomington: Indiana University Press, 1987.

McGann, Jerome J. "The Text, the Poem, and the Problem of Historical Method." *New Literary History* 12 (1981): 269–88.

McGee, Richard D. "John Wayne: Man with a Thousand Faces." *Literature/Film Quarterly* 16.1 (1988): 10–21.

Mead, Margaret. *Sex and Temperament in Three Primitive Societies*. New York: New American Libarary, 1935.

Meisner, Sanford, and Dennis Longwell. *Sanford Meisner on Acting*. New York: Vintage, 1987.

Mellen, Joan. *Big Bad Wolves: Masculinity in the American Film*. New York: Pantheon, 1977.

Merritt, Russell. "Rescued From a Perilous Nest: D. W. Griffith's Escape From Theatre Into Film." *Cinema Journal* 21.1 (1981): 2–30.

Messenger, Christian. *Sport and the Spirit of Play in American Literature*. New York: Columbia University Press, 1985.

Messner, Michael. "The Meaning of Success: The Athletic Experience and the Development of Male Identity." Brod 193–210.

Michaels, Lloyd. "Critical Survey." *Elia Kazan: A Guide to References and Resources*, 19–34. Boston: G. K. Hall, 1985.

Michie, Helena. *The Flesh Made Word: Female Figures and Women's Bodies*. New York: Oxford University Press, 1987.

Miles, Robert. *Racism*. New York: Routledge, 1989.

Miller, Christopher. *Blank Darkness: Africanist Discourse in French*. Chicago: University of Chicago Press, 1985.

Miller, Mark Crispin. "The Lives of the Stars." In *Boxed In: The Culture of TV*, 205–18. Evanston, Ill.: Northwestern University Press, 1988.

Mitchell, Juliet. *Psychoanalysis and Feminism*. New York: Pantheon, 1974.

Mitchell, W.T.J. "Going Too Far with the Sister Arts." In *Space, Time, Image, Sign: Essays on Literature and the Visual Arts*, edited by James A. W. Heffernan, 1–17. New York: Peter Lang, 1987.

———. "Seeing *Do the Right Thing*." *Critical Inquiry* 17.3 (1991): 596–608.

———. "The Violence of Public Art: *Do the Right Thing*." *Critical Inquiry* 16.4 (1990): 880–99.

Moch, Leslie Page, and Guy D. Stark. *Essays on the Family and Historical Change*. Arlington, Tex.: Texas A & M University Press, 1983.

Modell, John. "Dating Becomes the Way of American Youth." Moch and Stark 91–126.

Modleski, Tania. "A Father Is Being Beaten: Male Feminism and the War Film." *Discourse* 10.2 (1988): 62–77.

———, ed. *Studies in Entertainment: Critical Approaches to Mass Culture*. Bloomington: Indiana University Press, 1986.

———. *The Women Who Knew Too Much: Hitchcock and Feminist Theory*. New York: Methuen, 1988.

Monaco, James. *Celebrity: The Media as Image Makers*. New York: Delta Books, 1978.

Money, John. *Love and Love Stories: The Science of Sex, Gender Difference, and Pair Bonding*. Baltimore: Johns Hopkins University Press, 1981.

Mordden, Ethan. *Movie Star: A Look at the Women Who Made Hollywood*. New York: St. Martin's, 1983.

Morella, Joe, and Edward Z. Epstein. *Brando: The Unauthorized Biography*. London: Thomas Nelson, 1973.

———. *Rebels: The Rebel Hero in Film*. New York: Citadel, 1971.

Morin, Edgar. *The Stars*. Translated by Richard Howard. New York: Grove, 1960.

Morris, Desmond. *Manwatching*. New York: Abrams, 1978.

Mosse, George L. *Nationalism and Sexuality*. Madison: University of Wisconsin Press, 1985.

Mulvey, Laura. "Afterthoughts on 'Visual Pleasure and Narrative Cinema' Inspired by *Duel in the Sun*." *Framework* 15/16/17 (1981): 12–15.

———. "Visual Pleasure and Narrative Cinema." *Screen* 16.3 (1975): 6–18. (Reprinted in Rosen 198–209.)

Munden, Kenneth. "A Contribution to the Psychological Understanding of the Origin of the Cowboy and His Myth." *American Imago* 15.2 (1958): 103–48.

Munich, Adrienne. "Notorious Signs: Femininst Criticism and Literary Traditions." Green and Kahn 238–60.

Murray, Edward. "*On the Waterfront.*" *Ten Film Classics: A Re-Viewing*, 86–101. New York: Ungar, 1978.

Musser, Charles. "Moving Picture Actors: Their Status and Mode of Existence." Unpublished paper, 1984.

Myers, Sandra. *Westering Women: The Frontier Experience: 1800–1915*. Albuquerque: University of New Mexico Press, 1982.

Nachbar, Jack, ed. *Focus on the Western*. Englewood Cliffs, N.J.: Prentice-Hall, 1974.

———. "*Ulzana's Raid.*" In *Western Movies*, edited by William J. Pilkington and Don Graham, 139–48. Albuquerque: University of New Mexico Press, 1979.

Naremore, James. *Acting in the Cinema*. Berkeley: University of California Press, 1988.

———. "Authorship and the Cultural Politics of Film Criticism." *Film Quarterly* 44.1 (1980): 14–22.

———. "John Huston and *The Maltese Falcon.*" *Literature/Film Quarterly* 1.3 (1973): 235–49.

———. "*True Heart Susie* and the Art of Lillian Gish." *Quarterly Review of Film Studies* 6, no. 1 (1981): 91–104.

Nash, Mark, et al. "The Acting Tapes." Produced for Channel 4, Great Britain, 1985.

Navasky, Victor. *Naming Names*. New York: Viking, 1980.

Neale, Steve. *Cinema and Technology: Image, Sound, Colour*. Bloomington: Indiana University Press, 1985.

———. *Genre*. London: British Film Institute, 1980.

———. "Masculinity As Spectacle: Reflections on Men and Mainstream Cinema." *Screen* 24.4 (1983): 2–16.

———. "Questions of Genre." *Screen* 31.1 (1990): 45–66.

Nedelsky, Jennifer. "American Constitutionalism and the Paradox of Private Property." Elster and Slagstad 241–73.

———. "Law, Boundaries, and the Bounded Self." *Representations* 30 (1990): 162–89.

Neibaur, James L. *Tough Guy: The American Movie Macho*. Jefferson, N.C.: McFarland, 1989.

Neve, Brian. "The 1950s: The Case of Elia Kazan and *On the Waterfront.*" In *Cinema, Politics and Society in America*, edited by Philip Davies and Brian Neve, 97–118. Manchester: Manchester University Press, 1981.

Nichols, Bill, ed. *Movies and Methods*, vol. 1. Berkeley: University of California Press, 1976.

———. *Movies and Methods*, vol. 2. Berkeley: University of California Press, 1985.

Nolley, Ken. "Printing the Legend in the Age of MX: Reconsidering Ford's Military Trilogy." *Film Literature Quarterly* 14.2 (1986): 82–89.

Noose, Theodore. *Hollywood Film Acting*. Cranbury, N.J.: A. S. Barnes, 1979.

Nowell-Smith, Geoffrey. "Blackass Talk: *Do the Right Thing.*" *Sight and Sound* 58.4 (1989): 281.

———. "Minnelli and Melodrama." Gledhill 70–74.

O'Conner, John E. *The Hollywood Indian: Stereotypes of Native American in Films*. Trenton, N.J.: State Museum, 1980.

O'Dell, Paul, with Anthony Slide. *Griffith and the Rise of Hollywood*. New York: A. S. Barnes, 1970.

Omi, Michael, and Howard Winant. *Racial Formation in the United States: From the 1960s to the 1980s*. New York: Routledge and Kegan Paul, 1986.

Oppenheimer, J. Robert. *Science and the Common Understanding*. Simon and Schuster, 1954.

Orr, Christopher. "The Trouble with Harry: On the Hawks Version of *The Big Sleep*." *Wide Angle* 5.2 (1982): 66–71.

Ortner, Sherry. "Is Female to Male as Nature Is to Culture?" Rosaldo and Lamphere. 67–88.

———, and Harriett Whitehead. *Sexual Meanings: The Cultural Construction of Gender and Identity*. 1981.

Paredes, Raymond, ed. *The Cultural Atlas of Mexican-United States Border Studies*. Los Angeles: UCLA, forthcoming.

Parks, Rita. *The Western Hero in Film and Television: Mass Media Mythology*. Ann Arbor, Mich.: UMI Research Press, 1982.

Parry, Benita. *Delusions and Discoveries*. New Delhi: Orient Longman, 1972.

Pauly, Thomas. *Elia Kazan: An American Odyssey*. Philadelphia: Temple University Press, 1983.

———. "Howard Hughes and his Western: The Maverick and *The Outlaw*." *Journal of Popular Film and Television* 6.4 (1978): 350–68.

Pearson, Roberta E. "The Modesty of Nature: Performance Style in the Griffith Biographs." Ph.D. diss. New York University, 1987.

———. "O'rstep Not the Modesty of Nature: A Semiotic Approach to Acting in the Griffith Biographs." Zucker 1–27.

Peary, Danny, ed. *Close-Ups: The Movie Star Book*. New York: Workman, 1978.

Peary, Gerald, and Roger Shatzkin, eds. *The Modern American Novel and the Movies*. New York: Ungar, 1978.

Pechter, William S. "John Ford: A Persistance of Vision." Braudy and Dickstein 344–56.

Peiss, Kathy. *Cheap Amusements: Working Women and Leisure in Turn of the Century New York*. Philadelpia: Temple University Press, 1986.

———. "Making Faces: The Cosmetic Industry and the Cultural Construction of Gender, 1890–1930." *Genders* 7 (1990): 143–69.

Penley, Constance, ed. *Feminism and Film Theory*. New York: Routledge, 1988.

Perrot, Michelle, ed. *A History of Private Life*, vol. 4. Translated by Arthur Goldhammer. Cambridge, Mass.: Harvard University Press, 1988.

Person, Ethel Spector. *Dreams of Love and Fateful Encounters: The Power of Romantic Passion*. New York: W.W. Norton, 1988.

Pettit, Arthur G. *Images of the Mexican-American in Fiction and Film*. Edited by Dennis E. Showalter. College Station: Texas A & M University Press, 1980.

Pilkington, William T., and Don Graham. "Introduction: A Fistful of Westerns." Pilkington and Graham 1–13.

———, eds. *Western Movies*. Albuquerque: University of New Mexico Press, 1979.

Place, J. A. *The Western Films of John Ford*. Secaucus, N.J.: Citadel Press, 1974.

———. "Women in Film Noir." Kaplan 35–67.

Plech, Joseph. *The Myth of Masculinity*. Cambridge, Mass.: M.I.T. Press, 1981.

Polhemus, Robert. *Erotic Faith: Being in Love from Jane Austen to D. H. Lawrence*. Chicago: University of Chicago Press, 1990.

Pope, Kenneth S., ed. *On Love and Loving: Psychological Perspectives on the Nature and Experience of Romantic Love*. San Francisco: Jossey Bass Publishers, 1980.

Postlethwait, Thomas, and Bruce A. McConachie, eds. *Interpreting the Theatrical Past*. Iowa City: University of Iowa Press, 1989.

Powdermaker, Hortense. *Hollywood: The Dream Factory: An Anthropologist Looks at Moviemakers*. Boston: Little, Brown & Co., 1950.

Pratt, George C. "In the Nick of Time: D. W. Griffith and the 'Last-Minute Rescue.'" Deutelbaum 74–78.

Pratt, Mary Louise. "Conventions of Representation: When Discourse and Ideology Meet." Byrnes 139–55.

———. "Scratches on the Face of the Country; Or, What Mr. Barrow Saw in the Land of the Bushmen." *Critical Inquiry* 12.1 (1985): 119–43.

Pribram, E. Dierdre, ed. *Female Spectators: Looking at Film and Television*. New York: Verso, 1988.

Prindle, David. *The Politics of Glamour: Ideology and Democracy in the Screen Actors' Guild*. Madison, Wis.: University of Wisconsin Press, 1988.

Pudovkin, V. I. *Film Technique and Film Acting*. Translated and edited by Ivor Montague. New York: Grove Press, 1976.

———. "Stanislavsky's System in the Cinema." Translated by T. Shebunina. *Sight and Sound* 22.3 (1953): 115+. (Reprinted in *Pudovkin's Films and Film Theory*. Edited by Peter Dart, 186–206. New York: Arno, 1974.)

Pugh, D. *Sons of Liberty: The Masculine Mind in Nineteenth Century America*. Westport, Ct.: Greenwood Press, 1983.

Pye, Douglas. "Genre and History: *Fort Apache* and *Liberty Valance*." *Movie* 25 (1977–78): 1–11.

———. "The Western (Genre and Movies)." Grant.

Rabkin, Norman. *Shakespeare and the Common Understanding*. New York: The Free Press, 1967.

Radway, Janice. *Reading the Romance: Women, Patriarchy, and Popular Literature*. Chapel Hill: University of North Carolina Press, 1984.

Rahill, Frank. *The World of Melodrama*. University Park, Pa.: University of Pennsylvania Press, 1967.

Rainey, Brett. "Roy Rogers: The Yodeling Kid." *Heroes of the Range: Yesteryear's Saturday Matinee Movie Cowboys*. Metuchen, N.J.: Scarecrow Press, 1989. 291–311.

Ray, Robert. *A Certain Tendency in the Hollywood Cinema*. Princeton: Princeton University Press, 1985.

Reiter, Rayna, ed. *Toward an Anthropology of Women*. New York: Monthly Review Press, 1975.

Riggin, Judith, ed. "Interview: An American Voice." In *John Wayne: A Bio-Bibliography*, 31–67. New York: Greenwood Press, 1992.

Ringer, Benjamin B., and Elinor R. Lawless. *Race—Ethnicity and Society*. New York: Routledge, 1989.

Roach, Joseph R. "Power's Body: The Inscription of Morality as Style." Postlethwait and McConachie 99–118.

Robinson, Paul. *The Modernization of Sex*. Ithaca, N.Y.: Cornell University Press, 1989.

———. "The Women They Feared." *The New York Review of Books*, 21 June 1987, 14.

Roffman, Peter, and Jim Purdy. *The Hollywood Social Problem Film*. Bloomington: Indiana University Press, 1981.

"Rogers, Roy." In *Current Biography Yearbook:* 1983, 328–31. New York: The H. W. Wilson Co., 1983.

Rogin, Michael. "The Great Mother Domesticated: Sexual Difference and Sexual Indifference in D. W. Griffith's *Intolerance*." *Critical Inquiry* 15.3 (1989): 510–55.

———. "'The Sword Became a Flashing Vision': D. W. Griffith's *Birth of a Nation*." *Representations* 9 (1985): 150–95.

Rohdie, Sam. "Who Shot Liberty Valance? Notes on Structures of Fabrication in Realist Film." *Salmagundi* 29 (1975): 159–71.

Rorty, Richard. *Contingency, Irony, and Solidarity*. New York: Cambridge University Press, 1989.

Rosaldo, Michelle Zimbalist. "Women, Culture, and Society: A Theoretical Overview." Rosaldo and Lamphere 17–42.

———, and Louise Lamphere, eds. *Women, Culture and Society*. Stanford, Calif.: Stanford University Press, 1974.

Rosen, Marjorie. *Popcorn Venus: Women, Movies, and the American Dream*. New York: Coward, McCann and Geoghegan, 1973.

Rosen, Philip, ed. *Narrative, Apparatus, Ideology*. New York: Columbia University Press, 1986.

Ross, Andrew. "Ballots, Bullets, or Batman: Can Cultural Studies Do the Right Thing?" *Screen* 31.1 (1990): 26–44.

Ross, Ellen, and Rayna Rapp. "Sex and Society: A Research Note from Social History and Anthropology." In *Powers of Desire: The Politics of Sexuality*, edited by Ann Snitow, Christine Stansell, and Sharon Thompson, 51–73. New York: Monthly Review Press, 1983.

Ross, Lillian, and Helen Ross, eds. *The Player: Profile of an Art*. New York: Limelight, 1961.

Roth, Lane. "Vraisemblance and the Western Setting in Contemporary Science Fiction Film." *Literature/Film Quarterly* 13.3 (1985): 180–86.

Rothman, Ellen K. *Hands and Hearts: A History of Courtship in America*. New York: Basic Books, 1984.

Rubin, Gayle. "Traffic in Women: Notes Toward a Political Economy of Sex." Reiter 157–210.

Ruoff, Gene, ed. *The Romantics and Us*. New Brunswick, N.J.: Rutgers University Press, 1989.

Ruppert, Jeanne, ed. *Gender: Literary and Cinematic Representations*. Tallahassee: Florida State University Press, 1989.

Russo, Vito. *The Celluloid Closet: Homosexuality in the Movies*. New York: Harper and Row, 1981.

Sahlins, Marshall. "*La Pensée Bourgeoisie*: Western Society as Culture." In *Rethinking Popular Culture*, edited by Chandra Mukerji and Michael Schudson, 278–90. Berkeley: Univeristy of California Press, 1991.

Salt, Barry. "The Early Development of Film Form." In *Film Before Griffith*, edited by John L. Fell, 284–98. Berkeley: University of California Press, 1983.

Saragoza, Alex M. "The Border in American and Mexican Cinema." Paredes.

Sarris, Andrew. *The John Ford Movie Mystery*. Bloomington, Ind.: Indiana University Press, 1975.

———. "John Wayne's Strange Legacy: A Revisionist View." *The New Republic*, 4 August 1979, 33–36.

Saunders, David, and Ian Hunter. "Lessons for the 'Literatory': How to Historicize Authorship." *Critical Inquiry* 17.3 (1991): 479–509.

Sayre, Nora. "Behind the Waterfront." *Running Time: Films of the Fifties*, 151–72. New York: Dial, 1982.

Sayres, Janet, Mary Evans, and Nanneke Redclift, eds. *Engels Revisited: New Feminist Essays*. London: Tavistock, 1987.

Scarry, Elaine. *The Body in Pain: The Making and Unmaking of the World*. New York: Oxford University Press, 1985.

———. "Work and the Body in Hardy and Other Nineteenth Century Novelists." *Representations* 3 (1983): 90–123.

Schatz, Thomas. "The Western." Gehrig 105–24.

———. "The Western." *Hollywood Genres: Formulas, Filmmaking, and the Studio System*, 45–80. New York: Random House, 1981.

Schechner, Richard. "On Kinesic Analysis: A Discussion with Daniel Stern." *The Drama Review* 17.3 (1973): 102–8.

———. *Public Domain: Essays on the Theatre*. New York: Bobbs-Merrill, 1969.

———, with Cynthia Minz. "Kinesics and Performance." *TDR* 17.3 (1973): 102–8.

Schickel, Richard. *D.W. Griffith: An American Life*. New York: Simon and Schuster, 1984.

———. *His Picture in the Papers: A Speculation on Celebrity in America Based on the Life of Douglas Fairbanks*. New York: Charterhouse, 1973.

Schrader, Paul. *The Transcendental Style*. Berkeley: University of California Press, 1972.

Schneider, David M. *American Kinship: A Cultural Account*. 2d ed. Chicago: University of Chicago Press, 1980.

Schulberg, Budd. *On the Waterfront*. Carbondale: Southern Illinois University Press, 1980.

Schwartz, Hillel. *Never Satisfied: A Cultural History of Diets, Fantasies and Fat*. New York: The Free Press, 1986.

Sedgewick, Eve Kosofsky. *Between Men: English Literature and Male Homosocial Desire*. New York: Columbia University Press, 1985.

Seidler, Victor J. *Rediscovering Masculinity: Reason, Language, and Sexuality*. New York: Routledge, 1989.

Seidman, Steve. *Comedian Comedy: A Tradition in Hollywood Film*. Ann Arbor, Mich.: UMI Research Press, 1981.

Seigan, Bernard. *Economic Liberties and the Constitution*. Chicago: University of Chicago Press, 1980.

Self, Robert. "Robert Altman and the Theory of Authorship." *Cinema Journal* 25.1 (1985): 3–11.

Sennett, Richard. *The Fall of Public Man: On the Social Psychology of Capitalism*. New York: Knopf, 1977.

Shafer, Boyd C. *Nationalism and Internationalism*. Malabar, Fla.: Robert E. Krieger, 1982.

Shatzkin, Roger. "Who Cares Who Killed Owen Taylor?" Peary and Shatzkin 80–94.

Shepherd, Donald, Robert Slatzer, and Dave Grayson. *Duke: The Life and Times of John Wayne*. Garden City, N.Y.: Doubleday, 1985.

Sherrod, Drury. "The Bonds of Men: Problems and Possibilities in Close Male Relationships." Brod 213–40.

Shoos, Diane. "Female Spectatorship and *House of Games*: Case Her/History." Paper delivered at the Society for Cinema Studies Conference, Iowa City, 14 April 1989.

Shorter, Edward. *The Making of the Modern Family*. New York: Basic Books, 1975.

Silverman, Kaja. "Fragments of a Fashionable Discourse." Modleski 139–54.

Simpson, David. "Literary Critics and the Return to History." *Critical Inquiry* 14.1 (1988): 721–47.

Sinclair, Andrew. *John Ford: A Biography*. New York: Dial, 1979.

———. "Man on Horseback: The Seven Faces of John Wayne." *Sight and Sound* 44 (1979): 232–35.

Singer, Irving. *The Nature of Love*. Vol. 3, *The Modern Age*. Chicago: University of Chicago Press, 1984.

Singer, Jerome J. "Romantic Fantasy in Personality Development." Pope.

Sircello, Guy. "Beauty and Sex." Gustafson and Tapcott 229–40.

Siskin, Clifford. "Wordsworth Prescriptives: Romanticism and Professional Power." Ruoff.

Sklar, Robert. "'Oh! Althusser!': Historiography and the Rise of Cinema Studies." *Radical History Review* 41 (1988): 10–35.

Slide, Anthony. *The Griffith Actresses*. New York: A. S. Barnes, 1973.

Slotkin, Richard. *Regeneration through Violence: The Mythology of the American Frontier, 1600–1860*. Middleton, Ct.: Wesleyan University Press, 1973.

Smith, Henry Nash. *The Virgin Land*. New York: Vintage, 1952.

Smith-Rosenberg, Carroll. "The Female World of Love and Ritual: Relations Between Women in Nineteenth Century America." In *Disorderly Conduct*. New York: Oxford University Press, 1985.

———. "The New Woman As Androgyne: Social Disorder and Gender Crisis." In *Disorderly Conduct*, 245–96. New York: Oxford University Press, 1985.

———. "Puberty to Menopause: The Cycle of Femininity in Nineteenth-Century America." In *Disorderly Conduct*, 182–96. Oxford University Press, 1985.

Sollors, Werner S. *Beyond Ethnicity: Consent and Descent in American Culture*. New York: Oxford University Press, 1986.

Sontag, Susan. "The Double Standard of Aging." *Saturday Reivew*, 23 September 1972, 29–38.

Spivak, Gayatri. "Imperialism and Sexual Difference." Davis and Schleiffer 517–29.

Spolin, Viola. *Improvisation for the Theatre*. Evanston, Ill.: Northwestern University Press, 1983.

Spoto, Donald. *Camarado*. New York: New American Library, 1978.

———. *The Dark Side of Genius: The Life of Alfred Hitchcock*. New York: Ballantine, 1983.

Spurr, David. "Colonial Journalism: Stanley to Didion." *Raritan* 5.2 (1985): 35–40.

Staiger, Janet. "The Eyes Are Really the Focus: Photoplay Acting and Film Form and Style." *Wide Angle* 6.4 (1984): 14–24.

———. "Seeing Stars." *The Velvet Light Trap* 20 (1983): 10–16.

Stanfield, Peter. "The Western, 1909–14: A Cast of Villains." *Film History* 1 (1987): 97–112.

Stanislavsky, Constantin. *An Actor Prepares*. Translated by Elizabeth Reynolds Hapgood. New York: Theatre Arts Books, 1948.

———. *Stanislavsky's Legacy*. Edited and translated by Elisabeth Reynolds Hapgood. New York: Theater Arts Books, 1958.

Stanton, William. *The Leopard's Spots: Scientific Attitudes toward Race in America, 1815–1959*. Chicago: University of Chicago Press, 1970.

Stearns, Peter N. *Be a Man: Males in Modern Society*. New York: Holmes and Meier, 1979.

Stedman, Raymond. *Shadows of the Indian: Stereotypes in American Culture*. Norman: University of Oklahoma Press, 1982.

Steiger, Rod. Interview. In *Filmmakers Speak*, edited by Jay Leyda, 440–41. New York: Da Capo, 1984.

Steinberg, Cobbitt. *Reel Facts: the Movie Book of Records*. New York: Vintage, 1978.

Sternberg, Robert J., and Michael L Barnes, eds. *The Psychology of Love*. New Haven: Yale University Press, 1988.

Steven, Peter, ed. *Jump/Cut: Hollywood Politics and Counter Cinema*. Toronto: Between the Lines, 1985.

Stilgoe, John R. *Borderland: Origins of the American Suburb, 1820–1939*. New Haven: Yale University Press, 1988.

Stone, Lawrence. *The Family, Sex and Marriage in England* 1500–1800. New York: Harper and Row, 1977.

———. "Passionate Attachments in the West in Historical Perspective." Gaylin and Person 15–26.

Stowell, Peter. *John Ford*. Boston: Twayne, 1986.

Straayer, Amy Christine. "Sexual Subjects: Signification, Viewership, and Pleasure in Film and Video." Ph.D. diss., Northwestern University, 1989.

Strasberg, Lee. *A Dream of Passion: The Development of the Method*. Edited by Evangeline Morphos. Boston: Little Brown, 1987.

Studlar, Gaylyn. "The Perils of Pleasure? Fan Magazine Discourse as Women's Commodified Culture in the 1920s." *Wide Angle* 13.1 (1991): 6–23.

———. "Masochism, Masquerade, and the Erotic Metamorphosis of Marlene Dietrich." Gaines and Herzog 229–49.

———, and David Desser, eds. *Shadow Boxing: The Films of John Huston*. Washington, D.C.: Smithsonian Institution Press, forthcoming.

Suileman, Susan, ed. *The Female Body in Western Culture*. Cambridge, Mass.: Harvard University Press, 1986.

Sweet, Jeffrey. *Something Wonderful Right Away*. New York: Limelight, 1987.

Swindell, Larry. *Charles Boyer*. Garden City, N.Y.: Doubleday, 1983.

Tabouri, Lena. *Kisses*. New York: Citadel, 1991.

Theweleit, Klaus. *Male Fantasies*. Vol. 1, *Women, Floods, Bodies, History*. Translated by Stephen Conway et al. Minneapolis: University of Minnesota Press, 1987.

———. *Male Fantasies*. Vol. 2, *Male Bodies: Psychoanalyzing the White Terror*. Translated by Erica Carter et al. Minneapolis: University of Minnesota Press, 1989.

Thomas, Bob. *Golden Boy: The Untold Story of William Holden*. Wiedenfeldt & Nicholson, 1983.

Thompson, John O. "Beyond Commutation." *Screen* 26.5 (September–October 1985): 67–76.

———. "Screen Acting and the Commutation Test." *Screen* 19.2 (1978): 55–69.

Thompson, Kristin. "The 'American' Style of Acting." Bordwell, Staiger, and Thompson 189–92.

Todorov, Tvestan. *The Poetics of Prose*. Ithaca, N.Y.: Cornell University Press, 1977.

Tompkins, Jane. "Language and Landscape: An Ontology of the Western." *Artforum* (February 1990): 94–99.

Trebiliot, Joyce, ed. *Mothering: Essays in Feminist Theory*. Totowa N.J.: Rowan & Allanheld, 1984.

Turim, Maureen. "Designing Women: The Emergence of the New Sweetheart Line." Gaines and Herzog 212–28.

———. "Fashion Shapes: Film, the Fashion Industry, and the Image of Woman." *Socialist Review* (1983): 179–96.

Turner, Bryan S. *The Body and Society: Explorations in Social Theory*. Oxford: Basil Blackwell, 1984.

Turner, Chris, and Erica Carter. "Introduction." Theweleit, vol. 2.

Turner, Victor. *The Anthropology of Performance*. New York: Performing Arts Journal Publications, 1986.

———. *Dramas, Fields, and Metaphors: Symbolic Action in Human Society*. Ithaca, N.Y.: Cornell University Press, 1975.

———. *The Forest of Symbols: Aspects of the Ndemba Ritual*. Ithaca, N.Y.: Cornell University Press, 1967.

———. "Frame, Flow and Reflection: Ritual and Drama as Public Liminality." Benamou and Caramello. 33–58.

———. *From Ritual to Theatre: The Human Seriousness of Play*. New York: PAT Publications, 1982.

Tuska, Jon. *The American West in Film: Critical Approaches to the Western*. Westport, Ct.: Greenwood Press, 1985.

Van Wert, William F. "Psychoanalysis and Con Games: *House of Games*." *Film Quarterly* 43.4 (1990): 2–10.

Vardac, A. Nicholas. *Stage to Screen: Theatrical Method from Garrick to Griffith*. Cambridge, Mass.: Harvard University Press, 1949.

Variety. "Valance did 30% better overseas than US-Canada." 14 August 1963.

Veblen, Thorstein. *The Theory of the Leisure Class: An Economic Study of Institutions*. 1899. New York: New American Library, 1953.

Veeder, William S., and Gordon Hirsch, eds. *Dr. Jekyll and Mr. Hyde One Hundred Years Later*. Chicago: University of Chicago Press, 1988.

Vidor, King. *King Vidor on Filmmaking*. New York: David McKay, 1972.

Vineberg, Steve. "The Restored *Way Down East*." *Film Quarterly*, 39.3 (1986): 54–57.

Wagenknecht, Edward. "Lillian Gish: An Interpretation." In *The Movies in the Age of Innocence*. Norman, Okla.: University of Oklahoma Press, 1962. 246–56.

Wagley, Charles, and Marvin Harris. *Minorities in the New World*. New York: Columbia University Press, 1958.

Waldman, Diane. "From Midnight Shows to Marriage Vows: Women, Exploitation and Exhibition." *Wide Angle* 6.2 (1984): 40–49.

Walker, Alexander. *Stardom: The Hollywood Phenomenon*. London: Michael Joseph, 1970.

Warshow, Robert. "Movie Chronicle: The Westerner." Mast and Cohen 434–50.

Washburn, Wilcomb E. "American Indian Tribes and Their Relationship to the United States Government." Babu 126–33.

Weales, Gerald. *From Canned Goods to Caviar: American Film Comedy of the 1930s*. Chicago: University of Chicago Press, 1985.

Weeks, Jeffrey. "Questions of Identity." Caplan 31–51.

———. *Sex, Politics and Society: The Regulation of Sexuality Since 1800*. New York: Longman, 1981.

———. *Sexuality*. London: Tavistock, 1986.

———. *Sexuality and Its Discontents: Meanings, Myths and Modern Sexualities*. London: Routledge, 1985.

Weis, Elisabeth, ed. *The Movie Star*. New York: Penguin, 1981.

Wenders, Wim. *Emotion Pictures*. Translated by Sean Whiteside and Michael Hofman. London: Faber and Faber, 1989.

Westrum, Dexter. "Jane Russell Doesn't Figure: Male Bonding as True Love in Howard Hughes's *The Outlaw*." In *Sex and Love in Motion Pictures: Proceedings of the Second Annual Film Conference of Kent State University*, edited by Douglas Radcliff-Umstead, 14–17. Kent, Ohio: Kent State University Romance Languages Department, 1984.

Wexman, Virginia Wright. "The Critic as Consumer: Film Studies in the University, *Vertigo*, and the Film Canon." *Film Quarterly* 29.3 (Spring 1986): 32–41.

———. "Critical Survey." Wexman and Bisplinghoff 9–27.

———. "Horrors of the Body: Hollywood's Myth of Beauty and Rouben Mamoulian's *Dr. Jekyll and Mr. Hyde*." Veeder and Hirsch 283–307.

———. "An Interview with Mark Rydell." *Chicago Reader*, 22 April 1973.

———. "Kinesics and Film Acting: Humphrey Bogart in *The Maltese Falcon* and *The Big Sleep*." *The Journal of Popular Film and Television* 7.1 (1978): 42–55.

———. "Mastery Through Masterpieces: American Culture, the Male Body, and Huston's *Moulin Rouge*." Studlar and Desser, forthcoming.

———. Personal Interview with Martin Starger. Los Angeles, 5 October 1987.

———. "Returning from the Moon: Jackie Gleason, the Carnivalesque, and Television Comedy." *Journal of Film and Video* (1990): 35–45.

———. "The Rhetoric of Cinematic Improvisation." *Cinema Journal* 20.1 (1980): 29–41.

———. *Roman Polanski*. Boston: Twayne, 1984.

———, and Gretchen Bisplinghoff, eds. *Robert Altman: A Guide to References and Resources*. Boston: G. K. Hall, 1984.

White, Richard. *It's Your Misfortune and None of My Own: A New History of the American West*. Norman, Okla.: University of Oklahoma Press, 1991.

———. *Land Use, Environment and Social Change: The Shaping of Island County, Washington*. Seattle, Wash.: University of Washington, Press, 1980.

Wiles, Timothy. *The Theater Event: Theories of Modern Performance*. Chicago: University of Chicago Press, 1980.

Willemen, Paul. "Anthony Mann: Looking at the Male." *Framework* 15/16/17 (1981): 16.

Williams, Alan. "Is a Radical Genre Criticism Possible?" *Quarterly Review of Film Studies* 9.2 (1984): 121–25.

Williams, Linda. "Film Body: An Implantation of Perversions." *Cine-Tracts* 2 (n.d.): 19–35. (Reprinted in Rosen 507–34.)

———. *Hard Core: Power, Pleasure and the 'Frenzy of the Visible.'* Berkeley: University of California Press, 1989.

———. Lecture on *Way Down East*. Film Center of the School of the Art Institute of Chicago, 20 October 1987.

———. "When the Woman Looks." Doane, Mellencamp, and Williams. 83–99.

Williams, Martin. *Griffith: First Artist of the Movies*. New York: Oxford University Press, 1980.

Williams, Raymond. "Base and Superstructure in Marxist Cultural Theory." Davis and Schleiffer 378–90.

———. *The Sociology of Culture*. New York: Schocken Books, 1982.

Williamson, Alice. "Close-Up of Gloria Swanson." *Alice in Movieland*, 158–67. London: A. M. Philpot Ltd., 1927.

Wilson, Elizabeth. *Adorned in Dreams: Fashion and Modernity*. Berkeley: University of California Press, 1985.

Wilson, Rawden. "The Bright Chimera: Character as a Literary Term." *Critical Inquiry* 5.4 (1975): 725–49.

Winokur, Mark. "Improbable Ethnic Hero: William Powell and the Transformation of Ethnic Hollywood." *Cinema Journal* 27.1 (1987): 5–22.

Wolfe, Charles. "The Return of Jimmy Stewart: The Publicity Photograph as Text." *Wide Angle* 6.4 (1985): 44–52.

Wolfe, Naomi. *The Beauty Myth: How Images of Women Are Used Against Women*. New York: William Morrow, 1991.

Wolheim, Peter. "Limelight: The Hollywood Studio Portrait." *Photo Communique* 5.4 (1983/84): 7–19.

Woll, Allen L. "From Bandits to President: Latin Images in American Films, 1929–39." *Journal of Mexican History* 4 (1974): 28–40.

Wollen, Peter. *Signs and Meaning in the Cinema*. Bloomington: Indiana University Press, 1969.

Wood, Robin. "Acting." *Film Comment* (March-April 1976): 20–25.

———. "An Introduction to the American Horror Film." Nichols, *Movies and Methods*. Vol. 2. 195–219.

———. *Hollywood from Vietnam to Reagan*. New York: Columbia University Press, 1986.

———. "The Kazan Problem." *Movie* 19 (1971–72): 29–31.

———. "Responsibilities of a Gay Male Film Critic." Nichols, *Movies and Methods*, vol. 2. 649–60.

———. "Shall We Gather at the River? The Late Films of John Ford." *Film Comment* 7.3 (1971): 8–17.

Worthen, William. *The Idea of the Actor: Drama and the Ethics of Performance*. Princeton: Princeton University Press, 1984.

Wright, Will. *Sixguns and Society: A Structural Study of the Western*. Berkeley: University of California Press, 1975.

Yacowar, Maurice. "Actors as Conventions in the Films of Robert Altman." *Cinema Journal* 20.1 (1980): 14–28.

Yacowar, Maurice. "An Aesthetic Defense of the Star System." *Quarterly Review of Film Studies* 4.1 (1979): 39–51.

Yin, Robert K., ed. *Race, Creed, Color, or National Origin: A Reader on Racial and Ethnic Identities in American Society*. Itasca, Ill.: F. E. Peacock, 1973.

Zaratsky, William. "Epitaph for a Rebel." *Rolling Stone* 16 (October 1980): 50+.

Znaniecki, Florian. *Modern Nationalities*. Urbana, Ill.: University of Illinois Press, 1952.

Zucker, Carole, ed. *Making Visible the Invisible: An Anthology of Original Essays on Film Acting*. Metuchen, N.J.: Scarecrow Press, 1990.

INDEX